Beiträge zum
ausländischen öffentlichen Recht und Völkerrecht

Edited by

the Max Planck Society
for the Advancement of Science
represented by Prof. Dr. Armin von Bogdandy
and Prof. Dr. Anne Peters

Volume 350

Christoph Priess

The Settlement of Inter-State Disputes through ICJ Advisory Opinions

An Analysis of the Eastern Carelia Doctrine

Nomos

The Deutsche Nationalbibliothek lists this publication in the Deutsche Nationalbibliografie; detailed bibliographic data are available on the Internet at http://dnb.d-nb.de

a.t.: Hamburg, Bucerius Law School, Diss., 2025

Original title:
The Use of ICJ Advisory Opinions to Settle Inter-State Disputes: An Analysis of the Eastern Carelia Doctrine

1st Edition 2026

Published by
Nomos Verlagsgesellschaft mbH & Co. KG
Waldseestraße 3–5 | 76530 Baden-Baden
www.nomos.de

Production of the printed version:
Nomos Verlagsgesellschaft mbH & Co. KG

Waldseestraße 3–5 | 76530 Baden-Baden

ISBN (Print): 978-3-7560-4164-0
ISBN (ePDF): 978-3-7489-7114-6

DOI: https://doi.org/10.5771/9783748971146

Onlineversion
Inlibra

Für Alisa

Preface

I have written this dissertation largely between February 2019 and September 2022 during my time as a research assistant at the Chair of International Law, European Law and Public Law at Bucerius Law School in Hamburg. During this time, I had the privilege of completing a research stay at the PluriCourts Centre of Excellence at the University of Oslo from November to December 2021. After a nine-month break to complete an LL.M. degree at the University of Cambridge between September 2022 and June 2023, I have finished the dissertation in Berlin between July 2023 and October 2024. The dissertation was assessed by *Professor Dr Mehrdad Payandeh, LL.M. (Yale)* and *Professor Dr Dr h.c. Jörn-Axel Kämmerer* and accepted by Bucerius Law School in the summer term of 2025. The date of the oral examination at Bucerius Law School was 20 May 2025. The dissertation was nominated as one of three theses for the final selection of the Dissertation Prize of the German Society for the United Nations (DGVN).

I owe the success of this project to the kind support of many people. First of all, I would like to express my sincere gratitude to my doctoral supervisor, *Professor Dr Mehrdad Payandeh, LL.M. (Yale)*. Already when I was a student in one of his classes, he guided me in developing my own positions and questioning the positions of others. These encounters on an equal footing encouraged me to take on the dissertation project. From my initial ideas to the completion of the work, he gave me complete freedom while always being available as my most important mentor.

I would also like to thank *Professor Dr Dr h.c. Jörn-Axel Kämmerer* for promptly preparing his second opinion. My thanks also goes to *Professor Dr Geir Ulfstein* and *Professor Dr Andreas Føllesdal* for inviting me to the PluriCourts Centre at the University of Oslo and for the many enriching discussions that provided me with new insights into the study of international courts and tribunals. In this context, I would also like to thank the ZEIT STIFTUNG BUCERIUS for providing the financial support for my research stay.

I would also like to express my sincere thanks to the directors of the Max Planck Institute for Comparative Public Law and International Law, *Professor Dr Armin von Bogdandy* and *Professor Dr Dr h.c. mult. Anne Peters, LL.M. (Harvard)*, for including this work in the institute's series of publications.

I tested almost every new idea for the dissertation during numerous walks with *Dr Philipp Kleiner* through Hamburg's Stadtpark. I would like to thank him for his enormously important role as a critical sparring partner during this time. I would also like to thank *Dr Shpetim Bajrami* and *Dr Philipp Knitter* for critically proof-reading the book.

My special thanks goes to my family, especially my parents, *Ulrike* and *Dr Klaus-Peter Saake*. They have encouraged and supported me throughout my life, while allowing me to follow my own path.

Finally and most importantly, I would like to express my most heartfelt thanks to my wife, *Alisa Priess*. Throughout this entire process, she has been my discussion partner, editor, and coach all rolled into one. It is thanks to her that I have never lost faith in the success of this project.

Berlin, December 2025
Christoph Priess

Inhaltsverzeichnis

Table of abbreviations

ACHPR	African Commission on Human and Peoples' Rights
ACHR	American Convention on Human Rights
ACtHPR	African Court on Human and Peoples' Rights
AJICL	African Journal of International and Comparative Law
AJIL	American Journal of International Law
ALQ	Arab Law Quarterly
AU	African Union
AYBIL	Australian Yearbook of International Law
BIOT	British Indian Ocean Territory
BUILJ	Boston University International Law Journal
CJEU	Court of Justice of the European Union
CJTL	Columbia Journal of Transnational Law
CLJ	Cambridge Law Journal
CLR	California Law Review
CoE	Council of Europe
COSIS	Commission of Small Island States on Climate Change and International Law
ECHR	European Convention on Human Rights
ECOSOC	United Nations Economic and Social Council
ECtHR	European Court of Human Rights
EDC	European Defence Community
EEZ	Exclusive Economic Zone
FAO	Food and Agriculture Organization
FCC	Federal Constitutional Court of Germany
GLJ	German Law Journal
HRLR	Human Rights Law Review

IACHR	Inter-American Commission on Human Rights
IACtHR	Inter-American Court of Human Rights
IACtHR Statute	Statute of the Inter-American Court of Human Rights
IAEA	International Atomic Energy Agency
IBRD	International Bank for Reconstruction and Development
IC	International Court or Tribunal
ICAO	International Civil Aviation Organization
ICCPR	International Covenant on Civil and Political Rights
ICJ	International Court of Justice
ICJ Statute	Statute of the International Court of Justice
ICLQ	The International and Comparative Law Quarterly
IDA	International Development Association
IFAD	International Fund for Agricultural Development
IFC	International Finance Corporation
IHRL	International Human Rights Law
ILM	International Legal Materials
ILO	International Labour Organization
ILOAT	Administrative Tribunal of the International Labour Organization
IMF	International Monetary Fund
IMO	International Maritime Organization
ITLOS	International Tribunal for the Law of the Seas
ITU	International Telecommunication Union
JIDS	Journal of International Dispute Settlement
LJIL	Leiden Journal of International Law
LoN	League of Nations
MPYUNL	Max Planck Yearbook of United Nations Law
MULR	Monash University Law Review
NGO	Non-Governmental Organization

NZJPIL	New Zealand Journal of Public and International Law
OAS	Organization of American States
PCA	Permanent Court of Arbitration
PCIJ	Permanent Court of International Justice
PCIJ Statute	Statute of the Permanent Court of International Justice
RSFSR	Russian Soviet Federative Socialist Republic
SCOTUS	Supreme Court of the United States of America
SDC	Seabed Disputes Chamber
SRFC	Sub-Regional Fisheries Commission
UN	United Nations
UNC	Charter of the United Nations
UNCLOS	United Nations Convention on the Law of the Sea
UNESCO	United Nations Educational, Scientific and Cultural Organization
UNGA	United Nations General Assembly
UNIDO	United Nations Industrial Development Organization
UNRoD	United Nations Register of Damage Caused by the Construction of the Wall in the Occupied Palestinian Territory
UNSC	United Nations Security Council
UNSG	United Nations Secretary General
USSR	Union of Soviet Socialist Republics
VCCR	Vienna Convention on Consular Relations
VCLT	Vienna Convention on the Law of Treaties
WHO	World Health Organization
WIPO	World Intellectual Property Organization
WMO	World Meteorological Organization

Introduction

On 28 January 2021, a Special Chamber established under Article 15 para. 2 ITLOS Statute[1] ruled on the preliminary objections in an Annex VII arbitration between Mauritius and the Maldives.[2] The case concerned the delimitation of the maritime boundaries between the two states. Among other matters, the judges had to determine the territorial status of the Chagos Archipelago[3]. From the 19th to the 20th century, the Chagos Archipelago was part of the British colony of Mauritius. Before Mauritius became independent on 12 March 1968, the United Kingdom concluded the "Lancaster House Agreement" with its then colony of Mauritius on 23 September 1965. As a result of this agreement, the United Kingdom separated the Chagos Archipelago from the rest of the colony of Mauritius. The United Kingdom has administered the Chagos Archipelago as a separate colony under the name British Indian Ocean Territory (BIOT) and has leased parts of it to the USA for military purposes. There has been an ongoing dispute between the United Kingdom and Mauritius over the territorial sovereignty over the Chagos Archipelago since at least 1980, when Seewoosagur Ramgoolam, Prime Minister of Mauritius at the time, called for the reintegration of the Chagos Archipelago into the Mauritian territory before the UN General Assembly.

After Mauritius initiated proceedings before the ITLOS Special Chamber against the Maldives, the Maldives raised preliminary objections against the

1 The Statute of the International Tribunal for the Law of the Sea is listed in Annex VI to the Convention on the Law of the Sea (UNCLOS) and constitutes an integral part of the Convention pursuant to Art. 318 UNCLOS; United Nations Convention on the Law of the Sea (adopted on 10 December 1982, entered into force on 16 November 1994).

2 *Dispute concerning delimitation of the maritime boundary between Mauritius and Maldives in the Indian Ocean (Mauritius v. Maldives)*, Preliminary Objections, Judgment, ITLOS Reports 2021, 17.

3 The Chagos Archipelago is a group of islands, the largest of which is the island of Diego Garcia, which is about 27 km^2 in size and lies about 2,200 km north-east of Mauritius in the Indian Ocean, see *Legal Consequences of the Separation of the Chagos Archipelago from Mauritius in 1965*, Advisory Opinion, ICJ Reports 2019, 95 (107, paras. 25 et seq).

tribunal's jurisdiction.[4] Most notably, the Maldives invoked the Monetary Gold principle[5] arguing that the Special Chamber could not exercise its jurisdiction *ratione personae* because the United Kingdom was an indispensable party to the proceedings and had neither participated in nor consented to the proceedings in any other manner.[6] The Maldives argued that in proceedings between two states, during which the court would necessarily have to decide upon the legal position of a third state, the court could not exercise its jurisdiction without the participation of that third state.[7] The Maldives pointed out that the Special Chamber would necessarily have to rule on the legal position of the UK regarding the Chagos Archipelago. Since the United Kingdom had neither participated in nor agreed to the proceedings, the Special Chamber could not rule over the matter.[8] The Special Chamber accepted the doctrinal premise of this argument:

> "[I]f a sovereignty dispute over the Chagos Archipelago exists, the United Kingdom may be regarded as an indispensable party and the Monetary Gold principle would prevent the Special Chamber from exercising its jurisdiction. On the other hand, if such sovereignty dispute has been resolved in favour of Mauritius, the United Kingdom may not be regarded as an indispensable party and the Monetary Gold principle would not apply."[9]

The Special Chamber noted that while there had indeed been a dispute between Mauritius and the United Kingdom regarding the territorial sovereignty over the Chagos Archipelago, this dispute had been resolved

4 *Dispute concerning delimitation of the maritime boundary between Mauritius and Maldives in the Indian Ocean (Mauritius v. Maldives)*, Written Preliminary Objections of the Republic of Maldives, ITLOS Reports 2021 (15 et seq., paras. 45 et seq.).

5 *Case of the monetary gold removed from Rome in 1943 (Italy v. France, United Kingdom and United States) (Preliminary Question)*, Judgment, ICJ Reports 1954, 19; for an extensive study of the Monetary Gold principle, see *T. Thienel*, Drittstaaten und die Jurisdiktion des Internationalen Gerichtshofs. Die Monetary Gold-Doktrin, 2016. See also *infra*: §6.D.I.

6 *Dispute concerning delimitation of the maritime boundary between Mauritius and Maldives in the Indian Ocean (Mauritius v. Maldives)*, Written Preliminary Objections of the Republic of Maldives, ITLOS Reports 2021 (15 et seq., paras. 45 et seq.).

7 Ibid. (18, para. 52).

8 Ibid. (19, paras. 56-57).

9 *Dispute concerning delimitation of the maritime boundary between Mauritius and Maldives in the Indian Ocean (Mauritius v. Maldives)*, Preliminary Objections, Judgment, ITLOS Reports 2021, 17 (48, para. 99).

by the 2019 *Chagos* advisory opinion[10] of the International Court of Justice (ICJ):

> "The determinations made by the ICJ with respect to the issues of the decolonization of Mauritius in the *Chagos* advisory opinion have legal effect and clear implications for the legal status of the Chagos Archipelago. The United Kingdom's continued claim to sovereignty over the Chagos Archipelago is contrary to those determinations. [...] [The United Kingdom's] claim to sovereignty over the Chagos Archipelago is contrary to the authoritative determinations made in the advisory opinion."[11]

Although the ITLOS Special Chamber found that the ICJ advisory opinion was not binding in principle,[12] it nevertheless held that it had "legal effect" and that the ICJ had made "authoritative determinations". Specifically, the 2019 *Chagos* advisory opinion had the effect of settling the dispute between Mauritius and the United Kingdom regarding the territorial sovereignty over the Chagos Archipelago. If the dispute had continued to exist, the Special Chamber would have been forced to decline its jurisdiction in line with the *Monetary Gold* principle. Despite the fact that the ICJ had explicitly emphasized that its *Chagos* opinion did not serve to settle the territorial dispute between Mauritius and the UK,[13] the ITLOS Special Chamber found that the advisory opinion had precisely that effect. With the underlying dispute settled, the United Kingdom lost its status as an indispensable third party to the dispute between Mauritius and the Maldives concerning the sovereignty over the Chagos Archipelago and the ITLOS Special Chamber could consider the merits of the case.

The 2019 *Chagos* advisory opinion and the reliance thereupon by the ITLOS Special Chamber in its 2021 decision on preliminary objections bring to the fore a crucial question: What is the relationship between the ICJ's advisory opinion procedure and the judicial settlement of international legal disputes? As will be demonstrated below, the ICJ consistently emphasized that its advisory opinion procedure may not be used to settle

10 *Legal Consequences of the Separation of the Chagos Archipelago from Mauritius in 1965*, Advisory Opinion, ICJ Reports 2019, 95.

11 *Dispute concerning delimitation of the maritime boundary between Mauritius and Maldives in the Indian Ocean (Mauritius v. Maldives)*, Preliminary Objections, Judgment, ITLOS Reports 2021, 17 (88, para. 246).

12 Ibid. (62, para. 205).

13 *Legal Consequences of the Separation of the Chagos Archipelago from Mauritius in 1965*, Advisory Opinion, ICJ Reports 2019, 95 (117-118, para. 86).

international disputes as this would circumvent the principle of consent in international dispute settlement. States may not be forced to have their legal disputes with other states settled by judicial means. This is an expression of their sovereign equality. There are several safeguards within the procedural law of the ICJ to protect this fundamental right of states. Chief among them is the contentious procedure's strict consent requirement (see Article 36 ICJ Statute). To prevent this consent requirement from being circumvented, the Court developed the *Monetary Gold* doctrine. According to the Monetary Gold doctrine, the Court will not decide a dispute between two states that have given their consent to the contentious proceedings if doing so would require the Court to decide upon the legal rights and obligations of a third state which has not given or refused its consent.[14] The Court has developed a similar doctrine regarding its advisory opinion procedure: the Eastern Carelia doctrine.[15] According to the Eastern Carelia doctrine, the Court will refuse to give an advisory opinion if to do so would require the Court to decide a pending bilateral dispute against the will of the disputing states and thereby circumvent the principle according to which a state may not be forced to have its disputes settled by judicial means. The Eastern Carelia doctrine was first developed by the PCIJ in 1923 in the eponymous *Eastern Carelia* case.[16] Since then, states have invoked the Eastern Carelia doctrine in numerous PCIJ and ICJ cases, with some states continuing to adhere to its basic line of argument until today.[17]

The aim of this study is to analyze the relationship between the principle of consensual dispute settlement and the Court's advisory jurisdiction. The question at the heart of the study is whether there is – as the Eastern Carelia doctrine asserts – an inherent tension between the principle of consensual dispute settlement and the use of advisory opinions to address legal questions arising in inter-state disputes. To approach this question, the study first lays out the history of the international advisory function (§ 1). Finding that the application of advisory procedures to inter-state disputes

---

14 For a detailed account of the Monetary Gold doctrine, see *T. Thienel*, Drittstaaten und die Jurisdiktion des Internationalen Gerichtshofs. Die Monetary Gold-Doktrin, 2016.

15 Arguing that the Eastern Carelia doctrine (or "non-circumvention rule") is an application of the Monetary Gold doctrine in advisory proceedings, see *R. Kolb*, The International Court of Justice, 2013, 1073.

16 *Status of Eastern Carelia*, Advisory Opinion, PCIJ Series B 1923, 7.

17 The PCIJ and ICJ cases in which states have made arguments in line with or similar to the Eastern Carelia doctrine are analyzed below, see *infra* § 2 for the PCIJ and § 3 for the ICJ.

has been central to the advisory function from its inception, the study examines the Eastern Carelia doctrine as it emerged in the jurisprudence of the Permanent Court of International Justice (§ 2) and developed in the case law of the ICJ (§ 3). The study then compares the approach developed by the ICJ to approaches of other international courts and tribunals in dealing with inter-state disputes in their advisory capacity (§ 4). The study proceeds to examine if the Court's constituent instrument – the UNC and the ICJ Statute – provides a legal basis for the Eastern Carelia doctrine (§ 5). Finding that the Court's constituent instrument does not mandate a restrictive subject-matter advisory jurisdiction, the study examines other potential justifications for the Eastern Carelia doctrine, primarily the protection of the Court's judicial function (§ 6).

§ 1 History of the international advisory function

The advisory function of international courts and tribunals (ICs) has been a feature of the international judicial landscape for more than 100 years.[18] Advisory procedures are judicial procedures of ICs that have as their object not the settlement of a dispute but the clarification of a legal question and they result in advisory opinions that are non-binding.[19] The first IC with an advisory jurisdiction was the Permanent Court of International Justice (PCIJ),[20] which was established in 1920 as an independent international organization under the auspices of the League of Nations.[21] The decision to confer upon the PCIJ the power to render advisory opinions was by no means uncontroversial. The history of the advisory procedure and the controversies it sparked are highly elucidating for the question whether the ICJ may use its advisory procedure to address international legal disputes. That is the case for two reasons: first, the debate coined much of the vocabulary of today's debate on the use of ICJ advisory opinions to settle inter-state

18 *M. Giles Samson/D. Guilfoyle*, The Permanent Court of International Justice and the "Invention" of International Advisory Jurisdiction, in: C. J. Tams/M. Fitzmaurice (eds.), Legacies of the Permanent Court of International Justice, 2013, 41 (41). On the history of the advisory jurisdiction of the PCIJ and the ICJ, see *M. Pomerance*, The United States and the Advisory Function of the Permanent Court of International Justice, in: Y. Dinștein (ed.), International law at a time of perplexity, 1989, 567; *S. M. Schwebel*, Was the Capacity to Request an Advisory Opinion Wider in the Permanent Court of International Justice than it is in the International Court of Justice?, in: S. M. Schwebel (ed.), Justice in International Law: Selected Writings of Judge Stephen M. Schwebel, 1994, 27; *M. Giles Samson/D. Guilfoyle*, The Permanent Court of International Justice and the "Invention" of International Advisory Jurisdiction, in: C. J. Tams/M. Fitzmaurice (eds.), Legacies of the Permanent Court of International Justice, 2013, 41; *M. N. Shaw*, Rosenne's Law and Practice of the International Court: 1920-2015, 5th ed 2016, Vol. 1 Ch. 2; *M. Lando*, 61 CJTL 1 (2023), 67.

19 Cf. *R. Kolb*, The International Court of Justice, 2013, 1019 et seq.

20 *H. W. Thirlway*, The International Court of Justice, 2016, 61. There were certain non-judicial bodies that had an advisory function even earlier, including the International Bureau of the Universal Postal Union, the International South American Postal Bureau, and the International Commission for Air Navigation, see *K. Oellers-Frahm*, 12 GLJ 5 (2011), 1033 (footnote 2).

21 See Article 14, sentence 1 of the Covenant of the League of Nations: "The Council shall formulate and submit to the Members of the League for adoption plans for the establishment of a Permanent Court of International Justice." League of Nations, Covenant of the League of Nations, 28 April 1919.

disputes. Then like now, the advisory function was criticized for being incompatible with the Court's judicial function. Interestingly, however, while the debate around the PCIJ's advisory jurisdiction similarly centered on the term "judicial function" the underlying reasoning differed significantly. Secondly, while the creation of the advisory procedure of the PCIJ caused intense debates among scholars, practitioners and state representatives, when the ICJ took over the role of World Court as the quasi-successor of the PCIJ in 1945,[22] the matter of advisory opinions received very limited attention. For these two reasons, the origins of the international advisory function merit particular attention.

A. The international judicial landscape before the 20th century

Before examining the origins of the PCIJ's advisory jurisdiction, it is worth reflecting on the judicial landscape that existed prior to the creation of the PCIJ. This allows for a clearer appreciation of the significance of the creation of the PCIJ. International adjudication before the 20th century was mainly done by arbitration.[23] Arbitration is "a procedure for the settlement of disputes between States by a binding award on the basis of law and as the result of an undertaking voluntarily accepted" in which the parties may determine the arbitrators, the competence of the arbitral tribunal, the law to be applied, and the procedure to be followed.[24] As early as the Hellenistic Age, disputes between rival city states were resolved by impartial arbitrators.[25] In medieval Europe, the role of the arbitrator was often per-

22 See, for example, the report of Committee IV/1 to Commission IV at the 1945 San Francisco Conference: "The creation of the new Court will not break the chain of continuity with the past. Not only will the Statute of the new Court be based upon the Statute of the old Court, but this fact will be expressly set down in the Charter [Article 92]. In general, the new Court will have the same organization as the old, and the provisions concerning its jurisdiction will follow very closely those in the old Statute. [...] In a sense, therefore, the new Court may be looked upon as the successor to the old Court which is replaced.", Report of the Committee IV/1, 13 UNCIO 381, 383. On the San Francisco Conference, see *infra*: D.III.

23 On the difference between arbitration and judicial dispute settlement, see *S. Rosenne*, The law and practice of the International Court, 1920-2005, 4th ed. 2006, 9–14.

24 Report of the International Law Commission, [1953-II] ILCYB (A/2456), 202 para. 16.

25 *M. E. O'Connell/L. Vanderzee*, The History of International Adjudication, in: C. Romano/K. J. Alter/Y. Shany (eds.), The Oxford Handbook of International Adjudication, 2013 (42).

formed by the Pope or by a sovereign ruler of a neutral state that was not involved in the dispute.[26] Over the centuries, the procedure of inter-state arbitration evolved. Arbitrators no longer yielded religious or sovereign power. Instead, states increasingly chose commissions made up of nationals of the disputing parties to settle their disputes. An example of such an arbitration agreement was the 1794 Jay Treaty between the United States of America and Great Britain which created several arbitration commissions to settle disputes that arose as a consequence of the American War of Independence.[27] In the 19th century, the use of arbitration to settle inter-state disputes as a viable alternative to war became even more widespread.[28] A prominent example of a successful arbitration which settled an international dispute that could otherwise have resulted in military confrontation was the Alabama Claims arbitration of 1872.[29] The United States of America maintained that Great Britain violated its duties of neutrality during the American Civil War by not preventing the construction, equipment, and armament of several naval vessels - including the *Alabama* - which were then used as commerce raiders by the Confederate Navy. The international arbitration commission was composed of five arbitrators appointed by five states (Brazil, Italy, Switzerland, Great Britain, and the United States) and awarded the United States $ 15.5 million in damages[30] which Great Britain paid in full.[31] Considering the current geo-political landscape it is easy to overlook just how remarkable the compliance of Great Britain with the arbitration award was. Great Britain was the unchallenged hegemonial superpower of the 19th century. It could have easily ignored the decision of the arbitration commission. However, it decided to comply, a decision

26 Ibid., 43.

27 Treaty of Amity, Commerce, and Navigation, between His Britannic Majesty and the United States of America (Jay Treaty), 1795.

28 *M. E. O'Connell/L. Vanderzee*, The History of International Adjudication, in: C. Romano/K. J. Alter/Y. Shany (eds.), The Oxford Handbook of International Adjudication, 2013 (44).

29 In 1871, the United States and Great Britain concluded the Treaty of Washington in which they agreed to refer all claims "generically known as the Alabama claims" to an arbitral tribunal, see Treaty of Washington, 8 May 1871.

30 *Alabama claims of the United States of America against Great Britain*, Award rendered on 14 September 1872 by the tribunal of arbitration established by Article I of the Treaty of Washington of 8 May 1871, United Nations Reports of International Arbitral Awards, Volume XXIX, 125 (134).

31 *M. E. O'Connell/L. Vanderzee*, The History of International Adjudication, in: C. Romano/K. J. Alter/Y. Shany (eds.), The Oxford Handbook of International Adjudication, 2013 (45).

which strengthened the institution of arbitration as a means of peaceful settlement of inter-state disputes.

The end of the 19th century marked a shift from arbitration to the creation of permanent international courts. The fundamental difference between arbitral and judicial dispute settlement lies in the permanency or pre-established nature of judicial institutions.[32] This extends to the choice of judges, their competences, the rights of the disputing parties, the applicable law and procedure, as well as the publicity of the proceedings.[33] Permanent courts were believed to settle inter-state disputes and thus promote "peace through law" more effectively than ad-hoc arbitration commissions.[34] They could generate a standing body of case law which would make the outcome of proceedings more predictable and could accumulate greater prestige than individual arbitrators, which in turn was hoped to increase the likelihood of compliance.[35] The shift towards courts also signified a shift towards a greater desire for legal rather than diplomatic or political dispute resolution. The work of arbitration commissions was previously perceived as an endeavor focused on finding a political compromise between the disputing parties rather than a solution based on the law.[36] The establishment of disinterested permanent judicial institutions with pre-determined rules significantly limited the parties' power to adapt the procedure for political reasons.[37] The process of dispute settlement is thereby de-politicized to a certain extent.[38] One could therefore say the difference between arbitration and judicial dispute settlement is expressed in the degree of de-politicization.[39]

A first step towards the establishment of a permanent international court was the creation of the Permanent Court of Arbitration (PCA) in 1903 following the first Hague Peace Conference in 1899. The PCA continues to operate to this day and consists of three parts: an Administrative Coun-

---

32 *S. Rosenne*, The law and practice of the International Court, 1920-2005, 4th ed. 2006, 11.

33 Ibid., 11.

34 *M. E. O'Connell/L. Vanderzee*, The History of International Adjudication, in: C. Romano/K. J. Alter/Y. Shany (eds.), The Oxford Handbook of International Adjudication, 2013 (46).

35 Ibid., 46.

36 Ibid., 46.

37 *S. Rosenne*, The law and practice of the International Court, 1920-2005, 4th ed. 2006, 11–12.

38 Ibid., 11–12.

39 Ibid., 12.

cil made up of diplomatic representatives of the contracting State Parties which oversee the PCA's budget and policies, a list of arbitrators, known as 'Members of the Court', from which State Parties can select, and a registry, known as the 'International Bureau', which provides administrative support. Despite its name, the PCA has been aptly described as neither permanent nor a court.[40] The PCA is not a permanent court but rather an institutional framework which facilitates the creation of ad-hoc arbitration commissions. It has no judges, despite the somewhat misleading term 'Members of the Court', but rather a list of qualified arbitrators which can be called upon on an ad-hoc basis.

At both Hague Peace Conferences, the first in 1899 and the second in 1907, British and US-American delegates called for the creation of a permanent international arbitral tribunal to settle inter-state disputes.[41] However, both attempts proved unsuccessful as disagreement over the question of compulsory jurisdiction and the selection of judges persisted.[42] The first permanent court for the settlement of inter-state disputes was thus not a global, but rather a regional court: in 1908, the Central American Court of Justice was created.[43] Its jurisdiction was broadly defined and extended to any legal dispute between its Member States, to disputes between a Member State and the national of another Member State, and even, subject to an additional protocol, disputes between a Member State and its own nationals or disputes between a Member State and a third state. Despite its initial success, the Central American Court of justice ceased its operations ten years later when the United States terminated its support for the court and its mandate was not renewed.[44]

---

40 Quoting James Brown Scott, J Brown Scott, The Hague Court Reports (Oxford University Press 1916) xiii, see *M. E. O'Connell/L. Vanderzee*, The History of International Adjudication, in: C. Romano/K. J. Alter/Y. Shany (eds.), The Oxford Handbook of International Adjudication, 2013 (49).

41 Ibid., 48–51.

42 Ibid., 48–51.

43 Ibid., 51.

44 Ibid., 52.

B. The advisory function of the Permanent Court of International Justice

The Treaty of Versailles of 1919[45] marked not only the end of the First World War, but also the beginning of a new international organization and of the first "World Court". As part of the Treaty of Versailles, 33 signatory states, including Germany and the Allied states, concluded the Covenant of the League of Nations. It created the League of Nations, a new international organization to promote international cooperation, peace, and security. While previous generations of peace activists placed their hopes on international courts and arbitration mechanisms as guarantors of peace, the creation of the League of Nations indicated a turn towards governance institutions and collective political decision-making to secure peace.[46]

However, the Covenant also laid the foundation for the creation of the PCIJ. Article 14 of the Covenant charged the Council of the League to "formulate and submit to the Members of the League for adoption plans for the establishment of a Permanent Court of International Justice."

I. Relationship between the PCIJ and the League of Nations: Between formal independence and organic connection

The reason for the creation of the advisory function of the PCIJ is linked to the Court's relationship with the League of Nations. The relationship between the PCIJ and the League of Nations was characterized by formal independence and at the same time a close "organic" connection.[47] On the one hand, the PCIJ was designed as an independent judicial body. Unlike the ICJ in relation to the UN,[48] the PCIJ was not created as an organ of the

45 *Treaty of Versailles*, Washington, Govt. print. off, retrieved from the Library of Congress, https://www.loc.gov/item/43036001/.

46 Cf. *C. J. Tams*, Peace Through International Adjudication: The Permanent Court of International Justice and the Post-War Order, in: M. Erpelding/B. Hess/H. Ruiz Fabri (eds.), Peace Through Law, 2019, 215 (222 et seq.); *M. E. O'Connell/L. Vanderzee*, The History of International Adjudication, in: C. Romano/K. J. Alter/Y. Shany (eds.), The Oxford Handbook of International Adjudication, 2013 (52).

47 On the relationship between the PCIJ and the League of Nations, see in particular *M. N. Shaw*, Rosenne's Law and Practice of the International Court: 1920-2015, 5th ed 2016, Vol. 1, Ch. 3, § 21.

48 Art. 7 para. 1 UNC lists the ICJ as one of six organs of the UN. The other organs are the General Assembly, the Security Council, the Economic and Social Council, the Trusteeship Council, and the Secretariat.

League of Nations.[49] The PCIJ's constituent instrument, the PCIJ Statute, was formally independent from the League's Covenant.[50] Hence, the Member States of the League of Nations and the States Parties to the PCIJ Statute were not necessarily congruent.[51] The two instruments thus preserved the independence of the PCIJ from the League of Nations. Taking this into account, the Assembly of the League consistently referred to the PCIJ as an "autonomous institution".[52]

On the other hand, the PCIJ was integrated into the framework of the League of Nations.[53] The PCIJ was created by the Council and the Assembly of the League of Nations on the basis of Article 14 para. 1 of the Covenant.[54] The Covenant of the League of Nations made frequent references to the PCIJ, positioning it as the primary adjudicating body for the settlement of disputes between the League's Member States (Article 13 para. 3) and limiting access to the Court's advisory function to the League's organs (Article 14 sentence 3). The League's organs also had decisive powers to determine the staffing and financing of the Court as well as access to the Court of non-Member States of the League of Nations. The Council and Assembly were thus responsible for the election of the judges of the Court (Article 4 PCIJ Statute) and determined their remuneration (Article 32 para. 1 PCIJ Statute), their pension and the reimbursement of their travel expenses (Article 32 para. 2 PCIJ Statute). The budget of the PCIJ was determined and financed by the League (Article 33 PCIJ Statute). The Council determined the conditions under which non-Member States of the League of Nations could appear before the PCIJ (Article 35 PCIJ Statute).

---

49 According to Art. 2 of the Covenant of the League of Nations, the League's organs were the Assembly and the Council which were supported by a Secretariat.

50 *M. N. Shaw*, Rosenne's Law and Practice of the International Court: 1920-2015, 5th ed 2016, Vol. 1, Ch. 3, § 21. In contrast, the ICJ Statute "forms an integral part" of the UNC, see Art. 92 sentence 2 UNC.

51 Ibid., Vol. 1, Ch. 3, § 21.

52 *S. Rosenne*, The law and practice of the International Court, 1920-2005, 4th ed. 2006, 99, citing Financial Regulations, League of Nations, Records of the Third Assembly, II Plenary (doc. A.54(3) Ex) 207.

53 *M. N. Shaw*, Rosenne's Law and Practice of the International Court: 1920-2015, 5th ed 2016, Vol. 1, Ch. 3, § 21.

54 In 1920 the League's Council appointed an Advisory Committee of Jurists to prepare a draft Statute of the PCIJ. The Assembly of the League of Nations unanimously adopted the PCIJ Statute on 13 December 1920. The Statute of the PCIJ was opened for signature on 16 December 1920 and entered into force on 20 August 1921. On the work of the Advisory Committee of Jurists, see *O. Spiermann*, 73 British Yearbook of International Law 1 (2003), 187.

The overall picture is thus one of a special, "organic"[55] connection between the League of Nations and the PCIJ.[56] The two institutions clearly did not merely coexist but were significantly interconnected. In *Shaw's* words:

> "[T]he Court was established not as a disembodied dispenser of international justice but as one of the means for the pacific settlement of international disputes envisaged in the very conception of the League of Nations."[57]

Bestowing upon the PCIJ the function to give advisory opinions to the organs of the League of Nations underscores the special relationship between Court and organization. By means of the advisory function, the PCIJ was meant to become an advisor to the League of Nations.[58]

II. The PCIJ's advisory jurisdiction

During the drafting process of the Covenant of the League of Nations, the drafters initially proposed to limit the PCIJ's advisory jurisdiction to the interpretation of the Covenant and to exclude broader questions of international law or concrete disputes.[59] However, this proposal was rejected, and

55 Report of the Informal-Inter Allied Committee on the Future of the Permanent Court of Justice, 39 AJIL 1 (1945), 1 (4, para. 13).

56 According to Shaw, the PCIJ was "metaphysically part of the notion of the League", see *M. N. Shaw*, Rosenne's Law and Practice of the International Court: 1920-2015, 5th ed 2016, Vol.1, Ch. 3, § 21; Hudson speaks of the PCIJ as "part of the organization of the League", see *M. O. Hudson*, The Permanent Court of international justice, 1934, 111.

57 *M. N. Shaw*, Rosenne's Law and Practice of the International Court: 1920-2015, 5th ed 2016, Vol. 1, Ch. 3, § 21.

58 *Giles Samson* and *Guilfoyle* refer to it as "expert counsel", see *M. Giles Samson/D. Guilfoyle*, The Permanent Court of International Justice and the "Invention" of International Advisory Jurisdiction, in: C. J. Tams/M. Fitzmaurice (eds.), Legacies of the Permanent Court of International Justice, 2013, 41 (41).

59 *M. O. Hudson*, 37 Harvard Law Review 8 (1924), 970 (986); on the drafting history of the provisions on the PCIJ's advisory procedure in the Covenant of the League of Nations, see *M. Pomerance*, The Advisory Role of the International Court of Justice and its 'Judicial' Character: Past and Future Prisms, in: S. Muller/D. Raic/J. M. Thuránszky (eds.), The International Court of Justice, 1997, 271 (271 et seq.).

the Court was given a broad advisory jurisdiction.[60] Article 14 sentence 3 of the Covenant of the League of Nations thus stipulated:

> "The Court shall be competent to hear and determine any dispute of an international character which the parties thereto submit to it. The Court may also give an advisory opinion upon any dispute or question referred to it by the Council or by the Assembly."

One of the most controversial aspects of Article 14 was the question whether to extend the PCIJ's advisory jurisdiction to concrete disputes. Elihu Root, the US-American delegate of the Advisory Committee of Jurists tasked with drafting the PCIJ Statute, described this idea as "a violation of all juridical principles".[61] The idea behind giving the PCIJ the power to issue advisory opinions on existing disputes was that the Court could assist the League's organs, the Council and the Assembly, in their duty to peacefully settle international disputes.[62] The advisory procedure gave the League's organs access to the Court to clarify legal questions which lay at the heart of inter-state disputes. As *Hudson* stated in 1928:

> "The Council must deal with the political phases of the dispute. But political questions are frequently masked as legal questions, and to dispose of a political background it is sometimes necessary to deal with the legal foreground of a dispute. It is for this reason that during the past six years (...) the court's giving advisory opinions has proved so useful in the settlement of disputes."[63]

When drafting the PCIJ Statute in 1920, the Advisory Committee of Jurists proposed to pick up on the distinction contained in Article 14 between "disputes" and "questions" by creating different judicial procedures depending on which kind of request was brought before the Court.[64] Legal questions which did not refer to an existing dispute were to be answered by a chamber of three to five judges, while questions arising from actual disputes were

---

60 *M. Pomerance*, The Advisory Role of the International Court of Justice and its 'Judicial' Character: Past and Future Prisms, in: S. Muller/D. Raic/J. M. Thuránszky (eds.), The International Court of Justice, 1997, 271 (271 et seq.).

61 *M. O. Hudson*, 37 Harvard Law Review 8 (1924), 970 (987).

62 With further references, see *D. Pratap*, The advisory jurisdiction of the International Court, 1972, 229; so too *M. Lando*, 61 CJTL 1 (2023), 67 (92–93).

63 *M. O. Hudson*, 22 AJIL 4 (1928), 776 (790).

64 The proposed Article 36 PCIJ Statute read:
"The Court shall give an advisory opinion upon any question or dispute of an international nature referred to it by the Council or Assembly.

to be answered by the full Court.[65] For questions which form the subject of an existing dispute, the Committee proposed that the Court shall reply under the same conditions as if the case had been actually submitted to it for decision. However, this proposition was struck down by the Committee of the Assembly of the League which found that the distinction between disputes and questions was "lacking in clearness and likely to give rise to practical difficulties".[66]

In the early years of the Court, the PCIJ Statute did not contain any guidance for the Court on how to exercise its advisory jurisdiction. The only reference to the Court's advisory jurisdiction was contained in Article 1 which stipulated:

> "A Permanent Court of International Justice is hereby established in accordance with Article 14 of the Covenant of the League of Nations."

Article 14 sentence 3 of the Covenant of the League of Nations contained the legal basis for the PCIJ's advisory jurisdiction. Article 1 PCIJ Statute incorporated this legal basis into its text.[67]

When the Court shall give an opinion on a question of an international nature which does not refer to any dispute that may have arisen, it shall appoint a special Commission of from three to five members.
When it shall give an opinion upon a question which forms the subject of an existing dispute, it shall do so under the same conditions as if the case had been actually submitted to it for decision.", cited in *M. O. Hudson*, 37 Harvard Law Review 8 (1924), 970 (987).

65 On this proposal, see *M. Pomerance*, The Advisory Role of the International Court of Justice and its 'Judicial' Character: Past and Future Prisms, in: S. Muller/D. Raic/J. M. Thuránszky (eds.), The International Court of Justice, 1997, 271 (272 et seq.).

66 Records of First Assembly, Committee I, 534. See (3rd add) Ser D No 2 at 838, cited in: *M. Giles Samson/D. Guilfoyle*, The Permanent Court of International Justice and the "Invention" of International Advisory Jurisdiction, in: C. J. Tams/M. Fitzmaurice (eds.), Legacies of the Permanent Court of International Justice, 2013, 41 (58); on the discussions in the Committee of the first Assembly of the League of Nations, see *S. M. Schwebel*, Was the Capacity to Request an Advisory Opinion Wider in the Permanent Court of International Justice than it is in the International Court of Justice?, in: S. M. Schwebel (ed.), Justice in International Law: Selected Writings of Judge Stephen M. Schwebel, 1994, 27 (28–29).

67 *M. O. Hudson*, 22 AJIL 4 (1928), 776 (782).

III. Early criticism against the legal effects of PCIJ advisory opinions

Most of the early criticism against the PCIJ's advisory jurisdiction was directed against the uncertain the legal nature of the advisory opinions. Some authors feared that the non-binding nature of advisory opinions would cause tension with the Court's dispute settlement function: Since advisory opinions were non-binding, it was feared that the recipients of the opinions would simply ignore them.[68] This, in turn, would damage the reputation of the Court and thus undermine its capacity to authoritatively settle inter-state disputes. Especially US-American international lawyers regarded the activity of issuing advisory opinions primarily as an executive, not a judicial function.[69] Others criticized that the advisory opinion procedure would create a quasi-compulsory jurisdiction of the Court.[70] Although PCIJ advisory opinions were formally non-binding, they were regarded as being highly authoritative. The Court could thus find itself in the position of issuing an advisory opinion on an international dispute and later being asked to settle the same dispute by means of its contentious procedure. In such a situation, the decision on the dispute would be heavily influenced by the advisory opinion.[71]

The USA was among the most vocal critics of the Court's advisory jurisdiction fearing that the PCIJ advisory jurisdiction could be used to create a kind of compulsory jurisdiction under which the Court could adjudicate

68 *J. B. Moore*, The question of advisory opinions, 1922, PCIJ Series D. No. 2, 398.

69 With further references, see *M. Giles Samson/D. Guilfoyle*, The Permanent Court of International Justice and the "Invention" of International Advisory Jurisdiction, in: C. J. Tams/M. Fitzmaurice (eds.), Legacies of the Permanent Court of International Justice, 2013, 41 (44); see however Manley O. Hudson who points out that the US-American legal system already provided for similar procedures on state level before the state Supreme Courts of Massachusetts (since 1790), New Hampshire (since 1784), Maine (since 1820), Rhode Island (since 1842), Delaware (since 1852), Florida (since 1868), Colorado (since 1886), South Dakota (1889), Mississippi (1890), Oklahoma (1903), and Alabama (1923), *M. O. Hudson*, 22 AJIL 4 (1928), 776 (791). Other jurisdictions similarly provided for advisory procedures before domestic courts, including Austria, Bulgaria, Canada, Colombia, Ecuador, El Salvador, Finland, France, Honduras, Ireland, Nicaragua, Norway, Panama, Poland, Sweden and the United Kingdom, see *M. Giles Samson/D. Guilfoyle*, The Permanent Court of International Justice and the "Invention" of International Advisory Jurisdiction, in: C. J. Tams/M. Fitzmaurice (eds.), Legacies of the Permanent Court of International Justice, 2013, 41 (42 et seq.).

70 *M. Giles Samson/D. Guilfoyle*, The Permanent Court of International Justice and the "Invention" of International Advisory Jurisdiction, in: C. J. Tams/M. Fitzmaurice (eds.), Legacies of the Permanent Court of International Justice, 2013, 41 (45–46).

71 Ibid., 54.

matters against the will of the United States.[72] When US President Coolidge asked the US Senate for its approval to the adherence of the United States to the PCIJ Statute, the US Senate consented, however it placed its consent under several reservations.[73] Any one of these reservations would have created significant inequality between the United States and the other States Parties to the PCIJ Statute, for example by giving the United States special influence in the election process of the judges (reservation 2), or by allowing the United States to determine how much money it would contribute to covering the expenses of the Court (reservation 3). However, it was only the fifth reservation which created a deadlock between the United States and the other States Parties to the PCIJ[74] and which expressed most clearly the United States' opposition to the Court's advisory jurisdiction. The fifth US Senate reservation read:

> "That the Court shall not render any advisory opinion except publicly after due notice to all states adhering to the Court and to all interested states and after public hearing or opportunity for hearing given to any state concerned, nor shall it without the consent of the United States entertain any request for an advisory opinion touching any dispute or question in which the United States has or claims an interest."[75]

The first part of the reservation concerned procedural safeguards which by July of 1926 had already been enshrined into Articles 73 and 74 of the Rules of the Court.[76] However, the second part of the US reservation was highly controversial, so much so that the existing States Parties to the PCIJ Statute simply could not agree. The reservation would have allowed the United States to block any advisory proceedings which touched upon disputes or

---

72 Ibid., 45–46.

73 United States Senate Resolution 5 (The World Court) providing for adhesion on the part of the United States to the protocol of December 16, 1920, and the adjoined statute for the Permanent Court of International Justice, with reservations, 23 January 1926, printed in: Congressional Record, January 23, 1926, Vol. 67, Part. 3, 2656–2657, available at: https://www.congress.gov/bound-congressional-record/1926/01/23/senate-section.

74 *M. O. Hudson*, 22 AJIL 4 (1928), 776 (778).

75 Congressional Record, January 23, 1926, Vol. 67, Part. 3, 2657.

76 One potential reason why the US Senate included this first part of the reservation could be that it feared that the Court could change its Rules and eliminate these procedural safeguards. The US Senate might therefore have wanted to make them binding on the Court by incorporating them into the PCIJ Statute, cf. *M. O. Hudson*, 22 AJIL 4 (1928), 776 (783). This occurred during the revision of the PCIJ Statute in 1929.

questions in which the United States *had* or *claimed to have* an interest. As *Hudson* pointed out:

> "A mere claim of interest would disable the court, and would render it incompetent. Instead of an affirmative interposition of an objection to prevent the court from proceeding, it would take an affirmative yielding of consent to enable the court to proceed once an interest of the United States has been claimed or found to exist. Conceivably, the claim that the United States has an interest could be advanced by another state to bar an advisory opinion relating to a dispute to which two other states were parties."[77]

The US reservation, if accepted by the States Parties, would have created a far-reaching consent requirement which would have had the potential to completely incapacitate the Court's advisory jurisdiction. During the revision of the PCIJ Statute in 1929, the States Parties to the Statute thus deliberately decided against accommodating this request. While the United States eventually signed the PCIJ Statute on 9 December 1929, it never ratified it.

The Court was thus faced with two opposing criticisms concerning the legal nature of its advisory opinions: while some saw the lack of binding effect of its advisory opinions as a danger to the judicial character and authority of the Court, others feared precisely too high a degree of authority emanating from the Court's advisory opinions. The Court primarily addressed the first point of criticism: By procedurally converging the advisory opinion procedure with the contentious procedure, the Court sought to increase the authority of its advisory opinions, thereby ensuring the integrity of its judicial activity.[78] The convergence of the two procedures was an important factor to strengthen the reputation of the advisory opinion procedure.[79] Yet, this convergence came at a price. It reinforced the second of the two main concerns addressed at the advisory opinion procedure.

77 Ibid., 788.

78 *M. Giles Samson/D. Guilfoyle*, The Permanent Court of International Justice and the "Invention" of International Advisory Jurisdiction, in: C. J. Tams/M. Fitzmaurice (eds.), Legacies of the Permanent Court of International Justice, 2013, 41 (51 et seq., 60).

79 De Visscher in his 1929 Hague Lecture criticized the Court for taking the convergence of the two procedures too far, thereby depriving the advisory procedure of its unique value, *C. de Visscher*, Les avis consultatifs de la Cour permanente de justice internationale, Recueil des cours de l'Académie de La Haye / Hague Academy Collected Courses, 1 (58–59).

In this vein, *De Visscher* questioned whether the convergence of the two procedures had not turned the advisory opinion into a quasi-judgment.[80]

IV. Converging the Court's advisory and contentious procedure: Rules of the Court and revision of the PCIJ Statute

Initially, the PCIJ did not have any legal guidance on how to exercise its advisory jurisdiction beyond the broadly formulated Article 14 sentence 3 of the Covenant of the League of Nations. The PCIJ was thus left to find its own approach. The Court decided to orient itself towards its contentious procedure in the design of its advisory procedure.[81] This could be seen as an attempt by the Court to rebut the early criticism levied against its advisory jurisdiction.

An example of this orientation towards its contentious procedure can be seen in the Rules of the Court, which the PCIJ formulated on 24 March 1922 in accordance with Article 30 PCIJ Statute.[82] Article 71 of the 1922 Rules stipulated that advisory opinions were given after deliberation by the full Court, as is the case in contentious proceedings. Article 73 stipulated that the Registrar informs the Court, the League's Member States, and any international organizations which are likely to provide relevant information of any request for an advisory opinion. In formulating Article 73, the PCIJ deliberately decided against a proposition which would have limited the notification of a request for an advisory opinion to the Court.[83] Instead, the Court chose a more transparent procedure. This emphasized that the PCIJ in exercising its advisory jurisdiction is acting as a court of justice and performing a judicial function, instead of acting as a legal advisor to the requesting organ.[84] In other words, the PCIJ saw its role in giving advisory opinions more akin to regular contentious proceedings than to

80 Ibid., 60.

81 Cf. *M. Giles Samson/D. Guilfoyle*, The Permanent Court of International Justice and the "Invention" of International Advisory Jurisdiction, in: C. J. Tams/M. Fitzmaurice (eds.), Legacies of the Permanent Court of International Justice, 2013, 41 (48 et seq.).

82 1922 Rules of the Court, adopted 24 March 1922, PCIJ Series D, No. 1, 1926.

83 *M. Giles Samson/D. Guilfoyle*, The Permanent Court of International Justice and the "Invention" of International Advisory Jurisdiction, in: C. J. Tams/M. Fitzmaurice (eds.), Legacies of the Permanent Court of International Justice, 2013, 41 (48–49).

84 Ibid., 48–49.

a lawyer-client relationship.[85] In line with this, Article 74 of the Rules stipulated that both the request and the advisory opinion shall be printed and published, underlining the public function the Court performs in giving advisory opinions.

The 1922 Rules of the Court did not distinguish between advisory proceedings arising from abstract questions and those arising from existing inter-state disputes. Nevertheless, in practice the Court distinguished between the two by applying certain procedural safeguards when dealing with specific disputes in its advisory capacity[86]: The Court's registrar would inform all interested states about the request and invite them to submit memorials and counter-memorials, which the Court would then take into account before issuing the advisory opinion. Once the proceedings were concluded, the Court would deliver its advisory opinion in open court and provide extensive legal reasoning.

This practice found expression in the 1926 amendments to the Rules of the Court. The amendments further converged the Court's advisory jurisdiction with its contentious jurisdiction. For example, the 1926 revised version included provisions for states and certain international organizations to provide the Court with written and oral statements and comments on the submitted question(s) (Article 73 Revised Rules of the Court, 1926).[87] Also, advisory opinions were now read in open court and all immediately concerned states and international organizations had the possibility to be present (Article 74 Revised Rules of the Court, 1926). In 1927, the Court added another paragraph to Article 71, according to which

> "On a question relating to an existing dispute between two or more States or Members of the League of Nations, Article 31 of the Statute shall apply."[88]

---

85 Ibid., 48–49; see also *M. Pomerance*, The advisory function of the International Court in the League and U.N. eras, 1973, 287.

86 *M. Giles Samson/D. Guilfoyle*, The Permanent Court of International Justice and the "Invention" of International Advisory Jurisdiction, in: C. J. Tams/M. Fitzmaurice (eds.), Legacies of the Permanent Court of International Justice, 2013, 41 (50 et seq., 59-60).

87 1926 Rules of the Court, adopted 31 July 1931, PCIJ Series D, No. 1, 1926.

88 This addition to Art. 71 was based on a proposal made by Judge Dionisio Anzilotti, see *S. M. Schwebel*, Was the Capacity to Request an Advisory Opinion Wider in the Permanent Court of International Justice than it is in the International Court of Justice?, in: S. M. Schwebel (ed.), Justice in International Law: Selected Writings of Judge Stephen M. Schwebel, 1994, 27 (31).

Notably, the Court did not regard requests on inter-state disputes to be outside its competence. Instead, it proposed that in such situations Article 31 of the PCIJ Statute would apply, which allows parties to contentious proceedings to appoint a judge ad-hoc if none of their nationals is a judge on the Court. Through this amendment, the Court took a further step towards assimilating its advisory procedure with its contentious procedure.[89]

With the exception of the brief reference to the PCIJ's advisory jurisdiction in Article 14 sentence 3 of the League's Covenant, there were initially no binding provisions concerning the PCIJ's advisory jurisdiction.[90] When the Committee of Jurists was tasked to revise the PCIJ Statute in March of 1929, it decided to remedy the matter by incorporating the Court's practice pertaining to advisory opinions into the PCIJ Statute.[91] The Court's informal practice of converging its two procedures was thus formalized.[92] On 14 September 1929, the Assembly of the League of Nations adopted a revised version of the PCIJ Statute incorporating the proposals made by the Committee of Jurists half a year earlier.[93] Among other modifications, the revised statute contained a new "Chapter IV" on advisory opinions in Articles 65–68.[94] Articles 65–67 incorporated into the Statute provisions on the procedure which were previously part of Articles 72–74 of the Rules of the Court.[95] Article 68 PCIJ Statute established a dynamic link between

89 *M. O. Hudson*, 22 AJIL 4 (1928), 776 (782).

90 The Rules of the Court contained certain provisions on the Court's advisory jurisdiction, however, the Rules merely reflected the Court's practice.

91 *M. Giles Samson/D. Guilfoyle*, The Permanent Court of International Justice and the "Invention" of International Advisory Jurisdiction, in: C. J. Tams/M. Fitzmaurice (eds.), Legacies of the Permanent Court of International Justice, 2013, 41 (60).

92 Ibid., 60.

93 Resolution Concerning the Revision of the Statute of the Permanent Court of International Justice, adopted by the Assembly of the League of Nations on 14 September 1929, PCIJ Series D. No. 1, Statute and Rules of the Court, fourth edition (April 1940), 8.

94 Statute of the PCIJ, adopted on 14 September 1929, entry into force 1 September 1930, printed in: PCIJ Series D. No. 1, Statute and Rules of the Court, fourth edition (April 1940), 13. The fact that the PCIJ Statute did not contain any provisions on advisory opinions before was referred to by the President of the revising conference as merely "another slight omission in the Statute", League of Nations, Minutes of the conference regarding the revision of the Statute of the Permanent Court of International Justice and the accession of the United States of America to the Protocol of signature of that Statute, September 4th to 12th, 1929 (1929 Minutes), 43.

95 See on this the Minutes of the 1929 Conference of the Assembly of the League of Nations: "The aim of the new Articles 65, 66, 67 and 68 was, so to speak, to consecrate the usage which had grown by introducing into the Statute a number of

the Court's contentious and advisory procedures. The provision was not previously part of the Rules of the Court, but it could be argued that it encapsulated the core of all of the rules on the advisory jurisdiction as well as the Court's practice. Article 68 PCIJ Statute (which is identical to today's Article 68 ICJ Statute) stipulated:

> "In the exercise of its advisory functions, the Court shall further be guided by the provisions of the Statute which apply in contentious cases to the extent to which it recognizes them to be applicable."

Article 68 PCIJ Statute is the clearest illustration of the League's Assembly's aim to bring the PCIJ's advisory procedure in line with Court's contentious procedure.[96] Article 68 was added to the PCIJ Statute to ensure that the Court had all information it needed to issue the requested advisory opinion. This was intended to be achieved by giving the Court the same procedural techniques it used in contentious proceedings. When explaining the rationale of the new provision, *Henri Fromageot*, French delegate to the 1929 conference, declared:

> "In contentious cases, when a decision had to be pronounced, the procedure naturally had to provide for both parties to be heard; both parties stated their case, and the judges therefore had all the arguments before them. The same ought to be the case in advisory opinions. When an advisory opinion was asked for, the latter could have no value unless the person consulted could know all the relevant facts of the case in the same way as in contentious cases; he should know the arguments of *both parties* and *both parties* should adduce their evidence. It would be quite useless to give an advisory opinion after hearing only one side. For the opinion be useful *both parties* must be heard. It was therefore quite natural to lay down in the Statute of the Court that, in regard to advisory

very important articles which the Court had found itself obliged to include in its Rules.", see League of Nations, 1929 Minutes, 43.

96 When Sir Cecil Hurst, British delegate to the 1929 Conference of the Assembly of the League of Nations revising the PCIJ Statute, was approached by "an enthusiastic gentleman from across the Atlantic", who expressed US-American anxieties regarding "the whole question of advisory opinions" and who hoped that the advisory procedure would be assimilated, as much as possible, to the procedure in contentious cases, he replied "That is exactly what we have provided in the Statute", referring to Art. 68 PCIJ Statute, see League of Nations, 1929 Minutes, 46–47.

opinions, the Court should proceed in all respects in the same way as in contentious cases."[97]

The provision thus presumed that advisory proceedings may concern matters which were disputed between two parties in the same way as in contentious proceedings. Articles 65–68 PCIJ Statute did not pick up on the distinction between "disputes" and "questions" made in Article 14 of the Covenant. Instead, they only referred to "questions". However, there is no indication in the preparatory materials that the drafters of the revised Statute intended to exclude disputes from the Court's advisory jurisdiction.[98]

C. The collapse of the League of Nations and the beginning of a new world order

The Second World War ended the work of the PCIJ. Two months after the beginning of the war, the Court's administration had taken the first security measures and sent parts of the Court archives to Geneva. Later, the Court moved its operation to Geneva due to the invasion of the Netherlands by Germany.[99] However, since the election of new members of the Court, which had been scheduled for the fall of 1939, never took place, the last public session of the PCIJ was held on 4 December 1939.[100]

Nevertheless, even during the war years, intense discussions about the future of the international political and legal order continued.[101] In varying compositions, several meetings of the Allied states took place which would eventually culminate in the San Francisco Conference of 1945, during which the United Nations and the ICJ were created. The goal of these

97 League of Nations, 1929 Minutes, 48, emphasis added.

98 *M. Lando*, 61 CJTL 1 (2023), 67 (91).

99 President Guerrero, Registrar Oliván and three other PCIJ officials moved to Geneva as the "core" of the Court. The remaining judges returned to their home countries, see *G. Marston*, The London Committee and the Statute of the International Court of Justice, in: V. Lowe (ed.), Fifty years of the International Court of Justice, 1996, 40 (40–41).

100 *M. N. Shaw*, Rosenne's Law and Practice of the International Court: 1920-2015, 5th ed 2016, Vol. 1, Ch. 2, § 5.

101 Ibid., Vol. 1, Ch. 2, § 6.

meetings was to prepare a new post-war international legal and political order that could be implemented immediately after the end of the war.[102]

The first of these "Inter-Allied Meetings" took place in London on 12 June 1941. In the so-called St. James Agreement, delegates from 14 states and exile governments declared their mutual support in the fight against Germany and Italy and declared that "the only true basis of enduring peace is the willing co-operation of free peoples in a world in which, relieved of the menace of aggression, all may enjoy economic and social security; and that it is their intention to work together, and with other free peoples, both in war and peace to this end."[103] The delegates formulated a vision for the time after the war. International cooperation should form the basis of sustainable peace in the world.

Two months later, on 14 August 1941, President Roosevelt of the United States and Prime Minister Churchill of the United Kingdom signed the "Atlantic Charter". They committed themselves to "certain common principles in the national policies of their respective countries on which they base their hopes for a better future for the world."[104] The common principles included the respect for territorial sovereignty, the right of peoples to choose their own form of government, economic cooperation, and the renunciation of the use of force. In a modified form, these principles would eventually find their way into the Charter of the United Nations (UNC). Several Allied states joined the Atlantic Charter in the following months.[105]

In January 1942, 26 states, including the United States, the United Kingdom, the Union of Soviet Socialist Republics (USSR), and China signed the "Declaration by United Nations".[106] They committed themselves to a maximum war effort against the Axis states and declared their acceptance

102 Ibid., Vol. 1, Ch. 2, § 6.

103 St. James Agreement, Yearbook of the United Nations, 1946–47, 1.

104 Atlantic Charter, Yearbook of the United Nations, 1946–47, 2.

105 Yearbook of the United Nations, 1946–47, 2.

106 In the following months, many states signed the Declaration by United Nations, including Australia, Belgium, Canada, Costa Rica, Cuba, Czechoslovakia, Dominican Republic, El Salvador, Greece, Guatemala, Haiti, Honduras, India, Luxembourg, the Netherlands, New Zealand, Nicaragua, Norway, Panama, Poland, South Africa, and Yugoslavia. 21 more states joined over the next two and a half years. These included Bolivia, Brazil, Chile, Colombia, Ecuador, Egypt, Ethiopia, France, Iran, Iraq, Lebanon, Liberia, Mexico, Paraguay, Peru, the Philippines, Saudi Arabia, Syria, Turkey, Uruguay and Venezuela, Declaration by United Nations, Yearbook of the United Nations, 1946–47, 1–2.

of the principles of the Atlantic Charter.[107] The cornerstones of the future international organization thus found broad support for the first time.

In a joint declaration on 30 October 1943, China, the USSR, the United Kingdom, and the United States formulated a more precise concept of a general international organization. In their "Four Nations Declaration on General Security", also known as the "Moscow Declaration", they declared the need to establish as soon as possible a general international organization based on the principle of the sovereign equality of all peace-loving states, open to accession by these states and dedicated to the maintenance of international peace and security.[108]

While the governments of the Allied states discussed the post-war international order at these bi- and multilateral meetings, a group of legal experts deliberated on one essential part of this post-war order: the design of the new World Court. The "Informal Inter-Allied Committee of Experts" (also known as the "London Committee") was a group of international lawyers from eleven Allied states who met in 1943 to discuss the judicial organization of the post-war international order.[109] In particular they discussed whether the PCIJ ought to continue to exist or whether the world needed a new international court instead. The future of the League of Nations was subject of the London Committee's discussions only insofar as it directly concerned the Court.[110] In its final report of 10 February 1944, the London Committee found that a "new international agreement will be needed, whether the object be to set up a new Permanent Court or merely to continue the old one in existence."[111] The basis of this agreement should be the PCIJ Statute which "has worked well and should be retained as the general structure of the future Court".[112]

107 Declaration by United Nations, Yearbook of the United Nations, 1946–47, 1.

108 Four Nations Declaration on General Security, Yearbook of the United Nations, 1946–47, 3, para. 4.

109 For an extensive account of the London Committee, see *G. Marston*, The London Committee and the Statute of the International Court of Justice, in: V. Lowe (ed.), Fifty years of the International Court of Justice, 1996, 40.

110 The London Committee's isolated focus on the World Court was the reason for the United States' non-participation, cf. Ibid., 45–46.

111 United Nations, Report of the Informal Inter-Allied Committee on the Future of the Permanent Court of International Justice, 1945, 39 Am. j. int. law S1: Supplement Official Documents, 36, para. 115.

112 Ibid., 36, para. 113.

The London Committee criticized the PCIJ's "organic" relationship to the League of Nations, particularly its financial dependency.[113] It was believed that while there was no indication of undue influence on the judges of the PCIJ, the Court's institutional independence needed to be ensured by severing this organic connection.[114] Regarding the PCIJ's advisory jurisdiction, the London Committee voiced three points of criticism:

> "It was urged that the existence of this jurisdiction tended to encourage the use of the Court as an instrument for settling issues which were essentially of a political rather than of a legal character and that this was undesirable. Subsidiary objections were that the existence of this jurisdiction might promote a tendency to avoid the final settlement of disputes by seeking opinions, and might lead to general pronouncements of law by the Court not (or not sufficiently) related to a particular issue or set of facts."[115]

Despite these objections, the London Committee spoke out in favor of retaining the Court's advisory jurisdiction.[116] It even proposed to allow more entities to request an opinion from the Court, including "all international associations of an inter-state or inter-governmental character" as well as "any two or more States acting in concert".[117]

Individual states, however, should not be allowed to request advisory opinions as it was feared that a single state could otherwise indirectly impose a kind of compulsory jurisdiction on other states in circumvention of the principle of consensual dispute settlement.[118] However, the Committee accepted that two states acting in concert could request an advisory opinion on an inter-state dispute, even where the legal question was of particular interest to a third state.[119] This would not be problematic, the Committee found, as long as that third state had the opportunity to participate in

113 *G. Marston*, The London Committee and the Statute of the International Court of Justice, in: V. Lowe (ed.), Fifty years of the International Court of Justice, 1996, 40 (49, footnote 28).

114 United Nations, Report of the Informal Inter-Allied Committee on the Future of the Permanent Court of International Justice, 1945, 39 Am. j. int. law S1: Supplement Official Documents, 5-6, paras. 18-19.

115 Ibid., 20, para. 65.

116 Ibid., 21-22, para. 66.

117 Ibid., 40, para. 143.

118 Ibid., 22, para. 71.

119 Ibid., 23, para. 74.

the proceedings.[120] To ensure this, it would be sufficient to maintain the procedure of notification by the Registrar of the Court.

There were two other groups of experts that examined the future of the World Court during the war: The "Inter-American Juridical Committee" in Central and South America and the "Advisory Committee on Post-War Foreign Policy" in the United States.[121] While the Inter-American Juridical Committee advocated for retaining the PCIJ as the World Court, the US Advisory Committee on Post-War Foreign Policy advocated for the creation of a new Court that would also be the organ of a new international organization.[122]

D. The creation of the International Court of Justice

The early inter-allied meetings and works of legal experts laid the groundwork for what was to come next: the creation of the legal framework that would shape the post-war international order. Three conferences would develop more concrete proposals for a new world organization and a new World Court which would culminate in the creation of the UNC and the ICJ Statute: the Dumbarton Oaks Conversations from 21 August to 28 September 1944, the meeting of the Washington Committee of Jurists from 9 to 20 April 1945, and finally the San Francisco Conference on International Organization from 25 April to 26 June 1945. All three conferences addressed the role of the Court's advisory jurisdiction, although the focus was clearly on a variety of other issues.

I. Dumbarton Oaks Conversations (August to September 1944)

During the Dumbarton Oaks Conversations, Great Britain, the USA, the USSR, and China met to "informally" exchange views on a new world organization and the role of a new World Court within it.[123] The resulting Dum-

120 Ibid., 23, para. 74.

121 *M. N. Shaw*, Rosenne's Law and Practice of the International Court: 1920-2015, 5th ed 2016, Vol. 1, Ch. 2, § 6.

122 Ibid., Vol. 1, Ch. 2, § 6.

123 Ibid., Vol. 1, Ch. 2, § 7 The Dumbarton Oaks Conversations occurred in two phases: The Anglo-American-Soviet phase from 21 August to 28 September 1944 and the Anglo-American-Chinese phase from 28 September to 7 October 1944.

barton Oaks Proposals contained the foundation of the United Nations, a new international organization with the aim to ensure peace and security.[124] Contrary to the London Committee's proposal to cut the link between court and organization, the International Court of Justice was meant to become one of four main organs of the United Nations.[125] Chapter VII of the Dumbarton Oaks Proposals addressed the new International Court of Justice in more detail. In addition to being a principal organ, the Court was also to be the principal judicial organ of the organization (para. 1). Its Statute, which was proposed to be either a revised version of the PCIJ Statute or a new Statute based on the PCIJ Statute (para. 3), was to be part of the Charter of the new organization (para. 2). At the Dumbarton Oaks Conference, the states thus spoke out in favor of an even closer integration of the World Court within the World Organization than was previously the case.[126]

The Dumbarton Oaks Proposals also took up the Court's advisory jurisdiction, albeit in a curious fashion. Chapter VIII Section A para. 6 read:

> "Justiciable disputes should normally be referred to the International Court of Justice. The Security Council should be empowered to refer to the Court, for advice, legal questions connected with other disputes."

Several aspects are worth noting: The Dumbarton Oaks Proposals dealt with the Court's advisory jurisdiction exclusively in the context of dispute settlement. The above-cited paragraph is located within Chapter VIII, which is entitled "Arrangements for the maintenance of international peace and security including prevention and suppression of aggression" under section A "Pacific Settlement of Disputes". According to this paragraph, the envisioned Security Council could request advisory opinions on "legal questions connected with other disputes". The Court's advisory jurisdiction under this proposal thus expressly extended to disputes. However, the paragraph listed two types of disputes, without further explaining the difference: "justiciable disputes", which should be referred to the ICJ and "other disputes". The framing of the advisory opinion procedure as a method of

124 Dumbarton Oaks Proposals, preamble, Yearbook of the United Nations, 1946–47, 4.
125 Dumbarton Oaks Proposals, Chapter IV, Paragraph 1, Yearbook of the United Nations, 1946–47, 5. The other three envisaged organs were the General Assembly, the Security Council and the Secretariat.
126 *M. N. Shaw*, Rosenne's Law and Practice of the International Court: 1920-2015, 5th ed 2016, Vol. 1, Ch. 2, § 7.

dispute settlement was later discarded at the San Francisco Conference.[127] The Dumbarton Oaks Proposals did not pick up on the proposal of the Informal Inter-Allied Committee to extend the power to request advisory opinions to two or more states acting in concert. Some highly controversial questions were left open at the Dumbarton Oaks conference, including the question whether the new Court should have compulsory jurisdiction.[128]

II. Washington Committee of Jurists (9 to 20 April 1945)

The Dumbarton Oaks Proposals developed broad stroke proposals rather than drafting a detailed constituent instrument. The next step was thus to transform the Dumbarton Oaks Proposals into a binding legal instrument which would create the new world organization and the new World Court. This was the aim for the San Francisco Conference which was scheduled to commence on 25 April 1945. In preparation for this, the United States invited other Allied states to send experts to Washington for a preparatory meeting. This "Committee of Jurists" was tasked to write a draft Statute for the new International Court of Justice based on the PCIJ Statute and the Dumbarton Oaks Proposals. The newly drafted Statute would then serve as the basis for the discussions during the San Francisco Conference.[129] From 9 to 20 April 1945, the Committee developed a draft which was a revised version of the PCIJ Statute. However, several issues that were considered too political were deferred to the San Francisco Conference.[130] These included the question of the nomination and election of the judges of the Court, the role of the Court as principal judicial organ of the United Nations, the question of whether the International Court of Justice was a continuation of the PCIJ or a new court, and whether the Court should have compulsory jurisdiction.[131]

Regarding the Court's advisory jurisdiction, the Committee of Jurists simply incorporated Articles 65 to 68 of the PCIJ Statute into the draft for

127 Ibid., Vol. 1, Ch. 5, § 60.
128 Ibid., Vol. 1, Ch. 2, § 7.
129 Ibid., Vol. 1, Ch. 2, § 8.
130 Ibid., Vol. 1, Ch. 2, § 8.
131 Ibid., Vol. 1, Ch. 2, § 8.

the new ICJ Statute without making any substantial changes.[132] The Committee deferred the decision about which organs were entitled to request advisory opinions to the San Francisco Conference. However, it drafted the articles based on the presumption that the Security Council (UNSC) and the General Assembly (UNGA) would have this power, while other international organizations and states would not.[133]

Several states commented on the proposals made by the Washington Committee of Jurists. Guatemala, Mexico, and Norway supported the extension of the right to request advisory opinions to the UNGA,[134] the United Kingdom and Venezuela went even further and proposed an extension also to other international organizations connected to the United Nations, as well as two or more states acting in concert.[135] Norway addressed the question whether the advisory jurisdiction should extend to inter-state disputes:

> "The authority for the Security Council to request an advisory opinion of the International Court as formulated in the proposals must apply to legal questions arising out of *any dispute*. But the Security Council should have a similar authority to request an opinion of the Court also concerning legal questions unconnected with any particular dispute."[136]

During the discussions a debate erupted among the delegates whether the question of a compulsory jurisdiction of the Court rendered any debate about a liberal versus a restrictive advisory jurisdiction meaningless. The Iraqi delegate *Abass* argued that if the Court were given compulsory juris-

---

132 The Committee merely swapped references to the League of Nations for references to the United Nations and split some longer paragraphs into several shorter ones, United Nations, Doc. Jurists 59 G/47, Vol. 14, 564–565.

133 Washington Committee of Jurists, Doc. Jurists 86, G/73, Chapter IV; the Washington Committee of Jurists accepted the proposal to Proposal to grant the UNGA the power to request advisory opinions from the Court by 27 votes in favor and none opposed while disapproving the proposal to extend the same right to other international organizations by 16 votes to 4, Washington Committee of Jurists, Doc Jur.45; G/34 Vol. 14, p. 177, 183.

134 Committee of Jurists, Official comments, Doc Jur.1; G/1 vol. 14, 446–447.

135 Committee of Jurists, United Kingdom proposal regarding the Statute of the Permanent Court of International Justice, 10 April 1945, Doc. Jur.14; DP/4, Vol. 14, 319; Committee of Jurists, Memorandum presented by the delegation of Venezuela on basis for the organization of the International Court of Justice, 10 April 1945, Doc. Jur.16; G/12, Vol. 14, 373.

136 Committee of Jurists, Official comments, Doc Jur.1; G/1 vol. 14, 447 (emphasis added).

diction, advisory opinions would become unnecessary, since justiciable disputes would *ipso facto* be referred to the Court.[137] The British delegate *Fitzmaurice* responded that a compulsory jurisdiction would to the contrary increase the usefulness of advisory opinions, because states could avoid litigation by referring matters to the Court's advisory procedure before they reached the stage of a dispute.[138] The question of whether the ICJ should have compulsory jurisdiction occupied much of the debates of the Washington Committee of Jurists and during the San Francisco Conference. This focus was likely one reason, why the advisory jurisdiction of the Court received only passing attention. However, the record of the discussions does not indicate any intention of the delegates at the Washington Committee of Jurists to limit the new Court's advisory jurisdiction in comparison to the PCIJ.[139]

III. San Francisco Conference (25 April to 26 June 1945)

While the Second World War drew to an end in Europe, the founding conference of the United Nations took place in San Francisco. From 25 April to 26 June 1945, 850 delegates from 50 states[140] met with the aim of adopting the Charter of the United Nations as the constituent instrument of a new international organization and a Statute of the new World Court. The drafting of the UNC took place in four Commissions, whose work was subdivided into 12 Committees and numerous Subcommittees: the task of Commission I was to define the aims and principles of the new organization, determine its main organs and create rules governing membership and the work of the General Secretariat. Commission II was responsible

137 The United Nations Committee of Jurists, Summary of eighth meeting, Doc. 45; G/34, 178.

138 The United Nations Committee of Jurists, Summary of eighth meeting, Doc. 45; G/34, 178–9.

139 So too *S. M. Schwebel*, Was the Capacity to Request an Advisory Opinion Wider in the Permanent Court of International Justice than it is in the International Court of Justice?, in: S. M. Schwebel (ed.), Justice in International Law: Selected Writings of Judge Stephen M. Schwebel, 1994, 27 (58).

140 Yearbook of the United Nations, 1946–47, 12. Poland was invited but could not send delegates as it did not have a recognized government at the time of the conference, Yearbook of the United Nations, 1946–47, 12. Poland is nevertheless considered one of the founding members of the United Nations, https://www.un.org/en/about-us/history-of-the-un/san-francisco-conference.

for the General Assembly, Commission III for the Security Council, and Commission IV for the International Court of Justice.[141]

The San Francisco Conference brought about five important changes to the structure of the Court and its advisory jurisdiction:

First, Under pressure from the USSR and the USA, Commission IV decided against the continuation of the PCIJ and in favor of the creation of a new Court whose jurisdiction would be voluntary and thus subject to the consent of the states.[142] The idea of a compulsory international jurisdiction was explicitly rejected.

Secondly, and potentially most significantly, Article 7 para. 1 UNC establishes the ICJ as one of the six principal organs of the UN, among which there is no hierarchical order.[143] The ICJ also acts as the organization's principal judicial organ (see Article 92 UNC). The effects of this dual character of the Court, being one of the principal organs and a judicial organ at the same time, were not discussed during the conference. The reason for this might lie in the division of labor between Commission I, which dealt with the principal organs of the UN, and Commission IV, which dealt with the judicial organization.[144] This division of labor resulted in neither of the two Commissions considering in detail the interaction of the two features of the ICJ.[145] One of the most significant implications of the Court's character as an organ of the UN is that the ICJ, in exercising its judicial functions, must work towards the fulfilment of the aims of the Organization and to that effect cooperate with the other principal organs.[146] This "duty to cooperate" with other UN organs will be a guiding consideration in the Court's exercise of its advisory jurisdiction. Judge *Azevedo* emphasized this in the Court's first advisory opinion in the *Peace Treaties* case:

---

141 *M. N. Shaw*, Rosenne's Law and Practice of the International Court: 1920-2015, 5th ed 2016, Vol. 1, Ch. 2, § 9.

142 Ibid., Vol. 1, Ch. 2, § 10. Despite the fact that the PCIJ was discontinued, the ICJ is the PCIJ's quasi-successor. The final report of Committee IV/1 stated in this regard: "In a sense, therefore, the new Court may be looked upon as the successor to the old Court which is replaced.", Report of the Committee IV/1, 13 UNCIO 381, 383.

143 *M. Lippold*, in: B. Simma/D.-E. Khan/G. Nolte/A. Paulus (eds.), The Charter of the United Nations, 4. ed., 2024: Art. 7, para. 10.

144 *M. N. Shaw*, Rosenne's Law and Practice of the International Court: 1920-2015, 5th ed 2016, Vol. 1, Ch. 2, § 9.

145 Ibid., Vol. 1, Ch. 2, § 9.

146 *S. Rosenne*, The law and practice of the International Court, 1920-2005, 4th ed. 2006, 109.

> "The Court, which has been raised to the status of a principal organ and thus more closely geared into the mechanism of the U.N.O., must do its utmost to co-operate with the other organs with a view to attaining the aims and principles that have been set forth."[147]

The ICJ's duty to cooperate implies a duty to respond to requests for advisory opinions from the other UN organs as the Court considers that giving such advisory opinions "represents its participation in the activities of the Organization, and, in principle, should not be refused".[148] However, the Court's duty to cooperate and correlating duty to respond is limited by the Court's character as a judicial organ. How the Court reconciles these two elements of its character is examined below.[149]

Thirdly, the circle of entities authorized to request advisory opinions from the Court was widened to not only include the UNSC and the UNGA, but also "other organs of the United Nations and specialized agencies". Previous proposals to allow two or more states acting in concert to request advisory opinions from the Court were rejected during the negotiations in San Francisco.[150] It was feared that such a right "would afford a means whereby the State concerned could indirectly impose a species of compulsory jurisdiction on the rest of the world".[151]

Fourthly, all provisions on the power to request an advisory opinion from the ICJ have been consolidated in the provisions on the ICJ, instead of being distributed among the sections on the respective institutions. In earlier proposals, the provisions governing the ICJ's advisory jurisdiction were contained in the section on the UNSC's powers of pacific dispute settlement. During the drafting process the advisory procedure was relocated to the section on the competences of the ICJ. However, this relocation cannot be understood as a deliberate choice to restrict the ICJ from giving advisory opinions on inter-state disputes. Committee III/2, which was responsible for drafting the provisions relating to the UNSC, decided to delete any

---

147 *Interpretation of Peace Treaties with Bulgaria, Hungary and Romania (First Phase)*, Advisory Opinion, Separate Opinion Azevedo, ICJ Reports 1950, 79 (82).

148 *Interpretation of Peace Treaties with Bulgaria, Hungary and Romania (First Phase)*, Advisory Opinion, ICJ Reports 1950, 65 (71).

149 See *infra*: § 3.

150 United Nations Conference on International Organization, Fifteenth Meeting of Committee IV/1, 30 May 1945, Doc. 685, IV/1/52, vol. 13, 232.

151 United Nations Conference on International Organization, Report of the Informal Inter-Allied Committee on the Future of the Permanent Court of International Justice Source, Vol. 14, 22, 445.

reference to the advisory procedure in the chapter on the UNSC not to emphasize that advisory opinions may not concern disputes but for the simple reason that "Committee IV/1 had included an adequate provision on this subject in Chapter X dealing with the International court of Justice".[152]

And fifthly, during the drafting process, the participating states agreed upon a new wording to describe the Court's advisory jurisdiction *ratione materiae*. In departure from the text of the League's Covenant, which referred to any "dispute or question" (Article 14 Covenant), the newly drafted Articles 96 UNC and 65 ICJ Statute refer to "any legal question". The significance of this change in wording will be discussed later when the legal framework of the ICJ's advisory jurisdiction is analyzed in detail.[153]

E. Conclusions on the history of the advisory function

The ICJ – unlike the PCIJ – was created as an organ of an international organization. One of the most important consequences of this is that the ICJ has a duty to cooperate with the other UN organs.[154] This duty to cooperate finds its most concrete expression in the ICJ's advisory jurisdiction. How the Court ought to reconcile this duty to cooperate with the other UN organs with the requirements placed on the ICJ as a judicial organ, was neither discussed at the preparatory conferences nor the San Francisco Conference. However, exactly this tension between the two characteristics of the ICJ lies at the heart of the Eastern Carelia doctrine.

---

152 United Nations Conference on International Organization, Twelfth meeting of Committee III/2, Doc. 992; III/2/27, p. 105. The Rapporteur of Committee III/2 further stated: "The Committee recommends that there should be no reference to advisory opinions in this Chapter in view of the fact that Committee IV/1 has proposed the inclusion in the Chapter on the International Court of Justice of an article giving the Security Council and the General Assembly the power to request an advisory opinion of the Court on any legal question.", United Nations Conference on International Organization, Report of the Rapporteur of Committee III/2, Doc. 1027 III/2/31(1), vol. 12, 162.

153 See *infra*: § 5 Section D.V.

154 The ICJ implied such a duty to cooperate flowing from its status as an organ of the UN in its *Peace Treaties* advisory opinion when it stated that "the reply of the Court, itself an "organ of the United Nations", represents its participation in the activities of the Organization, and, in principle, should not be refused.", *Interpretation of Peace Treaties with Bulgaria, Hungary and Romania (First Phase)*, Advisory Opinion, ICJ Reports 1950, 65 (71).

§ 2 Origins of the Eastern Carelia doctrine

From the inception of the advisory jurisdiction of the PCIJ, legal scholars, practitioners, and state representatives have raised the concern that the Court's advisory jurisdiction clashes with the sovereign equality of states.[155] The sovereign equality of states protects a state from being forced to submit its international legal disputes to judicial settlement without its consent.[156] Critics of the Court's advisory jurisdiction are concerned that this fundamental principle is undermined by the power of the Court to issue advisory opinions on matters directly relating to inter-state disputes. States have consequently argued in several advisory proceedings that the Court may only give an advisory opinion if the affected states give their consent.[157] *Sloan* referred to this objection as "[t]he most important challenge to the competence of the Court".[158] This argument has entered the Court's case

155 See on this § 2 and § 3.

156 *Status of Eastern Carelia*, Advisory Opinion, PCIJ Series B 1923, 7 (27); on this, see also *J. Brunnée*, Consent (last updated 2010), in: A. Peters/R. Wolfrum (eds.), The Max Planck Encyclopedia of Public International Law, 2008 (4).

157 ICJ Pleadings, *Interpretation of Peace Treaties with Bulgaria, Hungary and Romania*, Written Statement of Bulgaria, 196–197; *Interpretation of Peace Treaties with Bulgaria, Hungary and Romania*, Written Statement of Romania, 203; *Interpretation of Peace Treaties with Bulgaria, Hungary and Romania*, Written Statement of Hungary, 211; *Reservations to the Convention on the Prevention and Punishment of the Crime of Genocide*, Written Statement of the Philippines, 296; *Legal Consequences for States of the Continued Presence of South Africa in Namibia (South West Africa) notwithstanding Security Council Resolution 276 (1970)*, Written Statement of South Africa, 377 (442 et seq.); *Western Sahara*, Vol. I, Written Statement of Spain, 202; *Legal Consequences of the Construction of a Wall in the Occupied Palestinian Territory*, Written Statement of Israel, 101–102, paras. 7.9 – 7.10; *Legal Consequences of the Separation of the Chagos Archipelago from Mauritius in 1965*, Written Statement of Australia, paras. 21, 32 et seq.; Written Statement of Chile, paras. 4 et seq.; Written Statement of France, para. 19; Written Statement of Israel, paras. 3.6 et seq.; Written Statement of the United Kingdom, paras. 7.14 et seq.; Written Comments of the United Kingdom, para. 3.3; Written Statement of the United States, paras. 1.2, 3.20 et seq.; Written Comments of the United States, para. 2.7; *Legal Consequences arising from the Policies and Practices of Israel in the Occupied Palestinian Territory, including East Jerusalem*, Written Statement of Israel, 2–3. For an analysis, see *infra*: § 3.

158 *F. B. Sloan*, 38 CLR 5 (1950), 830 (845); discussing state consent as a jurisdictional requirement of the Court's advisory procedure see *K. J. Keith*, The extent of

law under the name "Eastern Carelia doctrine"[159]. This doctrine originated in the 1923 *Eastern Carelia* advisory opinion of the PCIJ.[160] Since then, the Eastern Carelia doctrine has played an important role in the case law of both the PCIJ[161] and – in a significantly modified form – the ICJ[162]. The fundamental argument of the Eastern Carelia doctrine, which states have consistently invoked over the past 100 years, is the following: If two states have a legal dispute with each other, it is an expression of their sovereign equality to decide whether to submit the dispute to third party judicial settlement. If a party to the dispute refuses its consent, the dispute cannot be decided by any court or tribunal, even by non-binding means such as the advisory opinion procedure. This is a consequence of the sovereign equality of states. If an advisory opinion were given on a legal question which forms the subject-matter of the legal dispute pending between these two states, the issuing of the advisory opinion would circumvent the strict

---

the advisory jurisdiction of the International Court of Justice, 1971, 89 et seq; *D. Pratap*, The advisory jurisdiction of the International Court, 1972, 154 et seq.; *M. Pomerance*, The advisory function of the International Court in the League and U.N. eras, 1973, 287 et seq.; *K. J. Keith*, 16 AYBIL 39 (1996), 39-58 (43 et seq.); *C. F. Amerasinghe*, Jurisdiction of International Tribunals, 2003, 528 et seq.; *M. M. Aljaghoub*, The Advisory Function of the International Court of Justice 1946 - 2005, 2006, 97 et seq.; *M. M. Aljaghoub*, 24 ALQ 2 (2010), 191.

159 R. Kolb calls it the "anti-bypassing rule", *R. Kolb*, The International Court of Justice, 2013, 1074.

160 *Status of Eastern Carelia*, Advisory Opinion, PCIJ Series B 1923, 7. Although the PCIJ refused to give the requested advisory opinion, the PCIJ's response was published in the PCIJ's "Series B: Collection of Advisory Opinions" and subsequently referred to as an advisory opinion by the PCIJ, E 2, Second Annual Report, 164.

161 Ibid.; *Article 3, paragraph 2, of the Treaty of Lausanne (Frontier between Turkey and Iraq)*, Advisory Opinion, PCIJ Series B 1925, 6.

162 *Interpretation of Peace Treaties with Bulgaria, Hungary and Romania (First Phase)*, Advisory Opinion, ICJ Reports 1950, 65; *Reservations to the Convention on the Prevention and Punishment of the Crime of Genocide*, Advisory Opinion, ICJ Reports 1951, 15; *Legal Consequences for States of the Continued Presence of South Africa in Namibia (South West Africa) notwithstanding Security Council Resolution 276 (1970)*, Advisory Opinion, ICJ Reports 1971, 16; *Western Sahara*, Advisory Opinion, ICJ Reports 1975, 12; *Legal Consequences of the Construction of a Wall in the Occupied Palestinian Territory*, Advisory Opinion, ICJ Reports 2004, 136; *Legal Consequences of the Separation of the Chagos Archipelago from Mauritius in 1965*, Advisory Opinion, ICJ Reports 2019, 95; for an overview of the case law of the two Courts on the non-circumvention principle, see *K. J. Keith*, The extent of the advisory jurisdiction of the International Court of Justice, 1971, 89 et seq., 229; *D. Pratap*, The advisory jurisdiction of the International Court, 1972, 142 et seq.; *M. Pomerance*, The advisory function of the International Court in the League and U.N. eras, 1973, 287 et seq.; *M. M. Aljaghoub*, 24 ALQ 2 (2010), 191 (95 et seq.).

consent requirements of the Court's contentious procedure. To prevent this circumvention and to protect the legal interests of the disputing states, the Court may have to refuse to give the requested advisory opinion.

A. Eastern Carelia case (1923)

I. Background

The *Eastern Carelia* case[163] is the *locus classicus* of the delimitation of the PCIJ's advisory power.[164] The 1923 case also marks the beginning of the Eastern Carelia doctrine. At the heart of the *Eastern Carelia* case was a dispute between Finland and the USSR over the interpretation and application of the 1920 Treaty of Dorpat[165]. The Treaty of Dorpat was a peace treaty concluded in 1920 between Finland and the USSR's precursor – the Russian Soviet Federative Socialist Republic (RSFSR) – which transferred certain areas of the region of Eastern Carelia that were formerly under Finnish control to the RSFSR, while retaining certain autonomy rights.[166] Finland and the USSR were in dispute over whether a declaration made by the Russian delegation during the negotiation of the treaty became part of the treaty. Finland asked the League of Nations to take up the matter.[167] The Council of the League of Nations, through the good offices of Estonia, invited the USSR to accept the dispute resolution mechanism of the

163 *Status of Eastern Carelia*, Advisory Opinion, PCIJ Series B 1923, 7. Although the PCIJ refused to give the requested advisory opinion, the PCIJ's response was published in the PCIJ's "Series B: Collection of Advisory Opinions" and subsequently referred to as an advisory opinion by the PCIJ, E 2, Second Annual Report, p. 164; on the Eastern Carelia opinion, see *K. J. Keith*, The extent of the advisory jurisdiction of the International Court of Justice, 1971, 89–97; *M. Pomerance*, The advisory function of the International Court in the League and U.N. eras, 1973, 65–69; *J. Heliskoski*, Eastern Carelia (Request for Advisory Opinion) (last updated 2007), in: A. Peters/R. Wolfrum (eds.), The Max Planck Encyclopedia of Public International Law, 2008.

164 *G. Abi-Saab*, On Discretion: Reflections on the nature of the consultative function of the International Court of Justice, in: L. Boisson de Chazournes/P. Sands (eds.), International law, the World Court of justice and nuclear weapons, 1999, 36 (39).

165 *League of Nations Treaty Series*, vol. III, pp. 6–79, https://treaties.un.org/doc/Publication/UNTS/LON/Volume%203/v3.pdf. The Treaty is now commonly referred to as the Treaty of Tartu.

166 *Status of Eastern Carelia*, Advisory Opinion, PCIJ Series B 1923, 7 (18 et seq.).

167 Ibid. (23).

Covenant of the League of Nations and to submit its dispute with Finland to the Council in accordance with Article 17 of the Covenant.[168] However, the USSR refused its consent to any form of judicial dispute settlement.[169] Against this backdrop, the Council by resolution of 21 April 1923 requested an advisory opinion from the PCIJ on the question of whether Articles 10 and 11 of the Treaty of Dorpat between Finland and the RSFSR and the additional declaration of the Russian delegation were legally binding for Finland and the USSR.

II. Article 17 and the Council's competence to request advisory opinions from the PCIJ

Applying Article 14 of the League's Covenant, the PCIJ found that there was in fact a dispute between Finland and the USSR and that this dispute formed the subject-matter of the advisory request. The PCIJ held:

> "[t]hat both parties, while acknowledging the existence and obligatory force of the Treaty, differ as to the interpretation and legal effect of certain provisions, particularly Articles 10 and 11 relating to Eastern Carelia."[170]

Having established the existence of a dispute, the PCIJ then addressed the question whether this would prevent the Court from giving the requested advisory opinion. In particular, the Court raised the question whether it could give an advisory opinion relating to matters which form the subject-matter of a pending dispute between the two states without the consent of these states. Despite raising this question, the Court decided not to answer it:

> "There has been some discussion as to whether questions for an advisory opinion, if they relate to matters which form the subject of a pending dispute between nations, should be put to the Court without the consent of the parties. *It is unnecessary in the present case to deal with this topic.*"[171]

168 Ibid. (24).
169 Ibid.
170 Ibid. (22).
171 Ibid. (27), emphasis added.

Instead, the Court focused on the fact that the USSR was not a party to the League's Covenant and the legal consequences of this for the Council to act under Article 17. The PCIJ found:

> "As Russia is not a Member of the League of Nations, the case is one under Article 17 of the Covenant. According to this article, in the event of a dispute between a Member of the League and a state which is not a Member of the League, the state not a Member of the League shall be invited to accept the obligations of membership in the League for the purposes of such dispute, and, if this invitation is accepted, the provisions of Articles 12 to 16 inclusive shall be applied with such modifications as may be deemed necessary by the Council. [...] The submission, therefore, of a dispute between them and a Member of the League for solution according to the methods provided for in the Covenant, could take place only by virtue of their consent. Such consent, however, has never been given by Russia. [...] The Court therefore finds it impossible to give its opinion on a dispute of this kind."[172]

Article 17 para. 1 of the League's Covenant made the Council's competence to act regarding non-Member States subject to that states' consent.[173] Since the USSR – a non-Member State of the League – refused to give its consent, the Council was not competent to request an advisory opinion in relation to the dispute under Article 17 in connection with Article 15 of the Covenant.[174] The PCIJ's own lack of jurisdiction to give the requested advisory opinion was thus just a consequence of the Council's lack of jurisdiction to *request* the opinion. The Court thus addressed its own com-

172 Ibid. (27–28).

173 Art. 17 of the Covenant of the League of Nations read:
"In the event of a dispute between a Member of the League and a State which is not a Member of the League, or between States not Members of the League, the State or States not Members of the League shall be invited to accept the obligations of membership in the League for the purposes of such dispute, upon such conditions as the Council may deem just. If such invitation is accepted, the provisions of Articles 12 to 16 inclusive shall be applied with such modifications as may be deemed necessary by the Council."

174 *G. Abi-Saab*, Les exceptions préliminaires dans la procédure de la Cour internationale, 1966, 79; *K. J. Keith*, The extent of the advisory jurisdiction of the International Court of Justice, 1971, 96; *M. Pomerance*, The advisory function of the International Court in the League and U.N. eras, 1973, 287 et seq.; cf. *R. Kolb*, The Elgar companion to the International Court of Justice, 2014, 267–268.

petence to give the requested advisory opinion only to the extent it related to the competence of the Council to resolve the dispute brought before it.[175]

III. The birth of the Eastern Carelia doctrine by *obiter dictum*

Despite initially stating that it was "unnecessary" to address the question of state consent, the PCIJ made an *obiter dictum* that attracted much attention, and which was invoked in support of a general consent requirement in later cases.[176] The PCIJ declared:

> "[Article 17 of the Covenant], moreover, only accepts and applies a principle which is a fundamental principle of international law, namely, the principle of the independence of States. It is well established in international law that no State can, without its consent, be compelled to submit its disputes with other States either to mediation or to arbitration, or to any other kind of pacific settlement. Such consent can be given once and for all in the form of an obligation freely undertaken, but it can, on the contrary, also be given in a special case apart from any existing obligation. The first alternative applies to the Members of the League who, having accepted the Covenant, are under the obligation resulting from the provisions of this pact dealing with the pacific settlement of international disputes."[177]

The Court made two fundamental findings here: First, the principle of the independence of states – now more commonly referred to as sovereign equality of states[178] – requires that any kind of pacific settlement be subject to the consent of the disputing states. The PCIJ not only referenced binding dispute resolution mechanisms in this context, but also non-binding ones such as mediation as well as "any other kind of pacific dispute settlement". Without expressly saying so, by addressing this issue in its *Eastern Carelia* opinion, the PCIJ seems to regard its advisory procedure as such a non-binding "other kind of pacific dispute settlement" which may, in principle,

175 See *K. J. Keith*, The extent of the advisory jurisdiction of the International Court of Justice, 1971, 94 et seq.
176 See in particular the argumentation of Bulgaria, Hungary and Romania in the *Peace Treaties* case before the ICJ. See on this, §3.A.II.
177 *Status of Eastern Carelia*, Advisory Opinion, PCIJ Series B 1923, 7 (27).
178 Instead of many, see *J. Crawford*, Brownlie's Principles of Public International Law, 9. ed. 2019, 430 et seq.

trigger a consent requirement. The ICJ will depart from the idea that the principle of sovereign equality of states requires the consent of states that are affected from the proceedings regardless of the binding nature of the procedure.[179] Secondly, general consent to the Covenant and the Court's Statute and thus to the Court's advisory opinion procedure suffices as consent. By becoming a party to the League's Covenant and the Court's Statute, a state accepts the provisions governing the Court's advisory opinion procedure and also accepts that the PCIJ may address by means of its advisory procedure legal questions which form the subject of an inter-state dispute.

IV. Propriety of giving the requested advisory opinion

Although the PCIJ had already dismissed the competence of the League's Council to request an advisory opinion from the Court and thus decided that it could not give the requested advisory opinion, the Court nevertheless addressed a more general question: the question of judicial propriety. The refusal of the USSR to cooperate in the present case did not only lead to a lack of competence of the Council. It also affected the functioning of the Court. The Court found that because of the lack of cooperation by the USSR it would not have access to all the relevant facts of the case. The PCIJ held:

> "The Court is aware of the fact that it is not requested to decide a dispute, but to give an advisory opinion. This circumstance, however, does not essentially modify the above considerations. The question put to the Court is not one of abstract law, but concerns directly the main point of the controversy between Finland and Russia, and can only be decided by an investigation into the facts underlying the case. Answering

179 See in particular the Peace Treaties Advisory Opinion where the Court stated: "The consent of States, parties to a dispute, is the basis of the Court's jurisdiction in contentious cases. The situation is different in regard to advisory proceedings even where the Request for an Opinion relates to a legal question actually pending between States. The Court's reply is only of an advisory character: as such, it has no binding force. It follows that no State, whether a Member of the United Nations or not, can prevent the giving of an Advisory Opinion which the United Nations considers to be desirable in order to obtain enlightenment as to the course of action it should take.", *Interpretation of Peace Treaties with Bulgaria, Hungary and Romania (First Phase)*, Advisory Opinion, ICJ Reports 1950, 65 (71).

> the question would be substantially equivalent to deciding the dispute between the parties. The Court, being a Court of Justice, cannot, even in giving advisory opinions, depart from the essential rules guiding their activity as a Court."[180]

The PCIJ implied here an assimilation of its two procedures – the contentious procedure and the advisory procedure. The two procedures do not require two completely different modes of operation from the Court. Instead, the Court, even in giving advisory opinions, performs a judicial task which requires the Court to "investigate into the facts underlying the case". This is remarkable, as the PCIJ could also have understood its advisory function as only requiring the Court to state the abstract law without reference to the facts of the case.

V. Interim conclusions: (un)limited application of the Eastern Carelia 'precedent'

How could the *Eastern Carelia* advisory opinion serve as the main reference point for states in subsequent advisory proceedings to argue for a consent requirement when the PCIJ explicitly stated it was "unnecessary in the present case to deal with this topic"[181]? Maybe the answer lies in the fact that the Court did not say what it did and did not do what it said.[182] On the one hand, the Court emphasized that its reasoning only applied to the present case and that it was guided by the fact that the USSR was not a Member State of the League of Nations. Because of this, Article 17 of the Covenant made the Council's competence to request an advisory opinion subject to the prior consent of the USSR. If the Court's reasoning was limited to non-Member States of the League, the relevance of the *Eastern Carelia* advisory opinion for future advisory proceedings would be very limited.[183] On the other hand, the Court made an *obiter dictum* stating that even non-binding forms of dispute settlement including mediation and advisory opinions required the consent of the disputing states. The idea

180 *Status of Eastern Carelia*, Advisory Opinion, PCIJ Series B 1923, 7 (28–29).
181 Ibid. (27).
182 Cf. *R. Christensen*, Was heißt Gesetzesbindung?, 1989, 64.
183 Arguing that the Court only addressed the legal status of non-Member States, see *M. Pomerance*, The advisory function of the International Court in the League and U.N. eras, 1973, 289.

that the sovereign equality of states made non-binding forms of dispute settlement subject to state consent is far-reaching and forms the main reference-point for future arguments before the ICJ.[184]

B. Mosul case (1925)

The next step in the development of the Eastern Carelia doctrine was marked by the 1925 *Mosul* case.[185]

I. Background

At the time, Great Britain and Turkey had a dispute about the demarcation of Turkey's border with Iraq. The demarcation process was governed by the 1923 Treaty of Lausanne.[186] Article 3 para. 2 of the Treaty of Lausanne stipulated:

> "The frontier between Turkey and Iraq shall be laid down in friendly arrangement to be concluded between Turkey and Great Britain within nine months. In the event of no agreement being reached between the two Governments within the time mentioned, the dispute shall be referred to the Council of the League of Nations."

After Great Britain and Turkey could not agree upon such a "friendly arrangement" in due time, Great Britain asked the League's Secretariat to place the matter on the Council's agenda.[187] The Secretariat complied with this request and informed Turkey accordingly. Turkey, which was not a

---

184 Arguing that the PCIJ established a general consent requirement, see *Interpretation of Peace Treaties with Bulgaria, Hungary and Romania (First Phase)*, Advisory Opinion, Dissenting Opinion Krylov, ICJ Reports 1950, 65 (108–111).

185 *Article 3, paragraph 2, of the Treaty of Lausanne (Frontier between Turkey and Iraq)*, Advisory Opinion, PCIJ Series B 1925, 6; on the Mosul case, see *K. J. Keith*, The extent of the advisory jurisdiction of the International Court of Justice, 1971, 97–101; *M. Pomerance*, The advisory function of the International Court in the League and U.N. eras, 1973, 75–78.

186 Treaty of Lausanne, signed 24 July 1923, entry into force 6 August 1924, League of Nations Treaty Series, No. 701, Vol. XXVIII, 12–113.

187 *Article 3, paragraph 2, of the Treaty of Lausanne (Frontier between Turkey and Iraq)*, Advisory Opinion, PCIJ Series B 1925, 6 (15).

member of the League at the time,[188] agreed "in principle" to the inscription of the question on the Council's agenda[189] and then sent its representative to take part in the Council's discussions.[190] In the pursuing discussions, Great Britain and Turkey disagreed whether the Council could decide the question of delimitation in a binding manner. The Council decided to request an advisory opinion from the PCIJ on this question as well as the question of voting in the Council. Turkey continued to provide the Court with information – albeit under reservation[191] – and replied to certain questions which the Court had put to it in the lead-up to the public hearings,[192] but it did not consent to the judicial settlement of its dispute with Great Britain.[193] Turkey was "convinced that the questions (...) in regard to which Court's advisory opinion is asked are of a distinctly political character and, in the Turkish Government's opinion, cannot form the subject of a legal interpretation".[194]

Turkey thus consented to the Council's involvement, however not to that of the Court.

II. PCIJ reaffirms Eastern Carelia doctrine even where Article 17 is fulfilled

What is most interesting in the *Mosul* case is not so much what the Court addressed but rather what it decided not to address. Even though Turkey was not a member of the League of Nations and although Turkey refused to consent to the judicial settlement of the matter, the Court did not address the question of state consent. Rather, it emphasized that its answer to the request for an advisory opinion must not be understood as judicial settlement of the underlying bilateral dispute. The PCIJ held:

188 For a list of the Member States of the League of Nations, see https://www.britannica.com/topic/League-of-Nations/Members-of-the-League-of-Nations.

189 Article 3, paragraph 2, of the Treaty of Lausanne (Frontier between Turkey and Iraq), Advisory Opinion, PCIJ Series B 1925, 6 (15).

190 Ibid. (16).

191 *K. J. Keith*, The extent of the advisory jurisdiction of the International Court of Justice, 1971, 99.

192 *Article 3, paragraph 2, of the Treaty of Lausanne (Frontier between Turkey and Iraq)*, Advisory Opinion, PCIJ Series B 1925, 6 (9).

193 *K. J. Keith*, The extent of the advisory jurisdiction of the International Court of Justice, 1971, 99.

194 *Article 3, paragraph 2, of the Treaty of Lausanne (Frontier between Turkey and Iraq)*, Advisory Opinion, PCIJ Series B 1925, 6 (8).

> "Before proceeding to examine the questions put to it by the Council, the Court wishes to observe that it intends strictly to confine itself to consideration of these questions, without in any way prejudging the merits of the problem before the Council; nothing in the present opinion, therefore, is to be interpreted as anticipating the solution of that problem."[195]

The Court then proceeded to interpret Article 3 para. 2 of the Treaty of Lausanne concluding that the Council may decide the matter with binding force.[196]

Contrary to Russia in the *Eastern Carelia* case, Turkey gave its consent to the involvement of the League's Council by concluding Article 3 para. 2 sub-para. 2 of the Treaty of Lausanne and by actively participating in the Council's discussions after the dispute was referred to it.[197] Whereas in the *Eastern Carelia* case, the Council was not duly seized under Article 17 of the Covenant as Russia refused to give its consent, in the *Mosul* case, Turkey accepted the Council's involvement. The conditions of Article 17 of the Covenant were thus fulfilled, which allowed the Council to request an advisory opinion from the Court under Article 15 of the Covenant.[198] Although the Council was thus competent to request an advisory opinion from the Court, the Court nevertheless stressed that its answer may not be interpreted as a form of judicial dispute settlement. This is directed at Turkey's refusal of consent to any form of judicial dispute settlement. The Court thereby follows up on the *obiter dictum* it gave in the *Eastern Carelia* case. By stressing that the Court did not intend to settle the dispute between Turkey and Great Britain, it reaffirmed the principle that a state may not be forced to submit its matters to judicial settlement even by non-binding means.

The PCIJ thus made clear that two questions must be distinguished: the first question concerns the requesting organ's competence to request an advisory opinion from the Court. This competence results from an act of attribution by consent, either in the form of membership in the League of Nations and the Court's Statute or in the form of *ad-hoc* consent if non-members are involved. The other question concerns the use of advisory opinions as a means of dispute resolution. As the *Mosul* case highlights, the

---

195 Ibid. (18).

196 Ibid. (19).

197 *K. J. Keith*, The extent of the advisory jurisdiction of the International Court of Justice, 1971, 98.

198 Ibid., 101.

Court may not deduce its competence to settle a bilateral dispute by means of its advisory opinion procedure from the organ's competence to request an advisory opinion.

C. Conclusions on the origins of the Eastern Carelia doctrine

The PCIJ has introduced the Eastern Carelia doctrine as a potential argument for states to challenge the competence of the Court to issue an advisory opinion. The Court did so when it addressed the question of state consent in the context of non-binding advisory opinions and by linking it to the concept of sovereign equality of states. The transferability of this doctrine to the UN era seems questionable for multiple reasons: First, the relevant provision upon which the PCIJ based its decision not to give the advisory opinion in the *Eastern Carelia* case was Article 17 of the League's Covenant which made any request for an advisory opinion by the Council that related to the settlement of disputes involving non-Member States subject to the consent of the non-Member States. There is no comparable provision in the UNC or the ICJ's Statute. Secondly, the PCIJ – unlike the ICJ – did not address the most contentious matters of its time. As *Spiermann* put it, "[i]n the political history of the League of Nations, the Permanent Court is but a footnote, partly because it did not deal with the main political issues of the day."[199] In contrast, the ICJ addressed several highly controversial political disputes which attracted the attention of states

199 *O. Spiermann*, International legal argument in the permanent court of international justice, 2005, 132. See also *Hudson*, who commented on the role of the PCIJ in the settlement of international disputes in 1944: "Each of the cases had importance for the parties involved, and the successful disposition of it cleared the air in difficult situations. Yet few of the cases became the subject of popular interest. It would be difficult to say that any of the cases threatened to became a *casus belli*, though some of them related to differences which, if the Court had not been available and if they had been allowed to fester, might have led to serious consequences.", *M. O. Hudson*, International Tribunals, 1944, 239.

and the general public alike.[200] The *Kosovo* case[201] and the *Wall* case[202] are just two examples.[203]

Despite these differences, the notion that states may not be forced to have their disputes settled by an international court without their consent even by means of the advisory procedure continues to have relevance before the new World Court, the ICJ. As the next chapter will illustrate, the ICJ integrated the Eastern Carelia doctrine into its jurisprudence, not, however, without modifying the doctrine in the process.

---

200 Cf. *S. Rosenne*, The law and practice of the International Court, 1920-2005, 4th ed. 2006, 2.

201 *Accordance with international law of the unilateral declaration of independence in respect of Kosovo*, Advisory Opinion, ICJ Reports 2010, 403.

202 *Legal Consequences of the Construction of a Wall in the Occupied Palestinian Territory*, Advisory Opinion, ICJ Reports 2004, 136.

203 Both cases are examined in detail in the next chapter, see *infra*: § 3 Sections F. and G.

§ 3 Development of the Eastern Carelia doctrine by the ICJ

The ICJ addressed the Eastern Carlia doctrine in several cases with the first case being the 1950 *Peace Treaties* case and the most recent case being the 2024 *Palestine* case.[204] The aim of this chapter is to present an overview of the arguments that states have presented and the stance the ICJ has developed regarding the use of advisory opinions to settle inter-state disputes. One essential observation concerns a shift from arguments focusing on the protection of the interested states' rights towards the protection of the Court's judicial function. In line with this, the focus also shifted from arguments concerning the Court's jurisdiction to give the requested advisory opinion towards "softer" criteria such as the admissibility and propriety of giving it. As will be seen, this shift was prompted by the difference in the jurisdictional framework of the ICJ in comparison to the PCIJ. Whereas Article 17 of the League's Covenant stipulated express limitations to the giving of advisory opinions in relation to disputes that concerned non-consenting non-members of the League of Nations, no such provision exists for the ICJ.

204 *Interpretation of Peace Treaties with Bulgaria, Hungary and Romania (First Phase)*, Advisory Opinion, ICJ Reports 1950, 65; *Reservations to the Convention on the Prevention and Punishment of the Crime of Genocide*, Advisory Opinion, ICJ Reports 1951, 15; *Legal Consequences for States of the Continued Presence of South Africa in Namibia (South West Africa) notwithstanding Security Council Resolution 276 (1970)*, Advisory Opinion, ICJ Reports 1971, 16; *Western Sahara*, Advisory Opinion, ICJ Reports 1975, 12; *Applicability of Article VI, Section 22, of the Convention on the Privileges and Immunities*, Advisory Opinion, ICJ Reports 1989, 177; *Legal Consequences of the Construction of a Wall in the Occupied Palestinian Territory*, Advisory Opinion, ICJ Reports 2004, 136; *Legal Consequences of the Separation of the Chagos Archipelago from Mauritius in 1965*, Advisory Opinion, ICJ Reports 2019, 95; *Legal Consequences arising from the Policies and Practices of Israel in the Occupied Palestinian Territory, including East Jerusalem*, Advisory Opinion, Publication pending in ICJ Reports 2024, 1.

A. Peace Treaties case (1950)

The first example of states invoking the Eastern Carelia doctrine before the ICJ is the *Peace Treaties* case.[205]

I. Background

In 1947, Bulgaria, Hungary, and Romania – which were part of the former Axis powers – concluded peace treaties with the Allied states. In 1949, the UNGA asked the ICJ to interpret these peace treaties, in particular the provisions on dispute settlement.[206] The peace treaties established a so-called "Treaty Commission" which functioned as an arbitral tribunal to decide disputes on the implementation of the peace treaties.[207] Bulgaria, Hungary, and Romania, however, argued that the advisory proceedings really concerned another matter: the observance of human rights obligations by the three states.

II. Bulgaria, Hungary, and Romania challenge the Court's jurisdiction

Bulgaria, Hungary, and Romania challenged the jurisdiction of the Court arguing that the UNGA interfered in domestic matters by discussing the implementation of human rights within the three states.[208] The UNGA, they argued, acted *ultra vires*, and, therefore, the ICJ was not competent to issue the requested advisory opinion. Bulgaria employed the PCIJ's terminology in the *Eastern Carelia* opinion when it stated:

---

205 *Interpretation of Peace Treaties with Bulgaria, Hungary and Romania (First Phase)*, Advisory Opinion, Dissenting Opinion Winiarski, ICJ Reports 1950, 65; on the Peace Treaties case, see *K. J. Keith*, The extent of the advisory jurisdiction of the International Court of Justice, 1971, 111–119; *M. Pomerance*, The advisory function of the International Court in the League and U.N. eras, 1973, 98–103.

206 UNGA resolution 294(IV) of 22 October 1949, UN doc. A/RES/294(IV), para. 3. The resolution was adopted by 47 votes to 5 against, with 7 abstentions, see A/PV.235.

207 Cf. *Interpretation of Peace Treaties with Bulgaria, Hungary and Romania (First Phase)*, Advisory Opinion, ICJ Reports 1950, 65 (67 et seq).

208 ICJ Pleadings, *Interpretation of Peace Treaties with Bulgaria, Hungary and Romania*, Written Statement of Bulgaria, 196; Written Statement of Romania, 202; Written Statement of Hungary, 211.

> "The Bulgarian Government considers that the Court cannot issue the requested advisory opinion without seriously undermining the well-established principle in international law [...] namely, the principle that any judicial proceedings in a given case involving a legal issue pending between two parties [...] are only effective if the prior consent of all the parties to the proceedings is obtained."[209]

Romania also invoked a consent requirement for the Court's advisory jurisdiction. It argued:

> "The Romanian Government draws attention to the fact that in no case can the International Court of Justice have jurisdiction in a matter concerning Romania without the consent of the Romanian Government."[210]

Hungary, while not directly referring to the Eastern Carelia principle, nevertheless invoked the principle of sovereign equality of states to support its claim.[211]

All three states (Bulgaria and Romania explicitly, Hungary implicitly) argued that the ICJ could not issue the requested advisory opinion because the questions concerned a purely internal matter, and the three states did not consent to the proceeding. Bulgaria's comments, in particular, can be interpreted as a reference to the PCIJ's statements in the *Eastern Carelia* advisory opinion. The three states – just like, *mutatis mutandis*, the USSR

209 Translated by the author. The French original reads: "Gouvernement bulgare estime que Cour ne saurait émettre avis consultatif demandé sans porter grave atteinte au principe bien établi en droit international [...] à savoir principe selon lequel toute procédure judiciaire dans un cas déterminé, portant sur question juridique pendan-te entre deux parties [...] n'est opérante qu'à condition que consentement préalable de toutes les parties en cause soit acquis.", ICJ Pleadings, *Interpretation of Peace Treaties with Bulgaria, Hungary and Romania*, Written Statement of Bulgaria, 196–197; the PCIJ used a similar language when it stated: "Il est bien établi en droit international qu'aucun Etat ne saurait être obligé de soumettre ses différends avec les autres Etats soit à la médiation, soit à l'arbitrage, soit enfin à n'importe quel procédé de solution pacifique, sans son consentement.", *Status of Eastern Carelia*, Advisory Opinion, Series B, No. 5, 1923, 7 (27).

210 Translated by the author. The French original reads: "Le Gouvernement roumain attire l'attention qu'en aucun cas, la Cour internationale de Justice ne peut être compétente dans une question concernant la Roumanie sans que le Gouvernement roumain y eût donné son consentement", ICJ Pleadings, *Interpretation of Peace Treaties with Bulgaria, Hungary and Romania*, Written Statement of Romania, 203.

211 ICJ Pleadings, *Interpretation of Peace Treaties with Bulgaria, Hungary and Romania*, Written Statement of Hungary, 211.

in the *Eastern Carelia* case – were not Member States of the UN at the time of the advisory proceeding.[212]

III. Judges Azevedo, Krylov, Winiarski, and Zoričić agree with the objections

Several Judges recognized analogies between the *Peace Treaties* case and the *Eastern Carelia* case in their dissenting opinions. Judges *Azevedo*, *Krylov*, *Winiarski*, and *Zoričić* all agreed that an advisory opinion could not be given on a legal question relating to a bilateral dispute actually pending between two states without their consent and that this principle continued to apply under the UNC.[213] The four judges did not explicitly clarify whether their reasoning related to matters of jurisdiction or admissibility.

Judge *Azevedo* leant towards a "hard" jurisdictional requirement when he declared:

> "As was the case in 1923, the point which must primarily be borne in mind is that the Court cannot abandon the fundamental rules of international law in order to favour an indirect action designed to settle a dispute actually pending by way of a Request for an Advisory Opinion. A large measure of flexibility is admissible in seeking the consent of the parties; but this consent cannot be dispensed with altogether when the Court is confronted with a dispute actually pending. [...] To sum up, we must build a wall between the contentious and the advisory functions. [...] To abandon these elementary precautions would be to ignore the decisive refusal of the States to accept any rule of compulsory jurisdiction."[214]

Judge *Krylov* explicitly invoked the *Eastern Carelia* opinion and argued that the Court could not give the requested advisory opinion. He argued:

---

212 Bulgaria, Hungary, and Romania joined the United Nations on 14 December 1955, incidentally as a consequence of the Peace Treaties which form the subject-matter of the advisory proceedings.

213 *Interpretation of Peace Treaties with Bulgaria, Hungary and Romania*, Advisory Opinion, Separate Opinion Azevedo, ICJ Reports 1950, 65 (88); Dissenting Opinion Winiarski, ICJ Reports 1950, 65 (92); Dissenting Opinion Zoričić, ICJ Reports 1950, 65 (103); Dissenting Opinion Krylov, ICJ Reports 1950, 65 (108).

214 *Interpretation of Peace Treaties with Bulgaria, Hungary and Romania*, Advisory Opinion, Separate Opinion Azevedo, ICJ Reports 1950, 65 (88).

> "Therefore, there is a "legal question actually pending" between those five States. [...] In my opinion, the present request must be dealt with – in so far as possible – as a contentious case would be. I think that the Court *could not* exercise its consultative function in this case unless the interested States, including Bulgaria, Hungary and Romania, had expressly consented. This is demonstrated by the general meaning of the texts quoted and *especially by the precedent established by the P.C.I.J. on July 23rd, 1923*."[215]

By stating that the Court "could not" rather than "ought not" exercise its advisory function, Judge *Krylov* also implied that consent was required as a matter of jurisdiction. Judge *Winiarski* emphasized the danger of giving advisory opinions on pending bilateral disputes against the will of the affected states. Giving an advisory opinion in such situations could lead to the establishment of a compulsory jurisdiction as, according to Judge *Winiarski*, the advisory opinion would in effect settle the bilateral dispute. He regarded the consent requirement expressed in the *Eastern Carelia* advisory opinion as an attempt by the PCIJ to counter this danger. Judge *Winiarski* stated:

> "For the same reason, States see their rights, their political interests and sometimes their moral position affected by an opinion of the Court, and *their disputes are in fact settled by the answer* which is given to a question relating to them, which may be a "key question" of the dispute. [...] This is also why the *Permanent Court* did not hesitate to grant States the necessary guarantees, and, in order to exclude any possibility of introducing compulsory jurisdiction by the circuitous means of its advisory opinions, it deliberately laid down in Opinion No. 5 the principle of the consent of the parties (Article 36 of the Statute)."[216]

Judge *Zoričić* also invoked the "precedent of Eastern Carelia" to argue that consent of the affected states is necessary. He stated:

> "The precedent of Eastern Carelia constitutes, in my view, a convincing proof that the consent of the States is necessary, not only in regard to contentious cases, but also in advisory cases where the request for the

215 *Interpretation of Peace Treaties with Bulgaria, Hungary and Romania*, Advisory Opinion, Dissenting Opinion Krylov, ICJ Reports 1950, 65 (108), emphasis added.

216 *Interpretation of Peace Treaties with Bulgaria, Hungary and Romania*, Advisory Opinion, Dissenting Opinion Winiarski, ICJ Reports 1950, 65 (92), emphasis added.

> opinion relates to a dispute between States, so that the answer of the Court would decide the issue that is the subject of the dispute."[217]

All four judges saw the *Eastern Carelia* advisory opinion of the PCIJ as a kind of precedent which ought to guide the judicial work of the ICJ. The four judges cautioned that too liberal a recourse to the advisory opinion procedure may introduce a sort of compulsory jurisdiction and thus a form of judicial dispute settlement without consent.

IV. View of the Court majority: Distinction between jurisdiction and discretion

The Court majority did not share these concerns. Instead, the Court decided to give the requested opinion. How the Court responded to the challenges to its jurisdiction and the admissibility of the request would guide the Court's approach in all subsequent advisory proceedings.

1. Jurisdiction and state consent

The Court found that it had jurisdiction to give the requested advisory opinion. According to the Court and contrary to the arguments made by Bulgaria, Hungary, and Romania, the UNGA did not act *ultra vires*. Instead, it acted in accordance with the functions of the United Nations to promote the respect and realization of human rights and fundamental freedoms.[218] Additionally, the UNGA did not ask the Court to examine whether human rights and fundamental freedoms had actually been respected by the three states, nor to interpret the relevant human rights provisions. Instead, the Court was merely asked to interpret the provisions of the peace treaties regarding the dispute settlement mechanism. The dispute settlement mechanism agreed upon in the peace treaty, a multilateral treaty, was not an internal matter of the three states.[219]

The Court then picked up the thread left by the *Eastern Carelia* and *Mosul* advisory opinions of the PCIJ and unambiguously found that the

217 *Interpretation of Peace Treaties with Bulgaria, Hungary and Romania*, Advisory Opinion, Dissenting Opinion Zoričić, ICJ Reports 1950, 65 (103).

218 *Interpretation of Peace Treaties with Bulgaria, Hungary and Romania (First Phase)*, Advisory Opinion, ICJ Reports 1950, 65 (70).

219 Ibid. (70–71).

Court's *jurisdiction* to give advisory opinions did not depend on state consent. In one of the most crucial passages of its entire case law on the parameters of its advisory jurisdiction, the ICJ held:

> "The Court cannot, it is said, give the Advisory Opinion requested without violating the well-established principle of international law according to which no judicial proceedings relating to a legal question pending between States can take place without their consent. This objection reveals a confusion between the principles governing contentious procedure and those which are applicable to Advisory Opinions. The consent of States, parties to a dispute, is the basis of the Court's jurisdiction in contentious cases. The situation is different in regard to advisory proceedings even where the Request for an Opinion relates to a legal question actually pending between States. The Court's reply is only of an advisory character: as such, it has no binding force. It follows that no State, whether a Member of the United Nations or not, can prevent the giving of an Advisory Opinion which the United Nations considers to be desirable in order to obtain enlightenment as to the course of action it should take. The Court's Opinion is given not to the States, but to the organ which is entitled to request it; the reply of the Court, itself an 'organ of the United Nations', represents its participation in the activities of the Organization, and, in principle, should not be refused."[220]

The ICJ made several significant findings here. First, the Court stated in clear terms that in advisory proceedings (unlike in contentious proceedings) the jurisdiction of the Court did not depend on the consent of the states that are particularly affected by the proceedings. This holds true even if the advisory opinion relates to a legal question which forms the subject-matter of a pending dispute. Secondly, the Court linked the question of state consent with the question of the binding force of the judicial pronouncement in question. As the advisory opinions of the Court lack binding force, no consent of the disputing states is required. Finally, the Court found that the ICJ as an organ of the UN must participate in the activities of the organization. The principal way for the Court to participate is by replying to a request for an advisory opinion made by another UN organ. Recognizing that the giving of an advisory opinion is a duty of the

220 Ibid. (71).

Court is one of the most fundamental differences between the role of the ICJ within the UN and the role of the PCIJ within the League of Nations.[221]

2. Discretionary nature of the advisory competence

Notwithstanding the Court's clear rejection of a consent requirement, the ICJ nevertheless identified certain limits to its capacity to give advisory opinions. It held:

> "There are certain limits, however, to the Court's duty to reply to a Request for an Opinion. It is not merely an "organ of the United Nations", it is essentially the "principal judicial organ" of the Organization (Art. 92 of the Charter and Art. I of the Statute). It is on account of this character of the Court that its power to answer the present Request for an Opinion has been challenged. Article 65 of the Statute is permissive. It gives the Court the power to examine whether the circumstances of the case are of such a character as should lead it to decline to answer the Request. In the opinion of the Court, the circumstances of the present case are profoundly different from those which were before the Permanent Court of International Justice in the Eastern Carelia case (Advisory Opinion No. 5), when that Court declined to give an Opinion because it found that the question put to it was directly related to the main point of a dispute actually pending between two States, so that answering the question would be substantially equivalent to deciding the dispute between the parties, and that at the same time it raised a question of fact which could not be elucidated without hearing both parties."[222]

The Court found that it had a discretionary power to refuse to issue certain advisory opinions and it derived this discretion from its character as the principal judicial organ of the UN as well as the wording of Article 65 ICJ Statute. In accordance with the *Eastern Carelia* advisory opinion, the Court identified two scenarios in which it ought to exercise this discretionary power: first, if giving an advisory opinion settled a bilateral dispute and, secondly, if the Court lacked sufficient information. These are the same considerations the PCIJ previously raised in the *Eastern Carelia* case.

---

221 On the role of the PCIJ within the framework of the League of Nations, see *supra*: § 1 Section B.I.

222 *Interpretation of Peace Treaties with Bulgaria, Hungary and Romania (First Phase)*, Advisory Opinion, ICJ Reports 1950, 65 (71–72).

The ICJ denied that the requested advisory opinion would settle any pending dispute. According to the ICJ, the subject-matter of the dispute between Bulgaria, Hungary, Romania, and various western states was the observance of human rights by the three states. The submitted question in the advisory proceedings, on the other hand, concerned procedural questions relating to the dispute settlement mechanism under the peace treaty.[223] While the two aspects are connected, questions concerning the supervisory mechanism of human rights treaties are not identical to the question of the actual observance of human rights. As such, answering the request was not identical to deciding the underlying legal dispute.

V. Conclusion: Bringing the *Eastern Carelia* doctrine into the UN era

The *Peace Treaties* case is particularly interesting for the analysis of the Eastern Carelia doctrine as the arguments of the three states heavily relied on the statements made by the PCIJ in its *Eastern Carelia* advisory opinion. The case brought the Eastern Carelia doctrine into the UN era. The Court recognized that the Eastern Carelia doctrine continued to be relevant in the UN era despite the many institutional changes brought about by the creation of the UN. The Eastern Carelia doctrine continues to be important not for the *establishment* of the Court's jurisdiction (as argued by Bulgaria, Hungary, and Romania), but for the Court's discretionary *exercise* of its jurisdiction. The ICJ based its discretionary power on its character as an international judicial organ. Being an international judicial organ, there are certain requirements the Court must fulfil. These include that the Court must not settle a bilateral dispute against the will of the states involved and that it may only make judicial findings when it has access to all relevant facts of the case. The Court thus tentatively introduced the protection of its judicial function as the guiding principle of its discretionary power.[224] It is worth pointing out that the Court rejected a consent requirement for its advisory procedure based on the fact that its advisory opinions are non-binding. However, despite their non-binding nature, the Court found that its advisory opinions could settle bilateral disputes.

223 Ibid. (72).

224 On the ICJ's judicial function, see *infra*: § 6 Section B.

B. Reservations to the Genocide Convention case (1951)

The next step of the development of the Eastern Carelia doctrine is marked by the *Reservations to the Genocide Convention* case[225].

I. Background

In July of 1950, the Philippines have signed the Convention on the Prevention and Punishment of the Crime of Genocide (Genocide Convention).[226] The instrument of ratification submitted by the Philippines contained certain reservations to which Australia, a State Party to the Genocide Convention, objected. On 10 October 1950, the Australian representative before the UNGA stated that a state that had acceded to the Genocide Convention under reservation could, if a State Party objected to that reservation, only choose between withdrawing the reservation or not acceding to the Convention.[227] In November of 1950, the UNGA asked the ICJ to give an opinion on the legal relations between a state that has signed the Genocide Convention subject to a reservation and States Parties to the Convention that have objected to the reservation.[228]

Following the *Peace Treaties* advisory opinion, states could no longer hope to challenge the Court's *jurisdiction* based on the Eastern Carelia doctrine. Rather, states turned to arguments relating to the *admissibility* of giving the requested advisory opinion. Accordingly, the Philippines argued that the questions referred to the Court related to a dispute between the Philippines and Australia over the Philippines' accession to the Genocide Convention and that the Court should therefore exercise its discretion to decline to give the requested opinion. The Philippines stated:

---

225 *Reservations to the Convention on the Prevention and Punishment of the Crime of Genocide*, Advisory Opinion, ICJ Reports 1951, 15; on the Reservations opinion, see *K. J. Keith*, The extent of the advisory jurisdiction of the International Court of Justice, 1971, 119–120; *M. Pomerance*, The advisory function of the International Court in the League and U.N. eras, 1973, 117–125.

226 Convention on the Prevention and Punishment of the Crime of Genocide, 78 UNTS 277, entry into force 12 January 1951.

227 ICJ Pleadings, *Reservations to the Convention on the Prevention and Punishment of the Crime of Genocide*, Written Statement of the Philippines, 296.

228 UNGA resolution 478(V) of 16 November 1950, UN doc. A/RES/478(V). The resolution was adopted by 47 votes to 5 against, with 5 abstentions, see A/PV.305.

> "It follows that this Honourable Court, as the principal judicial organ of the United Nations, should decline to render an opinion as requested by the General Assembly for the reason that questions I and II put to it are directly related to the main point of a dispute actually pending between the Philippines and Australia, and that answering these questions would be substantially equivalent to deciding the dispute between the parties."[229]

II. ICJ focuses on the object and purpose of the request

The ICJ reaffirmed its position expressed in the *Peace Treaties* case that the existence of a bilateral dispute does not affect the Court's jurisdiction.[230] The Court then found that the Eastern Carelia doctrine would not hinder the Court from giving the requested advisory opinion: Without determining whether there was a dispute between Australia and the Philippines, the Court found that the request for an advisory opinion was at any rate *not directed* at settling a bilateral dispute.[231] The Court came to this conclusion not by comparing the submitted questions with the subject-matter of the dispute between Australia and the Philippines. Rather, it examined the object and purpose of the request for an advisory opinion and whether it was directed at guiding the UNGA in its work or whether it was directed at resolving a bilateral dispute.[232] The Court found that both the UNGA, as author of the Genocide Convention, and the UNSG, as depositary of the instruments of ratification and accession, had an interest in knowing the legal consequences of reservations made by states wishing to accede to the Convention and objections to these reservations made by Member States.[233]

It is important to note that by focusing on the object and purpose of the request, the Court modified its position developed in the *Peace Treaties* advisory opinion. In the *Peace Treaties* opinion, the Court had adopted

229 ICJ Pleadings, *Reservations to the Convention on the Prevention and Punishment of the Crime of Genocide*, Written Statement of the Philippines, 296.

230 *Reservations to the Convention on the Prevention and Punishment of the Crime of Genocide*, Advisory Opinion, ICJ Reports 1951, 15 (19); *Interpretation of Peace Treaties with Bulgaria, Hungary and Romania (First Phase)*, Advisory Opinion, ICJ Reports 1950, 65 (71).

231 *Reservations to the Convention on the Prevention and Punishment of the Crime of Genocide*, Advisory Opinion, ICJ Reports 1951, 15 (19).

232 Ibid.

233 Ibid.

the PCIJ's standard of what constitutes a circumvention of the principle of consensual dispute settlement by means of its advisory procedure, namely in situations where "the question put to it was directly related to the main point of a dispute actually pending between two States, so that answering the question would be substantially equivalent to deciding the dispute between the parties".[234] The Court implied in the *Peace Treaties* case that the congruence of subject-matters between advisory proceeding and bilateral dispute suffices for the Court to find that the giving of the opinion would constitute a circumvention of state consent.

In contrast, with the *Reservations to Genocide Convention* case, the ICJ started looking towards the *object and purpose* of the request to determine whether giving an advisory opinion would be substantially equivalent to deciding a pending bilateral dispute. Instead of comparing the subject-matter of the request with the subject-matter of the underlying dispute, the essential criterion became whether the request was *directed* at the settlement of the dispute. By doing so, the Court significantly reduced the scope of the Eastern Carelia doctrine by making the application of the doctrine subject to its own interpretation of the object and purpose of the request. This standard which looks at the object and purpose of the request as the central consideration would be taken up by the ICJ in its 1971 *Namibia* advisory opinion.

C. Judgments of the ILO Administrative Tribunal case (1956)

In the 1956 *Judgments of the Administrative Tribunal of the ILO* case[235] the UNESCO Executive Board asked the ICJ to examine the competences of the ILO Administrative Tribunal regarding complaints brought against the UNESCO by its staff members.[236] The case did not concern an inter-state dispute and thus does not directly relate to the Eastern Carelia doctrine. However, the Court further outlined the exercise of its advisory jurisdiction by introducing two important and related notions: the standard of compelling reasons and the "requirements of the Court's judicial character".

234 *Interpretation of Peace Treaties with Bulgaria, Hungary and Romania (First Phase)*, Advisory Opinion, ICJ Reports 1950, 65 (72).

235 *Judgments of the Administrative Tribunal of the ILO upon Complaints Made against UNESCO*, Advisory Opinion, ICJ Reports 1956, 77; on the Judgments of the ILO opinion, see *M. Pomerance*, The advisory function of the International Court in the League and U.N. eras, 1973, 125–130.

236 UNESCO Executive Board resolution 42 EX of 25 November 1955, 20–21.

The Court stated that it was not free in its exercise of discretion. Rather, it may only refuse to give a requested opinion if there were "compelling reasons". The Court found:

> "Notwithstanding the permissive character of Article 65 of the Statute in the matter of advisory opinions, *only compelling reasons* could cause the Court to adopt in this matter a negative attitude which would imperil the working of the régime established by the Statute of the Administrative Tribunal for the judicial protection of officials."[237]

Without explicitly connecting the two terms, the ICJ identified as the principal compelling reason on which it relied in all subsequent cases the protection of the Court's judicial character:

> "The Court is a judicial body and, in the exercise of its advisory functions, it is bound to remain faithful to the requirements of its judicial character."[238]

The ICJ emphasized here that the Court's advisory function is not disconnected from the Court's judicial function. Rather, the Court must at all times - even when issuing advisory opinions - act in accordance with its judicial character. The requirements of the Court's judicial character are the Court's guiding considerations when exercising its discretion.

D. Namibia case (1971)

I. Background

On 27 October 1966, the UNGA declared that South Africa's mandate for Namibia (then called "South-West Africa") had ended, and that South Africa had no legal right to continue its administration of Namibia.[239] After South Africa refused to end its administration of Namibia, the UNSC declared that the continued presence of South Africa in Namibia was illegal and that all acts taken by the government of South Africa on behalf of or concerning Namibia after the termination of the mandate were illegal

237 *Judgments of the Administrative Tribunal of the ILO upon Complaints Made against UNESCO*, Advisory Opinion, ICJ Reports 1956, 77 (86), emphasis added.

238 Ibid. (84).

239 UNGA resolution 2145 (XXI) of 27 October 1966, UN doc. A/RES/2145(XXI), para. 4.

and invalid.[240] The UNSC further called upon all states to refrain from any dealings with the government of South Africa which were inconsistent with this declaration.[241] Against this backdrop, in 1970 the UNSC made its first (and so far only) request for an advisory opinion from the ICJ, asking the Court to examine the legal consequences of the continued presence of South Africa in Namibia.[242] This request gave rise to the *Namibia* case.[243]

II. South Africa invokes the *Eastern Carelia* precedent

In the proceeding, South Africa invoked the Eastern Carelia doctrine and argued that the ICJ ought to refuse to give the requested advisory opinion.[244] South Africa argued that it was involved in a legal dispute with several UN Member States, including Ethiopia and Liberia about South Africa's mandate over Namibia. This legal dispute was already the subject-matter of the *South-West Africa* cases[245] before the Court and continued to exist when the UNSC requested the advisory opinion.[246] According to South Africa, a second dispute existed regarding the powers of the UNGA to terminate Namibia's status as a mandate territory.[247] This second dispute arose during the debates of the UNGA and constituted a pending legal dispute in the sense of the Eastern Carelia doctrine. Finally, South Africa argued that a third dispute arose when 40 states called upon the UNSC

240 UNSC resolution 276 (1970) of 30 January 1970, UN doc. S/RES/276(1970), para. 2.

241 UNSC resolution 276 (1970) of 30 January 1970, UN doc. S/RES/276(1970), para. 5.

242 UNSC resolution 284 (1970) of 29 July 1970, UN doc. S/RES/284(1970), para. 1. The resolution was adopted by 12 votes to none, with three abstentions, see UNSC official records, 25th year, 1550th meeting, 29 July 1970, UN doc. S/PV.1550, 16.

243 *Legal Consequences for States of the Continued Presence of South Africa in Namibia (South West Africa) notwithstanding Security Council Resolution 276 (1970)*, Advisory Opinion, ICJ Reports 1971, 16; on the Namibia opinion, see *M. Pomerance*, 67 The American journal of international law 3 (1973), 446; *M. Pomerance*, The advisory function of the International Court in the League and U.N. eras, 1973, 148–157.

244 ICJ Pleadings, *Legal Consequences for States of the Continued Presence of South Africa in Namibia (South West Africa) notwithstanding Security Council Resolution 276 (1970)*, Written Statement of South Africa, 377 (442 et seq.).

245 Cf. *South-West Africa Cases (Ethiopia v. South Africa; Liberia v. South Africa)*, Judgment, ICJ Reports 1966, 6.

246 ICJ Pleadings, *Legal Consequences for States of the Continued Presence of South Africa in Namibia (South West Africa) notwithstanding Security Council Resolution 276 (1970)*, Written Statement of South Africa, 377 (445, para. 38).

247 Ibid., 445–446, paras. 39 et seq.

to give effect to UNGA resolution 2145 (XXI) of 27 October 1966 which terminated South Africa's mandate over Namibia.[248] The UNSC complied with this request by passing Resolution 276. According to South Africa, the subject-matter of the advisory proceedings was identical to the subject-matter of the three pending disputes.[249] As such, responding to the advisory request would be substantially equivalent to deciding the pending legal disputes.[250]

III. Focus on the object and purpose of the request for an advisory opinion

The ICJ first emphasized that South Africa was a Member State of the UN. As such, South Africa accepted Article 96 UNC which gives the UNSC the power to request advisory opinions from the Court.[251] This distinguished the *Namibia* case from the *Eastern Carelia* case. In the Eastern Carelia case, the non-consenting state – the USSR – was not a member of the League of Nations.

The Court was doubtful whether there was a pending legal dispute between South Africa and other states in the sense of the Eastern Carelia doctrine. In particular, the Court found that a divergence of views is not the same as a legal dispute:

> "The fact that, in the course of its reasoning, and in order to answer the question submitted to it, the Court may have to pronounce on legal issues upon which radically divergent views exist between South Africa and the United Nations, does not convert the present case into a dispute [...] Differences of views among States on legal issues have existed in practically every advisory proceeding; if all were agreed, the need to resort to the Court for advice would not arise."[252]

Regardless of the existence of a pending bilateral dispute, the Court stated, in line with its 1951 *Reservations to the Genocide Convention* advisory opinion, that the advisory opinion was not *intended* to decide any such dispute.

248 Ibid., 446–447, para. 42.
249 Ibid., 447, para. 43.
250 Cf. ibid., 447, para. 43.
251 *Legal Consequences for States of the Continued Presence of South Africa in Namibia (South West Africa) notwithstanding Security Council Resolution 276 (1970)*, Advisory Opinion, ICJ Reports 1971, 16 (23-24, para. 31).
252 Ibid. (24, para. 34).

The Court, citing its *Reservations to the Genocide Convention* advisory opinion, stated that "[t]he object of this request for an Opinion is to guide the United Nations in respect of its own actions."[253]

According to the ICJ, the UNSC did not request the advisory opinion to decide a pending legal dispute but to receive legal guidance for its own actions.[254] The advisory opinion thus did not relate to a pending legal dispute in the sense of the Eastern Carelia doctrine. The ICJ established the object and purpose of the request by examining the wording of the UNSC resolution, in particular its preamble which stated that "an advisory opinion from the International Court of Justice would be useful for the Security Council in its further consideration of the question of Namibia and in furtherance of the objectives the Council is seeking".[255]

According to the Court, all disputes cited by South Africa were directly linked to the work of the UN: the mandate status of Namibia, the competence of the UNGA to revoke this status, and the ensuing UNSC resolution.[256]

The ICJ reaffirmed its position that an advisory opinion may only be regarded as a form of dispute settlement by other means if the opinion was *intended* to be used as a form of dispute settlement. Whether the opinion was intended in such a manner depends on the object and purpose of the request for an advisory opinion as determined by an interpretation of the requesting resolution. Through this approach, the Court can effectively give any advisory opinion regardless of a pending bilateral dispute if it can find an interest of the requesting organ in receiving the advisory opinion beyond the judicial settlement of the dispute. In later advisory opinions, the Court followed this approach by referring to certain legal questions as belonging to a "broader frame of reference".[257] In other words, a legal dispute which a state does not wish to settle by judicial means might nevertheless be linked to the activities of the UN with the result that giving an advisory opinion on the matter would not constitute a circumvention of that state's consent. The Court thus determines whether a request for an advisory

253 Ibid. (24, para. 32).
254 Ibid.
255 Ibid.
256 Ibid. (23-24, paras. 30 et seq.).
257 *Western Sahara*, Advisory Opinion, ICJ Reports 1975, 12 (26, para. 38); *Legal Consequences of the Construction of a Wall in the Occupied Palestinian Territory*, Advisory Opinion, ICJ Reports 2004, 136 (159, para. 50); *Legal Consequences of the Separation of the Chagos Archipelago from Mauritius in 1965*, Advisory Opinion, ICJ Reports 2019, 95 (118, para. 88).

opinion constitutes a circumvention of a state's will and thus a violation of the Eastern Carelia doctrine not by comparing the legal question submitted to the Court with the subject-matter of a pending bilateral dispute. Instead, the object and purpose of the requested advisory opinion becomes the Court's essential consideration.

E. Western Sahara case (1975)

I. Background

In 1974, the UNGA presented the Court with two questions on the legal status of Western Sahara.[258] It inquired whether Western Sahara was *terra nullius* at the time of colonization by Spain and, if that was not the case, what legal relations existed at that time between Western Sahara, the Kingdom of Morocco, and Mauritania.[259] The request for an advisory opinion was preceded by eight UNGA resolutions, in which the UNGA had called on Spain to implement the obligations contained in the "Declaration on the Granting of Independence to Colonial Countries and Peoples".[260] In particular the UNGA had called upon Spain to hold a referendum on the territorial status of Western Sahara.[261]

II. Spain invokes incompatibility of advisory opinion with judicial character of the ICJ

Spain invoked the *Eastern Carelia* case and argued that the Court ought not to give the advisory opinion as this would be incompatible with the Court's

---

258 UNGA resolution 3292 (XXIX) of 13 December 1974, UN doc. A/RES/3292(XXIX). The resolution was adopted by 87 votes to none, with 43 abstentions, see A/PV.2318.

259 UNGA resolution 3292 (XXIX) of 13 December 1974, UN doc. A/RES/3292(XXIX), para. 1.

260 UNGA resolution 1514 (XV) of 14 December 1960, UN doc. A/RES/1514(XV).

261 UNGA resolutions 2072 (XX) of 16 December 1965, UN doc. A/RES/2072(XX); 2229 (XXI) of 20 December 1966, UN doc. A/RES/2229(XXI); 2354 (XXII) of 19 December 1967, UN doc. A/RES/2354(XXII); 2428 (XXIII) of 18 December 1968, UN doc. A/RES/2428(XXIII); 2591 (XXIV) of 16 December 1969, UN doc. A/RES/2591(XXIV); 2711 (XXV) of 14 December 1970, UN doc. A/RES/2711(XXV); 2983 (XXVII) of 14 December 1972, UN doc. A/RES/2983(XXVII); 3162 (XXVIII) of 14 December 1973, UN doc. A/RES/3162(XXVIII).

judicial character.[262] Spain acknowledged that only the contentious procedure under Article 36 ICJ Statute was subject to state consent. However, if there is a bilateral dispute and the parties to that dispute refuse to have it settled by judicial means – as Spain did[263] – the ICJ must respect this refusal and cannot issue an advisory opinion on the same matter. Otherwise, the advisory procedure would be instrumentalized to circumvent the state's lack of consent to judicial dispute settlement.[264] Spain argued that using the advisory procedure in such a manner would eliminate the distinction between the contentious and the advisory procedure of the ICJ and violate the sovereign equality of states.[265]

III. The ICJ's standard of discretion

Building on its previous case law, the ICJ emphasized the importance of safeguarding its "judicial character"[266] while at the same time making sure to limit its exercise of discretion to "compelling reasons".[267] The Court reiterated that the giving of advisory opinions was an expression of the Court being an organ of the United Nations as well as the principal judicial organ in the sense of Article 92 UNC.[268] Relying on this standard, the Court accepted the premise of Spain's argument that the lack of consent of a disputing state to have its dispute settled by judicial means may be a compelling reason for the Court to refuse the requested advisory opinion:

---

262 ICJ Pleadings, *Western Sahara*, Vol. I, Written Statement of Spain, 202.

263 On 23 September 1974, the Moroccan Ministry of Foreign Affairs sent a letter from the Moroccan King to the Spanish Ministry of Foreign Affairs, in which Morocco proposed to Spain that the ICJ decide by contentious procedure whether Western Sahara was *terra nullius* at the time of Spanish colonization. Spain did not accept, *Western Sahara*, Advisory Opinion, ICJ Reports 1975, 12 (22, para. 26).

264 ICJ Pleadings, *Western Sahara*, Vol. I, Written Statement of Spain, 202.

265 ICJ Pleadings, *Western Sahara*, Vol. I, Written Statement of Spain, 202.

266 In its more recent advisory opinions the Court uses the term "judicial function" instead of "judicial character", see *Accordance with international law of the unilateral declaration of independence in respect of Kosovo*, Advisory Opinion, ICJ Reports 2010, 403 (416, para. 29); *Legal Consequences of the Separation of the Chagos Archipelago from Mauritius in 1965*, Advisory Opinion, ICJ Reports 2019, 95 (113, para. 64).

267 *Western Sahara*, Advisory Opinion, ICJ Reports 1975, 12 (21, para. 23).

268 Ibid.

> "Thus the Court recognized that lack of consent might constitute a ground for declining to give the opinion requested if, in the circumstances of a given case, considerations of judicial propriety should oblige the Court to refuse an opinion. In short, the consent of an interested State continues to be relevant, not for the Court's competence, but for the appreciation of the propriety of giving an opinion. In certain circumstances, therefore, the lack of consent of an interested State may render the giving of an advisory opinion incompatible with the Court's judicial character. An instance of this would be when the circumstances disclose that to give a reply would have the effect of circumventing the principle that a State is not obliged to allow its disputes to be submitted to judicial settlement without its consent."[269]

The ICJ did not elaborate on the meaning of the term "judicial character", nor why the giving of an advisory opinion could conflict with it. However, the Court gave its discretionary power some contours by stating that the Court must ensure that the advisory opinion is not used to circumvent the fundamental principle that judicial dispute settlement requires state consent. In other words, the advisory procedure must not be used to circumvent the Court's contentious procedure and the latter's consent requirement.

IV. Decolonization as an inherently multilateral matter

The ICJ recognized that there was a territorial dispute between Spain and Morocco and that Spain did not consent to the judicial settlement of this dispute.[270] However, this dispute was not bilateral in nature and for that reason giving the advisory opinion could not circumvent the principle of consensual dispute settlement. The reason for this, the Court found, lied in the origins of the dispute as well as its subject-matter.

First, the ICJ found that the dispute did not arise on the bilateral level, but during the sessions of the UNGA and in relation to matters before the UNGA.[271] It arose during an exchange of correspondences between Spain and the UNSG. In these correspondences Spain declared that it had no non-self-governing territories in Africa but only provinces which formed

269 Ibid. (25, paras. 32-33).
270 Ibid. (23, para. 29).
271 Ibid. (25, para. 34).

an integral part of Spain. Morocco responded with the "most explicit reservations" and declared to the UNSG that the territories currently controlled by Spain were an integral part of Morocco's territory.[272] In October 1961, both states reiterated their legal views before the UNGA.[273] The dispute remained in a state of limbo until 1974 when Morocco called on Spain to jointly submit the dispute to the ICJ on 23 September 1974.[274] The Court relied on this origin of the dispute within the UN to deny the bilateral nature of the dispute.[275]

Secondly, the subject-matter of the questions before the Court related to matters beyond the bilateral relations between Spain and Morocco. Spain argued that the Court was asked to address a bilateral territorial dispute. The Court, however, identified as the matter before it the decolonization process which was intrinsically linked to the activities of the UN. The UNGA emphasized this link between the UN and decolonization by referring to the "Declaration on the Granting of Independence to Colonial Countries and Peoples" in its request for the advisory opinion:

> "In any event, the terms of the request contain a proviso concerning the application of General Assembly resolution 1514 (XV). Thus the legal questions of which the Court has been seised are *located in a broader frame of reference than the settlement of a particular dispute* and embrace other elements."[276]

By referring to resolution 1514 (XV), the UNGA emphasized the continuity of the efforts made by the UN regarding the decolonization process. The ICJ regarded this as proof that the advisory opinion was not intended to settle a bilateral dispute between Spain and Morocco but to serve the UNGA in the exercise of its duties to support the decolonization process:

> "The object of the General Assembly has not been to bring before the Court, by way of a request for advisory opinion, a dispute or legal controversy, in order that it may later, on the basis of the Court's opinion, exercise its powers and functions for the peaceful settlement of that dispute or controversy. The object of the request is an entirely different one: to obtain from the Court an opinion which the General Assembly deems

272 Ibid.
273 Ibid. (25-26, para. 35).
274 Ibid. (26, para. 36).
275 Ibid.
276 Ibid. (26, para. 38), emphasis added.

> of assistance to it for the proper exercise of its functions concerning the decolonization of the territory."[277]

The combination of the origins of the dispute and the subject-matter of the request for an advisory opinion were the decisive reasons for the Court to deny that the matter before the Court was a purely bilateral matter. This is convincing considering the UN's special responsibility for the decolonization of colonized peoples which finds expression in the right of peoples to self-determination in Article 1 para. 2 UNC[278], the reporting procedure according to Article 73 UNC and numerous resolutions of the UNGA[279].

V. Judge Gros on the conditions of a bilateral dispute

Judge *Gros* underscored in his Declaration the finding of the majority that the advisory opinion does not settle a bilateral dispute by examining the requirements of a bilateral dispute. For this, Judge *Gros* relied on the definition of a bilateral dispute provided by Judge *Fitzmaurice* in the *Northern Cameroons* case:

> "[…] [T]he one party [or parties] should be making, or should have made, a complaint, claim or protest about an act, omission or course of conduct, present or past of the other party, which the latter refutes, rejects or denies the validity of, either expressly, or else implicitly by

277 *Western Sahara*, Advisory Opinion, ICJ Reports 1975, 12 (26–27, para. 39). In the *Wall* opinion, Judge Higgins regards the purpose of the request for an advisory opinion as the decisive factor in the assessment of whether circumvention in the meaning of the Eastern Carelia principle exists, see *Legal Consequences of the Construction of a Wall in the Occupied Palestinian Territory*, Advisory Opinion, Separate Opinion Higgins, ICJ Reports 2004, 136 (210, para. 12).

278 Art. 1 para. 2 UNC states as a purpose of the United Nations "To develop friendly relations among nations based on respect for the principle of equal rights and self-determination of peoples (…)".

279 See UNGA resolutions 1514 (XV) of 14. December 1960, UN doc. A/RES/1514(XV); 2072 (XX) of 16 December 1965, UN doc. A/RES/2072(XX); 2229 (XXI) of 20 December 1966, UN doc. A/RES/2229(XXI); 2354 (XXII) of 19 December 1967, UN doc. A/RES/2354(XXII); 2428 (XXIII) of 18 December 1968, UN doc. A/RES/2428(XXIII); 2591 (XXIV) of 16 December 1969, UN doc. A/RES/2591(XXIV); 2711 (XXV) of 14 December 1970, UN doc. A/RES/2711(XXV); 2983 (XXVII) of 14 December 1972, UN doc. A/RES/2983(XXVII); 3162 (XXVIII) of 14 December 1973, UN doc. A/RES/3162(XXVIII).

> persisting in the acts, omissions or conduct complained of, or by failing to take the action or make the reparation, demanded."[280]

Judge *Gros* argued that Spain could not possibly be a party to a legal dispute in this sense with Morocco because Spain could not bring about the legal consequence demanded by Morocco:

> "It is not enough that two States may have different or even opposing views as to an event or situation for there to be a contentious case, and the end of the passage quoted makes this clear: if it is not possible for any satisfaction for the claim of the one State to be obtained from the other, there is no dispute between them. Now what response could the Government of Spain make to a claim of the Government of Morocco concerning the right of reintegration of the Territory into the Kingdom of Morocco, when these two Governments have specifically agreed to effect the decolonization of the Territory by a procedure set in motion within the United Nations, except to reply that it had no competence to settle by itself this problem which the two Governments, along with many others, are debating in various United Nations bodies. Even if the Government of Spain had agreed to support the claim of the Government of Morocco, such an attitude would have been without any legal effect in the international sphere. The two Governments have explicitly chosen decolonization in the context of the United Nations, in order to study and ultimately settle the future of the Territory, with the other Members of the United Nations. There is no bilateral dispute which is detachable from the United Nations debate on the decolonization; there is no bilateral dispute at all, nor has there ever been any such dispute."[281]

Spain and Morocco agreed that the decolonization of the territory in question was to be achieved by UN procedures. Spain, as the administrative power of a non-self-governing territory, had no authority to dispose of the sovereignty of this territory. For this reason, Spain could not be a party to a legal dispute about it.

---

280 *Western Sahara*, Advisory Opinion, Declaration Gros, ICJ Reports 1975, 12 (71, para. 2), citing *Case concerning the Northern Cameroons (Cameroon v. United Kingdom)*, Judgment, Preliminary Objections, Separate Opinion Fitzmaurice, ICJ Reports 1963, 15 (109).

281 *Western Sahara*, Advisory Opinion, Declaration Gros, ICJ Reports 1975, 12 (71, para. 2).

VI. Conclusion

In the *Western Sahara* case, Spain tried to argue that the advisory opinion would effectively decide its bilateral dispute with Morocco as it had implications for the underlying legal questions. The ICJ opted for a functional assessment of when the giving of an advisory opinion would be substantially equivalent to the settlement of a dispute without state consent, taking into account the function of the advisory procedure to support the activities of the requesting UN organ. Consequently, the Court examined whether the legal questions submitted by the UNGA were of particular concern to the activities of the UNGA. The ICJ found that giving the advisory opinion would not violate the Eastern Carelia doctrine if it can be established that the requesting organ has an interest in receiving the legal guidance of the Court beyond dispute settlement. The Court effectively equated the scope of its advisory function with the scope of the functions of the UN. Once a matter falls within the functions of the requesting UN organ, giving the advisory opinion can almost never be understood as a violation of the Eastern Carelia doctrine as the opinion is not (primarily) directed at the settlement of a bilateral dispute but instead at supporting the UN organ in its functions. This radically reduces the possibility of states to challenge the admissibility of a request for an advisory opinion. While the Court majority approached the question from the perspective of the requesting organ and its functions, Judge *Gros* approached the matter from the opposite direction. He assessed whether the underlying dispute was bilateral by reference to the capacity of the states involved to bring about the legal consequences which the alleged dispute entails.

F. Wall case (2004)

The *Wall* case[282] is one of the most controversial advisory proceedings in recent years.[283]

---

282 *Legal Consequences of the Construction of a Wall in the Occupied Palestinian Territory*, Advisory Opinion, ICJ Reports 2004, 136.

283 On the *Wall* advisory opinion, see inter alia *R. J. Araujo*, 22 BUILJ 2 (2004), 349; *L. F. Damrosch/B. H. Oxman*, 99 AJIL 1 (2005), 1; *S. D. Murphy*, 99 AJIL 1 (2005), 62; *M. Pomerance*, 99 AJIL 1 (2005), 26; *I. Scobbie*, 16 EJIL 5 (2005), 941; *G. R. Watson*, 99 AJIL 1 (2005), 6; *A. M. Gross*, 19 Leiden Journal of International Law 2 (2006), 393; *A. Orakhelashvili*, 11 Journal of Conflict and Security Law 1 (2006),

I. Background

Following a sharp increase in suicide bombings by Palestinians against Israelis in 2000 (known as the Second Intifada), the Israeli government began building a wall in 2002 to separate Israel from the West Bank.[284] The construction of this wall attracted international attention when it became clear that it would extend into the West Bank, enclosing large Israeli settlements and fragmenting Palestinian communities.[285] In 2003, the UNGA requested an advisory opinion from the ICJ on the legal consequences of Israel's construction of the wall, in particular regarding international humanitarian law and previous UNGA and UNSC resolutions.[286]

Israel objected to the advisory proceeding arguing that the submitted question concerned a pending bilateral dispute between Israel and Palestine.[287] Israel stated that it did not agree to a judicial settlement of its dispute, as evidenced by Israel's attempts to seek a negotiated settlement of the dispute for years. Israel further argued that issuing the advisory opinion in these circumstances would circumvent the principle that a state may not be forced to settle its disputes against its will. Finally, Israel argued that the Court lacked sufficient information to answer the questions presented to it.[288]

119; *J. Dugard*, Advisory Opinions and the Secretary-General with Special Reference to the 2004 Advisory Opinion on the Wall, in: L. Boisson de Chazournes/M. G. Kohen/Boisson-de-Chazournes-Kohen (eds.), International law and the quest for its implementation, 2010, 403; *M. M. Aljaghoub*, 24 ALQ 2 (2010), 191; *A. Watts/ R. Jorritsma*, Israeli Wall Advisory Opinion (last updated 2019), in: A. Peters/R. Wolfrum (eds.), The Max Planck Encyclopedia of Public International Law, 2008.

284 *R. C. Williams*, 49 ILM 2 (2010), 620 (620).

285 Ibid., 620.

286 UNGA resolution ES-10/14 of 8 December 2003, UN doc. A/RES/ES-10/14. The resolution was adopted by 90 votes to 8 against, with 74 abstentions, see A/ES-10/ PV.23, 20.

287 ICJ Pleadings, *Legal Consequences of the Construction of a Wall in the Occupied Palestinian Territory*, Written Statement of Israel, 101–102, paras. 7.9 – 7.10.

288 Ibid., 107 et seq.

II. UNGA's permanent responsibility for the Israeli-Palestinian conflict places matter in "broader frame of reference"

The Court did not decide whether the questions submitted to it concerned a specific legal dispute between Palestine and Israel.[289] Instead, the Court turned to the question if the matter was even bilateral in nature. The ICJ rejected Israel's argument that the questions referred to it by the UNGA concerned a purely bilateral matter between Israel and Palestine, finding that the matter belonged to a "much broader frame of reference than a bilateral dispute".[290] The Court based its decision on two grounds: the powers and responsibilities of the UN in questions relating to international peace and security and the "permanent responsibility" of the UN regarding the Israeli-Palestinian conflict.[291] The Court found that this "permanent responsibility" has its origin in the UNGA "Partition Resolution concerning Palestine"[292] and has been manifested in many UNGA and UNSC resolutions as well as the creation of several subsidiary bodies to assist the realization of the rights of the Palestinian people.[293] Based on these two grounds, the ICJ decided that the purpose of the UNGA's request for an advisory opinion was not the judicial settlement of a bilateral dispute but the assistance of the UNGA in its work.[294] Consequently, the Court argued, there was no circumvention of the requirement of consent to the judicial settlement of disputes.[295]

At this point, it is worth taking a closer look at the ICJ's reasoning. The ICJ first referred to the powers and responsibilities of the UN in the field of international peace and security.[296] In this regard, Article 11 para. 2 UNC states:

> "The General Assembly may discuss any questions relating to the maintenance of international peace and security brought before it by any

289 *Legal Consequences of the Construction of a Wall in the Occupied Palestinian Territory*, Advisory Opinion, ICJ Reports 2004, 136 (158, para. 48).
290 Ibid. (159, para. 50).
291 Ibid. (159, para. 49).
292 UNGA resolution 181(II) of 29 November 1947, UN doc. A/RES/181(II)A-B.
293 *Legal Consequences of the Construction of a Wall in the Occupied Palestinian Territory*, Advisory Opinion, ICJ Reports 2004, 136 (159, para. 49).
294 Ibid. (159, para. 50).
295 Ibid.
296 These powers are enshrined, inter alia, in Art. 1 paras. 1 and 2, Art. 2 paras. 2, 3 and 6 UNC and, for the UNGA in Art. 11 UNC and, for the UNSC, in Art. 24 para. 1, Art. 26, Art. 39 et seq. UNC.

Member of the United Nations, or by the Security Council, or by a state which is not a Member of the United Nations [...]."

According to Article 35 para. 1 and Article 34 UNC, any Member State of the UN may bring to the attention of the UNGA "any dispute, or any situation which might lead to international friction or give rise to a dispute", regardless of whether the Member State is a party to such a dispute or not. As long as a Member State brings an inter-state incident before the UNGA, the incident falls within the UNGA's competence to discuss it. Following this reasoning, there is hardly a situation conceivable in which the UNGA could not invoke its responsibility to maintain peace and security which places a dispute in a "broader frame reference". The consequence of this reasoning is that any matter ceases to be "bilateral" in nature once the UNGA decides to exercises its competence with regard to it. If one accepts that the UNGA can exercise its competences regarding almost any international matter, the distinction developed by the ICJ between "bilateral disputes", which may not be settled by advisory opinions, and matters belonging to a "broader frame of reference" loses any analytical clarity. Following the ICJ's reasoning in the *Wall* opinion, it is questionable whether there remains any relevance for the Eastern Carelia doctrine.[297]

III. Access to necessary information and evidence

Israel made another objection which was indirectly linked to the matter of consent. It invoked the Court's lack of access to sufficient information as a reason for the Court to refuse the requested advisory opinion. Israel refused to make any submissions on the question submitted to the Court and argued that the Court was therefore forced to decide on the question without having recourse to all the relevant information and evidence. According to Israel, giving the advisory opinion without taking into account all relevant information violated the judicial character of the ICJ, and therefore the ICJ should refuse to issue the advisory opinion.[298]

297 Cf. *J. A. Frowein/K. Oellers-Frahm*, in: A. Zimmermann/C. Tomuschat/K. Oellers-Frahm/C. J. Tams/M. Kashgar/D. Diehl (eds.), The Statute of the International Court of Justice, 2. ed., 2012: Art. 65, paras. 36–37.

298 ICJ Pleadings, *Legality of the Use by a State of Nuclear Weapons in Armed Conflict*, Written Statement of Israel, 107 et seq.; in particular with a view to possible grounds of justifications, see also *Legal Consequences of the Construction of a Wall in the*

This argument had been raised in earlier advisory proceedings without developing any real significance. In the *Peace Treaties* case, the Court did not have to rule on the substantive legal issue; in the *Namibia* case, the Court could rely on a binding UNSC decision on the issue; and in the *Western Sahara* case, Spain filed extensive briefs despite its opposition to the proceedings. Only in the *Eastern Carelia* case of the PCIJ was this argument recognized by the Court as a significant consideration. The PCIJ found that because the USSR refused its cooperation, the Court would not have access to all the facts of the case.[299]

In line with its previous advisory opinions, the ICJ accepted Israel's argument in principle but rejected its relevance in the *Wall* case. The ICJ stated that it must determine in each case whether sufficient information and evidence were available, otherwise a judicial pronouncement would indeed violate its judicial character.[300] However, it is not necessary that the particularly affected state – in this case Israel – is the source of such information; reports by the UNSG or by special rapporteurs as well as written submissions by other states may likewise provide the necessary information.[301]

IV. The ICJ addresses the international responsibility of Israel

The ICJ held that Israel committed an internationally wrongful act by constructing the wall on Palestinian territory.[302] In particular, Israel violated its obligation to respect the Palestinian people's right to self-determination, its

Occupied Palestinian Territory, Advisory Opinion, Declaration Buergenthal, ICJ Reports 2004, 136 (240 et seq.).

299 *Status of Eastern Carelia*, Advisory Opinion, PCIJ Series B 1923, 7 (29), for a discussion of the Eastern Carelia opinion, see § 2 Section A.

300 *Legal Consequences of the Construction of a Wall in the Occupied Palestinian Territory*, Advisory Opinion, ICJ Reports 2004, 136 (161, para. 56).

301 Ibid. (161-162, para. 57).

302 Ibid. (197, para. 149); on the legal consequences of the *Wall* opinion, see *R. J. Araujo*, 22 BUILJ 2 (2004), 349 (382 et seq.); on the legal consequences of the *Wall* opinion for the UN and its Member States, see *I. Scobbie*, 16 EJIL 5 (2005), 941; for a general overview of the Israeli-Palestinian conflict, see *V. Kattan*, The Palestine question in international law, 2008; *Dinstein*, The International Law of Belligerent Occupation, 2009.

obligations under international humanitarian law[303] and its obligations under international human rights law.[304] As a consequence of these violations of international law, the ICJ found that Israel must cease the construction of the wall, dismantle those parts of the wall situated within the Occupied Palestinian territory, repeal all legislative and regulatory acts adopted with a view to its construction, and make reparation for the damage caused to all natural or legal persons harmed by the construction of the wall.[305]

This part of the Court's opinion, in which the Court addresses Israel's international responsibility, stands most in tension with the Court's Eastern Carelia doctrine, i.e., the position that the giving of an advisory opinion may not circumvent the principle of consensual dispute settlement. The ICJ not only found that Israel breached its international law obligations, it also laid out the legal consequences of these breaches under the law of international responsibility. While the Court's findings on the legal consequences of Israel's breaches of international law respond to the question submitted by the UNGA, Judges *Owada* and *Higgins* criticized the Court for doing so. Judge *Owada* stated in his separate opinion that "the Court (...) should focus its task on offering its objective findings of law to the extent necessary and useful to the requesting organ, the General Assembly, in carrying out its functions relating to this question, rather than adjudicating on the subject-matter of the dispute between the parties concerned".[306] Similarly, Judge *Higgins* stated the Court "revises, rather than applies, the existing case law" by not clearly addressing the question whether the UNGA requested the opinion to guide its functions concerning decolonization or to use the opinion to peacefully settle the dispute.[307]

---

303 The Court held that the construction of the Wall led to the destruction or requisition of properties in violation of Art. 46 and 52 of the Hague Regulations and Art. 53 of the fourth Geneva Convention.

304 *Legal Consequences of the Construction of a Wall in the Occupied Palestinian Territory*, Advisory Opinion, ICJ Reports 2004, 136 (197, para. 149).

305 Ibid. (197-198, paras. 150-152).

306 *Legal Consequences of the Construction of a Wall in the Occupied Palestinian Territory*, Advisory Opinion, Separate Opinion Owada, ICJ Reports 2004, 136 (265, para. 14).

307 *Legal Consequences of the Construction of a Wall in the Occupied Palestinian Territory*, Advisory Opinion, Separate Opinion Higgins, ICJ Reports 2004, 136 (210, paras. 12-13).

V. Legal consequences for states other than Israel and the UN

After finding that Israel violated several of its international law obligations and determining the legal consequences of these breaches for Israel, the ICJ turned to the legal consequences of Israel's violation for other states as well as for the UN as a whole.[308] The Court found that Israel violated several *erga omnes* obligations, including the right of self-determination of peoples and certain obligations under international humanitarian law.[309] Because Israel violated certain *erga omnes* obligations, the Court found that all states are under the obligations "not to recognize the illegal situation resulting from the construction of the wall" and "not to render aid or assistance in maintaining the situation created by such construction".[310] Additionally all states must "see to it that any impediment, resulting from the construction of the wall, to the exercise by the Palestinian people of its right to self-determination is brought to an end" and "ensure compliance by Israel with international humanitarian law".[311] With regard to the UN, the Court refrained from recognizing concrete obligations following from Israel's breaches of *erga omnes* obligations. Instead, it merely found that "the United Nations, and especially the General Assembly and the Security Council, should consider what further action is required to bring to an end the illegal situation resulting from the construction of the wall and the associated régime, taking due account of the present Advisory Opinion".[312]

308 *Legal Consequences of the Construction of a Wall in the Occupied Palestinian Territory*, Advisory Opinion, ICJ Reports 2004, 136 (199 et seq., paras. 154 et seq.).
309 Ibid. (199 et seq., 155 et seq.).
310 Ibid. (200, para. 159).
311 Ibid.
312 Ibid. (200, para. 160).

G. Kosovo case (2010)

The ICJ was again confronted with a request that directly touched upon the interests of several states in the *Kosovo* case.[313]

I. Background

On 17 February 2008, the "Assembly of Kosovo"[314] adopted a resolution in which it declared Kosovo's independence from Serbia.[315] Serbia was opposed to this move towards independence and presented to the UNGA a draft resolution to request an advisory opinion from the ICJ on the legality of the declaration of independence.[316] Serbia's Minister of Foreign Affairs asked the UNGA "to convey" Serbia's request to the Court and argued for a "right of any Member State of the United Nations to pose a simple, basic question on a matter it considers vitally important to the Court."[317] The UNGA adopted Serbia's draft resolution, asking the Court the following question:

---

313 *Accordance with international law of the unilateral declaration of independence in respect of Kosovo*, Advisory Opinion, ICJ Reports 2010, 403; on the *Kosovo* opinion, see *R. Wilde*, Kosovo (Advisory Opinion) (last updated 2011), in: A. Peters/R. Wolfrum (eds.), The Max Planck Encyclopedia of Public International Law, 2008; *R. Falk*, 105 American Journal of International Law 1 (2011), 50; *D. Jacobs/Y. Radi*, 24 Leiden Journal of International Law 2 (2011), 331-354; *M. D. Oberg*, 105 American Journal of International Law 1 (2011), 81; *A. Peters*, Has the Advisory Opinion's Finding that Kosovo's Declaration of Independence was not Contrary to International Law Set an Unfortunate Precedent?, in: M. Milanović/M. Wood (eds.), The Law and Politics of the Kosovo Advisory Opinion, 1. ed., 2015, 291.

314 On 17 November 2007, while negotiations about the legal status of Kosovo were still ongoing, elections were held for the "Assembly of Kosovo" as well as other public offices, Report of the Secretary-General on the United Nations Interim Administration Mission in Kosovo, United Nations doc. S/2007/768. The legal status of the Assembly of Kosovo was a contentious matter in the advisory proceeding before the ICJ, in particular if it was part of the "Provisional Institutions of Self-Government within the Constitutional Framework", see *Accordance with international law of the unilateral declaration of independence in respect of Kosovo*, Advisory Opinion, ICJ Reports 2010, 403 (444 et seq., paras. 102 et seq.).

315 Kosovo Declaration of Independence, published on 17 February 2008, http://old.kuvendikosoves.org/common/docs/Dek_Pav_e.pdf.

316 Request for an advisory opinion of the International Court of Justice on whether the unilateral declaration of independence of Kosovo is in accordance with international law, draft resolution submitted by Serbia, UN doc. A/63/L.2.

317 UNGA, 22nd Plenary Meeting, 8 October 2008, A/63/PV.22, 1.

"Is the unilateral declaration of independence by the Provisional Institutions of Self-Government of Kosovo in accordance with international law?"[318]

II. ICJ gives deference to requesting organ assuming its need for an advisory opinion

Several states argued that the Court ought to exercise its discretion to refuse to give the advisory opinion requested by the UNGA arguing that the advisory opinion was requested not in order to assist the UNGA but to serve the interests Serbia.[319] The advisory opinion procedure was being abused for the settlement of an inter-state dispute rather than for the assistance of a UN organ.[320] The states proposed that the Court look beyond the formalistic authorship of the UNGA resolution and determine the "real" author to decide on the propriety of issuing the requested advisory opinion.[321] The Court refuted this argument finding that the sponsorship of a resolution by a single state does not make that state the requesting entity. By adopting the resolution, the UNGA made the proposal its own matter:

> "*[T]he motives of individual States which sponsor, or vote in favour of, a resolution requesting an advisory opinion are not relevant to the Court's exercise of its discretion whether or not to respond.* As the Court put it in its Advisory Opinion on Legality of the Threat or Use of Nuclear Weapons, "once the Assembly has asked, by adopting a resolution, for an advisory opinion on a legal question, the Court, in determining whether there are any compelling reasons for it to refuse to give such an opinion, will not have regard to the origins or to the political history of the request, or to the distribution of votes in respect of the adopted resolution" (I.C.J. Reports 1996 (I), p. 237, para. 16)."[322]

By refusing to look for the "real" or material author of the request for an advisory opinion and thus applying a formalistic understanding of

---

318 UNGA resolution 63/3 of 8 October 2008, UN doc. A/RES/63/3. The resolution was adopted by 77 votes in favor, 6 votes against, with 74 abstentions, see A/63/PV.22, 10.

319 *Accordance with international law of the unilateral declaration of independence in respect of Kosovo*, Advisory Opinion, ICJ Reports 2010, 403 (416-417, para. 32).

320 Ibid.

321 Ibid.

322 Ibid. (417, para. 33), emphasis added.

the authorship, the ICJ further limited the scope of the Eastern Carelia doctrine. Even where the interest in receiving the advisory opinion seems to be limited to or at least driven by a single state, the Court will generally assume that the requesting organ has a legitimate interest in receiving the opinion which goes beyond the settlement of an inter-state dispute.

Vice-President *Tomka* criticized the Court's approach arguing that the Court should have exercised its discretion to decline to give the requested opinion.[323] *Tomka* did not see any "sufficient interest" for the UNGA in requesting the opinion while the UNSC was already dealing with the matter.[324] In particular, he raised the question whether an advisory opinion on the matter would in fact assist the UNGA in their activities, even if no prior activities regarding the matter could be discerned.[325]

H. Chagos case (2019)

In 2019, the ICJ issued its *Chagos* advisory opinion.[326] On the face of it, the *Chagos* case concerned a territorial dispute between two states over a small archipelago in a remote place, in the middle of the Indian Ocean about 2,200 km north-east of Mauritius. Yet, this simplified description neglects the highly important legal and geo-political questions underlying the case such as the Chagossian people's right to self-determination, the ongoing struggle of non-self-governing people and regional security interests claimed by the United Kingdom and the United States of America.[327] The *Chagos* case was not the first time the Court was asked to give an advisory

323 Accordance with international law of the unilateral declaration of independence in respect of Kosovo, Advisory Opinion, Declaration Vice-President Tomka, ICJ Reports 2010, 403 (454, para. 2).

324 Ibid. (455, para. 5).

325 *Accordance with international law of the unilateral declaration of independence in respect of Kosovo*, Advisory Opinion, Declaration Vice-President Tomka, ICJ Reports 2010, 403 (455, para. 5); see also Declaration Keith, ICJ Reports 2010, 403 (489, para. 17).

326 *Legal Consequences of the Separation of the Chagos Archipelago from Mauritius in 1965*, Advisory Opinion, ICJ Reports 2019, 95.

327 Ibid.; on the *Chagos* opinion, see *G. Puma*, 79 Zeitschrift für ausländisches öffentliches Recht und Völkerrecht (ZaöRV) (2019), 841; *F. L. Bordin*, 78 CLJ 2 (2019), 253; *V. Kattan*, 10 Asian Journal of International Law (2020), 12; *R. McCorquodale/J. Robinson/N. Peart*, 69 ICLQ 1 (2020), 221; *S. Allen*, 69 ICLQ 1 (2020), 203; *S. Allen*, Reflections on the Treatment of General Assembly Resolutions in the Chagos Advisory Opinion, in: T. Burri/J. Trinidad (eds.), The International Court of Justice and decolonisation, 2021, 41; *F. L. Bordin*, State Responsibility in Advisory Proceedings:

opinion in the context of decolonization. However, while the *South-West Africa* case, the *Namibia* case, and the *Western Sahara* took place in the 1950s and 1970s, the *Chagos* opinion was delivered in 2019, highlighting that the process of decolonizationis still ongoing. The *Chagos* case also marks an important stage in the development of the Eastern Carelia doctrine, with many states presenting arguments in their written and oral statements on the admissibility of the request.

I. Background

Mauritius has had a long and painful history of colonization by European powers.[328] Mauritius was occupied by the Netherlands in the 17th century and colonized by France in the 18th century. Under the Treaty of Paris of 1814, France ceded its colony of Mauritius, including all its dependencies, to Great Britain. Between 1814 and 1965, the Chagos Archipelago was a dependency of the colony of Mauritius and subject to British administration. On 23 September 1965, the United Kingdom and Mauritius concluded the Lancaster House Agreement which paved the way for Mauritian independence but also demanded painful concessions from Mauritius. In particular, Mauritius had to consent to the detachment of the Chagos Archipelago from the rest of its territory. The newly created colony was named "British Indian Ocean Territory" (BIOT) and was administered by the UK. On 30 December 1966, the UK and the USA concluded a separate agreement[329] in which the UK leased the BIOT to the USA for the purpose of establishing a military base. To this end, the UK forcibly resettled the Chagossian popu-

Thoughts on Judicial Propriety and Multilateralism in the Chagos Opinion, in: T. Burri/J. Trinidad (eds.), The International Court of Justice and decolonisation, 2021, 95; *Z. Crespi Reghizzi*, The Chagos Advisory Opinion and the Principle of Consent to Adjudication, in: T. Burri/J. Trinidad (eds.), The International Court of Justice and decolonisation, 2021, 51; *D. Snoxell*, Prospect of the Chagos Advisory Opinion and the Subsequent UN General Assembly Resolution Helping to Resolve the Future of the Chagos Archipelago and Its Former Inhabitants: A Political Perspective, in: T. Burri/J. Trinidad (eds.), The International Court of Justice and decolonisation, 2021, 262; *J. Summers*, Chagos, Custom and the Interpretation of UN General Assembly Resolutions, in: T. Burri/J. Trinidad (eds.), The International Court of Justice and decolonisation, 2021, 9.

328 *Legal Consequences of the Separation of the Chagos Archipelago from Mauritius in 1965*, Advisory Opinion, ICJ Reports 2019, 95 (107-111, paras. 25-53).

329 Agreement concerning the Availability for Defence Purposes of the British Indian Ocean Territory, 603 UNTS 1967, No 8737, 274.

lation, estimated at 1,500 to 2,000 people between 1967 and 1973.[330] When Mauritius gained its independence on 12 March 1968, the new Mauritian constitution defined Mauritius' territory without reference to the Chagos Archipelago.

Since at least 1980, when then Prime Minister of Mauritius Seewoosagur Ramgoolam called for the reintegration of the Chagos Archipelago into the Mauritian territory before the UNGA[331], there has been a dispute between the United Kingdom and Mauritius over the territorial affiliation of the Chagos Archipelago. In 2010, the United Kingdom declared the Chagos Archipelago and its surroundings a Marine Protected Area, whereupon Mauritius initiated UNCLOS Annex VII arbitration proceedings to establish *inter alia* that the United Kingdom was not a "coastal state" within the meaning of UNCLOS and thus not entitled to declare a Marine Protected Area.[332] The arbitral tribunal found that the dispute is "properly characterized as relating to land sovereignty over the Chagos Archipelago" and since such a dispute did not concern the interpretation or application of UNCLOS the tribunal declared that it lacked jurisdiction to decide on this first submission.[333]

In 2016, Mauritius inscribed the request for an advisory opinion on the matter into the provisional agenda of the 71st session of the UNGA.[334] Mauritius then asked that all discussions on the matter in the plenary were halted until June 2017 to allow for bilateral negotiations between Mauritius and the UK to take place. It was only when negotiations failed that Mauritius asked the plenary of the UNGA to discuss as soon as possible a draft resolution requesting an advisory opinion from the Court. The draft was prepared by Mauritius and formally presented to the plenary by the African Group without any modifications. The UNGA then adopted the resolution

---

330 The Guardian, Chagos islanders' exile is ongoing breach of human rights, court told, 12 May 2020, available at: https://www.theguardian.com/world/2020/may/12/chagos-islanders-exile-human-rights-breach-court-of-appeal-told.

331 *Legal Consequences of the Separation of the Chagos Archipelago from Mauritius in 1965*, Advisory Opinion, ICJ Reports 2019, 95 (110, para. 46).

332 See Mauritius' first submission, *Chagos Marine Protected Area Arbitration (Mauritius v. United Kingdom)*, Award, UNRIAA, Vol. XXXI (2015), 359 (para. 158).

333 Ibid., paras. 213 et seq.

334 UN doc. A/71/142. On the history of UNGA resolution 71/292 of 22 June 2017, see *Legal Consequences of the Separation of the Chagos Archipelago from Mauritius in 1965*, Advisory Opinion, Declaration Tomka, ICJ Reports 2019, 95 (149–150, para. 4).

– again without making any modifications – by majority vote.[335] On 22 June 2017, the UNGA requested an advisory opinion from the Court on two questions regarding the decolonization of Mauritius and the Chagos Archipelago.[336]

II. Position of the states participating in the proceeding

1. UK and others: Giving an advisory opinion violates the Eastern Carelia doctrine

Several states, first and foremost the United Kingdom, argued that the submitted questions concerned a purely bilateral dispute between the UK and Mauritius about the territorial sovereignty over the Chagos Archipelago and that, in the absence of the United Kingdom's consent, the Court could not decide this territorial dispute by way of an advisory opinion.[337] The UK pointed out that Mauritius had only pressed ahead in the UNGA with the application for the advisory opinion when bilateral negotiations with

---

335 UNGA resolution 71/292 of 22 June 2017, UN doc. A/RES/71/292. The resolution was adopted with 94 votes in favor, 15 votes against and 65 abstentions, see A/71/PV.88, 18.

336 UNGA resolution 71/292 of 22 June 2017, UN doc. A/RES/71/292:
"(a) Was the process of decolonization of Mauritius lawfully completed when Mauritius was granted independence in 1968, following the separation of the Chagos Archipelago from Mauritius and having regard to international law, including obligations reflected in General Assembly resolutions 1514 (XV) of 14 December 1960, 2066 (XX) of 16 December 1965, 2232 (XXI) of 20 December 1966 and 2357 (XXII) of 19 December 1967?;
(b) What are the consequences under international law, including obligations reflected in the above-mentioned resolutions, arising from the continued administration by the United Kingdom of Great Britain and Northern Ireland of the Chagos Archipelago, including with respect to the inability of Mauritius to implement a programme for the resettlement on the Chagos Archipelago of its nationals, in particular those of Chagossian origin?".

337 ICJ Pleadings, *Legal Consequences of the Separation of the Chagos Archipelago from Mauritius in 1965*, Written Statement of Australia, paras. 21, 32 et seq.; Written Statement of Chile, paras. 4 et seq.; Written Statement of France, para. 19; Written Statement of Israel, paras. 3.6 et seq.; Written Statement of the United Kingdom, paras. 7.14 et seq.; Written Comments of the United Kingdom, para. 3.3; Written Statement of the United States, paras. 1.2, 3.20 et seq.; Written Comments of the United States, para. 2.7.

the United Kingdom had failed.[338] The request for an advisory opinion was a strategy of Mauritius to circumvent the UK's opposition to dispute settlement by means of the advisory opinion procedure. While not every pending dispute would automatically have the Court refuse to give an advisory opinion, the UK argued that the specific questions referred to the Court in the *Chagos* case could not be answered without the Court resolving a long-standing bilateral dispute between the UK and Mauritius over the territorial sovereignty over the Chagos Archipelago.[339]

According to the UK, the Court could decide in the UK's favor and still adhere to its previous case law. The UK argued that the *Chagos* case was distinguishable from the *Peace Treaties* case in that the submitted legal questions in the *Chagos* case concerned the actual subject-matter of the pending dispute and not merely preliminary procedural questions, a point which the ICJ emphasized in the *Peace Treaties* Advisory Opinion when it held that "the present Request for an Opinion is solely concerned with the applicability to certain disputes of the procedure for settlement instituted by the Peace Treaties, and it is justifiable to conclude that it in no way touches the merits of those disputes".[340]

In contrast to the *Namibia* case, there was no binding UNSC resolution declaring the continued administration of the Chagos Archipelago by the UK illegal.[341] Unlike in the *Western Sahara* case, the dispute between the UK and Mauritius did not arise within the UNGA and the answer to the submitted questions would have a direct bearing on the current legal position of the UK as an administering power.[342] According to the UK, the decisive reason why the *Western Sahara* advisory opinion did not violate the Eastern Carelia doctrine was the opinion's lack of influence on Spain's

338 ICJ Pleadings, *Legal Consequences of the Separation of the Chagos Archipelago from Mauritius in 1965*, Written Statement of Israel, para. 3.8, citing UNGA official records of 22 June 2017, A/71/PV.88, 7 et seq.

339 ICJ Pleadings, *Legal Consequences of the Separation of the Chagos Archipelago from Mauritius in 1965*, Written Statement of the United Kingdom, para. 7.15.

340 *Interpretation of Peace Treaties with Bulgaria, Hungary and Romania (First Phase)*, Advisory Opinion, ICJ Reports 1950, 65 (72).

341 ICJ Pleadings, *Legal Consequences of the Separation of the Chagos Archipelago from Mauritius in 1965*, Written Statement of the United Kingdom, paras. 7.17 lit. b, 7.18 lit. a.

342 Ibid., paras. 7.17 lit. c, 7.18 lit. c.

legal position, not the decolonization context.[343] This, according to the UK, was different in the *Chagos* case, as the questions referred to the Court concerned the hitherto unresolved issue of territorial sovereignty over the Chagos Archipelago. Unlike in the *Wall* case, the questions referred and the subject-matter of the bilateral dispute were identical and there was no special and permanent responsibility of the UN for the dispute, so that the submitted questions could not be classified as belonging to a "broader frame of reference".[344] While the question submitted to the Court in the *Wall* case only concerned part of the Israeli-Palestinian conflict, the questions in the *Chagos* case concerned the very heart of the dispute between the United Kingdom and Mauritius.[345] The UNGA had not actively considered the Chagos Archipelago in the context of decolonization for several decades.[346] While the UNGA had a special responsibility for the Israeli-Palestinian conflict, no such responsibility existed in the *Chagos* case.[347] Similar to Israel in the *Wall* case, the UK also stressed that the advisory opinion procedure was not suitable for resolving complex questions of law and fact. Irrespective of whether the states particularly affected provided information, the special procedural rules of the contentious procedure, such as more extensive oral hearings and the rules on the burden of proof, do not apply in advisory procedures which is why complex questions of law and fact could not be adequately resolved.[348]

343 ICJ Pleadings, *Legal Consequences of the Separation of the Chagos Archipelago from Mauritius in 1965*, Written Comments of the United Kingdom, paras. 3.11, 3.18; Written Comments of the United States, para. 2.12.

344 ICJ Pleadings, *Legal Consequences of the Separation of the Chagos Archipelago from Mauritius in 1965*, Written Statement of the United Kingdom, paras. 7.17 lit. e, 7.18 lit. a; Written Comments of the United Kingdom, para. 3.21.

345 ICJ Pleadings, *Legal Consequences of the Separation of the Chagos Archipelago from Mauritius in 1965*, Written Statement of the United Kingdom, paras. 7.17 lit. e; 7.18 lit. a, lit. b; Written Statement of Israel, para. 3.14 – 3.15.

346 ICJ Pleadings, *Legal Consequences of the Separation of the Chagos Archipelago from Mauritius in 1965*, Written Statement of the United Kingdom, para. 7.18 lit. b.; Written Comments of the United Kingdom, para. 3.21 lit. b.

347 ICJ Pleadings, *Legal Consequences of the Separation of the Chagos Archipelago from Mauritius in 1965*, Written Comments of the United Kingdom, para. 3.21 lit. d.

348 ICJ Pleadings, *Legal Consequences of the Separation of the Chagos Archipelago from Mauritius in 1965*, Written Statement of the United Kingdom, para. 7.18 lit. e, f.

According to the United Kingdom, the Court thus ought to refuse the requested advisory opinion unless it wished to abandon the *Eastern Carelia* doctrine entirely.[349]

2. Mauritius and others: Advisory opinion concerns decolonization, not a territorial dispute

Mauritius and other states disagreed with the UK's reading of the case. They argued that giving the requested advisory opinion would not violate the Eastern Carelia doctrine. To support their claim, they relied on two conditions established in the Court's jurisprudence as a yardstick for determining when the giving of an advisory opinion would not circumvent state consent: first, the submitted questions are situated in a broader framework than a bilateral dispute and secondly, the purpose of the request for an advisory opinion is to assist the requesting organ in the proper performance of its duties.[350] Mauritius and the majority of states participating in the proceeding, as well as the African Union considered these conditions to be fulfilled in the *Chagos* case.[351] The broader frame of reference in which the submitted questions are placed was – as in the *Western Sahara* advisory opinion – decolonization. Mauritius argued that any dispute about the territorial sovereignty over the Chagos Archipelago was "entirely derivative of, subsumed within, and determined by the question of whether decolonization has or has not been lawfully completed".[352] The territorial dispute

349 ICJ Pleadings, *Legal Consequences of the Separation of the Chagos Archipelago from Mauritius in 1965*, Written Comments of the United Kingdom, para. 3.3.

350 ICJ Pleadings, *Legal Consequences of the Separation of the Chagos Archipelago from Mauritius in 1965*, Written Statement of Mauritius, para. 5.29.

351 ICJ Pleadings, *Legal Consequences of the Separation of the Chagos Archipelago from Mauritius in 1965*, Written Statement of Argentina, paras. 25–26; Written Statement of Brazil, paras. 11–12; Written Statement of Cyprus, paras. 26–27; Written Statement of Djibouti, paras. 21–22; cf. Written Statement of India, para. 6; Written Statement of Liechtenstein, para. 16; Written Statement of the Marshall Islands, para. 15; Written Comments of the Marshall Islands, para. 7; Written Statement of Mauritius, paras. 5.29 et seq.; Written Comments of Mauritius, paras. 2.15 et seq.; Written Statement of Namibia, 2; Written Comments of Nicaragua, paras. 15–16; Written Statement of Serbia, paras. 25 et seq.; Written Comments of Serbia, paras. 8 et seq.; cf. Written Statement of the African Union, para. 31.

352 ICJ Pleadings, *Legal Consequences of the Separation of the Chagos Archipelago from Mauritius in 1965*, Written Comments of Mauritius, para. 2.16.

was thus "completely and fully resolved exclusively by reference to the rules of international law on decolonization and self-determination".[353]

According to Mauritius, while it was true that disputes between the former colonial power and the former non-self-governing territory *also* have a bilateral component, they affect the entire community of states, which overrides any bilateral element.[354] Any legal question in the context of decolonization thus always falls within the remit of the UN and in particular the UNGA. This, Mauritius argued, follows from the fact that the right of peoples to self-determination creates *erga omnes* obligations and the decolonization process directly affects the UNGA due to its self-declared goal of eliminating colonialism.[355] In sum, according to Mauritius and the majority of participating states, the decisive factor in support of giving the requested opinion was that the submitted questions were located in the context of the decolonization of colonized territories. As evidence of the UNGA's ongoing efforts in this area, Mauritius referred to the UNGA resolution on the 50th anniversary of the Declaration on the Granting of Independence to Colonial Countries and Peoples,[356] in which the UNGA

> "[c]onsiders it incumbent upon the United Nations to continue to play an active role in the process of decolonization and to intensify its efforts for the widest possible dissemination of information on decolonization, with a view to the further mobilization of international public opinion in support of complete decolonization[...]".[357]

In contrast to the UK and the USA,[358] Mauritius did not see the decisive justification for issuing the *Western Sahara* advisory opinion in the fact that the advisory opinion had no influence on Spain's legal position. Rather, the decisive factor was that the matter of decolonization placed the submitted questions in a "broader frame of reference" than the settlement of a purely bilateral dispute, and that answering the submitted questions supported

353 Ibid., para. 2.17.
354 Ibid., paras. 2.30 – 2.31.
355 Ibid., para. 2.30.
356 ICJ Pleadings, *Legal Consequences of the Separation of the Chagos Archipelago from Mauritius in 1965*, Written Statement of Mauritius, para. 5.33.
357 UNGA resolution 65/118 of 10 December 2010, UN doc. A/RES/65/118, paras. 2, 9.
358 See ICJ Pleadings, *Legal Consequences of the Separation of the Chagos Archipelago from Mauritius in 1965*, Written Comments of the United Kingdom, paras. 3.11, 3.18; Written Comments of the United States, para. 2.12.

the UNGA in the performance of its tasks.[359] However, Mauritius did not provide an explanation for why the ICJ in the *Western Sahara* case emphasized that the advisory opinion did not affect Spain's legal position. Such a remark would have been superfluous if all that mattered was the broader frame of reference of decolonization.

3. Germany proposes compromise

Germany presented in its written submissions an interesting proposal to balance the interests of the requesting UN organ and of the states affected by the requested advisory opinion. At the same time, the proposal also tried to balance the two characteristics of the ICJ as an organ of the UN on the one hand and as a court of justice on the other. Germany pointed out that when the Court is confronted with a question which relates to a pending bilateral dispute, the Court does not only have the choice between issuing and not issuing the requested advisory opinion. The Court may also decide *to which extent* it answers the submitted questions.[360] Germany based its view on three essential premises:

First, the function of the advisory procedure is not to adjudicate bilateral disputes. Rather, the advisory procedure is intended to provide legal guidance to the requesting UN organ in the exercise of its powers under the UNC.[361] In this regard, Germany referred to previous statements the Court made in the *Western Sahara* advisory opinion in which the Court held:

> "The object of the General Assembly has not been to bring before the Court, by way of a request for advisory opinion, a dispute or legal controversy, in order that it may later, on the basis of the Court's opinion, exercise its powers and functions for the peaceful settlement of that dispute or controversy. The object of the request is an entirely different one: to obtain from the Court an opinion which the General Assembly deems of assistance to it for the proper exercise of its functions concerning the decolonization of the territory."[362]

359 ICJ Pleadings, *Legal Consequences of the Separation of the Chagos Archipelago from Mauritius in 1965*, Written Comments of Mauritius, para. 2.44.

360 ICJ Pleadings, *Legal Consequences of the Separation of the Chagos Archipelago from Mauritius in 1965*, Written Statement of Germany, paras. 123–124, 127 et seq.

361 Ibid., paras. 107–108.

362 *Western Sahara*, Advisory Opinion, ICJ Reports 1975, 12 (26-27, para. 39).

Second, the Court has the power to interpret and, if necessary, rephrase the submitted question.[363] The Court may reformulate the submitted question even if the question is formulated in a clear, narrow and specific manner and even if the reformulation would affect the content of the advisory opinion.[364] By reformulating the question, the Court could avoid making judicial pronouncements on the international responsibility of the states in question.

Third, Article 7 UNC imposes a duty of collegial cooperation on all UN organs. Because of this duty of cooperation, the requesting organ will only request an advisory opinion to the extent it deems necessary for the exercise of its powers.[365] The Court may therefore assume that the submitted question is limited in its extent to what is necessary for the work of the requesting UN organ.

In the case of a pending bilateral dispute, the Court should therefore only make statements on the legal position of individual states if the requesting body has explicitly requested this and if such statements are necessary for the work of the organ.[366] So far, this has only been assumed if the United Nations had a special responsibility for a certain territory.[367] Germany argued that the UNGA had not explicitly requested a statement on the legal consequences for the United Kingdom in the *Chagos* case and the UN – unlike in the case of Palestine or Namibia – did not have any special responsibility for the Chagos Archipelago which went beyond the general responsibility of the UN for the decolonization of colonized territories.[368] The Court should therefore limit its answer to those aspects of the submitted questions that were necessary for the UNGA in the exercise of its tasks in the context of decolonization and exclude, as far as possible, all bilateral

---

363 ICJ Pleadings, *Legal Consequences of the Separation of the Chagos Archipelago from Mauritius in 1965*, Written Statement of Germany, paras. 74 et seq.

364 ICJ Pleadings, *Legal Consequences of the Separation of the Chagos Archipelago from Mauritius in 1965*, Written Statement of Germany, paras. 88 et seq., citing Interpretation of the Agreement of 25 March 1951 between the WHO and Egypt, Advisory Opinion, ICJ Reports 1980, 73 (88, para. 35) and Accordance with international law of the unilateral declaration of independence in respect of Kosovo, Advisory Opinion, ICJ Reports 2010, 403 (423 et seq., paras. 50 et seq.).

365 ICJ Pleadings, *Legal Consequences of the Separation of the Chagos Archipelago from Mauritius in 1965*, Written Statement of Germany, paras. 120, 142.

366 Ibid., paras. 119 et seq.

367 Ibid., para. 123.

368 Ibid., paras. 121, 130 et seq.

aspects of the submitted question in particular questions concerning the international responsibility of the United Kingdom.[369]

III. The Court follows Mauritius' argumentation

The Court unanimously found that it had jurisdiction to give the requested advisory opinion and by twelve votes to two decided that it would not exercise its discretion to decline to give the opinion. Only Judge *Donoghue* and Judge *Tomka* voted against giving the requested advisory opinion.[370] Judge *Gevorgian*, while not voting against complying with the request for an advisory opinion, similarly argued that the Court overstretched its mandate by addressing the UK's international responsibility.[371]

1. Court majority

The overwhelming majority on the bench decided to give the requested advisory opinion on both questions. The Court reiterated its position formulated in the *Western Sahara* case that "there would be a compelling reason for [the Court] to decline to give an advisory opinion when such a reply 'would have the effect of circumventing the principle that a state is not obliged to allow its disputes to be submitted to judicial settlement without its consent'".[372] In doing so, the ICJ reaffirmed that it did not intend to abolish the Eastern Carelia doctrine.

The Court found that the object and purpose of the request for an advisory opinion was not to settle a bilateral dispute between Mauritius and the United Kingdom.[373] Rather, the purpose of the advisory opinion was to support the UNGA in its functions relating to the decolonization of

369 Ibid., para. 141.

370 *Legal Consequences of the Separation of the Chagos Archipelago from Mauritius in 1965*, Advisory Opinion, ICJ Reports 2019, 95 (140, para. 183).

371 *Legal Consequences of the Separation of the Chagos Archipelago from Mauritius in 1965*, Advisory Opinion, Separate Opinion Gevorgian, ICJ Reports 2019, 95 (336, para. 5).

372 *Legal Consequences of the Separation of the Chagos Archipelago from Mauritius in 1965*, Advisory Opinion, ICJ Reports 2019, 95 (117, para. 85), citing *Western Sahara*, Advisory Opinion, ICJ Reports 1975, 12 (25, para. 33).

373 Ibid. (117, para. 86). The ICJ developed the object and purpose test in its *Reservations to Genocide* advisory opinion, see *Reservations to the Convention on the Pre-*

Mauritius.[374] The ICJ referred to Article 1 para. 2 and Article 73 UNC as well as the active role the UNGA has played in the decolonization process as reflected in the work of the Fourth Committee[375] and the Committee of 24[376] to support its view.[377] The ICJ held:

> "The Court therefore concludes that the opinion has been requested on the matter of decolonization which is of particular concern to the United Nations. The issues raised by the request are located in the broader frame of reference of decolonization, including the General Assembly's role therein, from which those issues are inseparable."[378]

The Court did not distinguish between the role of the UNGA regarding decolonization in general and regarding the decolonization of Mauritius in particular. As Judge *Tomka* pointed out, the UNGA has not been actively involved in the matter of Mauritius. Nevertheless, the Court argued that the UNGA has a special responsibility for the completion of decolonization which justify a request for an advisory opinion on the matter. Irrespective of the existence of a bilateral dispute, the request for an advisory opinion is thus primarily directed at supporting the UNGA in its activities. The ICJ also rejected the argument that advisory proceedings are not suitable for

---

vention and Punishment of the Crime of Genocide, Advisory Opinion, ICJ Reports 1951, 15 (19).

374 *Legal Consequences of the Separation of the Chagos Archipelago from Mauritius in 1965*, Advisory Opinion, ICJ Reports 2019, 95 (117, para. 86).

375 The "Special Political and Decolonization Committee" or "Fourth Committee" deals with a variety of issues, including decolonization, the effects of atomic radiation, information issues, peacekeeping operations, reviews of special political missions, the United Nations Relief and Works Agency for Palestinian Refugees in the Near East (UNRWA), Israeli practices and settlement activities affecting the rights of Palestinians and other Arabs in the Occupied Territories, and international cooperation in the peaceful exploration of outer space, see Allocation of agenda items to the Special Political and Decolonization Committee (Fourth Committee), A/C.4/78/1.

376 The UNGA created the "Special Committee on the Situation with regard to the Implementation of the Declaration on the Granting of Independence to Colonial Countries and Peoples" also known as "Committee of 24" or "C-24" to monitor the application of the Declaration on the Granting of Independence to Colonial Countries and Peoples (UNGA resolution 1514 (XV) of 14 December 1960, UN doc. A/RES/1514(XV)) and to make suggestions and recommendations on the progress of the implementation of the Declaration, see UNGA resolution 1654 (XVI) of 27 November 1961, UN doc. A/RES/1654(XVI).

377 *Legal Consequences of the Separation of the Chagos Archipelago from Mauritius in 1965*, Advisory Opinion, ICJ Reports 2019, 95 (118, para. 87).

378 Ibid. (118, para. 88).

resolving complex questions of fact as the Court had been provided with sufficient information by UN organs and numerous participating states.[379] This, of course, does not address the issue of the burden of proof brought up by the United Kingdom.

The Court also rejected the suggestion made by Germany in its written submission that the Court should limit its answer to question (a) and not address the UK's international responsibility, so as not to circumvent the UK's lack of consent to dispute settlement. The Court found that "the Court is asked to state the consequences, under international law, of the continued administration by the United Kingdom of the Chagos Archipelago. By referring in this way to international law, the General Assembly necessarily had in mind the consequences for the subjects of that law, including States."[380]

The Court thus did not limit its answer to the finding that the decolonization process of Mauritius has not been completed (question a). It also found that the UK's continued administration of the Chagos Archipelago constituted an internationally wrongful act entailing the international responsibility of the UK (question b).[381] In doing so, one could argue that the Court went beyond what was "strictly necessary and useful" for the work of the UNGA in the realization of the decolonization of Mauritius. The international responsibility of the United Kingdom is not a prerequisite for the decolonization process but only for employing countermeasures, claiming reparation or invoking other legal remedies. It seems that the Court also felt uneasy about this point. As Judge *Gevorgian* pointed out in his declaration, while the Court includes a finding on the international responsibility of the UK in its reasoning, the "recitals" at the end of the advisory opinion make no mention of it.[382]

2. Separate opinions and Declarations by Vice-President Xue and Judges Gaja, Iwasawa, and Salam

Judges *Gaja*, *Iwasawa* and Judge *Salam* as well as Vice-President *Xue* added Separate Opinions and Declarations to the *Chagos* opinion in which they

379 Ibid. (114-115, paras. 73-74).

380 Ibid. (129, para. 136).

381 Ibid. (138, para. 177).

382 *Legal Consequences of the Separation of the Chagos Archipelago from Mauritius in 1965*, Advisory Opinion, Separate Opinion Gevorgian, ICJ Reports 2019, 95 (337, para. 7).

made specific references to the Eastern Carelia doctrine. The judges presented different proposals where to draw the line between the appropriate use of the advisory procedure to support the activities of the UNGA and its improper use to settle a bilateral dispute.

For Judge *Gaja,* the line would only have been crossed "[i]f the Court had chosen to express views on bilateral questions such as the alleged existence of an obligation for the United Kingdom to make reparation to Mauritius [...]."[383]In contrast, Judge *Salam* criticized the Court for not going far enough. According to him, the Court should have decided that the United Kingdom owes compensation to the Chagossian people.[384] Judge *Iwasawa* argued that the Court's reply did not constitute an adjudication of a bilateral territorial dispute because the Court left all the modalities of how the decolonization of Mauritius is to be achieved to the UNGA. The Court merely stated that the decolonization of Mauritius should be completed in a manner consistent with the Chagossian people's right to self-determination. The Court thus limited its response "to the extent necessary to assist the General Assembly in carrying out its function concerning decolonization".[385]

Vice-President *Xue* undertook the most detailed examination of the application of the Eastern Carelia doctrine in the *Chagos* case. According to Vice-President *Xue,* the mere existence of a bilateral dispute is not enough to render the giving of an advisory opinion on a certain matter inconsistent with the Eastern Carelia doctrine. Instead, "[w]hat is decisive is the object and nature of the request".[386] Accordingly, the giving of an advisory opinion only violates the Eastern Carelia doctrine, if the "object and nature" of the request is to settle a bilateral dispute.[387] If, on the other hand, the request's "object and nature" aims at assisting the UNGA in its functions, the Court ought to give the opinion. Vice-President *Xue* referred to three standards referenced in the Court's jurisprudence to determine the request's "object and nature". Accordingly, the Court must ascertain

383 Legal Consequences of the Separation of the Chagos Archipelago from Mauritius in 1965, Advisory Opinion, Separate Opinion Gaja, ICJ Reports 2019, 95 (269, para. 7).

384 Legal Consequences of the Separation of the Chagos Archipelago from Mauritius in 1965, Advisory Opinion, Declaration Salam, ICJ Reports 2019, 95 (339, paras. 6–7).

385 Legal Consequences of the Separation of the Chagos Archipelago from Mauritius in 1965, Advisory Opinion, Declaration Iwasawa, ICJ Reports 2019, 95 (342, para. 10).

386 *Legal Consequences of the Separation of the Chagos Archipelago from Mauritius in 1965,* Advisory Opinion, Declaration Vice-President Xue, ICJ Reports 2019, 95 (142, para. 4).

387 Ibid.

if the request concerns a matter located in a "broader frame of reference than the settlement of a dispute",[388] if the request aims at providing the UNGA with "enlightenment as to the course of action it should take" and if the dispute arose in proceedings before the UNGA or independently in bilateral relations.[389]

Applying these standards to the case, Vice-President *Xue* found that the object of the request was not to resolve a bilateral territorial dispute between Mauritius and the UK, but to assist the UNGA in the discharge of its functions relating to the decolonization of Mauritius.[390] Vice-President *Xue* argued that the "root cause " of the detachment of the Chagos Archipelago from Mauritius and thus of the dispute between the two states was the decolonization process of Mauritius.[391] Only because of the imminent independence of Mauritius did the United Kingdom separate the archipelago from the rest of the territory of Mauritius. The UK was aware that by detaching the archipelago and thus creating a new colony, it would provoke criticism by other states and the UN. The criticism soon followed suit in the form of resolution 2066 (XX) in which the UNGA declared that the creation of the BIOT and the establishment of a military base thereon were incompatible with the purposes and principles of the UNC and the Declaration on the Granting of Independence to Colonial Countries and Peoples.[392]

Vice-President *Xue* rejected the United Kingdom's argument that the dispute first arose in 1980, stating that this would "take the issue of the Chagos Archipelago out of its historical context".[393] During the administration of Mauritius, the United Kingdom never disputed that the Chagos Archipelago forms part of Mauritius and the United Kingdom agreed to return the archipelago once it was no longer needed for defense purposes in order to

---

388 Vice-President Xue referred to *Western Sahara*, Advisory Opinion, ICJ Reports 1975, 12 (26, para. 38); *Legal Consequences of the Construction of a Wall in the Occupied Palestinian Territory*, Advisory Opinion, ICJ Reports 2004, 136 (159, para. 50).

389 *Legal Consequences of the Separation of the Chagos Archipelago from Mauritius in 1965*, Advisory Opinion, Declaration Vice-President Xue, ICJ Reports 2019, 95 (142–3, para. 4).

390 Ibid., 143, paras. 5–6.

391 Ibid., 143, para. 7.

392 UNGA resolution 2066 (XX) of 16 December 1965, UN doc. A/RES/2066(XX).

393 *Legal Consequences of the Separation of the Chagos Archipelago from Mauritius in 1965*, Advisory Opinion, Declaration Vice-President Xue, ICJ Reports 2019, 95 (145, para. 11).

secure Mauritius' consent to the separation of the Chagos Archipelago.[394] The conduct of the United Kingdom, according to Vice-President *Xue*, thus supported the assumption that there existed no territorial dispute and that no sovereignty over the territory was intended to be transferred.[395] Vice-President *Xue* emphasized that the process of decolonization and the concomitant responsibility of the UN to support this process had no temporal limitation.[396] Even though more than fifty years had passed since the independence of Mauritius, unresolved questions concerning its decolonization still remained. The responsibility of the UN did not cease only because Mauritius sought to resolve its dispute with its former colonial power through bilateral or third-party procedures.[397]

3. Criticism by Judges *Donoghue*, *Tomka*, and *Gevorgian*

Judges *Donoghue*[398], *Tomka*[399], and *Gevorgian*[400] argued that the Court should have been more careful not to circumvent the United Kingdom's consent when giving the requested advisory opinion. While Judges *Donoghue* and *Tomka* in effect took up Germany's suggestion that the Court ought to limit its response to question (a) on the right of self-determination of the Chagossian people while not responding to question (b) on the legal consequences of the continued administration by the UK,[401]

394 Ibid., 145, para. 12.

395 Ibid., 145, paras. 13–14.

396 Ibid., 145, paras. 16–17.

397 Ibid., 145–6, para. 19.

398 *Legal Consequences of the Separation of the Chagos Archipelago from Mauritius in 1965*, Advisory Opinion, Dissenting Opinion Donoghue, ICJ Reports 2019, 95 (261 et seq.).

399 Legal Consequences of the Separation of the Chagos Archipelago from Mauritius in 1965, Advisory Opinion, Declaration Tomka, ICJ Reports 2019, 95 (148).

400 *Legal Consequences of the Separation of the Chagos Archipelago from Mauritius in 1965*, Advisory Opinion, Separate Opinion Gevorgian, ICJ Reports 2019, 95 (336, para. 4).

401 *Legal Consequences of the Separation of the Chagos Archipelago from Mauritius in 1965*, Advisory Opinion, ICJ Reports 2019, Dissenting Opinion Donoghue, 95 (266, para. 22); Declaration Tomka, ICJ Reports 2019, 95 (151–152, paras. 8–9).

Judge *Gevorgian* specifically criticized the Court's statements regarding the international responsibility of the United Kingdom.[402]

a) Dissenting opinion by Judge *Donoghue*

According to Judge *Donoghue*,

> "the Advisory Opinion has the effect of circumventing the absence of United Kingdom consent to judicial settlement of the bilateral dispute between the United Kingdom and Mauritius regarding sovereignty over the Chagos Archipelago and thus undermines the integrity of the Court's judicial function."[403]

Judge *Donoghue* acknowledged that the subject-matter of the proceeding is located within the "broader frame of reference of decolonization, including the General Assembly's role therein".[404] However, the question concerning decolonization could be separated from the territorial dispute over sovereignty over the Chagos Archipelago. The Court should be careful to avoid this "quintessentially bilateral"[405] dispute as rendering an advisory opinion on this matter would undermine the integrity of the Court's judicial function:

> "The Charter of the United Nations and the Statute of the Court give the Court the functions of settling legal disputes in contentious cases and of responding to requests for advisory opinions. To preserve the integrity of both functions, the distinctions between them must be respected. I consider that the Advisory Opinion fails to do so and instead signals that the advisory opinion procedure is available as a fall-back mechanism to be used to overcome the absence of consent to jurisdiction in contentious cases. Some may find this to be a welcome development, but I consider

402 *Legal Consequences of the Separation of the Chagos Archipelago from Mauritius in 1965*, Advisory Opinion, Separate Opinion Gevorgian, ICJ Reports 2019, 95 (336, para. 4).

403 *Legal Consequences of the Separation of the Chagos Archipelago from Mauritius in 1965*, Advisory Opinion, ICJ Reports 2019, Dissenting Opinion Donoghue, 95 (261, para. 1).

404 Ibid., 262, paras. 3–5.

405 Ibid., 266, para. 21.

that it undermines the integrity of the Court's judicial function. For this reason, I dissent."[406]

b) Declaration by Judge *Tomka*

Judge *Tomka* equally expressed his concern that the Court's advisory opinion procedure is being abused to bring an essentially bilateral dispute before the Court without the consent of one of the disputing parties:

> "I am concerned that advisory proceedings have now become a way of bringing before the Court contentious matters, with which the General Assembly had not been dealing prior to requesting an opinion upon an initiative taken by one of the parties to the dispute."[407]

Judge *Tomka* supported his concern by reference to the procedural history of the request for the advisory opinion.[408] The request was not the result of ongoing activities of the UNGA regarding the Chagos Archipelago. On the contrary, the UNGA has not dealt with the Chagos Archipelago or the decolonization process of Mauritius in the past 50 years prior to the adoption of resolution 71/292 in 2017.[409] It was only after the UNCLOS arbitral tribunal declared that it lacked jurisdiction to decide the dispute between Mauritius and the UK that Mauritius, in 2016, inscribed the request for an advisory opinion on the matter into the provisional agenda of the 71st session of the UNGA.[410] To allow for bilateral negotiations between Mauritius and the UK, Mauritius then asked that all discussions on the matter in the plenary of the UNGA were halted until June 2017. After negotiations failed, Mauritius asked that the plenary discussed as soon as possible a draft resolution requesting an advisory opinion from the Court. The draft was prepared by Mauritius and formally presented to the plenary by the African Group without any modifications. The UNGA then adopted the resolutions – again without making any modifications – by a majority vote. Judge *Tomka* depicts the request not as an instrument to guide the

406 Ibid., 266, para. 23.

407 Legal Consequences of the Separation of the Chagos Archipelago from Mauritius in 1965, Advisory Opinion, Declaration Tomka, ICJ Reports 2019, 95 (148, para. 2).

408 Ibid., 149–150, para. 4.

409 In fact, Judge Tomka started his Declaration by scolding the United Nations for having abandoned the Chagossian people in 1968, see ibid., 148, para. 1.

410 UN doc. A/71/142.

UNGA but rather as a strategy of Mauritius to bring its dispute with the United Kingdom before the Court.

Notwithstanding his criticism, Judge *Tomka* did not oppose the giving of the requested advisory opinion. Despite the request being the brainchild of Mauritius, the UNGA had, as a collective organ, made the request its own by adopting a resolution by majority vote in which it requested from the Court an advisory opinion. Consequently, the Court ought to respond to the request. However, Judge *Tomka* proposed a nuanced approach. He cautioned:

> "If one can accept this course of action, one must also exercise caution not to go further than what is strictly necessary and useful for the requesting organ. The Court must not forget that what looms in the background is a bilateral dispute over which the Court lacks jurisdiction."[411]

By limiting the Court's response to what is "strictly necessary and useful for the requesting organ", Judge *Tomka* did not propose that the Court should make its own assessment of what the requesting organ needs and considers useful. After all, the requesting organ is best suited to make this assessment. Rather, Judge *Tomka* emphasized that the Court must be careful in such a situation not to go beyond what the requesting organ has asked. The Court must carefully look at the wording of the request to determine what the requesting organ needs from the Court. In the *Chagos* case, Judge *Tomka* argued, the Court went beyond the request by not only answering whether the decolonization process was lawfully completed but also addressing matters of state responsibility.[412] The matter of state responsibility was not referred to the Court and a response on this was not necessary to answer the questions presented to the Court. Judge *Tomka* stated:

> "The Court, despite stating that it is not "dealing with a bilateral dispute" between Mauritius and the United Kingdom, makes an unnecessary pronouncement on "an unlawful act of a continuing character" of the latter [...]. Advisory proceedings are not an appropriate forum for making these kinds of determinations, especially when the Court is not asked to make them and they are not strictly necessary for providing advice to the requesting organ."[413]

---

411 Legal Consequences of the Separation of the Chagos Archipelago from Mauritius in 1965, Advisory Opinion, Declaration Tomka, ICJ Reports 2019, 95 (150–1, para. 6).

412 Ibid., 151–2, paras. 8–9.

413 Ibid., 151, para. 8.

Judge *Tomka's* nuanced approach which advocates for judicial restraint strikes a balance between the Court's duty to give advice to the requesting organ and the Court's duty to protect its judicial integrity.

c) Declaration by Judge *Gevorgian*

Judge *Gevorgian* also argued that the Court should limit its answer to the law of decolonization as enshrined in the UNC without addressing the international responsibility of the United Kingdom.[414] He criticized the Court for ruling that the United Kingdom's continued administration of the Chagos Archipelago constitutes a wrongful act entailing the UK's international responsibility:

> "I do not disagree with the substance of this conclusion, but in my view such a statement crosses the thin line separating the Court's advisory and contentious jurisdiction."[415]

Judge *Gevorgian* recognized that the Court made similar statements on the international responsibility of a state in the *Namibia* opinion and the *Wall* opinion.[416] However, these cases could be distinguished from the *Chagos* case on the fact that the Court could rely on binding resolutions of the UNSC declaring the respective conduct illegal.[417]

J. Policies and Practices of Israel in the Occupied Palestinian Territory case (2024)

The most recent example of a case in which a bilateral dispute arguably formed the subject-matter of an advisory proceeding is the *Policies and Practices of Israel in the Occupied Palestinian Territory* case.[418]

---

414 *Legal Consequences of the Separation of the Chagos Archipelago from Mauritius in 1965*, Advisory Opinion, Separate Opinion Gevorgian, ICJ Reports 2019, 95 (336, para. 4).

415 Ibid., 336, para. 5.

416 Ibid., 336–7, para. 6.

417 Ibid.

418 *Legal Consequences arising from the Policies and Practices of Israel in the Occupied Palestinian Territory, including East Jerusalem*, Advisory Opinion, Publication pending in ICJ Reports 2024, 1; for an analysis, see *Mehrdad Payandeh*, 79 JZ 18 (2024), 789.

I. Background

On 30 December 2022, the UNGA requested from the ICJ an advisory opinion on two questions:

> "(a) What are the legal consequences arising from the ongoing violation by Israel of the right of the Palestinian people to self-determination, from its prolonged occupation, settlement and annexation of the Palestinian territory occupied since 1967, including measures aimed at altering the demographic composition, character and status of the Holy City of Jerusalem, and from its adoption of related discriminatory legislation and measures?
> (b) How do the policies and practices of Israel referred to in paragraph 18 (a) above affect the legal status of the occupation, and what are the legal consequences that arise for all States and the United Nations from this status?"[419]

After written and oral proceedings have taken place, the ICJ issued its long-expected advisory opinion on 19 July 2024.

Israel voted against resolution 77/247 in which the UNGA requested the advisory opinion from the Court. During the written proceedings, in which an unprecedented number of states and international organizations participated,[420] Israel reiterated its opposition to the proceedings arguing that the question was tendentious and ignored Israel's security interests as well as efforts to find a diplomatic solution to the conflict.[421] Emphasizing its lack of consent, Israel alluded to the Eastern Carelia doctrine:

> "It follows that the present situation is not only one in which Israel, as an interested party, has not given its consent to judicial settlement of its dispute with the Palestinian side; it is also one in which both interested

419 UNGA resolution 77/247 of 30 December 2022, UN doc. A/RES/77/247, para. 18. The resolution was adopted with 87 votes in favor, 26 votes against with 53 abstentions, see A/77/400 DR I.

420 In total, 54 states and three international organizations submitted written statements. Additionally, 13 states and two international organizations submitted written comments in response to these written statements, see *Legal Consequences arising from the Policies and Practices of Israel in the Occupied Palestinian Territory, including East Jerusalem*, Advisory Opinion, Publication pending in ICJ Reports 2024, 1 (8–9).

421 ICJ Pleadings, *Legal Consequences arising from the Policies and Practices of Israel in the Occupied Palestinian Territory, including East Jerusalem*, Written Statement of Israel, 2–3.

> parties have given their express and binding consent to resolving that dispute through another settlement means. The request for the Court's advisory opinion perversely seeks to circumvent the lack of Israel's consent, and to make a dead letter of the fundamental international legal principle underlying the indispensable need for it."[422]

Most states and organizations participating in the written proceedings argued in favor of the Court rendering the requested advisory opinion. However, several participants urged the Court not to issue the requested opinion emphasizing the lack of consent by Israel. Among those states were Canada[423], Fiji[424], Hungary[425], the United Kingdom[426], Togo[427], and Zambia[428]. While most of these states only briefly touched upon the question of state consent to advisory proceedings, the United Kingdom extensively elaborated on the matter. The United Kingdom presented several arguments for why the principle of non-circumvention of state consent should continue to apply to advisory proceedings.[429] According to the United Kingdom, the formally non-binding nature of advisory opinions does not allow the ICJ to decide a bilateral dispute without consent by means of an advisory opinion.[430] While advisory opinions lack formal binding force, in issuing an advisory opinion the Court "makes statements of law, which may have

---

422 Ibid., 4.

423 ICJ Pleadings, *Legal Consequences arising from the Policies and Practices of Israel in the Occupied Palestinian Territory, including East Jerusalem*, Written Statement of Canada, 2–3.

424 ICJ Pleadings, *Legal Consequences arising from the Policies and Practices of Israel in the Occupied Palestinian Territory, including East Jerusalem*, Written Statement of Fiji, 4–5.

425 ICJ Pleadings, *Legal Consequences arising from the Policies and Practices of Israel in the Occupied Palestinian Territory, including East Jerusalem*, Written Statement of Hungary, 4–6.

426 ICJ Pleadings, *Legal Consequences arising from the Policies and Practices of Israel in the Occupied Palestinian Territory, including East Jerusalem*, Written Statement of the United Kingdom, 22–30.

427 ICJ Pleadings, *Legal Consequences arising from the Policies and Practices of Israel in the Occupied Palestinian Territory, including East Jerusalem*, Written Statement of Togo, 2.

428 ICJ Pleadings, *Legal Consequences arising from the Policies and Practices of Israel in the Occupied Palestinian Territory, including East Jerusalem*, Written Statement of Zambia, 2.

429 ICJ Pleadings, *Legal Consequences arising from the Policies and Practices of Israel in the Occupied Palestinian Territory, including East Jerusalem*, Written Statement of the United Kingdom, 22–25.

430 Ibid., 24.

legal consequences, even if not intended by the Court or required by the Statute."[431] The United Kingdom also criticized the "broader frame of reference"-standard developed by the Court in its *Western Sahara* advisory opinion arguing that "[e]very legal dispute falls within a broader context" and that this "says nothing about the test to be applied by the Court, *viz*, whether the specific request requires the Court to determine in effect the specific legal dispute between the parties in circumstances where to do so would circumvent the consent requirement."[432] The United Kingdom further argued that the mere fact that a UN organ has previously dealt with a matter, does not diminish the necessity of state consent to the proceedings.[433] Instead, the Court should "compare the subject-matter of the bilateral dispute with the issues presented by the request before the Court, recognising the significance of the "origin and scope of the dispute (...) in appreciating, from the point of view of the exercise of the Court's discretion, the real significance in this case of the lack of (...) consent".[434]

II. ICJ pays lip service to Eastern Carelia doctrine

In response to the arguments presented by the United Kingdom and others, the ICJ stated that it continued to adhere to the Eastern Carelia doctrine and reiterated its previous case law on the matter.[435] However, the ICJ declined to exercise its discretion finding that the subject-matter of the request was not merely a bilateral matter between Israel and Palestine.[436] The Court pointed to the long-standing involvement of the organs of the League of Nations and the United Nations in questions relating to Palestine.[437] Two issues stand out in the Court's response. First, the brevity of it. The ICJ did not engage with the subject-matter of the request to assess if it concerned

431 Ibid.

432 Ibid., 24–25.

433 Ibid., 25.

434 Ibid., citing *Western Sahara*, Advisory Opinion, ICJ Reports 1975, 12, (27, para. 42).

435 *Legal Consequences arising from the Policies and Practices of Israel in the Occupied Palestinian Territory, including East Jerusalem*, Advisory Opinion, Publication pending in ICJ Reports 2024, 1 (17, para. 34).

436 Ibid. (17, para. 35).

437 Ibid. The Court cited UNGA resolution 57/107 of 3 December 2002, UN doc. A/RES/57/107 which refers to "a permanent responsibility [of the UNGA] towards the question of Palestine until the question is resolved in all its aspects in a satisfactory manner in accordance with international legitimacy".

a bilateral dispute or if it was multilateral in nature. Instead, the Court referenced the long-standing involvement of the UN in matters concerning Palestine to justify that any question relating to Palestine is multilateral in nature. In doing so, the Court also did not engage with Judge *Donoghue's* dissenting opinion in the *Chagos* case in which she raised the concern that the Court's position effectively renders the Eastern Carelia doctrine meaningless. Secondly, the ICJ omitted its usual reference to a "broader frame of reference" which it used in previous advisory opinions when it rejected claims that a matter was bilateral in nature.[438] Maybe the Court recognized that this standard does not add any analytical clarity to deciding whether a matter is bilateral or multilateral in nature.

After finding that the lack of Israel's consent did not constitute a compelling reason for the Court not to render the requested advisory opinion, the Court rejected other grounds for exercising its discretion. These included that the opinion would not assist the UNGA in the performance of its functions,[439] that the opinion would undermine the negotiation process between Israel and Palestine,[440] that the opinion would be detrimental to the work of the UNSC,[441] that the Court lacked sufficient information to give an advisory opinion[442] and that the questions are formulated in a biased manner[443].

438 See *Western Sahara*, Advisory Opinion, ICJ Reports 1975, 12 (26, para. 38); *Legal Consequences of the Construction of a Wall in the Occupied Palestinian Territory*, Advisory Opinion, ICJ Reports 2004, 136 (159, para. 50); *Legal Consequences of the Separation of the Chagos Archipelago from Mauritius in 1965*, Advisory Opinion, ICJ Reports 2019, 95 (118, para. 88).

439 *Legal Consequences arising from the Policies and Practices of Israel in the Occupied Palestinian Territory, including East Jerusalem*, Advisory Opinion, Publication pending in ICJ Reports 2024, 1 (17-18, paras. 36-37).

440 Ibid. (18-19, paras. 38-40).

441 Ibid. (19-20, paras. 41-43).

442 Ibid. (20, paras. 44-47).

443 Ibid. (21, paras. 48-49).

K. Conclusions: Function, standard, and future of the Eastern Carelia doctrine

I. The Eastern Carelia doctrine's overarching function: safeguarding the integrity of the Court's judicial function

The ICJ exercises its advisory jurisdiction following a rule-exception-approach: As a rule, and as an expression of the Court's duty as an organ of the UN to cooperate with the other organs and to promote the activities of the UN, the ICJ will give the requested advisory opinion. Only exceptionally, when there are "compelling reasons" will the Court refuse to give an advisory opinion. However, as Judge *Bennouna* pointed out in his dissenting opinion to the *Kosovo* advisory opinion, the ICJ has not made "clear what it means by that".[444] This indeterminacy creates a certain risk of arbitrariness.

Nevertheless, the Court's case law provides guidance. The Court repeatedly emphasized that it will refuse to issue an advisory opinion if giving the opinion would be incompatible with its judicial function. An advisory opinion is incompatible with the Court's judicial function if giving the opinion would circumvent the principle that a state is not obliged to submit its dispute with another state to judicial dispute settlement without its consent.

II. The Eastern Carelia's three-pronged test: Bilateral dispute, lack of consent, dispute settlement by means of the advisory opinion procedure

The Court uses a three-pronged test to assess whether issuing an advisory opinion constitutes a circumvention of state consent in the sense of the Eastern Carelia doctrine: First, there must be a pending bilateral dispute which arose outside the organs of the United Nations and prior to the request for an advisory opinion. The Court denied the bilateral nature of the dispute between Spain and Morocco in the *Western Sahara* case precisely for the reason that the dispute did not originate outside the UN.[445]

---

444 *Accordance with international law of the unilateral declaration of independence in respect of Kosovo*, Advisory Opinion, Dissenting Opinion Bennouna, ICJ Reports 2010, 403 (501), para. 5; cf. *S. Rosenne*, The law and practice of the International Court, 1920-2005, 4th ed. 2006, 986–987.

445 *Western Sahara*, Advisory Opinion, ICJ Reports 1975, 12 (26, para. 36).

Secondly, at least one of the parties to the dispute must be opposed to the judicial settlement of the dispute within the contentious procedure of the Court. This requirement is usually met, as otherwise the matter would already be pending before the Court in contentious proceedings. Thirdly, the giving of the advisory opinion must be substantially equivalent to the judicial settlement of the bilateral dispute. The last of these conditions is the vaguest and most contentious among the three. To determine if giving the requested advisory opinion constitutes judicial dispute settlement, the ICJ does not compare the subject-matter of the dispute and the referred questions. Instead, it examines if the object and purpose of the request for an advisory opinion is to settle a bilateral dispute or if another object and purpose can be identified. Thus, for the ICJ, the central question is not whether the Court has to make judicial pronouncements on matters which are at the heart of a bilateral dispute but whether the advisory opinion was *intended* to be used as a method of dispute settlement. Only if an advisory opinion is being requested with the aim to settle a bilateral dispute, would the giving of the advisory opinion circumvent the interested state's consent.

Thus, the object and purpose of the request for the advisory opinion is the Court's central consideration when exercising its advisory jurisdiction. To determine a request's object and purpose, the Court interprets the requesting organ's resolution by reference to its wording in light of the request's procedural history. In doing so, the ICJ presumes that the authorized organs request advisory opinions only to the extent that this is necessary for the fulfilment of their functions. The Court views both its judicial restraint and the restraint of the requesting organ in requesting an advisory opinion as an expression of the inter-organ duty of cooperation under Article 7 UNC.

III. Abandoning or continuing the Eastern Carelia doctrine?

The ICJ regularly prioritizes the interest of the requesting UN body in receiving the requested advisory opinion over the interest of the affected states. The Court gave the requested opinion even in situations where the interest of the requesting organ in receiving the opinion was almost indistinguishable from the settlement of the underlying dispute. In the *Wall* case, the UNGA asked for an advisory opinion not only on the legal obligations of Israel but also on questions of state responsibility, thereby effectively asking the Court to adjudicate the case between Israel and Palestine. For Judge

Higgins, the Court crossed a line, effectively *revising* rather than *applying* the existing case law on the Eastern Carelia doctrine.[446] Similarly, in the *Chagos* case, the United Kingdom argued that the Court effectively abandoned the Eastern Carelia doctrine by deciding the territorial sovereignty over the Chagos Archipelago.[447]

One way of reading these decisions is that the Court recognized a community exception from the principle of consensual dispute settlement. Accordingly, even if the three-pronged test of the Eastern Carelia doctrine is fulfilled, the Court would not be required to refuse to give the requested opinion if the underlying dispute threatens international peace and security or when the referred question relates to *erga omnes* obligations.[448] In these circumstances the collective community interests prevail over individual interests of affected states because the international community has a legitimate interest in receiving an answer from the Court and a response cannot be regarded as a circumvention of state consent.[449] Read in this light, the Eastern Carelia doctrine illustrates a classic conflict at the heart of international law: the conflict between sovereignty and community. Whether this conflict can at all be resolved is questionable.[450] The Eastern Carelia doctrine originated in the case law of the PCIJ and in the context of the

---

446 *Legal Consequences of the Construction of a Wall in the Occupied Palestinian Territory*, Advisory Opinion, Separate Opinion Higgins, ICJ Reports 2004, 136 (210, paras. 12-13); see also *P. d'Argent*, in: A. Zimmermann/C. J. Tams/K. Oellers-Frahm/C. Tomuschat/D. W. K. Anderson (eds.), The Statute of the International Court of Justice, 3. ed., 2019: Article 65, 1806–1807.

447 Cf. ICJ Pleadings, *Legal Consequences of the Separation of the Chagos Archipelago from Mauritius in 1965*, Written Statement of the United Kingdom, para. 7.21.

448 Cf. *J. A. Frowein/K. Oellers-Frahm*, in: A. Zimmermann/C. Tomuschat/K. Oellers-Frahm/C. J. Tams/M. Kashgar/D. Diehl (eds.), The Statute of the International Court of Justice, 2. ed., 2012: Art. 65, paras. 33–37; *P. d'Argent*, in: A. Zimmermann/C. J. Tams/K. Oellers-Frahm/C. Tomuschat/D. W. K. Anderson (eds.), The Statute of the International Court of Justice, 3. ed., 2019: Article 65, 45.

449 Cf. *P.-M. Dupuy*, Recourse to the International Court of Justice for the Purpose of Settling a Dispute, in: L. Boisson de Chazournes/M. G. Kohen/J. Viñuales (eds.), Diplomatic and judicial means of dispute settlement, 2013, 61 (68); *P. d'Argent*, in: A. Zimmermann/C. J. Tams/K. Oellers-Frahm/C. Tomuschat/D. W. K. Anderson (eds.), The Statute of the International Court of Justice, 3. ed., 2019: Article 65, para. 45.

450 "It is the great merit of critical legal studies to have demonstrated that this tension between those two poles [sovereignty and community interests] is, really, unresolvable, at least given our normative apparatus which does not allow us to make normative choices.", *J. Klabbers*, An introduction to international organizations law, 3. ed. 2015, 5.

League of Nations which was still heavily influenced by the traditional Westphalian understanding of international law.[451] This context explains the doctrines focus on the protection of the sovereignty of individual states. The expanding scope of international law and modern conceptualizations of the sovereign equality of states focusing on interdependence and collective interests,[452] however, call the Eastern Carelia doctrine into question.

451 Cf. *S. Rosenne*, The law and practice of the International Court, 1920-2005, 4th ed. 2006, 7.

452 Cf. Ibid., 7.

§ 4 Eastern Carelia before other international courts and tribunals

The ICJ is not the only international court or tribunal (IC) with the jurisdiction to render advisory opinions. The stark expansion of the number of ICs in the second half of the 20th century[453] also brought about an expansion of the advisory function.[454] There are currently at least ten ICs with some kind of advisory function.[455] This chapter examines the advisory jurisdiction of some of these ICs. ICs are understood here as "permanent judicial bodies made up of independent judges who are entrusted with adjudicating international disputes on the basis of international law according to a pre-determined set of rules of procedure and rendering decisions which are binding on the parties."[456]

While it is a necessary condition of an IC that it *may* render binding decisions, not all of its pronouncements must have binding force. The focus of this study lies on advisory procedures, thus on procedures that regularly, though not always[457], lack binding force. Advisory procedures may generally be defined as judicial procedures in which an authorized body requests from an IC a non-binding legal opinion on a question of international law. This definition includes advisory opinions on abstract questions of law as well as concrete disputes.

This chapter examines the advisory function of three regional human rights courts – the European Court of Human Rights (ECtHR), the Inter-American Court of Human Rights (IACtHR), and the African Court on Human and Peoples' Rights (ACtHPR) – as well as of the International Tribunal for the Law of the Sea (ITLOS). The aim is to present an overview

453 On this, see *K. Oellers-Frahm*, 5 MPYUNL (2001), 67.

454 For an overview of the advisory function of different international courts and tribunals, see *A. Aust*, 1 JIDS 1 (2010), 123; *K. Oellers-Frahm*, 12 GLJ 5 (2011), 1033 (1034–1040); see also *A. Keene*, 14 NZJPIL 1 (2016), 67.

455 *K. Oellers-Frahm*, 12 GLJ 5 (2011), 1033 (1034–1040). *Benz* even lists 21 ICs with an advisory jurisdiction, see *E. Benz*, The Advisory Function of the Inter-American Court of Human Rights, 2024, 149–156.

456 *C. Tomuschat*, International Courts and Tribunals (last updated 2019), in: A. Peters/R. Wolfrum (eds.), The Max Planck Encyclopedia of Public International Law, 2008 (1).

457 On the concept of "binding" ICJ advisory opinions, see *R. Ago*, 85 AJIL 3 (1991), 439.

of the extent of the respective advisory jurisdiction and identify whether the legal framework of the respective advisory procedures provides guidance as to the use of advisory opinions for the settlement of international disputes.

The preliminary ruling procedure of the Court of Justice of the European Union is not considered here.[458] Not examined in this chapter are further the advisory procedures of the COMESA Court[459], the ECOWAS Court[460], the OAPEC Judicial Board[461], and the Badinter Commission[462]. While the Badinter Commission has issued 15 advisory opinions on important legal questions in the context of the dissolution of the former Socialist Federal Republic of Yugoslavia (SFRY), it has ceased its operations in 1993.[463] The advisory function of the other three ICs lays dormant.

A. European Court of Human Rights

The principal function of the ECtHR[464] is to ensure the observance under the obligations of the European Convention on Human Rights and Fundamental Freedoms[465] (ECHR). The ECHR was adopted by the Member States of the Council of Europe (CoE) on 4 November 1950 as the first comprehensive international convention on human rights. The ECtHR began its work in 1959, although it was not until 1998, with the entry into force of Protocol No. 11, that the ECtHR's jurisdiction became obligatory

458 The EU Member States have agreed to transfer a unique degree of sovereignty to the EU institutions. This makes it difficult to compare the powers of the EU institutions with those of the UN. Secondly, the powers of the ECJ are determined by European law, which is a distinct legal system and, because of its systematic nature, can only be compared to general international law to a limited extent.

459 See Article 32(1) of the Treaty Establishing the Common Market for Eastern and Southern Africa (COMESA Treaty).

460 See Article 10 of the Protocol A/P.l/7/91 on the Community Court of Justice, 6 July 1991.

461 See Article 25 of the Special Protocol for a Judicial Board for the settlement of disputes, adopted 9 May 1978, entered into force 20 April 1980.

462 UN/EC Geneva Conference of 27 January-26 April 1993.

463 *K. Oellers-Frahm*, 12 GLJ 5 (2011), 1033 (1039).

464 Since the ratification of Protocol 11 which abolished the Commission, there is no other body charged with monitoring the compliance with human rights in the Council of Europe system.

465 Convention for the Protection of Human Rights and Fundamental Freedoms, European Treaty Series No. 5, adopted 4 November 1950, entry into force 3 September 1953.

for CoE Member States and individual applicants had direct access to the Court.[466]

I. Overview of the ECtHR's advisory jurisdiction

The advisory jurisdiction of the ECtHR has evolved over time, culminating in three different types of advisory procedures: The first type of advisory procedure was bestowed upon the ECtHR by Article 47 of the ECHR which is limited in its personal scope to the Committee of Ministers of the CoE and concerns only the interpretation of non-substantive provisions of the ECHR. Recognizing a need for a procedure to also interpret the rights and freedoms under the ECHR, the CoE Member States later created an opt-in advisory procedure by passing Protocol No. 16 to the ECHR. A third type of advisory procedure is conferred upon the Court by the Oviedo Convention.[467] The first two advisory procedures are of particular interest for this study.

1. Article 47-procedure

The ECHR did not originally envision an advisory jurisdiction for the ECtHR. On 22 January 1960, the Consultative Assembly (now Parliamentary Assembly) of the CoE adopted Recommendation 232 in which it proposed to the Committee of Ministers to give to the ECtHR "the competence to interpret the Convention on Human Rights, when a doubt has arisen of a legal character, even though no case has been brought".[468]

---

466 Protocol No. 11 to the Convention for the Protection of Human Rights and Fundamental Freedoms, restructuring the control machinery established thereby (adopted 11 May 1994, entered into force 1 November 1998) ETS 155. On the history of the ECtHR, see *A. Nußberger*, The European Court of Human Rights, First edition 2020, 1 et seq. On the ratification of Protocol No. 11, see ibid., 27–28.

467 Any State Party to the 1997 Oviedo Convention as well as the Committee on Bioethics may ask the ECtHR for an advisory opinion on the interpretation of the Oviedo Convention, Convention for the protection of Human Rights and Dignity of the Human Being with regard to the Application of Biology and Medicine, European Treaty Series No. 164, adopted 4 April 1997, entry into force 1 December 1999, Articles 29 and 32.

468 CoE, Consultative Assembly Recommendation 232 of 22 January 1960.

The Committee of Ministers instructed a Committee of Experts to assess the desirability of introducing such a procedure and to produce a draft agreement.[469] The Committee of Experts prepared what became Protocol No. 2 to the ECHR, which gave the ECtHR the competence to give advisory opinions at the request of the Committee of Ministers on legal questions concerning the interpretation of the Convention and the Protocols thereto (Article 1 para. 1 Protocol 2).[470] With the adoption of Protocol No. 11, the advisory jurisdiction of the ECtHR was incorporated into the main text of the ECHR in Articles 47 to 49 ECHR.

The advisory jurisdiction lies with the Grand Chamber of the Court.[471] It was a deliberate decision not to allocate the advisory jurisdiction to smaller formations, as the Explanatory Report to Protocol No. 2 indicates:

> "The Committee [of Ministers] considered that the power conferred on the Court to give advisory opinions was such an important one that it ought to be exercised by the Court sitting in plenary session."[472]

Article 47 ECHR sets out the conditions for the advisory jurisdiction of the ECtHR. It stipulates:

> "1. The Court may, at the request of the Committee of Ministers, give advisory opinions on legal questions concerning the interpretation of the Convention and the Protocols thereto.

469 The Committee of Experts was a group of governmental experts instructed by the Committee of Ministers by resolution (60) 6 of 22 March 1960 to study problems relating to the ECHR, particularly regarding the introduction of an advisory competence of the ECtHR.

470 Protocol No. 2 to the Convention for the Protection of Human Rights and Fundamental Freedoms, conferring upon the European Court of Human Rights competence to give Advisory Opinions, European Treaty Series No. 44, adopted 6 May 1963, entry into force 21 September 1970. Interestingly, the Committee of Experts made another proposal in 1962 which would have introduced a prejudicial ruling procedure in which national courts or tribunals could have submitted questions of interpretation of the ECHR which arose in cases before them as well as an advisory opinion procedure in which governments of the Member States could request advisory opinions. This idea would be picked up some 50 years later in Protocol 16 to the ECHR.

471 See Article 87 Rules of Court.

472 Committee of Ministers, Explanatory Report to Protocol No. 2 to the Convention for the Protection of Human Rights and Fundamental Freedoms, conferring upon the European Court of Human Rights competence to give advisory opinions, 6 May 1963, 5.

> 2. Such opinions shall not deal with any question relating to the content or scope of the rights or freedoms defined in Section I of the Convention and the Protocols thereto, or with any other question which the Court or the Committee of Ministers might have to consider in consequence of any such proceedings as could be instituted in accordance with the Convention.
> 3. Decisions of the Committee of Ministers to request an advisory opinion of the Court shall require a majority vote of the representatives entitled to sit on the committee."

The ECtHR's advisory jurisdiction *ratione personae* under Article 47 ECHR is limited to the Committee of Ministers, which is composed of the Ministers for Foreign Affairs of the CoE Member States.[473] The CoE's other organ – the Parliamentary Assembly –, as well as the Secretary General are not authorized to request advisory opinions. During the drafting process of Protocol No. 2, the European Commission of Human Rights proposed that it too should be authorized to request advisory opinions from the ECtHR.[474] However, the proposal was rejected by the Committee of Ministers. Likewise, Member States of the ECtHR may also not request advisory opinions pursuant to Article 47 ECHR. They may, however, submit a proposal for such a request to the Committee of Ministers, which may then refer them by majority vote of its members[475] to the ECtHR.[476]

---

473 The original Art. 1 Protocol 2 to the ECHR contained a two-thirds majority for the vote of the Committee of Ministers.

474 Committee of Ministers, Explanatory Report to Protocol No. 2 to the Convention for the Protection of Human Rights and Fundamental Freedoms, conferring upon the European Court of Human Rights competence to give advisory opinions, 6 May 1963, 1.

475 See Article 47 para. 3 ECHR.

476 See Committee of Ministers, Explanatory Report to Protocol No. 2 to the Convention for the Protection of Human Rights and Fundamental Freedoms, conferring upon the European Court of Human Rights competence to give advisory opinions, 6 May 1963, 2. The Committee of Ministers has followed proposals made by the Parliamentary Assembly in the *Decision on the competence of the Court to give an advisory opinion*, 2 June 2004, A47–2004–001 (para. 14) and in the *Advisory opinion on certain legal questions concerning the lists of candidates submitted with a view to the election of judges to the European Court of Human Rights (No. 2)*, 22 January 2010, A47–2010–001 (paras. 17–18); similarly it has followed proposals made by a CoE Member State (Malta) in the *Advisory opinion on certain legal questions concerning the lists of candidates submitted with a view to the election of judges to the European Court of Human Rights*, 12 February 2008, A47–2008.

The ECtHR's advisory jurisdiction *ratione materiae* is governed by Article 47 paras. 1 and 2 ECHR. According to Article 47 para. 1, the ECtHR's advisory jurisdiction extends to "legal questions concerning the interpretation of the Convention and the Protocols thereto". The Committee of Ministers understands the term "legal questions" to have the same meaning as in other international instruments.[477] Legal questions concerning other international law instruments as well as policy matters such as amendments of the ECHR are excluded from the ECtHR's advisory jurisdiction.[478]

Article 47 para. 2 ECHR makes several important qualifications to the ECtHR's advisory jurisdiction. It firstly excludes from the ECtHR's advisory jurisdiction "any question relating to the content or scope of the rights or freedoms under Section I of the Convention and the Protocols thereto". The Committee of Ministers in its Commentary to Protocol 2 did not elaborate on the reasons for the exclusion. It merely referred to the reasons for the exclusion as being "self-evident".[479] It can be assumed that the CoE Member States were not willing to grant the ECtHR the competence to determine the scope of the Member States' substantive obligations under the ECHR.

Article 47 para. 2 ECHR secondly excludes from the ECtHR's advisory jurisdiction "any other question which the Court or the Committee of Ministers might have to consider in consequence of any such proceedings as could be instituted in accordance with the Convention". These "proceedings as could be instituted in accordance with the Convention" concern the inter-state cases under Article 33 ECHR as well as individual applications under Article 34 ECHR.[480] The wording "could be instituted" implies that this exclusion not only extends to past or presently pending cases, but also to future or merely hypothetical proceedings.[481] The ECtHR confirmed this extensive reading of Article 47 para. 2 ECHR in its first advisory opinion in 2004. The ECtHR found that Article 47 para. 2 prevented the court from answering any "legal question [...] which it *might* be called upon to address

477 Ibid., 2.

478 Cf. Ibid., 2.

479 Ibid., 3.

480 *Decision on the competence of the Court to give an advisory opinion*, 2 June 2004, A47–2004–001 (para. 26).

481 Committee of Ministers, Explanatory Report to Protocol No. 2 to the Convention for the Protection of Human Rights and Fundamental Freedoms, conferring upon the European Court of Human Rights competence to give advisory opinions, 6 May 1963, 4; *Decision on the competence of the Court to give an advisory opinion*, 2 June 2004, A47–2004–001 (para. 33).

in the future [...] in the examination of the admissibility or merits of a concrete case."[482]

The ECtHR based its interpretation on the wording of Article 47 para. 2 ECHR, the commentary to Protocol 2 issued by the Committee of Ministers and the provision's *travaux préparatoires*.[483] The underlying idea of such a stark separation of the proceedings was to "avoid the potential situation in which the Court adopts in an advisory opinion a position which might prejudice its later examination of an application brought under Articles 33 or 34 of the Convention".[484]

The exclusion does not only relate to the merits. The Court's task in proceedings under Articles 33 and 34 also includes ascertaining the admissibility of an application. Such questions concerning the admissibility of a potential application under Articles 33 and 34 ECHR are thus equally excluded from the ECtHR's advisory competence under Article 47 ECHR.[485] The ECtHR's advisory jurisdiction therefore only extends to questions about procedural matters such as the election of judges[486] and the duties of the Secretary General of the CoE.[487] Any questions which involve the Member States' obligations under the ECHR are excluded.[488]

The strict separation of the ECtHR'S advisory procedure from its contentious procedure is intended to prevent the advisory procedure from interfering with the ECtHR's primary function of deciding on inter-state cases and individual applications.[489] Notably, by creating Article 47 para. 2 ECHR, the Committee of Ministers intended to protect the ECtHR's "judicial function". The Committee regarded the ECtHR's "judicial function" as

482 *Decision on the competence of the Court to give an advisory opinion*, 2 June 2004, A47-2004-001 (para. 33). The case concerned the question of whether CoE Member States could join other, less robust human rights instruments.

483 Ibid.

484 Ibid.

485 Ibid., para. 27.

486 *Advisory opinion on certain legal questions concerning the lists of candidates submitted with a view to the election of judges to the European Court of Human Rights*, 12 February 2008, A47-2008-001.

487 *Decision on the competence of the Court to give an advisory opinion*, 2 June 2004, A47-2004-001 (para. 28).

488 Committee of Ministers, Explanatory Report to Protocol No. 2 to the Convention for the Protection of Human Rights and Fundamental Freedoms, conferring upon the European Court of Human Rights competence to give advisory opinions, 6 May 1963, 4.

489 *Decision on the competence of the Court to give an advisory opinion*, 2 June 2004, A47-2004-001 (para. 28); Ibid., 3.

being equivalent to the ECtHR's contentious function,[490] and thus excluding the Court's advisory procedure. However, the ECtHR has broadened the scope of its judicial function in its case law by referring to its contentious function as its *primary* rather than *only* judicial function.[491]

2. Protocol 16-procedure

Pursuant to the optional Protocol 16-procedure,[492] which has been ratified by 22 Member States of the CoE,[493] the highest courts and tribunals of the CoE Member States may request an advisory opinion from the ECtHR in the context of a pending case on "questions of principle relating to the interpretation or application of the rights and freedoms defined in the Convention or the protocols thereto" (Article 1 Protocol 16).

The Protocol 16-procedure fills the gap left by the Article 47-procedure which explicitly excludes requests relating to rights enshrined under the ECHR from the subject-matter jurisdiction of the Court.

A panel of five judges decides about the admissibility of a request (Article 2 Protocol 16) in accordance with the rules laid out in Article 1. Accordingly, the request must relate to an ongoing case, the requesting court must explain its reasons and provide relevant legal and factual context. Since these conditions are quite broad, the Court will need to further clarify when a request for an advisory opinion is admissible *vel non*.[494]

Advisory opinions rendered by the Court under its Protocol 16-Procedure are formally not binding (Article 5 Protocol 16). However, they have a "hybrid legal nature"[495]. As former Vice-President of the ECtHR *Nußberger* explained:

---

490 Explanatory Report to Protocol No. 2 to the Convention for the Protection of Human Rights and Fundamental Freedoms, conferring upon the European Court of Human Rights competence to give advisory opinions, 6 May 1963.

491 *Decision on the competence of the Court to give an advisory opinion*, 2 June 2004, A47–2004–001 (para. 33).

492 On the Protocol 16-procedure, see *J. Jahn*, 74 ZaöRV / HJIL (2014), 821; *A. Paprocka/M. Ziolkowski*, 11 European Constitutional Law Review 2 (2015), 274.

493 See the chart of signatures and ratifications of Protocol 16 on the CoE's website: https://www.coe.int/en/web/conventions/full-list?module=signatures-by-treaty&treatynum=214.

494 *A. Nußberger*, The European Court of Human Rights, First edition 2020, 56.

495 Ibid., 52.

> "[T]hey form part of the Court's case-law on an equal footing with other Grand Chamber judgments. They may have implicit *erga omnes* effects even for those Member States not parties to Protocol 16. In theory States requesting an advisory opinion may be free not to follow it, but might then be faced with individual complaints on the same issue."[496]

The Protocol 16-procedure was created for domestic courts to receive advisory opinions which shall be used to settle an ongoing dispute. The Protocol 16-procedure could thus be seen as an example of an advisory procedure that operates as a means of dispute settlement. Crucially, however, it is not the ECtHR that decides the pending dispute. The Court merely provides an authoritative interpretation of the ECHR.

The views on the Protocol 16-procedure differ: While some fear that the new advisory procedure could disturb the "existing balance between ordinary and Constitutional Courts in fundamental rights adjudication across Europe",[497] others argue that the new procedure could "help increase the acceptance of the ECtHR's jurisprudence as well as the homogeneity of human rights interpretation across Europe"[498].

II. Use of ECtHR advisory opinions to settle inter-state disputes

The ECtHR's Article 47-procedure strictly separates the ECtHR's contentious procedure from its advisory procedure. No matter that can be brought before the ECtHR by means of its contentious procedure may be the subject of the ECtHR's Article 47-procedure. This is to prevent the advisory procedure from interfering with the dispute settlement function of the ECtHR. This strict separation is somewhat reduced by the Protocol 16-procedure, which allows national courts of CoE Member States to refer the interpretation of substantive human rights provisions to the ECtHR. However, even under this procedure, the ECtHR's function is strictly limited to the interpretation of the human rights provision without deciding the underlying dispute that is before the national court.

---

496 Ibid., 52–53.

497 *M. Dicosola/C. Fasone/I. Spigno*, 16 German Law Journal 6 (2015), 1387 (1425).

498 *E. Benz*, The Advisory Function of the Inter-American Court of Human Rights, 2024, 142.

B. Inter-American Court of Human Rights

I. Overview of the IACtHR's advisory jurisdiction

The advisory jurisdiction of the IACtHR is governed by Article 64 of the American Convention on Human Rights (ACHR), Article 2 of the IACtHR Statute, and the Court's Rules of Procedure.[499]

Article 64 ACHR stipulates:

> "1. The member states of the Organization may consult the Court regarding the interpretation of this Convention or of other treaties concerning the protection of human rights in the American states. Within their spheres of competence, the organs listed in Chapter X of the Charter of the Organization of American States, as amended by the Protocol of Buenos Aires, may in like manner consult the Court.
> 2. The Court, at the request of a member state of the Organization, may provide that state with opinions regarding the compatibility of any of its domestic laws with the aforesaid international instruments."[500]

Under Article 64 ACHR, certain organs of the Organization of American States (OAS)[501] and all OAS Member States may request an advisory opinion from the IACtHR. By giving the OAS organs and Member States the right to request advisory opinions, the IACtHR's advisory procedure aims "to assist the American States in fulfilling their international human rights obligations and to assist the different organs of the inter-American system to carry out the functions assigned to them in this field."[502]

It is worth noting that the right to request advisory opinions is not limited to Member States of the IACtHR Statute or the ACHR but open

499 For an extensive study of the IACtHR's advisory function, see Ibid.; see also *J. M. Pasqualucci*, The practice and procedure of the Inter-American Court of Human Rights, 2nd ed. 2013, 37 et seq.

500 On the drafting history of Article 64 ACHR, see *E. Benz*, The Advisory Function of the Inter-American Court of Human Rights, 2024, 65 et seq.

501 The power to request advisory opinions from the IACtHR extends to all organs listed in Chapter X of the OAS Charter. These include the Meeting of Consultation of Ministers of Foreign Affairs (Art. 61), the Permanent Council of the OAS (Art. 62), the Advisory Defense Committee (Art. 66), the Organ of Consultation (Art. 66), and the General Assembly (Art. 69).

502 *"Other Treaties" Subject to the Consultative Jurisdiction of the Court*, Advisory Opinion OC-1/82, IACtHR Series A No. 1, para. 25.

to all OAS Member States.[503] States like Canada or the USA, which have ratified neither the ACHR nor the IACtHR Statute but are OAS Member States, could thus request advisory opinions from the IACtHR.[504]

The fact that individual Member States may request advisory opinions from the IACtHR provides an interesting counter-example to the ICJ's advisory jurisdiction, which deliberately excludes individual states from requesting advisory opinions from the Court.[505] It also significantly contributes to the number of advisory opinions requested from the IACtHR.[506] However, despite the possibility of individual states to present a question to the IACtHR, the IACtHR has made clear that the exercise of its advisory function is "multilateral rather than litigious":

> "The advisory jurisdiction of the Court differs from its contentious jurisdiction in that there are no "parties" involved in the advisory procedure nor is there any dispute to be settled. The sole purpose of the advisory function is "the interpretation of this Convention or of other treaties concerning the protection of human rights in the American states." (...) The Court therefore observes that the exercise of the advisory function assigned to it by the American Convention is multilateral rather than litigious in nature (...)."[507]

The IACtHR's advisory jurisdiction *ratione materiae* encompasses the interpretation of the ACHR as well as "other treaties concerning the protec-

503 *"Other Treaties" Subject to the Consultative Jurisdiction of the Court*, Advisory Opinion OC-1/82, IACtHR Series A No. 1, para. 35.

504 Such states could, for example, ask the IACtHR under Art. 64 para. 2 ACHR to issue an advisory opinion on the compatibility of their domestic laws with the ACHR or other human rights instruments. In theory, states that intend to join the ACHR could thereby ensure that their domestic laws are complying with the ACHR.

505 On the rejected proposals made by the Informal Inter-Allied Committee, the United Kingdom, and Venezuela to extend the ICJ's advisory jurisdiction *ratione personae* to two or more states acting in concert, see *supra*: § 1 Section D.II.

506 Of the 29 advisory opinions rendered until 2024, 21 have been requested by OAS Member States. Of these 21 requests, 17 requests were made in accordance with Art. 64 para. 1 ACHR, they thus concerned the interpretation of the ACHR or other treaties, while only four requests concerned the interpretation of the requesting state's domestic law under Art. 64 para. 2 ACHR. Costa Rica is the only OAS Member State that has asked the IACtHR to determine the compatibility of its own laws with the ACHR or other human rights treaties, which, incidentally, is also where the IACtHR is located. For a list of all advisory opinions rendered by the IACtHR, see https://www.corteidh.or.cr/opiniones_consultivas.cfm?lang=en.

507 *Reports of the Inter-American Commission on Human Rights*, Advisory Opinion OC-15/97, IACtHR Series A No. 15, paras. 25–6.

tion of human rights in the American states". The IACtHR interpreted this wording to mean that

> "the advisory jurisdiction of the Court can be exercised, in general, with regard to any provision dealing with the protection of human rights set forth in any international treaty applicable in the American States, regardless of whether it be bilateral or multilateral, whatever be the principal purpose of such a treaty, and whether or not non-Member States of the inter-American system are or have the right to become parties thereto."[508]

The IACtHR's advisory jurisdiction is thus open to applications concerning a wide range of treaties. For example, the IACtHR found that the ICCPR and the VCCR were "other treaties" in the sense of Article 64 para. 1 ACHR.[509]

Articles 70 to 75 of the Rules of Procedure, which the IACtHR adopted in accordance with Article 25 para. 1 of the IACtHR Statute, contain further provisions on the IACtHR's advisory jurisdiction. According to Article 74, the IACtHR "shall apply the provisions of Title II of these Rules [i.e., the rules concerning the IACtHR's contentious procedure] to advisory proceedings to the extent that it deems them to be compatible." The provision is similar to Article 68 ICJ Statute and Article 102 paras. 2–3 of the ICJ's Rules of the Court. However, unlike Article 102 of the ICJ's Rules of the Court, Article 74 Rules of Procedure of the IACtHR does not expressly refer to advisory opinions relating to "legal question[s] actually pending between two or more states", i.e. to inter-state disputes. The IACtHR's legal framework thus does not expressly address the question whether advisory opinions may be requested on matters relating to pending inter-state disputes.

---

508 *"Other Treaties" Subject to the Consultative Jurisdiction of the Court*, Advisory Opinion OC-1/82, IACtHR Series A No. 1, para. 52.

509 *The Right to Information on Consular Assistance in the Framework of the Guarantees of the Due Process of Law*, Advisory Opinion OC-16/99, IACtHR Series A No. 16, 36–37. In fact, the wording "other treaties concerning the protection of human rights in the American states" was likely included in Article 64 ACHR precisely to allow the Inter-American human rights system to be compatible with the international human rights treaties that were adopted shortly before the creation of the ACHR, see *E. Benz*, The Advisory Function of the Inter-American Court of Human Rights, 2024, 73–74.

Just like the ICJ, the IACtHR has held that it is not required to reply to all requests for advisory opinions.[510] Accordingly, the IACtHR found that its advisory jurisdiction is "permissive in character" which allows the IACtHR to assess whether to grant or deny a request for an advisory opinion on a case-by-case basis.[511] The IACtHR regards its "power of appreciation" not as a kind of "unfettered discretion to grant or deny a request".[512] Instead, the Court may only decline a request if there are "compelling reasons founded in the conviction that the request exceeds the limits of its advisory jurisdiction".[513] By echoing the "compelling reasons" standard, the IACtHR echoes the case law of the ICJ.

When determining the admissibility of a request for an advisory opinion, the IACtHR distinguishes between formal and substantive requirements of admissibility.[514] The formal requirements concern the formulation of the question, the identification of the provisions to be interpreted, the considerations that gave rise to the request, as well as the name and address of the agent (Art 70, 71 Rules of Procedure). The substantive admissibility requirements are less clearly defined. At this stage the IACtHR determines the admissibility of the request based on "considerations that exceed questions of mere form and that relate to the characteristics it has recognized for the exercise of its advisory function".[515]

Among these "characteristics for the exercise of its advisory function" the IACtHR is above all guided by the function of its advisory opinions

510 Cf. *The Right to Information on Consular Assistance in the Framework of the Guarantees of the Due Process of Law*, Advisory Opinion OC-16/99, IACtHR Series A No. 16, para. 31; *Rights and guarantees of children in the context of migration and/or in need of international protection*, Advisory Opinion OC-21/14, para. 25; *Entitlement of legal entities to hold rights under the Inter-American Human Rights System (Interpretation and scope of Article 1(2), in relation to Articles 1(2), 8, 11(2), 13, 16, 21, 24, 25, 29, 30, 44, 46 and 62(3) of the American Convention on Human Rights, as well as of Article 8(1)(A) and (B) of the Protocol of San Salvador)*, Advisory Opinion OC-22/16, IACtHR Series A No. 22, para. 21.

511 *"Other Treaties" Subject to the Consultative Jurisdiction of the Court*, Advisory Opinion OC-1/82, IACtHR Series A No. 1, paras. 27–29.

512 Ibid., para. 30.

513 Ibid.

514 *Gender identity, and equality and non-discrimination with regard to same-sex couples. State obligations in relation to change of name, gender identity, and rights deriving from a relationship between same-sex couples (interpretation and scope of Articles 1(1), 3, 7, 11(2), 13, 17, 18 and 24, in relation to Article 1, of the American Convention on Human Rights)*, Advisory Opinion OC-24/17, IACtHR Series A No. 24, paras. 19–22.

515 Ibid., para. 20.

to assist OAS Member States and OAS organs to effectively comply with their human rights obligations.[516] The IACtHR derived from this focus on the protection of human rights in the American states that any request for an advisory opinion is inadmissible "which is likely to undermine the Court's contentious jurisdiction or, in general, to weaken or alter the system established by the Convention, in a manner that would impair the rights of potential victims of human rights violations."[517] The IACtHR's concern to protect the integrity of its contentious procedure showcases a clear parallel to the ICJ's Eastern Carelia doctrine. The IACtHR's standard of admissibility is the result of a case law which has been shaped primarily by cases involving an inter-state dimension.

II. Use of IACtHR advisory opinions to settle inter-state disputes

The IACtHR's standard of admissibility insofar as it concerns the use of advisory opinions in the context of inter-state disputes has been shaped primarily by four cases: the 1983 *Death Penalty* case, the 1999 *Consular Assistance* case, the 2017 *Environment and Human Rights* case, and the 2018 *Asylum as a Human Right* case.

1. Death Penalty case (1983)

In 1983, the IACtHR was asked by the Inter-American Commission on Human Rights (IACHR) to interpret Article 4 paras. 2 and 4 ACHR which deals with the death penalty. At the time, a proceeding was pending before the IACHR against Guatemala regarding the interpretation of the provision.[518] Guatemala requested the Court to decline to exercise its advisory

516 *"Other Treaties" Subject to the Consultative Jurisdiction of the Court*, Advisory Opinion OC-1/82, IACtHR Series A No. 1, para. 25; cf. *Restrictions to the Death Penalty*, Advisory Opinion OC-3/83, IACtHR Series A No. 3, para. 22; *The institution of asylum, and its recognition as a human right under the Inter-American System of Protection (interpretation and scope of Articles 5, 22(7) and 22(8) in relation to Article 1(1) of the American Convention on Human Rights)*, Advisory Opinion OC-25/18, IACtHR Series A No. 25, para. 50.

517 *"Other Treaties" Subject to the Consultative Jurisdiction of the Court*, Advisory Opinion OC-1/82, IACtHR Series A No. 1, para. 31.

518 *Restrictions to the Death Penalty*, Advisory Opinion OC-3/83, IACtHR Series A No. 3, para. 10.

jurisdiction arguing that it had not consented to bringing its dispute with the ACHR before the Court in accordance with Article 62 para. 3 ACHR.[519]

The IACtHR found that Article 62 ACHR only applied to contentious proceedings, thereby rejecting Guatemala's claim that the provision also applied to advisory proceedings.[520] In considering whether the existing dispute between the IACHR and Guatemala constituted a compelling reason for the IACtHR to decline to exercise its advisory jurisdiction, the IACtHR focused on the purpose of its advisory jurisdiction to support the OAS organs in their functions. The IACtHR held:

> "The powers conferred on the Commission require it to apply the Convention or other human rights treaties. In order to discharge fully its obligations, the Commission may find it necessary or appropriate to consult the Court regarding the meaning of certain provisions whether or not at the given moment in time there exists a difference between a government and the Commission concerning an interpretation, which might justify the request for an advisory opinion. If the Commission were to be barred from seeking an advisory opinion merely because one or more governments are involved in a controversy with the Commission over the interpretation of a disputed provision, the Commission would seldom, if ever, be able to avail itself of the Court's advisory jurisdiction."[521]

The IACtHR also examined the wording of Article 64 ACHR:

> "The right to seek advisory opinions under Article 64 was conferred on OAS organs for requests falling "within their spheres of competence." This suggests that the right was also conferred to assist with the resolution of disputed legal issues arising in the context of the activities of an organ, be it the Assembly, the Commission, or any of the others referred to in Chapter X of the OAS Charter. It is clear, therefore, that the mere fact that there exists a dispute between the Commission and the Government of Guatemala regarding the meaning of Article 4 of the Convention does not justify the Court to decline to exercise its advisory jurisdiction in the instant proceeding."[522]

---

519 Ibid., para. 11.
520 Ibid., paras. 30–35.
521 Ibid., para. 38.
522 Ibid., para. 39.

The IACtHR recognized that there may be "legitimate interests of a State in the outcome of an advisory opinion proceeding", however such interests were adequately protected by the state's right to participate in the proceedings, to raise jurisdictional objections and to present its views on the matter to the court.[523] Consequently, the IACtHR found that the existence of a pending international dispute over the interpretation of a provision does not constitute a compelling reason for the Court to refuse to issue the requested advisory opinion.[524]

2. Consular Assistance case (1999)

In the *Consular Assistance* case,[525] Mexico requested from the IACtHR an advisory opinion on the obligations of states under the VCCR, the ICCPR, and the OAS Charter.[526] One of the most contentious questions during the proceeding concerned the interpretation of Article 36 para. 1 lit. b VCCR. The provision contains the right of nationals of a sending state to have their state of nationality informed of their arrest abroad. As a prerequisite to the IACtHR's jurisdiction to give the requested advisory opinion under Article 64 para. 1 ACHR, the IACtHR had to establish that the VCCR was a treaty "concerning the protection of human rights in the American States". To do so, the IACtHR had to decide whether the right enshrined in Article 36 para. 1 lit. b VCCR constituted a human right.[527]

523 *Restrictions to the Death Penalty*, Advisory Opinion OC-3/83, IACtHR Series A No. 3, para. 24.

524 See also *Certain Attributes of the Inter-American Commission on Human Rights (Arts. 41, 42, 44, 46, 47, 50 and 51 of the American Convention on Human Rights), Advisory Opinion OC-13/93, IACtHR Series A No. 13; International Responsibility for the Promulgation and Enforcement of Laws in Violation of the Convention (Arts. 1 and 2 of the American Convention on Human Rights)*, Advisory Opinion OC-14/94, IACtHR Series A No. 14, para. 28.

525 *The Right to Information on Consular Assistance in the Framework of the Guarantees of the Due Process of Law*, Advisory Opinion OC-16/99, IACtHR Series A No. 16.

526 Ibid.

527 *The Right to Information on Consular Assistance in the Framework of the Guarantees of the Due Process of Law*, Advisory Opinion OC-16/99, IACtHR Series A No. 16, paras. 68 et seq. In 2003, Mexico took the same matter to the ICJ and initiated contentious proceedings against the USA in the *Avena* case. While the ICJ left open the question of whether VCCR rights constitute human rights, it emphasized that it was skeptical about this, see *Avena and Other Mexican Nationals (Mexico v. United States of America)*, Judgment, ICJ Reports 2004, 12 (60–61, para. 124).

While Mexico phrased its questions to the IACtHR in abstract terms, the underlying issues arose from and related to a pending dispute pending between Mexico and the USA. The USA repeatedly failed to immediately notify Mexican nationals (as well as other foreign nationals) who were arrested, tried, and sentenced to death of their rights under Article 36 para. 1 lit. b VCCR and to immediately notify their home state of their arrests. In its request for an advisory opinion, Mexico referred to specific examples of Mexican nationals that have been detained by the USA and cited relevant US laws and practices.[528] The US practice was in fact so wide-spread that shortly after Mexico requested the advisory opinion from the IACtHR, Paraguay and Germany instituted similar proceedings against the USA before the ICJ.[529]

The United States requested the IACtHR to reject the requested opinion *inter alia* because of the close connection between Mexico's request for an advisory opinion and the pending cases before the ICJ.[530] The United States further argued that "Mexico has in fact presented a contentious case in the guise of a request for an advisory opinion. The Court has on several occasions expressed its concern over this possibility."[531] The United States argued that the IACtHR's advisory jurisdiction pursuant to Article 64 para. 1 ACHR is limited to interpreting the law, yet Mexico requested a legal assessment of specific facts which have not yet been established and which the IACtHR cannot establish by means of its advisory procedure.[532] The advisory procedure, the USA claimed, was unsuited to decide complex questions of fact because it lacked clear evidentiary rules.[533] The USA fur-

528 *The Right to Information on Consular Assistance in the Framework of the Guarantees of the Due Process of Law*, Advisory Opinion OC-16/99, IACtHR Series A No. 16, para. 46.

529 See *Vienna Convention on Consular Relations (Paraguay v. United States of America)*, Order, ICJ Reports 1998, 426 (discontinued on 2 November 1999); *LaGrand (Germany v. United States of America)*, Judgment, ICJ Reports 2001, 466.

530 IACtHR Pleadings, *Consular Assistance*, Written Observations of the United States of America, 1 June 1998, 4–5 (on file with the author). On the issue of parallel proceedings before ICs, see *Y. Shany*, The Competing Jurisdictions of International Courts and Tribunals, 2003; *J. Finke*, Die Parallelität internationaler Streitbeilegungsmechanismen, 2004.

531 IACtHR Pleadings, *The Right to Information on Consular Assistance in the Framework of the Guarantees of the Due Process of Law*, Written Observations of the United States of America, 1 June 1998, 9 (on file with the author).

532 Ibid., 9–10.

533 *The Right to Information on Consular Assistance in the Framework of the Guarantees of the Due Process of Law*, Advisory Opinion OC-16/99, IACtHR Series A No. 16, 26.

ther argued that the IACtHR would have to decide about several cases that were pending before US courts without access to the case files and without the participation of the relevant parties.[534] The USA concluded by repeating its claim that Mexico was abusing the IACtHR's advisory procedure:

> "Thus, the present case is patently an attempt to subject the United States to the contentious jurisdiction of this Court, notwithstanding that the United States is not a party to the American Convention and has not accepted the contentious jurisdiction of the Court under Article 62. An advisory opinion in the form sought here by Mexico will necessarily prejudice the rights and interests of the United States in any future contentious proceeding before this Court and in other international legal proceedings, as well as in its domestic legal system."[535]

The IACtHR agreed with the USA that it may not, in the course of its advisory proceeding, evaluate evidence against a state:

> "The Court observes that it may not rule on charges or evidence alleged against a State because to do so would be at variance with the nature of its advisory function and would deny the respective State the opportunities to defend itself that it would have in a contentious proceeding. This is one of the distinctive differences between the Court's contentious and advisory functions. (...) in exercising its advisory jurisdiction, the Court is not called upon to settle questions of fact, but rather to throw light on the meaning, object and purpose of international human rights norms."[536]

In doing so, the IACtHR demonstrated a divergence from the practice of the ICJ which has often made findings on questions of facts in the course of its advisory proceedings.[537] Nevertheless, the IACtHR decided to answer

---

534 IACtHR Pleadings, *The Right to Information on Consular Assistance in the Framework of the Guarantees of the Due Process of Law*, Written Observations of the United States of America, 1 June 1998, 10 (on file with the author).

535 Ibid., 10–11.

536 *The Right to Information on Consular Assistance in the Framework of the Guarantees of the Due Process of Law*, Advisory Opinion OC-16/99, IACtHR Series A No. 16, para. 47.

537 See for example *Legal Consequences of the Construction of a Wall in the Occupied Palestinian Territory*, Advisory Opinion, ICJ Reports 2004, 136; *Legal Consequences of the Separation of the Chagos Archipelago from Mauritius in 1965*, Advisory Opinion, ICJ Reports 2019, 95 See, however, the Separate Opinion of Judge Nolte in the *Policies and Practices of Israel in the Occupied Palestinian Territory* case, in

Mexico's reqeuest and, in doing so it decided not to ignore the request's factual context. The IACtHR regarded Mexico's specific references to ongoing judicial proceedings in the United States as a "use of examples [which] places the request in a particular context and illustrates the differences as to the interpretation that might be given of the legal issue raised in the present Advisory Opinion, without the Court having to rule on those examples."[538] The IACtHR thus limited itself to answering legal questions, while not deciding on "charges or evidence alleged against a State".[539]

This distinction between questions of law and questions of international responsibility seems persuasive in the context of the IACtHR. The IACtHR's subject-matter jurisdiction extends to the interpretation of the ACHR and "other treaties" containing human rights provisions as well as the compatibility of domestic law with these instruments. While questions of international responsibility are legal questions, they are not questions of interpretation of the ACHR or other human rights treaties. It may be noted that the IACtHR approach set an example for Germany's proposal in the *Chagos* case 20 years later, in which Germany argued that the ICJ may interpret the law even if it relates to pending bilateral disputes but it should be careful not to make findings on the international responsibility of the states involved.[540] However, unlike the IACtHR, the ICJ's advisory jurisdiction *ratione materiae* extends to "any legal question", which clearly encompasses questions of international responsibility.

---

which he argued for a limited fact-finding in advisory proceedings: "The particular purpose of advisory proceedings explains why the factual assessment in this Advisory Opinion has a different focus and depth than factual determinations made in contentious proceedings. (...) In advisory proceedings the Court will examine the facts only to the extent necessary for its response to the legal question posed, and it will draw legal conclusions only to the extent permitted by those facts.", see *Legal Consequences arising from the Policies and Practices of Israel in the Occupied Palestinian Territory, including East Jerusalem*, Advisory Opinion, Separate Opinion Nolte, Publication pending in ICJ Reports 2024, 1 (2, para. 5).

538 *The Right to Information on Consular Assistance in the Framework of the Guarantees of the Due Process of Law*, Advisory Opinion OC-16/99, IACtHR Series A No. 16, para. 49.

539 Ibid., para. 47.

540 Cf. ICJ Pleadings, *Legal Consequences of the Separation of the Chagos Archipelago from Mauritius in 1965*, Written Statement of Germany, para. 141. On the German proposal, see *supra*: § 3 Section H.II.3.

3. Environment and Human Rights case (2017)

In the *Environment and Human Rights* case,[541] Colombia requested an advisory opinion from the IACtHR on the interpretation of ACHR provisions in the context of Nicaragua's plan to construct a canal between the Atlantic and the Pacific Ocean. In its request, Colombia referred to "a danger that the construction and operation of major new infrastructure projects may have severe effects on the marine environment in the Wider Caribbean Region", specifically giving the example of the "construction, maintenance and expansions of canals for maritime traffic".[542] At the same time, the IACHR examined a petition concerning "alleged violations of the American Convention in the context of the project for the construction of the Grand Interoceanic Canal of Nicaragua".[543] Additional proceedings were pending before the ICJ between Nicaragua and Colombia over the alleged violations of Nicaragua's sovereign maritime waters by Colombia.[544]

Despite these other proceedings, the IACtHR found that the request for an advisory opinion was admissible. The Court held that petitions before the IACHR on the same subject-matter would not render a request for an advisory opinion inadmissible.[545] The same was true, the IACtHR held, for parallel contentious proceedings before the ICJ.[546] The reason for this, the Court argued, lied in the different function the IACtHR was exercising when giving advisory opinions:

> "The task of interpretation that the Court must perform in the exercise of its advisory function differs from its contentious competence because there is no litigation to be decided. The central purpose of the advisory function is to obtain a judicial interpretation of one or several provisions

541 *The Environment and Human Rights (State obligations in relation to the environment in the context of the protection and guarantee of the rights to life and to personal integrity – interpretation and scope of Articles 4(1) and 5(1) of the American Convention on Human Rights)*, Advisory Opinion OC-23/17, IACtHR Series A No. 23.

542 Ibid., para. 1.

543 Ibid., para. 25. IACHR, Petition 912/14, 17 June 2014.

544 *Alleged Violations of Sovereign Rights and Maritime Spaces in the Caribbean Sea (Nicaragua v. Colombia)*, Preliminary Objections, Judgment, ICJ Reports 2016, 3.

545 *The Environment and Human Rights (State obligations in relation to the environment in the context of the protection and guarantee of the rights to life and to personal integrity – interpretation and scope of Articles 4(1) and 5(1) of the American Convention on Human Rights)*, Advisory Opinion OC-23/17, IACtHR Series A No. 23, paras. 26–27.

546 Ibid.

of the Convention or of other treaties concerning the protection of human rights in the American States. (...) The citing of examples in the request for an advisory opinion serves the purpose of referring to a specific context and illustrating the different situations that may arise in relation to the legal issue that is the purpose of the advisory opinion, without this meaning that the Court is issuing a legal ruling on the situations described in such examples."[547]

4. Asylum as a Human Right case (2018)

In 2016, Ecuador presented the IACtHR with several questions for an advisory opinion on different aspects of the right to asylum, in particular in the context of foreign nationals seeking asylum within the diplomatic mission of a state.[548] Several states and organizations participating in the proceeding urged the IACtHR not to render the opinion because the subject-matter of the request related to a pending dispute between Ecuador and the UK involving Julian Assange, the founder of Wikileaks, who received asylum within the premises of the Ecuadorian embassy in the United Kingdom.[549] The situation surrounding Assange's stay in the Ecuadorian embassy had become a diplomatic minefield involving not only Ecuador and the UK, but also the USA, which urged the UK to extradite Assange to the US to face criminal charges. To determine whether Ecuador's request for an advisory opinion was intended to resolve a contentious matter, the IACtHR examined the "substantial purpose of the request" and whether it claimed "general validity and transcend[ed] all American States, beyond the reasons that may have given rise to it or reference made to particular facts".[550] The IACtHR found that a request may refer to the facts of an actual dispute, as this merely demonstrated that the advisory opinion was not used for "purely academic speculation, without a foreseeable application to concrete situations justifying the need for an advisory opinion".[551]

547 Ibid.

548 *The institution of asylum, and its recognition as a human right under the Inter-American System of Protection (interpretation and scope of Articles 5, 22(7) and 22(8) in relation to Article 1(1) of the American Convention on Human Rights)*, Advisory Opinion OC-25/18, Series A No. 25, para. 3.

549 Ibid., paras. 20, 22.

550 Ibid., para. 52.

551 Ibid., para. 51.

III. Interim conclusions

The IACtHR has developed a differentiated standard of admissibility for requests for advisory opinions.[552] In determining the admissibility of a request, the Court is guided by the purpose of its advisory function, which the Court identified as the effective promotion of human rights in the American states.[553] Accordingly, a request for an advisory opinion is inadmissible if it has "the effect of altering or weakening the system established by the Convention in a manner detrimental to the individual human being".[554] Among other considerations of admissibility, the IACtHR found that its advisory opinions "cannot be used to conceal a contentious case nor prematurely obtain a ruling on a matter that could eventually be submitted to the Court as a contentious case" or to "resolve questions of fact".[555] However, the IACtHR has also stated on multiple occasions that the fact that a request relates to an existing dispute would not necessarily prevent

---

552 The IACtHR defines its standard of admissibility along six criteria: "The Court has developed the following jurisprudential standards regarding the admissibility of a request for an advisory opinion: (1) it cannot be used to conceal a contentious case nor prematurely obtain a ruling on a matter that could eventually be submitted to the Court as a contentious case; (2) it cannot be used as a mechanism to obtain an indirect domestic ruling on a matter being litigated or is subject to a controversy; (3) it cannot be used as an instrument of a domestic political debate; (4) it cannot exclusively concern matters on which the Court has already ruled in its jurisprudence and, (5) it cannot be used to resolve questions of fact, but only to untangle the sense, purpose and meaning of inter-national norms on human rights and, above all, (6) it is to assist the OAS Member States and organs to fully and effectively comply with their international obligations.", see *Differentiated approaches with respect to certain groups of persons in detention (Interpretation and scope of Articles 1(1), 4(1), 5, 11(2), 12, 13, 17(1), 19, 24 and 26 of the American Convention on Human Rights and other human rights instruments)*, Advisory Opinion OC-29/22, IACtHR Series A No. 29, para. 21.

553 Cf. *Restrictions to the Death Penalty, Advisory Opinion OC-3/83, IACtHR Series A No. 3, para. 22; The institution of asylum, and its recognition as a human right under the Inter-American System of Protection (interpretation and scope of Articles 5, 22(7) and 22(8) in relation to Article 1(1) of the American Convention on Human Rights)*, Advisory Opinion OC-25/18, IACtHR Series A No. 25, para. 50.

554 *The Right to Information on Consular Assistance in the Framework of the Guarantees of the Due Process of Law*, Advisory Opinion OC-16/99, IACtHR Series A No. 16, para. 43.

555 *Differentiated approaches with respect to certain groups of persons in detention (Interpretation and scope of Articles 1(1), 4(1), 5, 11(2), 12, 13, 17(1), 19, 24 and 26 of the American Convention on Human Rights and other human rights instruments)*, Advisory Opinion OC-29/22, IACtHR Series A No. 29, para. 21.

the Court from issuing an advisory opinion.[556] The Court thus regularly answered requests even if they relate to existing disputes, emphasizing that it does not render a judicial decision about the underlying controversy but only interprets the relevant human rights instruments.

C. African Court on Human and Peoples' Rights

In 1998, the ACtHPR was created to complement the work of the African Commission on Human and Peoples' Rights (ACHPR).[557] Until the Statute of the African Court of Justice and Human Rights enters into force,[558] the ACtHPR serves as the regional human rights court of Africa.[559]

I. Overview of the ACtHPR's advisory jurisdiction

The ACtHPR's advisory jurisdiction is enshrined in Article 4 para. 1 Protocol to the African Charter on Human and Peoples' Rights (Banjul Protocol).[560] It stipulates:

> "At the request of a Member State of the OAU, the OAU, any of its organs, or any African organization recognized by the OAU, the Court

556 *Restrictions to the Death Penalty, Advisory Opinion OC-3/83, IACtHR Series A No. 3, para 38; Compatibility of Draft Legislation with Article 8(2)(h) of the American Convention on Human Rights*, Advisory Opinion OC-12/91, IACtHR Series A No. 12, para. 28; *The Right to Information on Consular Assistance in the Framework of the Guarantees of the Due Process of Law*, Advisory Opinion OC-16/99, IACtHR Series A No. 16, para. 45.

557 *Murray* points out that while concerns that the newly established court would undermine the ACHPR proved unwarranted, the relationship between the two human rights bodies has not been without tension, see *R. Murray*, The African Charter on Human and Peoples' Rights: A Commentary, 2019, 11.

558 The Protocol on the Statute of the African Court of Justice and Human Rights was adopted on 1 July 2008. Its purpose is to merge the African Court on Human and Peoples' Rights and the Court of Justice of the African Union into a single court, called the African Court of Justice and Human Rights, see Art. 2 Protocol on the Statute of the African Court of Justice and Human Rights. However, the Protocol has not yet entered into force as its entry into force requires the ratification by 15 AU Member States. By 2024, only 8 AU Member States have ratified the Protocol, see https://au.int/en/treaties/protocol-statute-african-court-justice-and-human-rights.

559 *A. P. van der Mei*, 18 LJIL 1 (2005), 113 (114).

560 On the advisory jurisdiction of the ACtHPR, see *A. P. van der Mei*, 5 African Human Rights Law Journal 1 (2005), 27; *L. Chenwi*, 38 Nordic Journal of Human Rights 1 (2020), 61.

> may provide an opinion on any legal matter relating to the Charter or any other relevant human rights instruments, provided that the subject matter of the opinion is not related to a matter being examined by the Commission."

Being a regional human rights court, the ACtHPR's advisory jurisdiction *ratione materiae* is limited to the interpretation of the African Charter on Human and Peoples' Rights (Banjul Charter) and other human rights instruments. The ACtHPR thus rejects requests for advisory opinions which "raise issues of general Public International Law and not human rights law".[561] Article 4 of the Banjul Protocol contains a particularly broad advisory jurisdiction *ratione materiae*. Note the difference in wording between Article 4 Banjul Protocol and the previously discussed Article 64 para. 1 ACHR. While Article 4 refers to "any relevant human rights instrument", Article 64 para. 1 ACHR more specifically refers to "other treaties concerning the protection of human rights in the American states". The advisory jurisdiction of the ACtHPR therefore arguably extends even further than that of the IACtHR and includes any human rights instrument, regardless of its application to AU Member States.[562] However, it seems likely that the ACtHPR will interpret its advisory jurisdiction under Article 4 of the Banjul Protocol in a similar way to the IACtHR's interpretation of its advisory jurisdiction under Article 64 para. 1 ACHR. This reading is also supported by Article 7 of the Banjul Protocol which lists as the sources of law the Court shall apply the Banjul Charter and "any other relevant human rights instrument ratified by the States concerned". The ACtHPR's advisory jurisdiction *ratione materiae* is further limited by Article 4 para. 1 Banjul Protocol to matters that are not currently pending before the ACHPR. This provision is echoed in the Rules of Court, which the ACtHPR has adopted pursuant to Article 33 of the Banjul Protocol.[563] According to Rule 82 para. 3, "[t]he subject matter of the request for advisory opinion shall not relate to a Communication pending before the Commission". Article 4 para. 1 Banjul Protocol and Rule 82 para. 3 aim to harmonize the ACtHPR's

561 *Request for Advisory Opinion by the Coalition for the International Criminal Court, the Legal Defence & Assistance Project (LEDAP), the Civil Resource Development & Documentation Center (CIRDDOC) and the Women Advocates Documentation Center (WARDC)*, No. 001/2014, Order, para. 13.

562 *A. P. van der Mei*, 5 African Human Rights Law Journal 1 (2005), 27 (38).

563 ACtHPR, Rules of Court, 1 September 2020, https://www.african-court.org/wpafc/wp-content/uploads/2021/04/Rules-Final-Revised-adopted-Rules-eng-April-2021.pdf.

activities with the activities of the ACHPR, the other international body charged with the protection of human rights on the African continent. In accordance with these provisions, the ACtHPR's Registry enquires from the ACHPR whether the subject-matter of a request for an advisory opinion relates to a matter pending before the ACHPR. If there is a parallel proceeding pending before the ACHPR, the ACtHPR will reject the request for an advisory opinion.[564]

Interestingly, and unlike the ICJ, the ACtHPR's broad advisory jurisdiction *ratione materiae* is not counterbalanced by a narrow jurisdiction *ratione personae*. Instead, the ACtHPR has the broadest advisory jurisdiction *ratione personae* of any of the ICs extending to the AU, any AU organ, any AU Member State,[565] as well as "any African organization recognized by the OAU [now AU]".[566] The term "African organization" includes non-governmental organizations.[567] The advisory procedure under the Banjul Protocol thus provides a forum for civil society actors to exert pressure on states on human rights issues. The respective NGO must be "African", which the ACtHPR interprets to mean that the NGO must be registered in one African state and operate in at least one other African state[568] and it must be recognized by the AU, i.e. it must have been granted observer status before the AU or have signed a "Memorandum of Understanding and Cooperation" with the AU.[569] Recognition by an AU organ, such as the IACHR, is not sufficient.[570]

564 The ACtHPR thus rejected the request by the for an advisory opinion by the Pan African Lawyer's Union and the Southern African Litigation Centre in the case *Request for advisory opinion by Pan African Lawyers' Union and Southern African Litigation Center*, No. 002/2012, because the subject-matter of the request related to a matter that was already being examined by the Commission (i.e., the suspension of the SADC Tribunal).

565 *Request for Advisory Opinion by the Pan African Lawyers Union (PALU) on the compatibility of vagrancy laws with the African Charter on Human and Peoples' Rights and other human rights instruments applicable in Africa*, No. 001/2018, Advisory Opinion, para. 37. All 55 states in Africa are Member States of the African Union.

566 The fact that article 4 lists the AU separately from its organs seems to perform no particular purpose as the AU could in any event only act through its organs, see *A. P. van der Mei*, 5 African Human Rights Law Journal 1 (2005), 27 (32).

567 *Request for Advisory Opinion by the Socio-Economic Rights and Accountability Project (SERAP)*, No. 001/2013, Advisory Opinion, para. 46.

568 Ibid., para. 48.

569 Ibid., para. 65; *Request for Advisory Opinion by Rencontre Africain pour la Defense des Droits de l'Homme*, No. 002/2014, Advisory Opinion, para. 36.

570 *Request for Advisory Opinion by the Socio-Economic Rights and Accountability Project (SERAP)*, No. 001/2013, Advisory Opinion, para. 65; *Request for Advisory*

II. Use of ACtHPR advisory opinions to settle inter-state disputes

To date, the ACtHPR has not received any request for an advisory opinion on a question relating to a pending inter-state dispute. Nor has the ACtHPR been asked to give an advisory opinion on the lawfulness of specific state conduct. However, the ACtHPR has indicated that it would follow a similar approach to the IACtHR in that it will respond to requests which concern the human rights situation in a specific state and treat specific references to the facts of a case as mere examples which illustrate the human rights problem at hand. The ACtHPR thus held that "[i]n exercising its advisory jurisdiction, the Court does not resolve factual disputes between opposing parties. (...) Any use of examples simply serves to highlight the practical dimensions of the opinion and does not amount to a decision on any factual situation described in those illustrations."[571] In doing so, the ACtHPR does not examine the lawfulness of any specific conduct.[572]

D. International Tribunal for the Law of the Sea

The advisory function of the ITLOS is divided into two separate procedures: The advisory procedure of the Seabed Disputes Chamber (SDC) under Article 191 UNCLOS[573] and the advisory procedure of the ITLOS in full plenum.[574] The latter is a particularly interesting example, as not

---

Opinion by l'Association Africaine de Défense des Droits de l'Homme, No. 002/2016, Advisory Opinion, para. 32.

571 *Request by the Pan African Lawyers Union (PALU) on the right to participate in the government of one's country in the context of an election held during a public health emergency or a pandemic, such as the COVID-19 Crisis, NO. 001/2020*, Advisory Opinion, para. 45 citing Juridical Condition and Rights of the Undocumented Migrants, Advisory Opinion OC-18/03, IACtHR Series A No. 18, para. 65.

572 Cf. *Request by the Pan African Lawyers Union (PALU) on the right to participate in the government of one's country in the context of an election held during a public health emergency or a pandemic, such as the COVID-19 Crisis*, No. 001/2020, Advisory Opinion, para. 47.

573 On the advisory function of the SDC, see *L. B. Sohn*, Advisory Opinions by the International Tribunal for the Law of the Sea or Its Seabed Disputes Chamber, in: Moore (ed.), Oceans Policy, 1999, 61; *T. Treves*, Advisory Opinions under the Law of the Sea Convention, in: J. N. Moore/M. H. Nordquist (eds.), Current Marine Environmental Issues and the International Tribunal for the Law of the Sea, 1st ed., 2001, 81.

574 On the advisory function of the ITLOS in full plenum, see *K.-J. You*, 39 Ocean Development & International Law 4 (2008), 360; *T. M. Ndiaye*, 9 Chinese Journal

only its extent but its very existence is contested. A close examination of the two procedures provides valuable insights into the nature of advisory procedures in general. Many of the same critiques voiced against the ICJ's advisory jurisdiction are echoed in relation to the ITLOS.

I. Overview of the ITLOS's advisory jurisdiction

1. Seabed Disputes Chamber

The SDC was established in accordance with Part XI, Section 5, of UNCLOS as well as Article 14 ITLOS Statute. The SDC is composed of eleven ITLOS judges and has jurisdiction to decide disputes relating to activities in the Area (Article 187 UNCLOS). The Area refers to the "seabed and ocean floor and subsoil thereof, beyond the limits of national jurisdiction" (Article 1 para. 1 subpara. 1 UNCLOS). Article 191 UNCLOS confers advisory jurisdiction upon the SCD:

> "The Seabed Disputes Chamber shall give advisory opinions at the request of the Assembly or the Council on legal questions arising within the scope of their activities. Such opinions shall be given as a matter of urgency."[575]

Accordingly, the SDC's advisory jurisdiction *ratione personae* extends to the Assembly and the Council of the International Seabed Authority. The SDC's advisory jurisdiction *ratione materiae* extends to legal questions aris-

---

of International Law 3 (2010), 565; *J. L. Kateka*, 17 Max Planck Yearbook of United Nations Law 1 (2013), 159; *G. Le Floch* Annuaire français de droit international (2015), 669; *M. García García-Revillo*, The contentious and advisory jurisdiction of the International Tribunal for the law of the sea, 2015, 311; *M. A. Becker*, 109 Am. j. int. law 4 (2015), 851; *T. Ruys/A. Soete*, 29 Leiden Journal of International Law 1 (2016), 155; *M. Lando*, 29 LJIL 2 (2016), 441; *A. von Rebay/C. Oberle*, 83 ZaöRV / HJIL 2 (2023), 283.

575 Another advisory procedure is enshrined in Art. 159 para. 10 UNCLOS which allows for the SDC to review proposals before the Assembly on their conformity with UNCLOS. *Wolfrum* further identified the procedure under Art. 188 UNCLOS as a type of advisory procedure, see *R. Wolfrum*, Advisory Opinions: Are they a Suitable Alternative for the Settlement of International Disputes, in: R. Wolfrum/I. Gatzschmann (eds.), International Dispute Settlement: Room for Innovations?, 2013, 35 (55).

ing within the requesting organ's scope of activities.[576] For this, the request must fall within the competence of the International Seabed Authority and the requesting organ.[577]

Article 191 UNCLOS stipulates that the SDC "*shall* give advisory opinions". This wording stands in contrast to the wording "may give" employed in Article 65 ICJ Statute and Article 4 of the Banjul Charter. Some states have argued that this wording indicates that the SDC has a duty to give any advisory opinion if the jurisdictional requirements of Article 191 UNCLOS are fulfilled.[578] The wording would thus exclude any discretion of the SDC in the exercise of its advisory jurisdiction.[579] In its first (and so far only) advisory opinion, the SDC has noted the difference in wording between Article 191 UNCLOS and Article 65 ICJ Statute but decided to leave the question of discretion unanswered.[580]

The function of the SDC's advisory opinions is to assist the Authority in its duties regarding the administration of the Area. As the SDC stated:

> "In order to exercise its functions properly in accordance with the Convention, the Authority may require the assistance of an independent and impartial judicial body. This is the underlying reason for the advisory jurisdiction of the Chamber. In the exercise of that jurisdiction, the Chamber is part of the system in which the Authority's organs operate, but its task within that system is to act as an independent and impartial body."[581]

The first request for an advisory opinion to the SDC exemplifies this function. In 2008, the Authority received two applications for seabed exploration in the Area which were sponsored by the Republic of Nauru and the Kingdom of Tonga. Nauru, unsure about the legal ramifications

576 Cf. *Responsibilities and obligations of States with respect to activities in the Area*, Advisory Opinion, ITLOS Reports 2011, 10 (paras. 31–32).

577 *R. Wolfrum*, Advisory Opinions: Are they a Suitable Alternative for the Settlement of International Disputes, in: R. Wolfrum/I. Gatzschmann (eds.), International Dispute Settlement: Room for Innovations?, 2013, 35 (50).

578 Cf. ITLOS Pleadings, *Responsibilities and obligations of States with respect to activities in the Area*, Written Statement of Mexico paras. 50–54; Written Statement of Australia para. 5.

579 So also *R. Wolfrum*, Advisory Opinions: Are they a Suitable Alternative for the Settlement of International Disputes, in: R. Wolfrum/I. Gatzschmann (eds.), International Dispute Settlement: Room for Innovations?, 2013, 35 (52).

580 *Responsibilities and obligations of States with respect to activities in the Area*, Advisory Opinion, ITLOS Reports 2011, 10 (para. 48).

581 Ibid., para. 26.

of sponsoring such an application and fearing an overburdening financial liability, asked the Authority to postpone its decision and to request an advisory opinion from the SDC on the legal obligations of sponsoring states. The Council modified Nauru's questions and submitted a request for an advisory opinion on three issues: the obligations of UNCLOS Member States sponsoring activities in the area, on the specific measures Member States must take when sponsoring activities in the area and on the liability of sponsoring states for the sponsored entities' failures to comply with relevant UNCLOS provisions.[582] The requested advisory opinion was intended to guide the Authority's decision whether to permit the activities sponsored by Nauru and Tonga.

2. ITLOS

While the legal basis of the SDC's advisory jurisdiction is expressly enshrined in Article 191 of UNCLOS, the legal basis for an advisory jurisdiction of the Tribunal in plenum is more nebulous.[583] Lacking an express legal basis within UNCLOS or the ITLOS Statute, not only the extent of the Tribunal's advisory jurisdiction is contested, but also its very existence.[584] Several states challenged the existence of the Tribunal's advisory jurisdiction when the Sub-Regional Fisheries Commission (SRFC) requested the first advisory opinion from the Tribunal in 2013.[585]

---

582 Cf. Ibid., para. 1.

583 On the advisory jurisdiction of the ITLOS in full plenum, see *K.-J. You*, 39 Ocean Development & International Law 4 (2008), 360; *T. M. Ndiaye*, 9 Chinese Journal of International Law 3 (2010), 565; *J. L. Kateka*, 17 Max Planck Yearbook of United Nations Law 1 (2013), 159.

584 For a critical account, see *G. Le Floch* Annuaire français de droit international (2015), 669; *M. A. Becker*, 109 Am. j. int. law 4 (2015), 851; *M. Lando*, 29 LJIL 2 (2016), 441; *T. Ruys/A. Soete*, 29 Leiden Journal of International Law 1 (2016), 155. Favorable to the advisory jurisdiction of the ITLOS, see *M. García García-Revillo*, The contentious and advisory jurisdiction of the International Tribunal for the law of the sea, 2015, 311; *A. von Rebay/C. Oberle*, 83 ZaöRV / HJIL 2 (2023), 283.

585 The states that voiced their opposition to an advisory jurisdiction of ITLOS during the SRFC proceeding were Argentina, Australia, China, Ireland, Spain, Thailand, the UK, and the US. Additionally, France, the Netherlands, and Portugal raised their doubts over an advisory jurisdiction of the full plenum without taking a clear position on the topic. Other states argued in favor of a plenary advisory jurisdiction. These were Chile, Cuba, Germany, Japan, Micronesia, Montenegro, New Zealand, Saudi Arabia, Somalia, Sri Lanka, and Switzerland.

The objections of states against the existence of a plenary advisory jurisdiction of the ITLOS can be summarized as follows: First, neither UNCLOS nor the ITLOS Statute provide for an express conferral of an advisory jurisdiction on the ITLOS.[586] Second, Article 288 UNCLOS and Article 21 ITLOS Statute, which contain rules governing the Tribunal's jurisdiction, cannot be interepretd to allow for an advisory jurisdiction of the full Tribunal. This follows from a comparison of the different authentic texts of Article 21 ITLOS Statute[587], its *travaux préparatoires*[588], and the fact that the UNCLOS States Parties did not omit the matter of advisory opinions, but decided to limit its scope to the SDC[589]. Third, the Tribunal cannot, by means of creating its own rules of procedure in accordance with Article 16 ITLOS Statute, confer upon itself a jurisdiction which is not provided for under UNCLOS.[590] Finally, neither the doctrine of inherent powers nor the doctrine of implied powers can provide for an advisory jurisdiction of the Tribunal.[591] It is worth exploring these arguments in more detail since they provide an interesting perspective on the matter of jurisdiction of ICs.

The ITLOS bases its advisory jurisdiction primarily on Article 21 of its Statute. The provision stipulates:

> "The jurisdiction of the Tribunal comprises all disputes and all applications submitted to it in accordance with this Convention and all matters

586 ITLOS Pleadings, *Request for Advisory Opinion submitted by the Sub-Regional Fisheries Commission*, Written Statement of Australia para. 13; Written Statement of the United States of America para. 13.

587 ITLOS Pleadings, *Request for Advisory Opinion submitted by the Sub-Regional Fisheries Commission*, Written Statement of Australia paras. 23 et seq.; Written Statement of the United Kingdom para. 24.

588 ITLOS Pleadings, *Request for Advisory Opinion submitted by the Sub-Regional Fisheries Commission*, Written Statement of China para. 36; Written Statement of the United Kingdom para. 7; Written Statement of the United States para. 18.

589 ITLOS Pleadings, *Request for Advisory Opinion submitted by the Sub-Regional Fisheries Commission*, Written Statement of Australia para. 13; Written Statement of the United Kingdom para. 24; United States para. 13.

590 ITLOS Pleadings, *Request for Advisory Opinion submitted by the Sub-Regional Fisheries Commission*, Written Statement of the United Kingdom para. 12.

591 ITLOS Pleadings, *Request for Advisory Opinion submitted by the Sub-Regional Fisheries Commission*, Written Statement of Australia para. 7; Written Statement of China paras. 9–15; Written Statement of Spain para. 6; Written Statement of the United Kingdom paras. 9–12. See also ITLOS Pleadings, *Request for an Advisory Opinion submitted by the Commission of Small Island States on Climate Change and International Law*, Written Statement of China para. 21.

> specifically provided for in any other agreement which confers jurisdiction on the Tribunal."

The provision refers to three elements of the Tribunal's jurisdiction: "disputes", "applications", and "matters". While Article 21 thus does not expressly refer to advisory opinions, it refers to "all matters". According to the ITLOS

> "the words all "matters" (...) should not be interpreted as covering only 'disputes', for if that were to be the case, article 21 of the Statute would simply have used the word 'disputes'. Consequently, it must mean something more than only 'disputes'. That something more must include advisory opinions, if specifically provided for in 'any other agreement which confers jurisdiction on the Tribunal.'"[592]

The ITLOS found that by including the reference to "all matters", the ITLOS Statute allowed for the conferral of an advisory jurisdiction on the full Tribunal.[593] However, Article 21 on its own is not a sufficient legal basis for the Tribunal's advisory jurisdiction. As the ITLOS clarified, Article 21 ITLOS Statute merely recognizes the possibility of an international agreement conferring an advisory jurisdiction on the Tribunal. What is needed, therefore, is another international agreement which confers a specific advisory jurisdiction on the Tribunal.[594] As the ITLOS held, "Article 21 and the "other agreement" conferring jurisdiction on the Tribunal are interconnected and constitute the substantive legal basis of the advisory jurisdiction of the Tribunal."[595]

This dual legal basis of the Tribunal's advisory jurisdiction stands independently from other provisions in UNCLOS. As such, Article 288 UNCLOS which governs the Tribunal's and the SDC's jurisdiction in contentious matters does not invalidate the assumption of an advisory jurisdiction of the Tribunal.[596]

---

592 *Request for Advisory Opinion submitted by the Sub-Regional Fisheries Commission*, Advisory Opinion, ITLOS Reports 2015, 4 (para. 56).

593 Ibid., para. 58.

594 Ibid.

595 Ibid.

596 Ibid., para. 52.

However, as Judge *Cot* pointed out in his Declaration, the wording "all matters" is quite ambiguous and can support arguments both in favor and against an advisory jurisdiction of the Tribunal.[597]

To decipher the meaning of the wording "all matters", one could thus compare the wording of Article 21 ITLOS Statute in the six authentic versions.[598] As a rule of treaty interpretation, it is presumed that the terms used in each six versions have the same meaning (see Article 33 para. 3 VCLT). Where two language versions differ from each other in their meaning, the meaning which can be harmonized with both versions prevails.[599] One must therefore look for a common meaning among all six versions of UNCLOS. As *Lando* has demonstrated, of the six authentic texts of Article 21 ITLOS Statute, four employ a broad wording which can be read to extend the Tribunal's jurisdiction to include advisory opinions.[600] However, the Chinese and French versions of Article 21 ITLOS Statute seem to contain a reference to Article 288 UNCLOS which would limit the Tribunal's jurisdictional scope to the settlement of disputes.[601] *Lando* therefore argued that the two narrowest versions, the Chinese and the French version, are to be preferred as they reconcile all authentic texts of UNCLOS.[602]

The idea that UNCLOS refers to an advisory jurisdiction of the Tribunal by employing the wording "all matters" becomes even less convincing if one considers that UNCLOS expressly mentions the advisory jurisdiction of the SDC in Article 191 UNCLOS. This begs the question why the same instrument would expressly mention the advisory jurisdiction regarding the SDC but merely imply it regarding the Tribunal.[603] It seems likely that had the States Parties to UNCLOS intended to confer advisory jurisdiction on the plenary Tribunal as well, they would have expressly stated it, as they did

597 "The ambiguity of the provision is blindingly obvious", see *Request for Advisory Opinion submitted by the Sub-Regional Fisheries Commission*, Advisory Opinion, Declaration Judge Cot, ITLOS Reports 2015, 73 (para. 3); see also *M. Lando*, 29 LJIL 2 (2016), 441 (446).

598 *M. Lando*, 29 LJIL 2 (2016), 441 (453).

599 *Mavrommatis Palestine Concessions (Greece v. United Kingdom)*, Judgment, 1924, PCIJ Series A, no. 2, 5 (19).

600 According to Lando, the Arabic, English, Russian, and Spanish versions are in line with a broad interpretation of Art. 21 ITLOS Statute which is compatible with an advisory jurisdiction of the Tribunal, *M. Lando*, 29 LJIL 2 (2016), 441 (453).

601 Ibid., 453.

602 Ibid., 453.

603 ITLOS Pleadings, *Request for Advisory Opinion submitted by the Sub-Regional Fisheries Commission*, Written Statement of Australia para. 13; Written Statement of the United States of America para. 13.

with the SDC.[604] However, such an inference from the express mentioning of one jurisdiction to the exclusion of all not-mentioned jurisdictions (*expressio unius est exclusio alterius*) is only compelling if one can demonstrate not only that UNCLOS confers advisory jurisdiction on the SDC, which it does, but also that it confers advisory jurisdiction *only* on the SDC.[605]

During the advisory proceeding instituted by the SRFC, several states referred to the preparatory materials of UNCLOS which indicate that the question of the Tribunal giving advisory opinions has not been discussed by the negotiating states at any stage.[606] One could counter this argument, as *von Rebay* and *Oberle* did, by arguing that the ITLOS advisory jurisdiction is not an advisory jurisdiction under UNCLOS but under another agreement in conjunction with Article 21 ITLOS Statute.[607] As such, it is hardly surprising that UNCLOS only refers to the advisory jurisdiction of the SDC.

While UNCLOS itself does not expressly mention the Tribunal's advisory jurisdiction, Article 138 of the Rules of ITLOS does.[608] Based on this provision, the ITLOS found that its advisory jurisdiction was subject to three conditions: (1) there must be an international agreement related to the purposes of the Convention specifically providing for the submission of a request for an advisory opinion to the Tribunal; (2) the request must be transmitted to the Tribunal by a body authorized by or in accordance with

604 ITLOS Pleadings, *Request for Advisory Opinion submitted by the Sub-Regional Fisheries Commission*, Written Statement of the United Kingdom para. 24. One could also argue the opposite, i.e. that the parties could have included more express language in Article 21 ITLOS Statute, if they had intended to exclude the Tribunal from issuing advisory opinions, see *A. von Rebay/C. Oberle*, 83 ZaöRV / HJIL 2 (2023), 283 (288).

605 Cf. *K. Larenz*, Methodenlehre der Rechtswissenschaft, 6. ed. 1991, 390.

606 ITLOS Pleadings, *Request for Advisory Opinion submitted by the Sub-Regional Fisheries Commission*, Written Statement of China para. 36; Written Statement of the United Kingdom para. 7; Written Statement of the United States of America para. 18.

607 *A. von Rebay/C. Oberle*, 83 ZaöRV / HJIL 2 (2023), 283 (289).

608 Art. 138 of the Rules of ITLOS reads:
"1. The Tribunal may give an advisory opinion on a legal question if an international agreement related to the purposes of the Convention specifically provides for the submission to the Tribunal of a request for such an opinion.
2. A request for an advisory opinion shall be transmitted to the Tribunal by whatever body is authorized by or in accordance with the agreement to make the request to the Tribunal.
3. The Tribunal shall apply mutatis mutandis articles 130 to 137."

the agreement; and (3) an opinion may only be given on a legal question.[609] However, as the ITLOS found in its *SRFC* advisory opinion,[610] Article 138 of the ITLOS Rules is not the legal basis for the Tribunal's advisory jurisdiction, it merely stipulates certain prerequisites for the exercise of it.[611] While Article 16 ITLOS Statute authorizes the Tribunal to formulate rules on how to carry out its functions, it cannot by doing so create *new* functions.

Nevertheless, by adopting Article 138 of the ITLOS Rules, the Tribunal clearly indicated its understanding that Article 21 ITLOS Statute in conjunction with other agreements provide a legal basis for the Tribunal's advisory jurisdiction. Furthermore, no state objected to Article 138 prior to the *SRFC* advisory proceedings. One could thus argue that the States Parties to UNCLOS by not objecting to Article 138 ITLOS Rules acquiesced to the Tribunal's advisory capacity.[612] The UNCLOS States Parties could also be said to have formed a subsequent practice (see Article 31 para. 3 lit. b VCLT) in the application of UNCLOS which modified the meaning of Article 21 ITLOS Statute to include advisory opinions among the Tribunal's powers.[613] However, the subsequent practice of the parties to a treaty must be "in the application of the treaty" and it must "establish the agreement of the parties" (Article 31 para. 3 lit. b VCLT).[614] The third element enshrined in Article 21 ITLOS Statute ("all matters") was applied for the first time when the first advisory opinion was requested from the Tribunal in the *SRFC* case at which point several states objected to the Tribunal's advisory

609 *Request for Advisory Opinion submitted by the Sub-Regional Fisheries Commission*, Advisory Opinion, ITLOS Reports 2015, 4 (para. 60).

610 Ibid., para. 59.

611 See however, Rüdiger Wolfrum, who argues that "Art. 138 of the Rules establishes a consensual solution. If the jurisdiction of international courts and tribunals is based upon the consensus of the parties concerned there is no reason to deny them to establish an additional jurisdiction.", *R. Wolfrum*, Advisory Opinions: Are they a Suitable Alternative for the Settlement of International Disputes, in: R. Wolfrum/I. Gatzschmann (eds.), International Dispute Settlement: Room for Innovations?, 2013, 35 (54).

612 Cf. *Request for Advisory Opinion submitted by the Sub-Regional Fisheries Commission*, Advisory Opinion, Declaration Judge Cot, ITLOS Reports 2015, 73 (para. 4).

613 So *A. von Rebay/C. Oberle*, 83 ZaöRV / HJIL 2 (2023), 283 (290–291).

614 Subsequent practice which falls below this threshold can be used as a supplementary means of interpretation under Article 32 VCLT, see ILC, Draft conclusions on subsequent agreements and subsequent practice in relation to the interpretation of treaties, 2018, Article 4 para. 3.

jurisdiction.[615] This objection seriously undermines the claim that there was an agreement of the parties expressed by subsequent practice.

Several states convincingly argued that neither the *doctrine of inherent powers* nor the *doctrine of implied powers* can provide a legal basis for the plenary advisory jurisdiction of the ITLOS.[616] While the two doctrines have sometimes been used as synonymous, they have distinct applications:

The idea that a certain power is an "inherent power" concerns the nature of the power in question.[617] Inherent powers are those powers which are inherent in any organ of a particular nature.[618] Inherent to any judicial organ are thus those powers which derive from its nature as a judicial organ.[619] Examples of this are the power of a court to determine its own jurisdiction in a certain case and the power to rule on provisional measures and preliminary objections.[620]

Implied powers, on the other hand, are powers "which, though not expressly provided in the [constituent instrument], are conferred upon it by necessary implication as being essential to the performance of its duties."[621] The doctrine of implied powers refers to the idea that certain powers may be implicitly contained within an organ's constituent instrument and need to be revealed by interpreting the organ's functions and objectives.[622] The

615 So *M. Lando*, 29 LJIL 2 (2016), 441 (448); *T. Ruys/A. Soete*, 29 Leiden Journal of International Law 1 (2016), 155 (162).

616 See ITLOS Pleadings, *Request for Advisory Opinion submitted by the Sub-Regional Fisheries Commission*, Written Statement of Australia para. 7; Written Statement of China paras. 9–15; Written Statement of Spain para. 6; Written Statement of the United Kingdom paras. 9–12. See also ITLOS Pleadings, *Request for an Advisory Opinion submitted by the Commission of Small Island States on Climate Change and International Law*, Written Statement of China para. 21.

617 *M. Paparinskis*, Inherent Powers of ICSID Tribunals: Broad and Rightly So, in: I. A. Laird/T. Weiler (eds.), Investment treaty arbitration and international law, 2012 (14–15).

618 *C. Brown*, Inherent Powers in International Adjudication, in: C. Romano/K. J. Alter/Y. Shany (eds.), The Oxford Handbook of International Adjudication, 2013, 828-847 (832–833).

619 Ibid., 834.

620 *M. Paparinskis*, Inherent Powers of ICSID Tribunals: Broad and Rightly So, in: I. A. Laird/T. Weiler (eds.), Investment treaty arbitration and international law, 2012 (14–15).

621 *Reparation for Injuries Suffered in the Service of the United Nations*, Advisory Opinion, ICJ Reports 1949, 174 (182).

622 *M. Paparinskis*, Inherent Powers of ICSID Tribunals: Broad and Rightly So, in: I. A. Laird/T. Weiler (eds.), Investment treaty arbitration and international law, 2012 (14–15); *C. Brown*, Inherent Powers in International Adjudication, in: C. Romano/K. J.

doctrine examines which powers the States Parties to that instrument must have intended to confer on that organ in order for it to effectively perform its functions and achieve its objectives. The doctrine of implied powers thus is a kind of effective treaty interpretation.[623] These implied powers may (but do not have to) go beyond the powers that are inherent to the respective organ.[624]

In practice, the two doctrines often overlap. The nature of the organ which forms the basis for its inherent powers is necessarily influenced by the content of its constituent instrument. While within a domestic context there may be an abstract concept of a judicial organ, the contours of an international court or tribunal are mostly determined by its constituent instrument. The constituent instrument also specifies that organ's functions which in turn determine which powers may have been implied by the constituent instrument's drafters.

It seems convincing to argue that the power to issue advisory opinions is not a competence which is inherent to an IC because the proper administration of justice does not necessarily rely on the existence of such a function.[625] The inherent powers doctrine assumes that a judicial organ has those powers which it requires to exercise its existing functions, not however to extend its functions to include new ones. Arguing for the existence of such an inherent power also goes against international practice, since there are several ICs that do not possess an advisory function.[626] Similarly, an advisory competence is not necessary for a judicial organ to effectively exercise its functions and achieve its objectives in the sense of the implied

Alter/Y. Shany (eds.), The Oxford Handbook of International Adjudication, 2013, 828-847 (840).

623 *C. Brown*, Inherent Powers in International Adjudication, in: C. Romano/K. J. Alter/Y. Shany (eds.), The Oxford Handbook of International Adjudication, 2013, 828-847 (839).

624 *M. Paparinskis*, Inherent Powers of ICSID Tribunals: Broad and Rightly So, in: I. A. Laird/T. Weiler (eds.), Investment treaty arbitration and international law, 2012 (14–15).

625 ITLOS Pleadings, *Request for Advisory Opinion submitted by the Sub-Regional Fisheries Commission*, Written Statement of Australia para. 7; Written Statement of China paras. 9–15; Written Statement of Spain para. 6; Written Statement of the United Kingdom para. 9.

626 ICs without an advisory jurisdiction include the Court of Justice of the European Union (CJEU), the Appellate Body of the World Trade Organization (WTO AB) and the International Criminal Court (ICC).

powers doctrine.[627] Thus, neither the inherent powers doctrine nor the implied powers doctrine provide a legal basis for the Tribunal's advisory jurisdiction.[628]

It seems that UNCLOS neither permits nor prohibits the ITLOS from giving advisory opinions.[629] Considering that international organizations and their organs have only those powers which have been expressly or implicitly conferred upon them (principle of specialty)[630], this finding seems to indicate that ITLOS has no plenary advisory jurisdiction. However, Article 21 ITLOS Statute indicates that the Tribunal's functions are not conclusively determined by UNCLOS and its Annexes. Instead, by including Article 21 in the ITLOS Statute, the States Parties clearly intended for the Tribunal's jurisdiction to be malleable to a certain extent.[631]

The Tribunal's advisory practice is still in its infancy. It seems too early to tell whether the Tribunal was successful in asserting its advisory jurisdiction *vis-à-vis* the UNCLOS States Parties. On the one hand, only one of the nine states that rejected the Tribunal's advisory jurisdiction during the first advisory proceeding also did so during the second advisory proceeding.[632] Most states participating in the second advisory proceeding only addressed the specific conditions of the Tribunal's advisory jurisdiction, not its existence. However, many of the "doubters" did not participate in the second advisory proceeding at all.[633] What is more, some states, while not submitting arguments on this point, prefaced their submissions with a statement expressing doubt as to the existence of the Tribunal's advisory

627 ITLOS Pleadings, *Request for Advisory Opinion submitted by the Sub-Regional Fisheries Commission*, Written Statement of the United Kingdom paras. 11–12. See also ITLOS Pleadings, Request for an Advisory Opinion submitted by the Commission of Small Island States on Climate Change and International Law, Written Statement of China para. 21.

628 So also *M. Lando*, 29 LJIL 2 (2016), 441 (457).

629 Cf. *Request for Advisory Opinion submitted by the Sub-Regional Fisheries Commission*, Advisory Opinion, Declaration Judge Cot, ITLOS Reports 2015, 73 (paras. 3–4).

630 On the principle of specialty, see *infra*: § 5 Section B.II.

631 *A. von Rebay/C. Oberle*, 83 ZaöRV / HJIL 2 (2023), 283 (294–295).

632 ITLOS Pleadings, *Request for an Advisory Opinion submitted by the Commission of Small Island States on Climate Change and International Law*, Written Statement of China paras. 6–21.

633 Among the states not participating in the *COSIS* advisory proceeding were Argentina, Ireland, Spain, and the United States of America.

jurisdiction.[634] However, considering that the Tribunal has clearly found that it has an advisory jurisdiction, it seems unlikely that the Tribunal will backpedal on this matter. The existence of the Tribunal's advisory jurisdiction thus seems settled for now. The focus of jurisdictional arguments thus shift to the *extent* of this advisory jurisdiction as can already be seen in the written submissions during the second advisory proceeding before the Tribunal.[635]

II. Use of ITLOS advisory opinions to settle inter-state disputes

1. Seabed Disputes Chamber

In principle, nothing in UNCLOS or ITLOS Statute prevents the SDC from giving advisory opinions on pending bilateral disputes, as long as the SDC receives a request which satisfies the jurisdictional requirements laid down in Article 191 UNCLOS. On the contrary, certain provisions in the Statute and the Tribunal's Rules speak in favor of such a broad advisory jurisdiction. Article 140 para. 2 ITLOS Statute states that the SDC shall be guided by the provisions relating to the Tribunal's contentious procedure when exercising its advisory function. Even more pertinent, Article 130 para. 2 ITLOS Rules expressly refers to the SDC advisory jurisdiction extending to pending disputes. It states:

> "The Chamber shall consider whether the request for an advisory opinion relates to a legal question pending between two or more parties.

634 Australia submitted its views in the *COSIS* case "without prejudice to Australia's position on the advisory jurisdiction of the Tribunal", see ITLOS Pleadings, *Request for an Advisory Opinion submitted by the Commission of Small Island States on Climate Change and International Law*, Written Statement of Australia para. 4. The United Kingdom repeated its arguments against an advisory jurisdiction of the Tribunal and merely "recognize[d] (...) that in that case, ITLOS found that it did have advisory jurisdiction" and asked the Tribunal to "clarify its reasoning with respect to the basis of its advisory jurisdiction in these proceedings", Written Statement of the United Kingdom paras. 15a-16. France similarly did not expressly recognize the Tribunal's advisory jurisdiction but merely recognized that "the Tribunal's advisory jurisdiction now seems to be accepted", Written Statement of France para. 9.

635 See ITLOS Pleadings, *Request for Advisory Opinion submitted by the Sub-Regional Fisheries Commission*, Written Statement of Argentina para. 17; Written Statement of Australia para. 27; Written Statement of China para. 77; Written Statement of Ireland para. 2.11; Written Statement of the Netherlands paras. 2.3 et seq.; Written Statement of the United States paras. 36–7.

When the Chamber so determines, article 17 of the Statute applies, as well as the provisions of these Rules concerning the application of that article."

It is worth noting that Article 130 para. 2 ITLOS Rules, which is based upon Article 102 para. 3 of the ICJ Rules[636], does not oblige the SDC to reject requests for advisory opinions relating to pending disputes. Instead it merely stipulates that when the SDC determines that the request relates to a pending dispute, Article 17 ITLOS Statute applies, allowing the disputing states to appoint a judge ad-hoc of their nationality. One can derive from this provision that the fact that an advisory opinion relates to a pending bilateral dispute is not considered a problem *per se* as long as the procedural rights of the states that are directly affected by the outcome of the proceedings are protected.

While the ITLOS Rules are not binding treaty law, they are relevant for two reasons: First, the States Parties to UNCLOS have authorized ITLOS to formulate the ITLOS Rules in Article 16 ITLOS Statute.[637] The ITLOS Statute "forms an integral part" of UNCLOS (Article 318 UNCLOS) and thus enjoys the same legal status as UNCLOS.[638] The States Parties to UNCLOS are thus bound by Article 16 ITLOS Statute which authorizes the Tribunal to formulate its own rules on how to carry out its functions. Secondly, the ITLOS Rules reflect the practice and legal opinion of the ITLOS. They are thus a reliable guide on how the ITLOS and the SDC will deal with future cases. It is therefore likely that the SDC will not reject requests relating to pending bilateral disputes. Instead, the SDC will likely develop its own approach on how to deal with such requests. Considering the central role of discretion in the ICJ's handling of such requests, the SDC will have to develop its position on whether the wording of Article 191 UNCLOS is compatible with exercising a similar kind of discretion.

636 *R. Wolfrum*, Advisory Opinions: Are they a Suitable Alternative for the Settlement of International Disputes, in: R. Wolfrum/I. Gatzschmann (eds.), International Dispute Settlement: Room for Innovations?, 2013, 35 (50).

637 Art. 16 ITLOS Statute stipulates: "The Tribunal shall frame rules for carrying out its functions. In particular it shall lay down rules of procedure."

638 *Request for Advisory Opinion submitted by the Sub-Regional Fisheries Commission*, Advisory Opinion, ITLOS Reports 2015, 4 (para. 52).

2. ITLOS

The question whether advisory opinions may be requested from the ITLOS to settle inter-state disputes has not explicitly been raised so far. However, a related issue was raised during the second advisory proceeding before the ITLOS. It concerned the question whether the ITLOS advisory jurisdiction *ratione materiae* was limited to the interpretation of the "other agreement" which confers advisory jurisdiction on the ITLOS or also to other treaties including UNCLOS.

Several states argued that the Tribunal's subject-matter jurisdiction is limited to the interpretation and application of the "other agreement" in the sense of Article 21 ITLOS Statute.[639] Supporters of this view highlighted the wording "matters specifically provided for" in Article 21 ITLOS Statute.[640] Accordingly, Article 21 ITLOS Statute limits the advisory jurisdiction to these matters governed by the separate agreement. Proponents of this view further argued that giving the Tribunal the power to interpret UNCLOS through another agreement outside UNCLOS would constitute an *inter se* agreement affecting the rights of third states, as it would require the Tribunal to interpret UNCLOS without the consent of the UNCLOS States Parties.[641] In principle, any question or treaty provision could thus be brought before ITLOS by means of a separate agreement. Such a conferral by another agreement would be at odds with the decision of UNCLOS not to confer an express competence upon the Tribunal to interpret UNCLOS in advisory proceedings.[642] Australia expressed this point most succinctly:

639 ITLOS Pleadings, *Request for Advisory Opinion submitted by the Sub-Regional Fisheries Commission*, Written Statement of Argentina para. 17; Written Statement of Australia para. 27; Written Statement of China para. 77; Written Statement of Ireland para. 2.11; Written Statement of the Netherlands paras. 2.3 et seq.; Written Statement of the United States paras. 36–7.

640 ITLOS Pleadings, *Request for Advisory Opinion submitted by the Sub-Regional Fisheries Commission*, Written Statement of the Netherlands para. 2.3.

641 "Permitting States Parties of one treaty to ask for an advisory opinion about questions under another treaty violates the consent of the States Parties to the other treaty", ITLOS Pleadings, *Request for Advisory Opinion submitted by the Sub-Regional Fisheries Commission*, Written Statement of the United States para. 37; see also Written Statement of Australia paras. 27–30.

642 ITLOS Pleadings, *Request for Advisory Opinion submitted by the Sub-Regional Fisheries Commission*, Written Statement of Australia para. 28; cf. Written Statement of Ireland para. 2.11.

> "Simply put, any form of jurisdiction to be exercised by an international court or tribunal must be based upon the consent of the relevant parties. The giving of an advisory opinion at the request of a limited number of States which will focus primarily on the interpretation and application of the provisions of other treaties without the consent of the States parties to those other treaties would be inconsistent with this principle."[643]

Other states argue for a broader interpretation of Article 21 ITLOS Statute.[644] Accordingly, the Tribunal's advisory jurisdiction *ratione materiae* extends not only to the interpretation and application of the other agreement (as long as it relates to UNCLOS, see Article 138 ITLOS Rules) but also to all matters which have a "sufficient connection with the purposes and principles" of that agreement.[645] Accordingly, the Tribunal may also interpret treaty provisions which relate to the other agreement's subject-matter. The ITLOS particularly rejected the argument that it should not pronounce on the rights and obligations of third states not members to the other agreement without their consent.[646] It argued that such consent was not necessary, as the advisory opinion had no binding force and was given only to the requesting organ in order to assist it in the performance of its activities under its constituent instrument (i.e., the other agreement).[647]

The ITLOS was clearly inspired by the jurisprudence of the ICJ. Like the Den Haag Court, the Hamburg Court rebutted the allegation of circumventing state consent by pointing out that its opinions were non-binding and not addressed to states but only to the requesting organ. Irrespective of the merit of this argument,[648] this nonchalant reference to the ICJ's advisory jurisprudence seems questionable at best. The ICJ's advisory jurisdiction is expressly enshrined in the UNC and the ICJ Statute. As such,

643 ITLOS Pleadings, *Request for Advisory Opinion submitted by the Sub-Regional Fisheries Commission*, Written Statement of Australia para. 30.

644 *Request for Advisory Opinion submitted by the Sub-Regional Fisheries Commission*, Advisory Opinion, ITLOS Reports 2015, 4 (paras. 68 et seq.); cf. ITLOS Pleadings, Request for Advisory Opinion submitted by the Sub-Regional Fisheries Commission, Written Statement of Germany para. 12.

645 *Request for Advisory Opinion submitted by the Sub-Regional Fisheries Commission*, Advisory Opinion, ITLOS Reports 2015, 4 (para. 68), citing ICJ, *Legality of the Use by a State of Nuclear Weapons in Armed Conflict*, Advisory Opinion, ICJ Reports 1996, 66, (77, para. 22).

646 *Request for Advisory Opinion submitted by the Sub-Regional Fisheries Commission*, Advisory Opinion, ITLOS Reports 2015, 4 (paras. 75–77).

647 Ibid.

648 See on this in detail *infra*: § 6 Section D.II.

it has been directly accepted by all UN Member States.[649] What is more, the ICJ is an organ of the UN. When the ICJ states in its case law that it has a duty to give the requested advisory opinion and may only refuse to do so when there are compelling reasons, it refers to its duty as an organ of the UN to promote the activities of the UN and support the other UN organs in their activities. Furthermore, the ICJ advisory jurisdiction *ratione personae* is significantly more restricted than that of the ITLOS under Article 21 ITLOS Statute.[650] Access to the ICJ's advisory jurisdiction is limited to the UNSC and the UNGA as well as certain UN organizations with the express authorization of the UNGA. As such, only UN organs and certain organizations that are linked to the UN have the right to request advisory opinions from the ICJ. The requesting organizations thus have quasi-universal state membership and resolutions of the organizations' organs are generally preceded by prolonged debates which allow for broad participation by the organization's Member States and are carried by a majority of the organization's Member States. As such, the views and concerns of a large number of states are taken into account early in the process of requesting an advisory opinion from the ICJ which bestows upon these requests significant legitimacy.[651] The idea to allow individual states or two or more states acting in concert to request advisory opinions from the ICJ was deliberately rejected, as it was feared that this would entice states to abuse the advisory jurisdiction to circumvent state consent to dispute settlement procedures.[652]

In contrast, the ITLOS's advisory jurisdiction under Article 21 ITLOS Statute in conjunction with other international agreements enables any "body" (see Article 138 ITLOS Rules) authorized by an international agreement to request an advisory opinion from the Tribunal. While Article 21 ITLOS Statute could be read to allow only organs of an international organization created by another agreement to request advisory opinions from the ITLOS, it could also be read to extend to individual states which are so authorized by an international agreement.[653] Read broadly individual

649 Highlighting this important difference between the advisory jurisdiction of the two courts, see *T. Ruys/A. Soete*, 29 Leiden Journal of International Law 1 (2016), 155 (169–170).

650 So also Ibid., 170.

651 So also Ibid., 170.

652 See *supra*: § 1 Section D.II.

653 *T. Ruys/A. Soete*, 29 Leiden Journal of International Law 1 (2016), 155 (164); arguing for such a broad reading, see *R. Wolfrum*, Advisory Opinions: Are they a

states could thereby have recourse to the ITLOS advisory procedure. States could conclude such agreements merely for the reason of requesting an advisory opinion from the ITLOS.[654] In contrast to requests for advisory opinions from the ICJ, the plenary advisory jurisdiction of the ITLOS thus allows a small number of states (as the requests by the *SRFC* and the *COSIS illustrate*)[655] to request an advisory opinion on matters affecting a large number of states without the direct or indirect participation of those states. There is thus a significant potential for states to abuse the Tribunal's advisory jurisdiction by bringing a dispute with a third state before the ITLOS in the guise of advisory proceedings under Article 21 ITLOS Statute.[656]

III. Interim conclusions

The recent developments regarding the plenary advisory jurisdiction of the ITLOS raise several important aspects of advisory jurisdictions of ICs in general. First, it illustrates how ICs can use their power to formulate their own rules of procedure not only to specify but also assert their advisory function. By means of Article 138 ITLOS Rules, the Tribunal asserted its competence to give advisory opinions in full plenum, a power which was only implied by its constituent instrument. Secondly, it provides guidance on the role of state consent in the context of advisory proceedings. While state consent is not required for the *exercise* of advisory jurisdiction, it is required for the initial *creation* of the advisory jurisdiction.[657] Thirdly, by indirectly enabling states to request advisory opinions via newly formed international organizations, the plenary advisory jurisdiction raises questions of legitimacy in advisory proceedings. The ITLOS will have to defend its extensive advisory jurisdiction against states that see it as a means for a small number of states to bring their international disputes before the ITLOS.

Suitable Alternative for the Settlement of International Disputes, in: R. Wolfrum/I. Gatzschmann (eds.), International Dispute Settlement: Room for Innovations?, 2013, 35 (54).

654 *T. Ruys/A. Soete*, 29 Leiden Journal of International Law 1 (2016), 155 (165).

655 The SRFC had seven Member States, the COSIS had six Member States when requesting the respective advisory opinion.

656 So also *Request for Advisory Opinion submitted by the Sub-Regional Fisheries Commission*, Advisory Opinion, Declaration Judge Cot, ITLOS Reports 2015, 73 (para. 9).

657 On this, see *M. Lando*, 29 LJIL 2 (2016), 441 (454 et seq.).

E. Conclusions on the Eastern Carelia doctrine before other ICs

All the ICs examined in this chapter share a common concern: to ensure that their advisory procedures do not adversely affect their other procedures, in particular their dispute settlement and individual complaint procedures. This concern about safeguarding the integrity of the dispute settlement procedure is also the driving force behind the ICJ's Eastern Carelia doctrine.[658] The different ICs have developed different approaches to ensure the integrity of their respective procedures.

In the case of the ECtHR, the relationship between its advisory and its contentious procedures is explicitly regulated by its legal framework. The ECtHR maintains a strict separation between its contentious procedure and its advisory procedures. This strict separation is most apparent in the ECtHR's Article 47-procedure, under which the ECtHR may not deal with substantive human rights provisions or any matter which may come before the ECtHR through its other procedures. While under the Protocol 16-procedure, the ECtHR may deal with substantive human rights obligations that are the subject of a dispute pending before domestic courts, the ECtHR has made clear that its function is limited to providing legal guidance and not to settling the underlying dispute.

Lacking an express provision in its constituent instrument, the IACtHR had to develop its own approach on how to reconcile its different procedures. Similarly to the ICJ, the IACtHR found that its advisory opinions "cannot be used to conceal a contentious case nor prematurely obtain a ruling on a matter that could eventually be submitted to the Court as a contentious case" or to "resolve questions of fact".[659] The IACtHR thus follows a similar doctrine to the Eastern Carelia doctrine, in that it does not allow its advisory function to be used to circumvent its contentious function. Another feature the IACtHR shares with the ICJ is its reluctancy to reject requests for advisory opinions. The IACtHR has stated on several occasions that the fact that a request relates to an existing dispute would not necessarily prevent the Court from issuing an advisory opinion.[660]

658 See *infra*: § 6 Section D.

659 *Differentiated approaches with respect to certain groups of persons in detention (Interpretation and scope of Articles 1(1), 4(1), 5, 11(2), 12, 13, 17(1), 19, 24 and 26 of the American Convention on Human Rights and other human rights instruments)*, Advisory Opinion OC-29/22, IACtHR Series A No. 29, para. 21.

660 *Restrictions to the Death Penalty, Advisory Opinion OC-3/83, IACtHR Series A No. 3, para 38; Compatibility of Draft Legislation with Article 8(2)(h) of the American*

The IACtHR has thus regularly responded to requests, even when they relate to existing disputes. The IACtHR has emphasized that it does not make a judicial decision on the underlying dispute, but merely interprets the relevant human rights instruments. However, there is an important difference between the approaches of the IACtHR and the ICJ: In contrast to the ICJ, the IACtHR refrains from making any findings on questions of fact or international responsibility. As indicated above, this is in line with the IACtHR's subject-matter jurisdiction which, unlike that of the ICJ, expressly limits the Court's powers to the interpretation of human rights provisions. By limiting the content of its advisory opinions to the interpretation of human rights instruments, the IACtHR draws a sharper distinction between its advisory and its contentious procedures. Only in contentious proceedings does the IACtHR make findings on questions of fact and international responsibility. In advisory proceedings, the Court will refer to the facts of a case only to demonstrate the practical relevance of its legal guidance on the interpretation of the applicable human rights instruments.[661] The IACtHR's approach resembles the approach proposed by Germany in the *Chagos* case, in which Germany asked the ICJ not to rule on the UK's international responsibility.[662]

There are several important lessons to be drawn from this excursus into other ICs for the study of the ICJ's advisory function: First, the ICJ is not the only IC that is concerned about a negative spill-over effect between its advisory and contentious procedures. This makes the approaches taken by other ICs an interesting reference point. Secondly, other ICs found that the mere fact that a request relates to an existing dispute does not necessarily prevent the Court from issuing an advisory opinion. They recognized a certain flexibility of the Court in deciding whether or not to give a requested advisory opinion. Thirdly, other ICs deal with the question of whether a request for an advisory opinion negatively affects

Convention on Human Rights, Advisory Opinion OC-12/91, IACtHR Series A No. 12, para. 28; *The Right to Information on Consular Assistance in the Framework of the Guarantees of the Due Process of Law*, Advisory Opinion OC-16/99, IACtHR Series A No. 16, para. 45.

661 Cf. *International Responsibility for the Promulgation and Enforcement of Laws in Violation of the Convention (Arts. 1 and 2 of the American Convention on Human Rights)*, Advisory Opinion OC-14/94, IACtHR Series A No. 14, para. 27; *The Right to Information on Consular Assistance in the Framework of the Guarantees of the Due Process of Law*, Advisory Opinion OC-16/99, IACtHR Series A No. 16, para. 49.

662 ICJ Pleadings, *Legal Consequences of the Separation of the Chagos Archipelago from Mauritius in 1965*, Written Statement of Germany, paras. 120, 141.

the Court's other procedures as a question of admissibility. This echoes the ICJ's approach. Fourthly, a practical way of preventing a negative spill-over effect between advisory and contentious proceedings in this context is for the IC to refrain from making findings on the international responsibility of the states involved.

§ 5 Legal framework of the Eastern Carelia doctrine

The core tenet of the Eastern Carelia doctrine is that the ICJ's advisory procedure may not be used with the aim to settle inter-state legal disputes. This chapter assesses the merit of this argument by reference to the legal framework of the ICJ's advisory jurisdiction. As will be demonstrated, the Court's legal framework in no way prevents the Court from issuing advisory opinions on inter-state disputes.

A. Relevant provisions

The advisory jurisdiction of the Court is governed by Article 96 UNC, Articles 65–68 ICJ Statute, Articles 102–109 of the Rules of the Court (the Rules)[663], and Practice Direction XII[664].

The UNC and the ICJ Statute form a single instrument (Article 92 sentence 2 UNC)[665] and constitute the ICJ's constituent instrument.[666] Article 96 UNC and Article 65 para. 1 ICJ Statute contain the conditions of the Court's jurisdiction *ratione personae* and *ratione materiae*, while the other provisions relate to procedural questions.[667]

Article 96 UNC stipulates:

> "The General Assembly or the Security Council may request the International Court of Justice to give an advisory opinion on any legal question. Other organs of the United Nations and specialized agencies, which may at any time be so authorized by the General Assembly, may also request

663 See Art. 30 para. 1 ICJ Statute.

664 Since 2001, the Court has issued Practice Directions as guidance for the States appearing before the Court. These Practice Directions do not amend the Rules of the Court, but supplement them.

665 *S. Rosenne*, The law and practice of the International Court, 1920-2005, 4th ed. 2006, 106.

666 *M. N. Shaw*, Rosenne's Law and Practice of the International Court: 1920-2015, 5th ed 2016, Vol. 3, Ch. 16, § 255.

667 *P. d'Argent*, in: A. Zimmermann/C. J. Tams/K. Oellers-Frahm/C. Tomuschat/D. W. K. Anderson (eds.), The Statute of the International Court of Justice, 3. ed., 2019: Article 65, para. 1.

> advisory opinions of the Court on legal questions arising within the scope of their activities."

Article 65 para. 1 ICJ Statute stipulates:

> "The Court may give an advisory opinion on any legal question at the request of whatever body may be authorized by or in accordance with the Charter of the United Nations to make such a request."

B. Methods of treaty interpretation

Before examining the relevant legal provisions, it is worth taking a step back and reflecting on the rules that apply when interpreting constituent instruments of international organizations. While the basic rules of treaty interpretation apply to all international treaties, there are certain principles that are particularly important when it comes to the interpretation of constituent instruments of international organizations: the principle of specialty and principle of implied powers.

I. Basic rules of treaty interpretation

Constituent instruments of international organizations are multilateral treaties and as such – in principle – subject to the rules of treaty interpretation codified in Articles 31–33 VCLT.[668] However, the VCLT only applies to treaties that have been concluded after the VCLT's entry into force (Article 4 VCLT). This excludes the application of Articles 31 and 32 VCLT to the interpretation of the UNC and the ICJ Statute, which were concluded prior to the entry into force of the VCLT. However, the ICJ held that Articles 31 and 32 VCLT codify customary international law and applied the rules enshrined therein to treaties concluded prior to the entry into force of

668 Art. 5 VCLT stipulates that the VCLT applies to the constituent instruments of international organizations "without prejudice to any relevant rules of the organization". E contrario, the rules of the organization may deviate from this general rule, *G. Nolte*, Third report on subsequent agreements and subsequent practice in relation to the interpretation of treaties, 7. April 2015, UN Docs A/CN.4/683, 8, paras. 21 et seq. See also *Legality of the Use by a State of Nuclear Weapons in Armed Conflict*, Advisory Opinion, ICJ Reports 1996, 66 (74, para. 19).

the VCLT.[669] The methods of interpretation listed in Article 31 VCLT are of equal status, there is no hierarchy among them.[670]

In addition to the "primary"[671] methods of treaty interpretation contained in Article 31 VCLT, Article 32 VCLT codifies "supplementary means of interpretation". These supplementary means of interpretation, which include the treaties' preparatory work and the circumstances of their conclusion, may only be applied if the application of the primary methods leaves ambiguity or obscurity (Article 32 lit. a VCLT) or the result is manifestly absurd or unreasonable (Article 32 lit. b VCLT).

II. Principle of specialty and principle of implied powers

Constituent instruments of international organizations are treaties of a special kind. States conclude such treaties to create new subjects of international law that possess international legal personality.[672] The signatory states want these new subjects of international law to achieve certain common objectives and in order to do so they confer on them certain powers.[673] Importantly, international organizations and their organs possess only those powers which have been conferred on them by the States Parties to the organization's constituting instrument. This principle is commonly referred

669 *Arbitral Award of 31 July 1989 (Guinea-Bissau v. Senegal)*, Judgment, ICJ Reports 1991, 53 (69-70, para. 48); *Legality of the Use by a State of Nuclear Weapons in Armed Conflict*, Advisory Opinion, ICJ Reports 1996, 66 (75, para. 19); *Kasikili/Sedudu Island (Botswana v. Namibia)*, Judgment, ICJ Reports 1999, 1045 (1059, para. 18); *LaGrand (Germany v. United States of America)*, Judgment, ICJ Reports 2001, 466 (501, para. 99); *Legality of Use of Force (Serbia and Montenegro v. Belgium)*, Preliminary Objections, Judgment, ICJ Reports 2004, 279 (318, para. 100). Arguing that it was only the conclusion of the VCLT itself that rendered the principles of treaty interpretation customary, see *J.-M. Sorel/V. Eveno Boré*, in: O. Corten/P. Klein (eds.), The Vienna Conventions on the law of treaties, 2011: Art. 31, para. 15.

670 *M. E. Villiger*, in: M. E. Villiger (ed.), Commentary on the 1969 Vienna Convention on the Law of Treaties, 2009: Art. 31, para. 29; *J.-M. Sorel/V. Eveno Boré*, in: O. Corten/P. Klein (eds.), The Vienna Conventions on the law of treaties, 2011: Art. 31, para. 8.

671 *M. E. Villiger*, in: M. E. Villiger (ed.), Commentary on the 1969 Vienna Convention on the Law of Treaties, 2009: Art. 31, para. 9 et seq.

672 *G. Nolte*, Third report on subsequent agreements and subsequent practice in relation to the interpretation of treaties, 7. April 2015, UN Docs A/CN.4/683, 4, para. 8.

673 *Legality of the Use by a State of Nuclear Weapons in Armed Conflict*, Advisory Opinion, ICJ Reports 1996, 66 (75, para. 19).

to as the *principle of specialty* or the *principle of conferred powers.*[674] As the organization is a product of the states' collective will, it has only those powers that the states conferred on it.

The powers of an organization are not limited to those powers which are explicitly stated in the organization's constituent instrument. By means of treaty interpretation, one can also deduce an organization's competences from its objectives. In other words, all those powers are considered to have been implicitly conferred by the signatory states to the organization which are deemed essential for the fulfilment of the organization's objectives.[675] This deduction from the objectives of the organization to its powers is called the *principle of implied powers.*[676]

Precursors to the principle of implied powers can be traced back to the case law of the United States Supreme Court. In a case from 1819, the Court examined the relationship between US federal states and the US federal government. The US Supreme Court held:

> "Many particular means are, of course, involved in the general means necessary to carry into effect the powers expressly granted [...]. It was impossible for the framers of the constitution to specify, prospectively, all these means, both because it would have involved an immense variety of details, and because it would have been impossible for them to foresee the infinite variety of circumstances, in such an unexampled state of political society as ours, for ever changing and for ever improving."[677]

---

674 Ibid. (78, para. 25); *M. Virally*, La notion de fonction dans la théorie de l'organisation internationale, in: M. Virally (ed.), Le droit international en devenir, 1990 (para. 71); *N. M. Blokker*, International Organizations or Institutions, Implied Powers (last updated 2021), in: A. Peters/R. Wolfrum (eds.), The Max Planck Encyclopedia of Public International Law, 2008 (1–2); *H. G. Schermers/N. Blokker*, International institutional law, 6. edition 2018, paras. 209-210.

675 *Reparation for Injuries Suffered in the Service of the United Nations*, Advisory Opinion, ICJ Reports 1949, 174 (182); *Legality of the Use by a State of Nuclear Weapons in Armed Conflict*, Advisory Opinion, ICJ Reports 1996, 66 (78, para. 25); on the principle of implied powers with further references, see *H. G. Schermers/N. Blokker*, International institutional law, 6. edition 2018, paras. 232 et seq.

676 Some commentators distinguish between powers being implied from explicit powers and powers being implied from the purpose or functions of an organization, see on this *H. G. Schermers/N. Blokker*, International institutional law, 6. edition 2018, para. 233.

677 *McCulloch v. Maryland, 17 U.S. 316 (1819)*, U.S. Supreme Court decision (384 et seq), cited in *N. M. Blokker*, International Organizations or Institutions, Implied Powers (last updated 2021), in: A. Peters/R. Wolfrum (eds.), The Max Planck Encyclopedia of Public International Law, 2008 (7).

The two central ideas which underlie the principle of implied powers are exemplified in the US Supreme Court's decision: First, as a matter of drafting technique, the drafters of a treaty cannot conclusively list all the powers which an organization needs to achieve its objectives as this would amount to an incomprehensively long list. Secondly, it is equally impossible for the drafters to predict all the powers that may become necessary in the future under changed circumstances. The latter notion is also known as the idea that constituent instruments of international organizations are "living instruments".[678]

It is important to emphasize that the principle of conferred powers and the principle of implied powers do not contradict each other. Rather, the principle of implied powers serves to effectuate the will of the States Parties by giving the organization the powers which are necessary to fulfil the objectives set by the States Parties.[679] Instead of contradicting the principle of conferred powers, the principle of implied powers thus builds on and supplements it. This clarity in principle becomes blurred when applied in practice. It may be difficult to distinguish between powers implicitly conferred by the States Parties onto the organization to achieve the organization's objectives on the one hand and an unauthorized assumption of powers by the organization (in the sense of a "*Kompetenz-Kompetenz*") on the other hand.[680] The latter would be contrary to the principle of conferred powers. To navigate this field, it is important to bear in mind that the implied powers doctrine cannot establish an interpretation of a treaty provision that is incompatible with the text of the treaty.[681] The implied powers doctrine thus finds its limits in the ordinary meaning of the text of the treaty.[682]

678 *M. N. Shaw*, International law, 7. ed. 2014, 946. On the concept of treaties as living instruments, see *T. Thienel*, The 'Living Instrument' Approach in the ECHR and Elsewhere: Some Remarks on the Evolutive Interpretation of International Treaties, in: J. Delbrück/U. E. Heinz/K. Odendahl/N. Matz-Lück/A. von Arnauld (eds.), Aus Kiel in die Welt: Kiel's Contribution to International Law, 1. ed., 2014, 165 (165).

679 Cf. *H. G. Schermers/N. Blokker*, International institutional law, 6. edition 2018, para. 233.

680 *O. Dörr*, in: O. Dörr/K. Schmalenbach (eds.), Vienna convention on the law of treaties, 2012: Art. 31, para. 76.

681 Cf. *O. Dörr*, in: O. Dörr/K. Schmalenbach (eds.), Vienna Convention on the Law of Treaties, 2. ed., 2018: Art. 31, para. 57.

682 Cf. Ibid., para. 57.

C. General scope of the ICJ's advisory jurisdiction

Article 65 ICJ Statute and Article 96 UNC address the Court's advisory jurisdiction from different perspectives: Article 96 UNC focuses on the power of the authorized UN organ to *request* an advisory opinion from the ICJ, whereas Article 65 ICJ Statute focuses on the Court's power to *give* an advisory opinion.[683] Together, the two provisions lay down two conditions for the Court's advisory jurisdiction[684]: First, there must be a request from an authorized organ on a matter within that organ's scope of activities (*jurisdiction ratione personae*). Secondly, the request must relate to a legal question (*jurisdiction ratione materiae*). The Court's jurisdiction or power to give an advisory opinion can be distinguished from the Court's discretion *not* to give an advisory opinion. The Court's discretion will be addressed separately.[685]

I. Jurisdiction ratione personae – request from an "authorized organ"

Article 96 UNC distinguishes between two categories of authorized organs. Paragraph 1 grants the UNGA and the UNSC the power to request advisory opinions from the Court. Paragraph 2 extends this power to "other organs of the United Nations and specialized agencies", however under two further conditions: prior authorization by the UNGA and the request for an advisory opinion must relate to a legal question "arising within the scope of [the authorized organ's] activities". While the first paragraph resembles Article 14 sentence 3 of the Covenant of the League of Nations, which empowered the League's Council and Assembly to request advisory

683 See the discussions during the sixteenth meeting of Committee IV/1 during the San Francisco Conference of 1945, during which the delegate of Australia suggested that provisions on advisory opinions should be in both the Charter and in the ICJ Statute and that the Charter should indicate the power of certain bodies to seek advisory opinions, while the Statute should define the power of the Court to render advisory opinions, United Nations, Sixteenth Meeting of Committee IV/1, 31 May 1945, Doc. 714, IV/1/57, p. 241.

684 *P. d'Argent*, in: A. Zimmermann/C. J. Tams/K. Oellers-Frahm/C. Tomuschat/D. W. K. Anderson (eds.), The Statute of the International Court of Justice, 3. ed., 2019: Article 65, paras. 6–40; *M. M. Aljaghoub*, The Advisory Function of the International Court of Justice 1946 - 2005, 2006, 38–63; *D. Pratap*, The advisory jurisdiction of the International Court, 1972, 121 et seq.

685 See *infra* in this Chapter Section E.

opinions from the PCIJ, the second paragraph extends the power to request advisory opinions to a broader category of entities.[686]

1. Authorization

The UNSC and the UNGA are authorized *per se* to request advisory opinions from the ICJ. For the UNSC, the necessary quorum to request an advisory opinion from the Court is stipulated in Article 27 paras. 2 and 3 UNC.[687] If the request constitutes a "procedural matter" within the meaning of Article 27 para. 2 UNC, a simple majority of nine votes is sufficient. If it qualifies as "other matters" within the meaning of Article 27 para. 3 UNC, the affirmative vote of all permanent members is required. The UNSC has so far only requested one advisory opinion[688] and the request was decided without the affirmative vote of two permanent members thus indicating that a request constitutes a procedural matter.[689]

With regards to the UNGA, it was the initial position of the UNGA that a request for an advisory opinion constituted an "important question" within the meaning of Article 18 para. 2 UNC and thus requires a two-thirds-majority.[690] However, when the UNGA requested an advisory opinion on the *Legality of the Threat or Use of Nuclear Weapons*[691], it did so by simple

686 For further comments on the genesis of Art. 96 UNC during the 1945 San Francisco Conference see for example *M. N. Shaw*, Rosenne's Law and Practice of the International Court: 1920-2015, 5th ed 2016, Vol. 1, Ch. 2, § 9; *M. Giles Samson/ D. Guilfoyle*, The Permanent Court of International Justice and the "Invention" of International Advisory Jurisdiction, in: C. J. Tams/M. Fitzmaurice (eds.), Legacies of the Permanent Court of International Justice, 2013, 41 (62).

687 On this, see *R. Kolb*, The International Court of Justice, 2013, 1044.

688 *Legal Consequences for States of the Continued Presence of South Africa in Namibia (South West Africa) notwithstanding Security Council Resolution 276 (1970)*, Advisory Opinion, Separate opinion de Castro, ICJ Reports 1971, 170.

689 UNSC resolution 284 (1970) of 29 July 1970, UN doc. S/RES/284(1970) which requested the *Namibia* advisory opinion was passed by 12 votes in favor to none against with three abstentions (Poland, the UK and the USSR). Arguing that a request for an advisory opinion constitutes a "procedural matter" in the sense of Article 27 para. 2 UNC, see *R. Kolb*, The International Court of Justice, 2013, 1044.

690 UNGA resolution 44(I) of 8 December 1946, UN doc. A/RES/44(I).

691 *Legality of the Threat or Use of Nuclear Weapons*, Advisory Opinion, ICJ Reports 1996, 226.

majority vote.[692] Nevertheless, the ICJ gave the requested advisory opinion without addressing the issue of the quorum, thus implicitly finding that a request for an advisory opinion is not an "important question" within the meaning of Article 18 para. 2 UNC.[693] This practice was confirmed in the *Wall* case, the *Kosovo* case and the *Chagos* case.[694] It thus seems accepted practice that the UNGA may request advisory opinions by simple majority.[695]

Other UN organs and specialized agencies require an authorization by the UNGA to request advisory opinions from the ICJ. It seems convincing to treat the authorization of other organs by the UNGA as a matter which falls within the purview of Article 18 para. 3 UNC and thus requiring a simple majority. The UNGA may grant conditional authorization,[696] although it has never made use of this right.[697] The UNGA has granted authorization to two principal organs of the UN: the ECOSOC[698] and the Trusteeship Council[699]. Thus, among the principal organs of the UN only the ICJ and the UNSG are not authorized to request advisory opinions, the former because it is unable to seize itself, the latter because it was generally feared that such a power could shift the balance of powers within the UN too much in favor of the UNSG.[700] The UNGA has further authorized

692 UNGA resolution 49/75(K) of 15 December 1994, UN doc. A/RES/49/75(K), which requested the *Legality of the Threat or Use of Nuclear Weapons* advisory opinion, was passed by 78 votes in favor and 43 votes against with 38 abstentions.

693 *K. Oellers-Frahm/E. Lagrange*, in: B. Simma/D.-E. Khan/G. Nolte/A. Paulus (eds.), The Charter of the United Nations, 4. ed., 2024: Art. 96, para. 13.

694 Ibid., para. 13.

695 *R. Kolb*, The International Court of Justice, 2013, 1043; *K. Oellers-Frahm/E. Lagrange*, in: B. Simma/D.-E. Khan/G. Nolte/A. Paulus (eds.), The Charter of the United Nations, 4. ed., 2024: Art. 96, para. 13; *Keith* argues that the necessary quorum depends on the subject-matter of the request, see *K. J. Keith*, The extent of the advisory jurisdiction of the International Court of Justice, 1971, 45 et seq.

696 *K. J. Keith*, The extent of the advisory jurisdiction of the International Court of Justice, 1971, 39; *M. N. Shaw*, Rosenne's Law and Practice of the International Court: 1920-2015, 5th ed 2016, Vol. 1 Ch. 5 § 60.

697 *R. Kolb*, The Elgar companion to the International Court of Justice, 2014, 263. If the UNGA grants its authorization subject to further conditions, the fulfilment of these conditions may be examined by the ICJ, *M. N. Shaw*, Rosenne's Law and Practice of the International Court: 1920-2015, 5th ed 2016, Vol. 1 Ch. 5 § 60.

698 UNGA resolution 89(I) of 11 December 1946, UN doc. A/RES/89(I).

699 UNGA resolution 171(II) of 14 November 1947, UN doc. A/RES/171(II).

700 *R. Kolb*, The Elgar companion to the International Court of Justice, 2014, 265.

one subsidiary organ of the UNGA[701], 15 specialized agencies[702] and one independent related organization[703].

2. Question arising within the requesting organ's scope of activities

Article 96 para. 2 UNC further stipulates that the legal question on which an advisory opinion is requested must arise within the requesting organ's scope of activities. An organ's "scope of activities" or "field of jurisdiction"[704] is determined by the organization's constituent instrument.[705] In order to determine an organ's scope of activities one must therefore interpret the organization's constituent instrument, particularly the provisions relating to the powers of the organization and its organs.

701 The UNGA authorized the Interim Committee of the General Assembly in resolutions 196(III) of 3 December 1948, UN doc. A/RES/196(III) and 295(IV) of 21 November 1949, UN doc. A/RES/295(IV).

702 The authorized specialized agencies of the UN are: the International Labour Organization (ILO), the Food and Agriculture Organization (FAO), the United Nations Educational, Scientific and Cultural Organization (UNESCO), the International Civil Aviation Organization (ICAO), the World Health Organization (WHO), the International Bank for Reconstruction and Development (IBRD), the International Finance Corporation (IFC), the International Development Association (IDA), the International Monetary Fund (IMF), the International Telecommunication Union (ITU), the World Meteorological Organization (WMO), the International Maritime Organization (IMO), the World Intellectual Property Organization (WIPO), the International Fund for Agricultural Development (IFAD), and the United Nations Industrial Development Organization (UNIDO). For a list of all authorized organs, see Report of the International Court of Justice (2022–2023), 14, https://www.icj-cij.org/sites/default/files/2023-10/2022-2023-en_0.pdf.

703 The UNGA authorized the International Atomic Energy Agency (IAEA) in UNGA resolution 1146(XII) of 14 November 1957, UN doc. A/RES/1146(XII).

704 *R. Kolb*, The Elgar companion to the International Court of Justice, 2014, 263.

705 Ibid., 263; *P. d'Argent*, in: A. Zimmermann/C. J. Tams/K. Oellers-Frahm/C. Tomuschat/D. W. K. Anderson (eds.), The Statute of the International Court of Justice, 3. ed., 2019: Article 65, para. 33.

a) ICJ interprets "scope of activities" narrowly

In the 1996 *Nuclear Weapons* case[706], the ICJ refused to give the advisory opinion requested by the WHO finding that the question did not arise within the WHO's scope of activities:

> "Having arrived at the view that the request for an advisory opinion submitted by the WHO does not relate to a question which arises "within the scope of [the] activities" of that Organization in accordance with Article 96, paragraph 2, of the Charter, the Court finds that an essential condition of founding its jurisdiction in the present case is absent and that it cannot, accordingly, give the opinion requested."[707]

In particular, the ICJ found that the question of the *legality* of the use of nuclear weapons was beyond the scope of the WHO's activities. The Court reasoned that the WHO is only competent to assess the *effects* of the use of nuclear weapons on the health of human beings.[708] However, this assessment of the effects of nuclear weapons, according to the Court, is independent from the *legal assessment* of the use of nuclear weapons.[709] The WHO may fulfil its functions regarding the protection of human health without knowing whether the specific use of nuclear weapons violates international law.[710] For this reason, the WHO was not competent to ask the Court for a legal opinion on the lawfulness of the use of nuclear weapons.

The reasoning of the Court is plausible but not beyond reproach. Article 2 lit. (v) of the WHO Constitution[711] states that the function of the WHO is "generally to take all necessary action to attain the objective of the Organization". The objectives of the WHO are described in Article 1 WHO

---

706 *Legality of the Use by a State of Nuclear Weapons in Armed Conflict*, Advisory Opinion, ICJ Reports 1996, 66; on the Nuclear Weapons (WHO) opinion, see *D. Akande*, 9 EJIL 3 (1998), 437; on both Nuclear Weapons opinions, see L. Boisson de Chazournes, P. Sands (eds.), International law, the World Court of justice and nuclear weapons, 1999.

707 *Legality of the Use by a State of Nuclear Weapons in Armed Conflict*, Advisory Opinion, ICJ Reports 1996, 66 (84, para. 31).

708 Ibid. (76 para. 21).

709 Ibid.; in favor *R. Kolb*, The Elgar companion to the International Court of Justice, 2014, 267.

710 *Legality of the Use by a State of Nuclear Weapons in Armed Conflict*, Advisory Opinion, ICJ Reports 1996, 66 (77 para. 22).

711 Constitution of the World Health Organization, signed 22 July 1946, entry into force 7 April 1948, 14 UNTS 185.

Constitution as the "attainment by all peoples of the highest possible level of health".

It seems at least possible that an advisory opinion of the ICJ on the general illegality of the use of nuclear weapons could deter states from using nuclear weapons. The request could thus be seen as a preventative measure by the WHO. This line of reasoning is supported by Article 2 lit. (k) WHO Constitution, according to which the WHO is empowered "to propose conventions, agreements and regulations, and make recommendations with respect to international health matters".

It seems unclear how the WHO is supposed to meaningfully contribute to the development of conventions without knowing the legal *status quo*. The opinion indicates that the ICJ interprets the requirement that the question must arise within the requesting organ's scope of activities narrowly – at least where it concerns requests from specialized organizations such as the WHO.

b) Applying the "scope of activities" limitation to the UNSC and the UNGA

The wording of Article 96 para. 2 UNC seems to indicate that only the specifically authorized organs must meet the additional requirement that the question they refer to the Court must arise within their scope of activity.[712] However, many commentators argue that the UNSC and the UNGA are also limited by their scope of activities when requesting advisory opinions from the ICJ.[713]

According to *Kolb*, the difference in wording between "any legal question" in para. 1 and "legal questions arising within the scope of the

712 *A. Zimmermann*, Uniting-for-Peace und Gutachtenanfragen der Generalversammlung: Anmerkungen aus Anlaß des Gutachtens des Internationalen Gerichtshofes zur Zulässigkeit des Sicherheitszaunes zwischen Israel und den palästinensischen Gebieten, in: K. Dicke/S. Hobe/K.-U. Meyn/A. Peters/E. Riedel/H.-J. Schütz/C. Tietje (eds.), Weltinnenrecht, 2005, 909 (918); *T. Thienel*, Drittstaaten und die Jurisdiktion des Internationalen Gerichtshofs. Die Monetary Gold-Doktrin, 2016, 205.

713 *H. Kelsen*, The law of the United Nations, 2. ed. 1951, 546; *R. Kolb*, The International Court of Justice, 2013, 1046–1047; *M. N. Shaw*, Rosenne's Law and Practice of the International Court: 1920-2015, 5th ed 2016, Vol. 1 Ch. 5 § 60; cf. *J. A. Frowein/K. Oellers-Frahm*, in: A. Zimmermann/C. Tomuschat/K. Oellers-Frahm/C. J. Tams/M. Kashgar/D. Diehl (eds.), The Statute of the International Court of Justice, 2. ed., 2012: Art. 65, para. 16.

activities" in para. 2 is merely intended to emphasize the special importance of the UNSC and the UNGA as well as their equal status with the ICJ.[714] *Shaw* argues that the difference is intended to emphasize that the UNGA and UNSC have broad competences, while the bodies mentioned in para. 2 have specialized competences.[715] Nonetheless, no organ, including the UNGA and the UNSC, could act outside their own competences, even when requesting advisory opinions from the Court.[716]

The ICJ initially rejected the argument that questions referred to the Court by the UNGA or the UNSC must also arise within the organs' scope of activities.[717] More recently, however, the ICJ left the question either unanswered,[718] or – without explicitly making it a jurisdictional requirement – examined if the question related to the UNGA's scope of activities.[719] Despite the difference in wording, it thus seems that the UNSC and the UNGA are also limited by their respective scope of activities when requesting advisory opinions.

In practice, however, the scope of activities of the two organs as formulated in the UNC is so broad that hardly any request could be considered *ultra vires*.[720] The UNSC's scope of activities extends to the "maintenance of international peace and security" (Article 24 UNC). In particular, the UNSC's broad understanding of the term "threats to peace" in Article 39 UNC[721] extends the scope of its activities significantly. The UNGA's scope

---

714 *R. Kolb*, The International Court of Justice, 2013, 1046–1047.

715 *M. N. Shaw*, Rosenne's Law and Practice of the International Court: 1920-2015, 5th ed 2016, Vol. 1 Ch. 5 § 60.

716 Ibid., Vol. 1 Ch. 5 § 60.

717 *Application for Review of Judgment No. 273 of the United Nations Administrative Tribunal*, Advisory Opinion, ICJ Reports 1982, 325 (333-334, para. 21).

718 *Legality of the Threat or Use of Nuclear Weapons*, Advisory Opinion, ICJ Reports 1996, 226 (233, para. 11).

719 *Legal Consequences of the Construction of a Wall in the Occupied Palestinian Territory*, Advisory Opinion, ICJ Reports 2004, 136 (145, paras. 15 et seq.); *Accordance with international law of the unilateral declaration of independence in respect of Kosovo*, Advisory Opinion, ICJ Reports 2010, 403 (413-414, paras. 21 et seq.).

720 *K. Oellers-Frahm*, in: B. Simma/D.-E. Khan/G. Nolte/A. Paulus (eds.), The Charter of the United Nations, 3. ed., 2012: Art. 96, para. 14; arguing that requests made by the UNSC and the UNGA are not limited to the organs' scope of activities, see in the most recent edition *K. Oellers-Frahm/E. Lagrange*, in: B. Simma/D.-E. Khan/G. Nolte/A. Paulus (eds.), The Charter of the United Nations, 4. ed., 2024: Art. 96, para. 11.

721 See on this *K. Wellens*, 8 Journal of Conflict and Security Law 1 (2003), 15.

of activities potentially extends even further.[722] According to Article 10 UNC, the UNGA may discuss "any question or any matter" within the scope of the UNC. According to Article 11 para. 2 UNC, this explicitly extends to questions relating to the maintenance of international peace and security.[723]

c) Relationship between the UNGA and the UNSC

While any matter within the scope of the UNC also falls within the scope of activities of the UNGA, this does not mean that the UNGA can always request an advisory opinion on such a matter. Instead, the UNGA's competence to request advisory opinions from the ICJ is also limited by the relationship between the UNGA and the UNSC. Article 12 para. 1 UNC gives the UNSC priority when dealing with "disputes or situations". It stipulates:

> "While the Security Council is exercising in respect of any dispute or situation the functions assigned to it in the present Charter, the General Assembly shall not make any recommendation with regard to that dispute or situation unless the Security Council so requests."

In the *Wall* case, Israel relied on this provision to argue that the UNGA acted *ultra vires* when it requested an advisory opinion on the legal consequences of the construction of the wall in the occupied Palestinian territory while the UNSC was also actively engaged in the Israel-Palestine-conflict.[724] The case was preceded by various resolutions of the two organs.[725] On 14 October 2003, the USA vetoed a resolution by the UNSC which would have declared the Israeli construction of the wall in the occupied

722 *M. Lippold*, in: B. Simma/D.-E. Khan/G. Nolte/A. Paulus (eds.), The Charter of the United Nations, 4. ed., 2024: Art. 7, para. 10.

723 See on this *Legal Consequences of the Construction of a Wall in the Occupied Palestinian Territory*, Advisory Opinion, ICJ Reports 2004, 136 (145, para. 17).

724 Ibid. (148, para. 24).

725 For a description of the chronology of UNSC and UNGA involvement in the case, see *A. Zimmermann*, Uniting-for-Peace und Gutachtenanfragen der Generalversammlung: Anmerkungen aus Anlaß des Gutachtens des Internationalen Gerichtshofes zur Zulässigkeit des Sicherheitszaunes zwischen Israel und den palästinensischen Gebieten, in: K. Dicke/S. Hobe/K.-U. Meyn/A. Peters/E. Riedel/H.-J. Schütz/C. Tietje (eds.), Weltinnenrecht, 2005, 909 (910–911).

territories illegal under international law.[726] Following this veto, the UNGA reconvened the Tenth Emergency Special Session and passed a resolution in which it declared the border facilities to violate international law.[727] Shortly afterwards, the UNSC passed a resolution in which it called on the parties to the dispute to fulfil their obligations under the "Roadmap"[728] and decided to "remain seized of the matter".[729] A few days later, the UNGA requested an advisory opinion from the Court on the legal consequences of the construction of wall by Israel.[730] Israel argued the UNGA acted *ultra vires* when it convened the Tenth Emergency Special Session, because the requirements of the Uniting for Peace Resolution were not fulfilled.[731] Israel further argued that the UNGA could not have requested the advisory opinion under its general competence because of the active involvement of the UNSC.[732] The Court thus had to address the question whether Article 12 UNC prohibits the UNGA from requesting an advisory opinion about a matter of which the UNSC was already seized.[733]

Article 12 para. 1 UNC prohibits the UNGA from making recommendations regarding a dispute or situation while the UNSC exercises its functions regarding that dispute or situation. This is a reflection of the UNSC's "primary responsibility for the maintenance of international peace and security" enshrined in Article 24 para. 1 UNC.

In the early years of the UN, the UNSC and the UNGA interpreted Article 12 para. 1 UNC as prohibiting the UNGA from making recommen-

726 UNSC draft resolution S/2003/973 of 9 October 2003.

727 UNGA resolution ES-10/13 of 27 October 2003, UN doc. A/RES/ES-10/13.

728 The so-called "Quartet", consisting of representatives of the United States of America, the European Union, Russia and the United Nations, prepared a proposal to resolve the Israeli-Palestinian conflict entitled "A performance-based road map to a permanent two-State solution to the Israeli-Palestinian conflict", see S/2003/529, Annex.

729 UNSC resolution 1515 (2003) of 19 November 2003, UN doc. S/RES/1515(2003).

730 UNGA resolution ES-10/14 of 3 December 2003, UN doc. A/RES/ES-10/14.

731 ICJ Pleadings, *Legal Consequences of the Construction of a Wall in the Occupied Palestinian Territory*, Written Statements of Israel, paras. 4.28 et seq.

732 Ibid., paras. 4.46 et seq.

733 See on this also *A. Zimmermann*, Uniting-for-Peace und Gutachtenanfragen der Generalversammlung: Anmerkungen aus Anlaß des Gutachtens des Internationalen Gerichtshofes zur Zulässigkeit des Sicherheitszaunes zwischen Israel und den palästinensischen Gebieten, in: K. Dicke/S. Hobe/K.-U. Meyn/A. Peters/E. Riedel/H.-J. Schütz/C. Tietje (eds.), Weltinnenrecht, 2005, 909 (917 et seq).

dations on any issue that was on the agenda of the UNSC.[734] On several occasions, the UNSC removed items from its agenda to allow the UNGA to make recommendations.[735] Over time, the UNGA started interpreting the words "is exercising the functions" in Article 12 UNC as meaning "is exercising the functions at this moment".[736] The UNGA thus started to make recommendations on matters that were on the UNSC's agenda, but on which the Council has not recently acted.[737] This interpretation led to the two organs dealing in parallel with the same matters, often focusing on different sub-topics.[738]

Based on this developed practice, the Court found in the *Wall* case, that the request made by the UNGA was in line with Article 12 para. 1 UNC.[739] A recent example of this "complementary relationship"[740] between the UNSC and the UNGA are the actions taken by the UNGA in the context of Russia's war of aggression against Ukraine. After a UNSC resolution condemning Russia's invasion of Ukraine was vetoed by Russia, the UNSC called for an emergency special session of the UNGA.[741] The UNGA subsequently adopted resolutions "deplor[ing] in the strongest terms the aggression by the Russian Federation against Ukraine in violation of Article 2(4) of the Charter"[742] and deciding that whenever a permanent member

734 In 1949, the UNGA thus did not comment on the question of Indonesia because the UNSC was already seized of the matter, see Official Records of the General Assembly, Fourth Session, Ad Hoc Political Committee, Summary Records of Meetings, 56th Meeting, 3 December 1949, 339 para. 118.

735 Official Records of the Security Council, First Year: Second Series, No. 21, 79th Meeting, 4 November 1946, 498 (regarding Spain); Second Year: No. 89, 202nd Meeting, 15 September 1947, 2404–2405 (regarding the Greek border); Fifth Year, No. 48, 506th Meeting, 29 September 1950, 5 (regarding Taiwan); Sixth Year, S/PV.531, 541st Meeting, 31 January 1951, 11–12, para. 57 (Republic of Korea).

736 UNGA, Twenty-third Session, Third Committee, 1637th meeting, A/C.3/SR.1637, para. 9.

737 See UNGA resolution 1600 (XV) of 15 April 1961, UN doc. A/RES/1600(XV) (on the Congo) and UNGA resolution 1913 (XVIII) of 3 December 1963, UN doc. A/RES/1913(XVIII) (on Portuguese colonies).

738 *Legal Consequences of the Construction of a Wall in the Occupied Palestinian Territory*, Advisory Opinion, ICJ Reports 2004, 136 (149-150, para. 27).

739 Ibid. (150, para. 28).

740 *M. Lippold*, in: B. Simma/D.-E. Khan/G. Nolte/A. Paulus (eds.), The Charter of the United Nations, 4. ed., 2024: Art. 7, para. 11.

741 UNSC resolution 2623 of 27 Feburary 2022, UN doc. S/RES/263(2022).

742 UNGA resolution ES-11/1 of 2 March 2022, UN doc. A/RES/ES-11/1, para. 2.

of the UNSC vetoes a resolution, the UNGA will "hold a debate on the situation as to which the veto was cast"[743].

The Court also found that a request for an advisory opinion was not in itself a "recommendation" by the UNGA with regard to a dispute or situation.[744] This view finds support in literature.[745] The ordinary meaning (cf. Article 31 para. 1 VCLT) of the word "recommendation" implies a non-binding legal act expressing a desire.[746] A request for an advisory opinion, however, goes beyond a mere non-binding desire as it compels the Court to issue the requested advisory opinion unless there are compelling reasons not to.[747]

II. Jurisdiction ratione materiae – "any legal question"

According to Article 96 para. 1 UNC and Article 65 para. 1 ICJ Statute, the ICJ may address "any legal question" by means of its advisory opinions, including questions of interpretation of the provisions of the UNC.[748]

---

743 UNGA resolution 79/262 of 26 April 2022, UN doc. A/RES/76/262, para. 1.

744 *Legal Consequences of the Construction of a Wall in the Occupied Palestinian Territory*, Advisory Opinion, ICJ Reports 2004, 136 (148, para. 25); *Accordance with international law of the unilateral declaration of independence in respect of Kosovo*, Advisory Opinion, ICJ Reports 2010, 403 (414, para. 24).

745 *A. Zimmermann*, Uniting-for-Peace und Gutachtenanfragen der Generalversammlung: Anmerkungen aus Anlaß des Gutachtens des Internationalen Gerichtshofes zur Zulässigkeit des Sicherheitszaunes zwischen Israel und den palästinensischen Gebieten, in: K. Dicke/S. Hobe/K.-U. Meyn/A. Peters/E. Riedel/H.-J. Schütz/C. Tietje (eds.), Weltinnenrecht, 2005, 909 (917 et seq).

746 *E. Klein/S. Schmahl*, in: B. Simma/D.-E. Khan/G. Nolte/A. Paulus (eds.), The Charter of the United Nations, 3. ed., 2012: Art. 10, para. 48.

747 *A. Zimmermann*, Uniting-for-Peace und Gutachtenanfragen der Generalversammlung: Anmerkungen aus Anlaß des Gutachtens des Internationalen Gerichtshofes zur Zulässigkeit des Sicherheitszaunes zwischen Israel und den palästinensischen Gebieten, in: K. Dicke/S. Hobe/K.-U. Meyn/A. Peters/E. Riedel/H.-J. Schütz/C. Tietje (eds.), Weltinnenrecht, 2005, 909 (918–919).

748 *Conditions of Admission of a State to Membership in the United Nations (Article 4 of the Charter)*, Advisory Opinion, ICJ Reports 1948, 57 (61); *Competence of the General Assembly for the Admission of a State to the United Nations*, Advisory Opinion, ICJ Reports 1950, 4 (6) In 1947, the UNGA called upon all authorized organs of the UN to make use of the Court's advisory jurisdiction to receive guidance on the interpretation of the UNC, see UNGA resolution 171(II) of 14 November 1947, UN doc. A/RES/171(II).

1. Political questions

The only express restriction of the Court's subject-matter jurisdiction is contained in the word "legal". The Court distinguishes between legal questions on the one hand and political or moral questions on the other hand.[749] Purely political questions do not fall within the purview of the Court.[750] The first time the Court had to do distinguish between political and legal questions was in the two *Admissions* advisory opinions.[751] In the first case, the UNGA requested advice on whether a UN Member State could make its consent to the admission of new Member States subject to conditions that are not explicitly mentioned in Article 4 para. 1 UNC.[752] In the second opinion, the UNGA inquired whether it could admit a new Member State without a recommendation from the UNSC.[753] The questions concerned the admission to the UN and the voting procedure of a political body of the UN, which lent them a political dimension.[754] However, the ICJ found that they were questions of interpretation of Article 4 UNC and thus legal questions in the sense of Article 96 UNC and Article 65 ICJ Statute. The ICJ held:

749 *Conditions of Admission of a State to Membership in the United Nations (Article 4 of the Charter)*, Advisory Opinion, ICJ Reports 1948, 57 (58); *Competence of the General Assembly for the Admission of a State to the United Nations*, Advisory Opinion, ICJ Reports 1950, 4 (5); *Western Sahara*, Advisory Opinion, ICJ Reports 1975, 12 (18, para. 15); *Interpretation of the Agreement of 25 March 1951 between the WHO and Egypt*, Advisory Opinion, ICJ Reports 1980, 73 (87, para. 33); *Legality of the Threat or Use of Nuclear Weapons*, Advisory Opinion, ICJ Reports 1996, 226 (234, para. 13); *Accordance with international law of the unilateral declaration of independence in respect of Kosovo*, Advisory Opinion, ICJ Reports 2010, 403 (415, para. 27); on the distinction between legal and political questions, see *D. W. Greig*, 15 ICLQ 2-3 (1966), 325.

750 *J. A. Frowein/K. Oellers-Frahm*, in: A. Zimmermann/C. Tomuschat/K. Oellers-Frahm/C. J. Tams/M. Kashgar/D. Diehl (eds.), The Statute of the International Court of Justice, 2. ed., 2012: Art. 65, para. 22; *P. d'Argent*, in: A. Zimmermann/C. J. Tams/K. Oellers-Frahm/C. Tomuschat/D. W. K. Anderson (eds.), The Statute of the International Court of Justice, 3. ed., 2019: Article 65, para. 21.

751 *Conditions of Admission of a State to Membership in the United Nations (Article 4 of the Charter)*, Advisory Opinion, ICJ Reports 1948, 57; *Competence of the General Assembly for the Admission of a State to the United Nations*, Advisory Opinion, ICJ Reports 1950, 4.

752 *Conditions of Admission of a State to Membership in the United Nations (Article 4 of the Charter)*, Advisory Opinion, ICJ Reports 1948, 57 (58).

753 *Competence of the General Assembly for the Admission of a State to the United Nations*, Advisory Opinion, ICJ Reports 1950, 4 (5).

754 *F. B. Sloan*, 38 CLR 5 (1950), 830 (843).

> "The Court cannot attribute a political character to a request which, framed in abstract terms, invites it to undertake an essentially judicial task, the interpretation of a treaty provision. It is not concerned with the motives which may have inspired this request [...]."[755]

The Court has continuously emphasized that a political dimension of a question will not deprive the Court of its competence to answer the question, if the question has a legal element to it.[756] If the Court can clearly distinguish between a legal and a political part of a question, the Court will only answer the legal part. The controversial *International Status of South-West Africa* advisory opinion[757] provides an example of this. After the Court rejected a legal obligation of the Union of South Africa to place the administration of then South-West Africa (Namibia) under the system of the UN Trusteeship Council, it declined to elaborate on the political consequences:

> "It is not for the Court to pronounce on the political or moral duties which these considerations may involve."[758]

2. Questions of fact, historical questions, interpretation of the UN Charter

While the Court lacks the resources, in particular the personnel, to conduct its own fact-finding missions, it may nevertheless address factual questions which underlie the legal question it is asked to answer. As the Court held in its *Namibia* advisory opinion:

> "[T]he contingency that there may be factual issues underlying the question posed does not alter its character as a 'legal question' as envis-

755 *Conditions of Admission of a State to Membership in the United Nations (Article 4 of the Charter)*, Advisory Opinion, ICJ Reports 1948, 57 (61).

756 *Legality of the Threat or Use of Nuclear Weapons*, Advisory Opinion, ICJ Reports 1996, 226 (234, para. 13); *Accordance with international law of the unilateral declaration of independence in respect of Kosovo*, Advisory Opinion, ICJ Reports 2010, 403 (415, para. 27); *R. Kolb*, The Elgar companion to the International Court of Justice, 2014, 267.

757 *International Status of South-West Africa*, Advisory Opinion, ICJ Reports 1950, 128; on the opinion, see *C. Heyns/M. Killander*, South West Africa/Namibia (Advisory Opinions and Judgments) (last updated 2007), in: A. Peters/R. Wolfrum (eds.), The Max Planck Encyclopedia of Public International Law, 2008 (9 et seq.).

758 *International Status of South-West Africa*, Advisory Opinion, ICJ Reports 1950, 128 (140).

> aged in Article 96 of the Charter. The reference in this provision to legal questions cannot be interpreted as opposing legal to factual issues. Normally, to enable a court to pronounce on legal questions, it must also be acquainted with, take into account and, if necessary, make findings as to the relevant factual issues."[759]

The ICJ held that "[i]t is for the Court to assess the sufficiency of the information available to it."[760] Furthermore, the Court is not limited to address existing rights and obligations, but it may also address relevant historical legal questions. This was confirmed by the Court in its *Western Sahara* opinion:

> "[T]here is nothing in the Charter or Statute to limit either the competence of the General Assembly to request an advisory opinion, or the competence of the Court to give one, to legal questions relating to existing rights or obligations. [...] [T]he references to "any legal question" in the above-mentioned provisions of the Charter and Statute are not to be interpreted restrictively."[761]

D. The question of state consent

States have claimed in various advisory proceedings that the ICJ may only give an advisory opinion on their legal disputes with their consent.[762] This idea which lies at the heart of the Eastern Carelia doctrine has been referred to as "[t]he most important challenge to the competence of the Court".[763]

---

759 *Legal Consequences for States of the Continued Presence of South Africa in Namibia (South West Africa) notwithstanding Security Council Resolution 276 (1970)*, Advisory Opinion, ICJ Reports 1971, 16 (27, para. 40).

760 *Legal Consequences of the Construction of a Wall in the Occupied Palestinian Territory*, Advisory Opinion, ICJ Reports 2004, 136 (20, para. 47).

761 *Western Sahara*, Advisory Opinion, ICJ Reports 1975, 12 (27, para. 40).

762 See in detail *supra*: § 3.

763 *F. B. Sloan*, 38 CLR 5 (1950), 830 (845); discussing state consent as a jurisdictional requirement of the Court's advisory procedure see *K. J. Keith*, The extent of the advisory jurisdiction of the International Court of Justice, 1971, 89 et seq; *D. Pratap*, The advisory jurisdiction of the International Court, 1972, 154 et seq.; *M. Pomerance*, The advisory function of the International Court in the League and U.N. eras, 1973, 287 et seq.; *K. J. Keith*, 16 AYBIL 39 (1996), 39-58 (43 et seq.); *C. F. Amerasinghe*, Jurisdiction of International Tribunals, 2003, 528 et seq.; *M. M. Aljaghoub*, The Advisory Function of the International Court of Justice 1946 - 2005, 2006, 97 et seq.; *M. M. Aljaghoub*, 24 ALQ 2 (2010), 191.

However, an interpretation of the legal framework of the Court's advisory jurisdiction demonstrates that there is no basis for such an objection. The wording of Article 96 UNC and Article 65 ICJ Statute indicate no consent requirement. Considering the provision's context, it becomes apparent that the ICJ has the power to address inter-state disputes without the affected states' consent.

I. Grammatical interpretation

Despite there being no hierarchical order between the different methods of treaty interpretation, the logical starting point for interpreting a treaty is the text of the treaty provision in light of its ordinary meaning.[764] Neither Article 96 UNC nor Article 65 ICJ Statute expressly stipulate a condition of state consent or expressly exclude bilateral disputes from the purview of the Court's advisory jurisdiction. According to the two provisions, the advisory opinion procedure is a procedure which takes place between two entities: the ICJ and the requesting UN organ. Article 96 para. 1 UNC and Article 65 para. 1 ICJ Statute stipulate that the Court may address within its advisory opinions "any legal question". The inclusion of the word "any" indicates a broad subject-matter jurisdiction. Bilateral legal disputes clearly entail legal questions. A first reading of the text of Articles 96 UNC and 65 ICJ Statute thus seems to indicate that the Court may address inter-state disputes within its advisory jurisdiction without the consent of the disputing states.[765]

The Court's subject-matter jurisdiction is further qualified by Article 96 para. 2 UNC. Accordingly, the legal question which forms the subject-mat-

764 "[T]he first duty of a tribunal which is called upon to interpret and apply the provisions of a treaty, is to endeavour to give effect to them in their natural and ordinary meaning in the context in which they occur. If the relevant words in their natural and ordinary meaning make sense in their context, that is an end of the matter. If, on the other hand, the words in their natural and ordinary meaning are ambiguous or lead to an unreasonable result, then, and then only, must the Court, by resort to other methods of interpretation, seek to ascertain what the parties really did mean when they used these words.", *Competence of the General Assembly for the Admission of a State to the United Nations*, Advisory Opinion, ICJ Reports 1950, 4 (8); Gardiner argues that the ICJ recognized here the interpretation in accordance with a term's ordinary meaning as "the starting point of an interpretation", *R. K. Gardiner*, Treaty interpretation, 2nd ed. 2015, 185.

765 Cf. *P. d'Argent*, in: A. Zimmermann/C. J. Tams/K. Oellers-Frahm/C. Tomuschat/D. W. K. Anderson (eds.), The Statute of the International Court of Justice, 3. ed., 2019: Article 65, paras. 27–30.

ter of the request for an advisory opinion must arise within the requesting organ's scope of activities. If inter-state legal disputes necessarily fell outside the scope of activities of the requesting UN organs, Article 96 para. 2 UNC would support the Eastern Carelia doctrine.[766] The organ's scope of activities is determined by the organ's constituent instrument.[767] To determine whether the UNGA or the UNSC could request an advisory opinion on a legal question which forms the subject-matter of an inter-state dispute, one must therefore refer to other provisions within the UNC. We thus move to the second method of treaty interpretation, the provision's context.

II. Context

The entire text of the treaty is to be taken into account as the provision's "context".[768] This includes the treaty's title, preamble, annexes and potential protocols, as well as the systematic position of the relevant provision within the treaty.[769]

766 On limiting an organ's power to request advisory opinions to its scope of activities, see *H. Kelsen*, The law of the United Nations, 2. ed. 1951, 546; *S. Rosenne*, The law and practice of the International Court, 1920-2005, 4th ed. 2006, 290; *R. Kolb*, The International Court of Justice, 2013, 1046–1047; *M. N. Shaw*, Rosenne's Law and Practice of the International Court: 1920-2015, 5th ed 2016, § 60; cf. *J. A. Frowein/K. Oellers-Frahm*, in: A. Zimmermann/C. Tomuschat/K. Oellers-Frahm/C. J. Tams/M. Kashgar/D. Diehl (eds.), The Statute of the International Court of Justice, 2. ed., 2012: Art. 65, para. 16; arguing for an unlimited material scope, see *A. Zimmermann*, Uniting-for-Peace und Gutachtenanfragen der Generalversammlung: Anmerkungen aus Anlaß des Gutachtens des Internationalen Gerichtshofes zur Zulässigkeit des Sicherheitszaunes zwischen Israel und den palästinensischen Gebieten, in: K. Dicke/S. Hobe/K.-U. Meyn/A. Peters/E. Riedel/H.-J. Schütz/C. Tietje (eds.), Weltinnenrecht, 2005, 909 (918); *T. Thienel*, Drittstaaten und die Jurisdiktion des Internationalen Gerichtshofs. Die Monetary Gold-Doktrin, 2016, 205.

767 *R. Kolb*, The Elgar companion to the International Court of Justice, 2014, 263; *P. d'Argent*, in: A. Zimmermann/C. J. Tams/K. Oellers-Frahm/C. Tomuschat/D. W. K. Anderson (eds.), The Statute of the International Court of Justice, 3. ed., 2019: Article 65, para. 33.

768 *O. Dörr*, in: O. Dörr/K. Schmalenbach (eds.), Vienna Convention on the Law of Treaties, 2. ed., 2018: Art. 31, para. 44.

769 Ibid., para. 44.

1. Provisions governing the scope of activities of the UNGA and UNSC

Having regard to the UNC provisions, it becomes apparent that inter-state legal disputes regularly fall within the scope of activities of both the UNGA and the UNSC.

Article 10 UNC stipulates that the UNGA "may discuss *any questions* or *any matters* within the scope of the present Charter".[770] According to Article 14 UNC, the UNGA "may recommend measures for the peaceful adjustment of *any situation*, regardless of origin, which it deems likely to impair the *general welfare* or *friendly relations* among nations, including situations resulting from a violation of the provisions of the present Charter setting forth the Purposes and Principles of the United Nations".[771] While this responsibility of the UNGA may be superseded by the UNSC if the latter decides to exercise its functions (Article 12 UNC), Article 14 UNC nevertheless clearly stipulates a *prima facie* responsibility of the UNGA to address "any situation" which may negatively affect the "general welfare or friendly relations among nations".[772] Inter-state legal disputes have the potential to negatively affect the general welfare or friendly relations among nations and thus fall within the scope of activities of the UNGA.

Even more so than the UNGA's activities are the UNSC's activities geared towards the settlement of specific inter-state disputes. The UNSC has the "primary responsibility for the maintenance of international peace and security" (Article 24 UNC), which it fulfils through exercising its competences under Chapters VI to VIII. Chapter VI is entitled "Pacific Settlement of Disputes" and gives the UNSC a pivotal role in the settlement of inter-state disputes. The UNSC "may investigate any dispute, or any situation which might lead to international friction or give rise to a dispute" (Article 34 UNC) and "may, at any stage of a dispute (...) recommend appropriate procedures or methods of adjustment" (Article 36 para. 1 UNC). Chapter VII grants the UNSC the power to "determine the existence of any threat to the peace, breach of the peace, or act of aggression" and to "make recommendations, or decide what measures shall be taken (...) to maintain or restore international peace and security" (Article 39 UNC).

---

770 Emphasis added.

771 Emphasis added.

772 Even if the UNSC decides to exercise its functions over a situation or dispute, the UNGA may nevertheless request an advisory opinion on the matter. On the relationship between the UNSC and the UNGA, see *supra*: § 5 Section C.I.2.c).

Thus, inter-state legal disputes regularly fall within the scope of activities of the UNGA and the UNSC.[773]

2. No consent requirement in Articles 66–68 ICJ Statute

Inter-state disputes may be brought before the ICJ by means of the Court's contentious procedure. In such a case, the disputing states' consent is required, see Article 36 ICJ Statute. However, the consent requirement enshrined in Article 36 ICJ Statute does not apply to the Court's advisory procedure, as a closer look at the Articles 66 to 68 ICJ Statute reveals.

The only example the ICJ Statute references states in the context of the advisory procedure is in Articles 66 and 67. According to Article 66 ICJ Statute, once a request for an advisory opinion has been made, the Court's Registrar notifies all states that are entitled to appear before the Court (para. 1), particularly those which are likely to furnish information on the submitted question (para. 2). According to Article 67 ICJ Statute, the Court's Registrar notifies all states that are "immediately concerned" prior to delivering its advisory opinion. None of these provisions contain any form of consent requirement, even though Article 67 ICJ Statute acknowledges that certain states may be "immediately concerned" by ICJ advisory proceedings. The provision thus presupposes that the Court may issue advisory opinions on matters that affect certain states more than others.

Whereas the ICJ's contentious jurisdiction is subject to the prior consent of the disputing states (Article 36 ICJ Statute), there is no similar provision regarding the Court's advisory jurisdiction. One may be tempted to read Article 68 ICJ Statute as a reference to the consent requirement found in Article 36 ICJ Statute. Article 68 ICJ Statute states:

> "In the exercise of its advisory functions the Court shall further be guided by the provisions of the present Statute which apply in contentious cases to the extent to which it recognizes them to be applicable."

However, both the wording and the structure of the provision speak against the notion that the provision incorporates the contentious procedure's consent requirement into the advisory opinion procedure. Firstly, Article 68 ICJ Statute does not state that the Court "shall apply" the provisions which

773 Cf. *Legal Consequences of the Construction of a Wall in the Occupied Palestinian Territory*, Advisory Opinion, ICJ Reports 2004, 136 (145, para. 17).

apply in contentious cases, but that it "shall further be guided by" these provisions. If Article 68 ICJ Statute were to establish a consent requirement to the Court's advisory jurisdiction, this would not be aptly described as "mere guidance". Jurisdictional requirements are a *conditio sine qua non* for the Court's competence, not flexible guidelines.[774] Secondly, the Court shall only be guided "to the extent to which it recognizes [the provisions] to be applicable". In other words, the Court has discretion when applying the provisions applicable to contentious proceedings. As such, Article 68 ICJ Statute was designed to allow the Court a flexible recourse to the provisions which govern contentious cases.[775] Such flexibility, however, stands in contrast to the function of jurisdictional clauses which outline and delimit the competences of the Court and which apply without discretion.[776]

Articles 66–68 ICJ Statute thus do not contain any consent requirement nor incorporate the consent requirement into the advisory opinion procedure. In contrast, they indicate a broad advisory competence of the Court extending to inter-state disputes.

3. Rules of the Court expressly refer to inter-state disputes

The finding that the UNC and the ICJ Statute stipulate a broad advisory jurisdiction extending to inter-state disputes is further supported by reference to the Rules of the Court.

While the Rules of the Court are not binding treaty norms, they provide important legal guidance. Article 30 para. 1 ICJ Statute authorizes the Court to "frame rules for carrying out its functions" and in particular to "lay down rules of procedure". These rules of procedure, which are norms of a "delegated character",[777] are designed to fill gaps left by the

774 So also *Y. Shany*, Jurisdiction and Admissibility, in: C. Romano/K. J. Alter/Y. Shany (eds.), The Oxford Handbook of International Adjudication, 2013, 779 (787).

775 *J.-P. Cot/S. Wittich*, in: A. Zimmermann/C. J. Tams/K. Oellers-Frahm/C. Tomuschat/D. W. K. Anderson (eds.), The Statute of the International Court of Justice, 3. ed., 2019: Art. 68, para. 11.

776 So also *K. J. Keith*, The extent of the advisory jurisdiction of the International Court of Justice, 1971, 110.

777 *M. N. Shaw*, Rosenne's Law and Practice of the International Court: 1920-2015, 5th ed 2016, Vol. 3, Ch. 16, § 255.

Court's Statute.[778] However, the extent of the Court's delegated powers is not clear. The Informal Inter-Allied Committee[779] distinguished between "fundamental points of principle" which must be decided by the Court's Statute (and thus by the States Parties) and other procedural matters which are left to be decided by the Court.[780] What seems clear from the gap-filling function of the Rules of the Court is that the Court may not create rules that are in conflict with its Statute.[781] Whether the Rules are binding on the States Parties to the ICJ Statute is a matter of dispute.[782] On the one hand, the States Parties have not given their consent to the express terms of the Rules which argues against any binding force. However, they have given their consent to delegate to the Court the power to lay down procedural rules by including Article 30 in the Court's Statute which in turn has binding effect.[783] The Court has dealt with this question pragmatically in its judgment in the *Northern Cameroons* case:

> "The Court cannot be indifferent to any failure, whether by Applicant or Respondent, to comply with its Rules which have been framed in accordance with Article 30 of its Statute."[784]

As the Rules constitute the Court's written, generalized, and practical interpretation of the UNC and the Statute, the ICJ will likely follow them and

778 *H. W. Thirlway*, in: A. Zimmermann/C. J. Tams/K. Oellers-Frahm/C. Tomuschat/D. W. K. Anderson (eds.), The Statute of the International Court of Justice, 3. ed., 2019: Article 30, para. 6.

779 The "Informal Inter-Allied Committee" was an independent group of experts during the Second World War that set itself the task of conceptualizing the organization of the International Court of Justice, in particular by assessing whether the structures of the PCIJ should be maintained. On this, see *M. N. Shaw*, Rosenne's Law and Practice of the International Court: 1920-2015, 5th ed 2016, Vol. 1, Ch. 2, § 6.

780 Ibid., Vol. 3, Ch. 16, § 255.

781 Cf. *H. W. Thirlway*, in: A. Zimmermann/C. J. Tams/K. Oellers-Frahm/C. Tomuschat/D. W. K. Anderson (eds.), The Statute of the International Court of Justice, 3. ed., 2019: Article 30, para. 7.

782 *M. N. Shaw*, Rosenne's Law and Practice of the International Court: 1920-2015, 5th ed 2016, Vol. 3, Ch. 16, § 255.

783 *Thirlway* argues that because of the States Parties' consent to the PCIJ Statute, the Rules are also binding, see *H. W. Thirlway*, in: A. Zimmermann/C. J. Tams/K. Oellers-Frahm/C. Tomuschat/D. W. K. Anderson (eds.), The Statute of the International Court of Justice, 3. ed., 2019: Article 30, 4.

784 *Northern Cameroons (Cameroon v. United Kingdom) (Preliminary Objections)*, Judgment, ICJ Reports 1963, 15 (27).

only depart from them in special circumstances.[785] Thus, the Court's Rules at least constitute an important source of guidance when interpreting the UNC and the ICJ Statute.

Article 102 paras. 2 and 3 of the Rules is particularly important for the purposes of this analysis. The provision stipulates:

> "The Court shall also be guided by the provisions of the Statute and of these Rules which apply in contentious cases to the extent to which it recognizes them to be applicable. For this purpose, it shall above all consider whether the request for the advisory opinion relates to a legal question actually pending between two or more States.
> When an advisory opinion is requested upon a legal question actually pending between two or more States, Article 31 of the Statute shall apply, as also the provisions of these Rules concerning the application of that Article."

Article 102 para. 2 of the Rules takes up the phrasing employed in Article 68 ICJ Statute ("shall also be guided by..."). The key consideration shall be whether the request "relates to a legal question actually pending between two or more States".

Article 102 para. 3 specifies that in such instances the Court shall apply Article 31 ICJ Statute which allows each disputing party in contentious proceedings before the Court to appoint a judge *ad hoc*. Two important takeaways may be drawn from this reference: Firstly, Article 102 clearly expresses the ICJ's understanding that its advisory jurisdiction may extend to legal questions which form the subject-matter of an inter-state dispute.[786] The ICJ thus believes that inter-state disputes are not categorically excluded from its advisory jurisdiction. Secondly, the only provision the Court shall apply according to Article 102 para. 3 of the Rules when advisory opinions concern pending inter-state disputes is Article 31 ICJ Statute. Notably, Article 102 para. 3 does not refer to Article 36 ICJ Statute which stipulates the contentious jurisdiction's consent requirement. *E contrario*, the Court does not assume that Article 36 applies to the Court's advisory opinion procedure, even if an opinion is requested upon a legal question pending between two or more states. The Rules of the Court thus also speak in

785 *M. N. Shaw*, Rosenne's Law and Practice of the International Court: 1920-2015, 5th ed 2016, Vol. 3, Ch. 16, § 255.

786 *P. d'Argent*, in: A. Zimmermann/C. J. Tams/K. Oellers-Frahm/C. Tomuschat/D. W. K. Anderson (eds.), The Statute of the International Court of Justice, 3. ed., 2019: Article 65, paras. 27–30.

favor of a broad understanding of the Court's advisory jurisdiction which does not require state consent when addressing inter-state disputes. The Rules of the Court thus do not provide a legal basis for the Eastern Carelia doctrine.[787]

III. Subsequent agreements and subsequent practice

Further guidance on the meaning of Article 96 UNC and Article 65 ICJ Statute could be drawn from subsequent agreements regarding the interpretation of the provisions (Article 31 para. 3 lit. a VCLT) and subsequent practice in the application of the provisions (Article 31 para. 3 lit. b VCLT). Constituent instruments of international organizations have the unique quality that they regularly create new subjects of international law. As such, they are inherently forward-looking and practice-oriented. This finds expression in the particular importance of the subsequent agreements and subsequent practice of the parties.[788]

1. Subsequent agreements relating to the use of ICJ advisory opinions to settle international disputes

Article 31 para. 3 lit. a VCLT allows recourse to subsequent agreements between the parties to a treaty as a method of interpreting a treaty.[789] As *Wolfrum* pointed out, there are several international treaty provisions which provide for the recourse to ICJ advisory opinions as a means to settle international disputes.[790] The Headquarters Agreement between the United States of America and the United Nations contains a dispute settlement

787 Cf. Ibid., paras. 27–30.

788 Cf. *R. Kolb*, The International Court of Justice, 2013, 1060; *P. d'Argent*, in: A. Zimmermann/C. J. Tams/K. Oellers-Frahm/C. Tomuschat/D. W. K. Anderson (eds.), The Statute of the International Court of Justice, 3. ed., 2019: Article 65, para. 33; *N. Blokker*, Constituent Instruments, in: J. K. Cogan/I. Hurd/I. Johnstone (eds.), The Oxford Handbook of International Organizations, 2016 (955 et seq.).

789 Art. 31 para. 3 lit. a VCLT stipulates: "There shall be taken into account, together with the context: [...] a. any subsequent agreement between the parties regarding the interpretation of the treaty or the application of its provisions."

790 *R. Wolfrum*, Advisory Opinions: Are they a Suitable Alternative for the Settlement of International Disputes, in: R. Wolfrum/I. Gatzschmann (eds.), International Dispute Settlement: Room for Innovations?, 2013, 35 (48).

provision, according to which any dispute between the United Nations and the United States concerning the agreement shall be decided by an arbitral tribunal.[791] If a proceeding is pending before the arbitral tribunal, the UNGA and the USA may ask the ICJ for an advisory opinion on any legal question arising in the course of such a proceeding and the arbitral tribunal shall render its decision "having regard to the opinion" of the ICJ.[792] Disputes between the United Nations and States Parties to the "Convention on the Privileges and Immunities of the United Nations" are also settled by recourse to the ICJ's advisory procedure.[793] Furthermore, advisory opinions of the ICJ reviewing the activity of the ILO Administrative Tribunal are binding under the ILO Statute.[794] *Wolfrum* argued that these examples demonstrate that the ICJ may issue advisory opinions to settle international disputes.[795] However, one may equally conclude from these examples that where states intend for ICJ advisory opinions to be used in such a manner, a special agreement to that extent is required which expresses the States Parties' consent to it.

2. Subsequent practice in the application of Article 96 UNC and Article 65 ICJ Statute

The subsequent practice in the application of the UNC and the ICJ Statute – by the UNGA in requesting advisory opinions, by the states in voting for the UNGA request and in participating in the advisory proceedings and by the ICJ in giving the requested opinions – may provide further guidance as to the question if advisory opinions may be used to settle inter-state disputes.

---

791 Agreement between the United Nations and the United States of America regarding the Headquarters of the United Nations, 31 October 1947, Art. VIII Section 21(a).

792 Ibid., Art. VIII Section 21(b).

793 Convention on the Privileges and Immunities of the United Nations, 13 February 1946, 1 UNTS 15, Art. VIII Section 30.

794 Statute of the Administrative Tribunal of the International Labour Organization, 9 October 1946, Art. XII.

795 *R. Wolfrum*, Advisory Opinions: Are they a Suitable Alternative for the Settlement of International Disputes, in: R. Wolfrum/I. Gatzschmann (eds.), International Dispute Settlement: Room for Innovations?, 2013, 35 (48).

Subsequent practice as a method of treaty interpretation is codified in Article 31 para. 3 lit. b VCLT[796] and applies to the interpretation of constituent instruments of international organizations.[797] The ICJ[798] (and the PCIJ before it[799]) regularly examined the subsequent practice of the parties in the application of a treaty to determine the "true meaning"[800] of a treaty provision. The idea of Article 31 para. 3 lit. b VCLT is that the parties as the "masters of the treaty"[801] collectively have the legal capacity to authentically interpret the treaty's provisions.[802] This collective will, or in the words of Article 31 para. 3 lit. b VCLT "agreement of the parties", is expressed through "subsequent practice in the application of the treaty". There must

796 Art. 31 para. 3 lit. b VCLT stipulates: "There shall be taken into account, together with the context: [...] any subsequent practice in the application of the treaty which establishes the agreement of the parties regarding its interpretation."

797 See ILC, Draft conclusions on subsequent agreements and subsequent practice in relation to the interpretation of treaties, with commentaries, 2018, A/73/10, Conclusion 12 para. 1.

798 *Corfu Channel (United Kingdom v. Albania)*, Merits, Judgment, ICJ Reports 1949, 4 (25); *Arbitral Award made by the King of Spain on 23 December 1906 (Honduras v. Nicaragua)*, Judgment, ICJ Reports, 192 (206–207); *Case concerning the Temple of Preah Vihear (Cambodia v. Thailand) (Merits)*, Judgment, ICJ Reports 1962, 6 (33–35); *Certain Expenses of the United Nations (Article 17, paragraph 2, of the Charter)*, Advisory Opinion, ICJ Reports 1962, 151 (160–161); *Case Concerning Military and Paramilitary Activities in and against Nicaragua (Nicaragua v. United States of America) (Jurisdiction and Admissibility)*, Judgment, ICJ Reports, 392 (408-413, paras. 36-47); *Territorial Dispute (Libyan Arab Jamahiriya v. Chad)*, Judgment, ICJ Reports 1994, 6 (34-37, paras. 66-71); *Legality of the Use by a State of Nuclear Weapons in Armed Conflict*, Advisory Opinion, ICJ Reports 1996, 66 (75, para. 19); *Kasikili/Sedudu Island (Botswana v. Namibia)*, Judgment, ICJ Reports 1999, 1045 (1076, para. 50).

799 *Competence of the ILO in Regard to International Regulation of the Conditions of Labour of Persons Employed in Agriculture*, Advisory Opinion, PCIJ Series B 1922, 8 (39–41); cf. *Case Concerning the Payment in Gold of Brazilian Federal Loans Contracted in France*, PCIJ Series A 1929, 93 (119–120).

800 *Competence of the ILO in Regard to International Regulation of the Conditions of Labour of Persons Employed in Agriculture*, Advisory Opinion, PCIJ Series B 1922, 8 (39).

801 See *O. Dörr*, in: O. Dörr/K. Schmalenbach (eds.), Vienna Convention on the Law of Treaties, 2. ed., 2018: Art. 31, para. 77.

802 *Villiger*, Mark Eugen (Hg.): Commentary on the 1969 Vienna Convention on the Law of Treaties 2009, Art. 31, para. 16; *O. Dörr*, in: O. Dörr/K. Schmalenbach (eds.), Vienna Convention on the Law of Treaties, 2. ed., 2018: Art. 31, para. 77.

be uniform and repeated practice to which all parties to the treaty have expressly or implicitly consented.[803]

While the wording of Article 31 para. 3 lit. b VCLT is clear that there must be agreement of the parties, the provision does not explicitly state whose practice is the relevant practice. There are potentially three different sources of practice[804]: the practice of the States Parties to the treaty,[805] the practice of the organization and its organs[806] and a combination of the two[807].[808]

803 *M. E. Villiger*, in: M. E. Villiger (ed.), Commentary on the 1969 Vienna Convention on the Law of Treaties, 2009: Art. 31, para. 22; *A. Aust*, Modern treaty law and practice, 3rd ed. 2013, 215; see, however, *Dörr* who argues for a more flexible approach, which allows for a lower threshold of practice and agreement which then results in a lower "interpretative value", see *O. Dörr*, in: O. Dörr/K. Schmalenbach (eds.), Vienna Convention on the Law of Treaties, 2. ed., 2018: Art. 31, 80 et seq.

804 See *G. Nolte*, Third report on subsequent agreements and subsequent practice in relation to the interpretation of treaties, 7. April 2015, UN Docs A/CN.4/683, 12, para. 30 et seq.

805 *Land and Maritime Boundary between Cameroon and Nigeria (Cameroon v. Nigeria)*, Preliminary Objections, Judgment, ICJ Reports 1998, 275 (305, paras. 65 ff.).

806 *Competence of the General Assembly for the Admission of a State to the United Nations*, Advisory Opinion, ICJ Reports 1950, 4 (9); *Constitution of the Maritime Safety Committee of the Inter-Governmental Maritime Consultative*, Advisory Opinion, ICJ Reports 1960, 150 (168–169); *Certain Expenses of the United Nations (Article 17, paragraph 2, of the Charter)*, Advisory Opinion, ICJ Reports 1962, 151 (175); *Applicability of Article VI, Section 22, of the Convention on the Privileges and Immunities*, Advisory Opinion, ICJ Reports 1989, 177 (194, para. 48); *Legality of the Use by a State of Nuclear Weapons in Armed Conflict*, Advisory Opinion, ICJ Reports 1996, 66 (74-75, para. 19).

807 *Legal Consequences for States of the Continued Presence of South Africa in Namibia (South West Africa) notwithstanding Security Council Resolution 276 (1970)*, Advisory Opinion, ICJ Reports 1971, 16 (22); *Legal Consequences of the Construction of a Wall in the Occupied Palestinian Territory*, Advisory Opinion, ICJ Reports 2004, 136 (149–150).

808 See also ILC, Draft conclusions on subsequent agreements and subsequent practice in relation to the interpretation of treaties, with commentaries, 2018, A/73/10, Conclusion 12 para. 2: "Subsequent agreements and subsequent practice of the parties under article 31, paragraph 3, or subsequent practice under article 32, may arise from, or be expressed in, the *practice of an international organization* in the application of its constituent instrument." (emphasis added).

a) UNGA requests for advisory opinions on inter-state disputes

Several requests for an advisory opinion by the UNGA explicitly concern the rights and obligations of specific states in the context of a pending inter-state dispute. Such requests could be regarded as a form of subsequent practice of the UN in the application of the UNC and ICJ Statute.

The ICJ regularly examines the practice of the organization in applying its constitutive instrument when interpreting that treaty.[809] A notable example is the ICJ's interpretation of Article 27 para. 3 UNC.[810] By relying on the practice of the organization to determine how far its conferred competences extend, the ICJ allows the organization significant influence on the interpretation of its own powers. This creates a certain tension between the principle of conferred powers and the implied powers doctrine.[811] To prevent the organization from assuming powers by way of subsequent practice without the consent of the States Parties to the constituent instrument, Article 31 para. 3 lit. b VCLT further qualifies the required practice: The practice must establish the *agreement* of the parties regarding the interpretation of the provision.

The practice of an organization in the application of a treaty is regularly the combination of a multitude of individual decisions of its organs. These decisions are the result of the decision-making process of the respective organ as determined by the organization's constitutive instrument. The Member States have given their consent to the constitutive instrument, and they are generally involved in the organization's decision-making process, so that the decisions of the organization are an expression of the will of the Member States. The resulting practice of the organization thus reflects the

---

809 *Legality of the Use by a State of Nuclear Weapons in Armed Conflict*, Advisory Opinion, ICJ Reports 1996, 66 (75, para. 19); *A. von Arnauld*, Völkerrecht, 5. ed. 2023, 51, para. 126.

810 According to Art. 27 para. 3 UNC, decisions by the UNSC on non-procedural matters require the "affirmative vote of nine members including the concurring votes of all permanent members". The ICJ interpreted the words "concurring votes" in accordance with the practice of the UNSC and its permanent members as meaning "non-rejection". Thus, if a permanent member wishes to prevent a UNSC resolution, it must actively vote against the decision, i.e. veto it. See *Legal Consequences for States of the Continued Presence of South Africa in Namibia (South West Africa) notwithstanding Security Council Resolution 276 (1970)*, Advisory Opinion, ICJ Reports 1971, 16 (22, para. 22).

811 Cf. *A. von Arnauld*, Völkerrecht, 5. ed. 2023, 51, para. 126. On the implied powers doctrine, see *supra*: § 5 Section B.II.

agreement of the Member States on the interpretation of the constitutive instrument. This inference of consent is unproblematic if the respective decision is taken unanimously.[812]

The situation becomes less clear when decisions are reached by majority vote. According to *Amerasinghe*, majority vote decisions can constitute relevant state practice if the decision is supported by a large majority of the Member States of the organization.[813] He argues that the Member States have given their consent to the decision-making process of the organization at the time of signing the treaty and thus have accepted that decisions can be reached against their will with a simple majority.[814] The decision is thus an expression of the implicit consent of the Member States. If the majority decision is opposed by a large number of Member States, however, such implicit consent may not be assumed. According to *Amerasinghe*, one can assume that the Member States have implicitly agreed that a small opposition cannot prevent the organization from forming a certain practice but if a larger number of Member States oppose a decision, practice cannot be formed.[815]

Amerasinghe's view is based on the idea that the subsequent practice of the organization, despite the contrary vote of some Member States, still represents the agreement of the Member States of the organization because the outvoted Member States implicitly consented to the decision-making process at the time of the conclusion of the treaty. However, it seems that this implicit consent is given to all decisions that have been reached in accordance with the procedural rules laid down in the constituent instrument. To distinguish, as proposed by *Amerasinghe*, between decisions made by a large majority (which represent the agreement of the parties) and a decision made by a small majority (which does not), seems inconsistent.

Amerasinghe's argument raises another question: How does the implicit consent to the decision-making process at the time of the conclusion of the treaty relate to the explicitly expressed disapproval of the outvoted states at the moment of the vote? In other words, can implicit consent

---

812 Cf. Whaling in the Antarctic (Australia v. Japan: New Zealand intervening), Judgment, ICJ Reports 2014, 226 (257, para. 83).

813 *C. F. Amerasinghe*, Principles of the institutional law of international organizations, Second edition 2005, 51. See also *Loizidou v Turkey*, Judgment of 23 March 1995, Series A, no. 310, paras. 79–89, where the ECtHR relied on "practice denoting *practically* universal agreement amongst Contracting Parties" (emphasis added).

814 Ibid., 53.

815 Ibid., 54.

to the procedure outweigh explicit dissent when it comes to identifying the states' agreement on treaty interpretation? In particular if the organization's competences (possibly even in its relations to its Member States) are further expanded through the subsequent practice, the assumption of such far-reaching implicit consent seems questionable.[816] The implicit consent to the procedure seems to be only that: a consent to the decision-making procedure of the organization. The decisions made by the organization in this way may result in a subsequent practice of the organization (see above). However, this practice – if it is not supported by all Member States – does not represent the agreement of the Member States regarding the interpretation of the treaty provisions as required by Article 31 para. 3 lit. b VCLT.[817]

Some commentators argue that the term "agreement" in Article 31 para. 3 lit. b VCLT constitutes a lower threshold than in the context of lit. a of the same provision.[818] However, even according to this view "agreement" in lit. b requires the absence of dissent.[819] Such absence of dissent can only be assumed for acts of international organizations if there are no contrary acts or statements by the States Parties.[820] As soon as there are dissenting votes of individual Member States, dissent exists. Only if the practice of the organization can be traced back to decisions that are supported by all Member States, can it be ensured that a change of the organization's powers through subsequent practice is an expression of the will of the State Parties.

---

816 So also Dörr, who argues that the practice of an organization is only relevant "if it is not counteracted by acts or representations of the parties to the treaty in question", see *O. Dörr*, in: O. Dörr/K. Schmalenbach (eds.), Vienna Convention on the Law of Treaties, 2. ed., 2018: Art. 31, para. 87.

817 Whaling in the Antarctic (Australia v. Japan: New Zealand intervening), Judgment, ICJ Reports 2014, 226 (257, para. 83); Certain Expenses of the United Nations (Article 17, paragraph 2, of the Charter), Advisory Opinion, Separate Opinion Spender, 182 (191–192); cf. Certain Expenses of the United Nations (Article 17, paragraph 2, of the Charter), Advisory Opinion, Dissenting Opinion Fitzmaurice, 198 (201–202). See also *G. Nolte*, Third report on subsequent agreements and subsequent practice in relation to the interpretation of treaties, 7. April 2015, UN Docs A/CN.4/683, 30; *O. Dörr*, in: O. Dörr/K. Schmalenbach (eds.), Vienna Convention on the Law of Treaties, 2. ed., 2018: Art. 31, para. 88.

818 *O. Dörr*, in: O. Dörr/K. Schmalenbach (eds.), Vienna Convention on the Law of Treaties, 2. ed., 2018: Art. 31, para. 87, citing *Kasikili/Sedudu Island Case (Botswana v. Namibia)*, Judgment, ICJ Reports 1999, p. 1045 (1087), para. 63.

819 Ibid., para. 88.

820 Ibid., para. 88.

UNGA requests for advisory opinions on legal questions relating to pending inter-state disputes which are not passed unanimously thus do not constitute practice of the UN which establishes the agreement of the States Parties. Such practice could, however, be used as a supplementary means of interpretation according to Article 32 VCLT.[821] The ICJ has relied on UNGA resolutions that were passed against the opposition of individual Member States as supplementary means of interpretation under Article 32 VCLT.[822]

b) Practice of the Court

The ICJ has held on multiple occasions that by giving an advisory opinion it participates in the activities of the UN.[823] One could thus be tempted to regard the ICJ's advisory practice as subsequent practice in the application of Article 96 UNC, Article 65 ICJ Statute. However, relying on judicial pronouncements as subsequent practice in the sense of Article 31 para. 3 lit. b VCLT poses challenges.

First, the ICJ Statute clearly sets out the legal effects of the Court's pronouncements. Article 59 ICJ Statute stipulates that the "decision of the Court has no binding force except between the parties and in respect of that particular case". Accordingly, only decisions of the Court[824] have binding force and this binding force extends only to the parties of a case and in relation to a particular case. Outside these confines, judicial pronouncements of the ICJ have no binding force. Allowing judicial pronouncements of the Court to constitute subsequent practice in accordance with Article 31

821 *G. Nolte*, Third report on subsequent agreements and subsequent practice in relation to the interpretation of treaties, 7. April 2015, UN Docs A/CN.4/683, 17-19, para. 49-51; *O. Dörr*, in: O. Dörr/K. Schmalenbach (eds.), Vienna Convention on the Law of Treaties, 2. ed., 2018: Art. 31, para. 90.

822 *Legal Consequences of the Construction of a Wall in the Occupied Palestinian Territory*, Advisory Opinion, ICJ Reports 2004, 136 (149); *G. Nolte*, Third report on subsequent agreements and subsequent practice in relation to the interpretation of treaties, 7. April 2015, UN Docs A/CN.4/683, 18.

823 *Interpretation of Peace Treaties with Bulgaria, Hungary and Romania (First Phase)*, Advisory Opinion, ICJ Reports 1950, 65 (71).

824 "Decisions" in the sense of Article 59 ICJ Statute are the final judgements on the merits of a case, judgments on preliminary objections as well as certain orders, see *C. Brown*, in: A. Zimmermann/C. J. Tams/K. Oellers-Frahm/C. Tomuschat/D. W. K. Anderson (eds.), The Statute of the International Court of Justice, 3. ed., 2019: Article 59 ICJ Statute, paras. 35–36.

para. 3 lit. b VCLT would circumvent the express provisions within the ICJ Statute governing the legal effects of ICJ decisions (and advisory opinions).

Secondly, while the ICJ is an organ of the UN, it is not a collective organ in which the UN members are represented. Instead, it is composed of independent judges (Article 2 ICJ Statute). As such, their conduct cannot be attributed to the States Parties to the UNC and ICJ Statute and therefore cannot constitute a practice of the organization capable of establishing the agreement of the States Parties. The ILC held in its Draft conclusions on subsequent agreements and subsequent practice in relation to the interpretation of treaties (2018) that the pronouncements of expert treaty bodies cannot constitute subsequent practice under Art 31 para. 3 lit. b VCLT.[825] The reason for this lies in the fact that these bodies are composed of independent experts acting in their personal capacity, whose views are not attributable to States Parties.[826] While the ILC Conclusions did not expressly address independent expert bodies that are organs of an international organization (such as the ICJ), the same considerations apply *mutatis mutandis.*[827] The ILC emphasized that the "relevance of a pronouncement of an expert treaty body for the interpretation of a treaty is subject to the applicable rules of the treaty".[828] The same is true for pronouncements of the ICJ whose legal effects are governed by the ICJ Statute.

The ILC stated in their Conclusions that the pronouncements of UN treaty bodies, while not constituting subsequent practice themselves, may *give rise* to the practice of States Parties or the UN, for example in the form of actions taken in response to the respective pronouncement.[829] Applied to the advisory proceedings of the ICJ, the views expressed by the States Parties during the advisory proceedings and their actions taken in response to advisory opinions can constitute subsequent practice in the sense of Article 31 para. 3 lit. b VCLT.

---

825 ILC, Draft conclusions on subsequent agreements and subsequent practice in relation to the interpretation of treaties, with commentaries, 2018, A/73/10, Conclusion 13 para. 3 and commentary to Conclusion 13 para. 10.

826 *O. Dörr*, in: O. Dörr/K. Schmalenbach (eds.), Vienna Convention on the Law of Treaties, 2. ed., 2018: Art. 31, para. 85.

827 ILC, Draft conclusions on subsequent agreements and subsequent practice in relation to the interpretation of treaties, with commentaries, 2018, A/73/10, Commentary to draft conclusion 13 para. 4.

828 Ibid., Conclusion 13 para. 2.

829 Ibid., Conclusion 13 para. 2, commentary to Cocnlusion 13 para. 7.

However, the practice of the States Parties to the ICJ Statute on the question whether ICJ advisory opinions may address the subject-matter of pending bilateral disputes is far from uniform.

c) Practice of States Parties

Whenever a state invoked the Eastern Carelia doctrine to challenge the admissibility of a request for an advisory opinion, the ensuing arguments between the participating states did not center on the question whether the Court may use its advisory procedure to settle an inter-state dispute. Instead, those states that urged the Court to give the requested opinion argued either that there was no inter-state dispute to begin with or that the object and purpose of the request was not to settle such a dispute.

The *Chagos* case provides the most recent example of this dynamic. The United Kingdom argued that the request for an advisory opinion related to a purely bilateral dispute between the UK and Mauritius.[830] In response, Mauritius argued that the request did not relate to a bilateral matter at all, but to the broader frame of reference of decolonization, which directly relate to the work of the UNGA.[831] Both states thus accepted the premise that advisory opinions in general ought not address purely bilateral disputes. This is in line with the majority of states participating in the *Chagos* advisory proceeding. While there was a disagreement whether the Court ought to give the requested advisory opinion or not, the vast majority of states phrased their arguments within the framework of the Eastern Carelia doctrine.[832]

830 ICJ Pleadings, *Legal Consequences of the Separation of the Chagos Archipelago from Mauritius in 1965*, Written Statement of the United Kingdom, para. 7.15; Written Comments of the United Kingdom, para. 3.3.

831 ICJ Pleadings, *Legal Consequences of the Separation of the Chagos Archipelago from Mauritius in 1965*, Written Statement of Mauritius, paras. 5.29 – 5.35; Written Comments of Mauritius, para. 2.13.

832 See ICJ Pleadings, *Legal Consequences of the Separation of the Chagos Archipelago from Mauritius in 1965*, Written Statement of Australia, paras. 32–48; Written Statement of Brazil, paras. 11–12; Written Statement of Chile, para. 9; Written Statement of Cyprus, paras. 26–27; Written Comments of Cyprus, paras. 5–6; Written Statement of Djibouti, paras. 22–23; Written Statement of France, paras. 6, 19; Written Statement of Lesotho; Written Statement of Liechtenstein, para. 16; Written Statement of the Marshall Islands, paras. 15–16; Written Statement of Mauritius, paras. 5.29 – 5.35; Written Comments of Mauritius, para. 2.13; Written Statement of Namibia; Written Comments of Nicaragua, paras. 15–16; Written Statement of

However, not all states accepted this premise: some states did not refer to the Eastern Carelia framework at all,[833] others rejected the doctrine entirely,[834] or proposed a different framework.[835] Germany, for example, argued that the question was not whether the Court was entitled to give an advisory opinion on purely bilateral matters, but whether one can presume that the requesting UN organ intended to focus its question on bilateral aspects of the legal question. Germany argued that since one may presume that requesting organs request advisory opinions only to the extent that it is necessary for their work, the Court ought to focus its response on matters that are "necessary and relevant for the General Assembly to exercise its own competences."[836]

The *Chagos* case thus demonstrates that there is no uniform practice among States Parties to the ICJ Statute on the question whether advisory opinions may be used to settle inter-state legal disputes *vel non*. Interpreting Article 96 UNC and Article 65 ICJ Statute in accordance with Article 31 para. 3 lit. b VCLT thus provides no clear guidance on the question whether ICJ advisory opinions may address pending bilateral disputes without the consent of the disputing states.

IV. Object and purpose

Article 31 para. 1 VCLT stipulates that the provisions of a treaty are to be interpreted in light of the treaty's "object and purpose". A treaty's "object" describes its content, whereas its "purpose" is what the parties to the treaty

Niger; Written Statement of China, paras. 15–18; Written Statement of the Republic of Korea, para. 16; Written Statement of Russia, para. 17; Written Statement of Serbia, para. 25; Written Statement of the United Kingdom, para. 7.15; Written Comments of the United Kingdom, para. 3.3, Written Statement of the United States of America, paras. 3.3, 3.20 et seq.; Written Comments of the United States of America, paras. 2.12 et seq.

833 See ICJ Pleadings, *Legal Consequences of the Separation of the Chagos Archipelago from Mauritius in 1965*, Written Statements of India, Madagascar, the Netherlands, the Seychelles, and Vietnam.

834 See ICJ Pleadings, *Legal Consequences of the Separation of the Chagos Archipelago from Mauritius in 1965*, Written Statement of Guatemala, paras. 22–23; Written Statement of South Africa, para. 52.

835 See ICJ Pleadings, *Legal Consequences of the Separation of the Chagos Archipelago from Mauritius in 1965*, Written Statement of Germany, paras. 39–40, 48.

836 Ibid., para. 48.

aim to achieve by concluding the treaty.[837] In practice, however, there is no sharp distinction between the two elements.[838] Instead, ICs usually identify the treaty's aim and then interpret the provisions of the treaty in a way that best achieves this aim.[839] The use of the singular in Article 31 para. 1 VCLT ("its object and purpose") also indicates that it is the interpreter's task to find a single overarching object and purpose of the treaty, i.e., a singular *telos* which (most of) the treaty provisions aim to advance.[840] Particularly, when it comes to interpreting the constituent instruments of international organizations, ICs have shown a tendency to apply a teleological interpretation.[841] In general, all provisions of a treaty are relevant when interpreting a treaty's object and purpose.[842] However, usually the treaty's title, its preamble as well as the type of treaty (for example a boundary treaty instead of a trade treaty), provide a good indication about the aim the parties try to achieve.[843]

Interpreting Article 96 UNC and Article 65 ICJ Statute in accordance with the instrument's object and purpose supports a broadly defined subject-matter advisory jurisdiction that extends to inter-state disputes. The purpose of the UN as enshrined in Art. 1 UNC is to maintain peace and security (Article 1 para. 1 UNC), develop friendly relations among nations (Article 1 para. 2 UNC), and to promote economic, social, cultural, and humanitarian co-operation and human rights (Article 1 para. 3 UNC). The UN's focus on peace and security is further reflected in the Charter's preamble which declares as an "end" of the UN to "save succeeding generations from the scourge of war".

Article 1 para. 1 UNC particularly highlights as the organization's aim "to bring about by peaceful means, and in conformity with the principles

---

837 *O. Dörr*, in: O. Dörr/K. Schmalenbach (eds.), Vienna Convention on the Law of Treaties, 2. ed., 2018: Art. 31, para. 54.

838 Ibid., para. 54.

839 Ibid., paras. 52-54.

840 Ibid., para. 54.

841 See for example *Reparation for Injuries Suffered in the Service of the United Nations*, Advisory Opinion, ICJ Reports 1949, 174 (174); *Effect of Awards of Compensation Made by the United Nations Administrative Tribunal*, Advisory Opinion, ICJ Reports 1954, 47 (47); *J.-M. Sorel/V. Eveno Boré*, in: O. Corten/P. Klein (eds.), The Vienna Conventions on the law of treaties, 2011: Art. 31, para. 14; *O. Dörr*, in: O. Dörr/K. Schmalenbach (eds.), Vienna Convention on the Law of Treaties, 2. ed., 2018: Art. 31, para. 56.

842 *O. Dörr*, in: O. Dörr/K. Schmalenbach (eds.), Vienna Convention on the Law of Treaties, 2. ed., 2018: Art. 31, para. 55.

843 Ibid., para. 55.

of justice and international law, adjustment or settlement of international disputes or situations which might lead to a breach of the peace."

The responsibility for the maintenance of peace and security lies with the UNSC and the UNGA, the UNSC having the primary (Article 24 para. 1 UNC), the UNGA having a complimentary responsibility (Articles 11, 12 UNC) for this. To this end, the UNSC may investigate any dispute, or any situation which might lead to international friction or give rise to a dispute (Article 34 UNC), call upon the parties to an international dispute to settle their dispute by peaceful means (Article 33 para. 2 UNC), recommend appropriate procedures or methods of adjustment (Articles 36–38 UNC), or make binding decisions under Chapter VII. Likewise, the UNGA may discuss any questions relating to the maintenance of international peace and security brought before it by members of the UN, by the UNSC, or – under certain conditions – by a non-Member State (Article 11 para. 2 UNC).

In order to perform these dispute-prevention and dispute-settlement functions, the two UN organs need a profound understanding of the respective international dispute they are dealing with. Regularly, inter-state disputes revolve around legal questions. Article 96 UNC gives the two UN organs a tool to receive legal guidance and to adapt their conduct accordingly in order to address a certain dispute more effectively.[844] As the ICJ has continuously stated since 1950, it has a duty to support the political organs of the UN in their functions by giving advisory opinions:

"the reply of the Court, itself an 'organ of the United Nations', represents its participation in the activities of the Organization, and, in principle, should not be refused."[845]

An interpretation of Article 96 UNC in light of the UNC's object and purpose to prevent and resolve inter-state disputes argues for an extensive subject-matter advisory jurisdiction which allows the Court to address legal questions that arise within the context of a pending inter-state dispute. After all, it is pending inter-state disputes and not abstract legal questions which are likely to endanger international peace and security.

844 *K. Oellers-Frahm/E. Lagrange*, in: B. Simma/D.-E. Khan/G. Nolte/A. Paulus (eds.), The Charter of the United Nations, 4. ed., 2024: Art. 96, para. 7.

845 *Interpretation of Peace Treaties with Bulgaria, Hungary and Romania (First Phase)*, Advisory Opinion, ICJ Reports 1950, 65 (71).

V. Preparatory work of the UNC and ICJ Statute

While the grammatical and contextual interpretation of Article 96 UNC and Article 65 ICJ Statute argues for a broad subject-matter advisory jurisdiction extending to inter-state disputes, taking into account subsequent practice casts some doubt on this finding. Recourse to the preparatory works of the respective provisions as supplementary means of treaty interpretation under Article 32 lit. a VCLT may resolve this remaining ambiguity.[846]

Several states have invoked the difference in wording between Article 14 sentence 3 of the Covenant of the League of Nations (which laid out the PCIJ's advisory jurisdiction), on the one hand, and Article 96 UNC and Article 65 ICJ Statute, on the other hand, to argue that pending bilateral disputes fall outside the ICJ's subject-matter advisory jurisdiction. Whereas the PCIJ's advisory jurisdiction under Article 14 of the League's Covenant extended to "any dispute or question", Article 96 UNC and Article 65 ICJ Statute refer to "any legal question". While the word "any" seems to indicate a particularly broad subject-matter jurisdiction, the comparison between the two texts could also indicate the opposite interpretation. One could argue that the deletion of the reference to "disputes" in the UNC and the ICJ Statute indicates the drafters' intention to frame the ICJ's advisory jurisdiction more narrowly and exclude pending disputes from the Court's advisory jurisdiction *ratione materiae*.

Germany argued along these lines during the *Chagos* advisory proceeding:

> "In contrast to the Covenant of the League, Art. 96 of the Charter of the United Nations does not refer to disputes, but rather to 'any legal question'. This constitutes a deliberate alteration of the terms of that provision allowing the almost obvious assumption that under the system of the Charter a bilateral dispute should not be made the subject of a request for an advisory opinion."[847]

---

846 On the drafting history of the ICJ Statute, see also *M. Lando*, 61 CJTL 1 (2023), 67 (89 et seq.).

847 ICJ Pleadings, *Legal Consequences of the Separation of the Chagos Archipelago from Mauritius in 1965*, Written Statement of Germany, para. 43.

The United States of America presented a similar argument in the same proceeding:

> "The Court's advisory jurisdiction is limited to "any legal question" asked by an authorized U.N. organ or agency. This language reflects a deliberate decision by the drafters of the Statute of the Court to adopt a narrower formulation of the provision granting advisory jurisdiction as compared to that of the Permanent Court."[848]

Both states argue that there was a "deliberate decision" to exclude disputes from the Court's advisory jurisdiction.

At first glance, the references to the change in wording seem persuasive. The deletion of the express reference to disputes could indicate the intention of the drafters of the UNC and ICJ Statute to exclude dispute from the Court's advisory jurisdiction *ratione materiae* and thereby create a stricter separation between the Court's contentious procedure and its advisory opinion procedure. However, a closer look at the drafting history of Article 96 UNC and Article 65 ICJ Statute reveals that the change in wording was not meant to restrict the ICJ's advisory jurisdiction.

The current wording of Articles 96 UNC, 65 para. 1 ICJ Statute was drafted and agreed upon by Committee IV/1 during the San Francisco Conference of 1945. Committee IV/1 dealt with the judicial organization of the envisioned new organization. Several states made propositions for the Court's advisory jurisdiction. Norway for example proposed that the UNGA should have the power to request advisory opinions "on any legal question where it needs an authoritative opinion, including questions relating to the interpretation of the Charter".[849] At another occasion Norway referred to the right of the UNGA to request advisory opinions on "any legal question arising in matters on which it has the right to make recommendations."[850] As illustrated above, the UNGA may make recommendations on inter-state disputes, which would mean that it could also request advisory opinions on such disputes.

848 ICJ Pleadings, *Legal Consequences of the Separation of the Chagos Archipelago from Mauritius in 1965*, Written Statement of the United States of America, para. 3.6.

849 United Nations Conference on International Organization, Comments on the Dumbarton Oaks Proposals submitted by Norway, 6 May 1945, Doc. 2, G/7(j), Vol. 3, 356.

850 United Nations Conference on International Organization, Suggested Modifications to Dumbarton Oaks Proposals submitted by Norway, Doc. 2, G/7(n)(1), Vol. 3, 6.

Similarly, the Netherlands proposed that "[t]he Court shall give an advisory opinion on any legal question referred to it by the General Assembly or the Security Council".[851]

With respect to the UNSC, Norway stated:

> "The authority for the Security Council to request an advisory opinion of the International Court as formulated in the proposals must apply to legal questions arising out of any dispute. But the Security Council should have a similar authority to request an opinion of the Court also concerning legal questions unconnected with any particular dispute."[852]

Ecuador expressly stated that both organs should have the right to request advisory opinions on disputes:

> "All disputes between the States, whatever their nature, are justiciable before the International Court of Justice. The Security Council or the General Assembly shall be empowered to refer to the Court, for advice, questions brought in any controversy."[853]

None of these proposals saw it as problematic that the Court could issue advisory opinions on existing inter-state disputes. Some, like the Norwegian and the Ecuadorian proposals even made express references to the use of advisory opinions on matters arising out of concrete legal disputes. These proposals were also not challenged by other states for extending the Court's advisory jurisdiction to inter-state disputes.

Amongst the various proposals, Committee IV/1 decided to vote in favor of a joint Colombian-Cuban proposal which changed the wording to "any legal question".[854] Nothing indicates that this change in wording was moti-

---

851 United Nations Conference on International Organization, Amendments to the Dumbarton Oaks Proposals submitted by the Netherlands, 1 May 1945, Doc. 2, G/7(j), Vol. 3, 327.

852 United Nations Conference on International Organization, Comments on the Dumbarton Oaks Proposals submitted by Norway, 6 May 1945, Doc. 2, G/7(j), Vol. 3, 360.

853 United Nations Conference on International Organization, Proposal submitted by Ecuador, 1 May 1945, Doc. 2, G/7(p), Vol. 3, 436.

854 The joint Columbian-Cuban proposal read:
"[To be inserted into the UNC, now Art. 96 UNC]: The General Assembly and the Security Council may request the International Court of Justice to give an advisory opinion on any legal question.
[Art. 65 para. 1 ICJ Statute]: The Court may give an advisory opinion on any legal question at the request of whoever may be authorized by the Charter of the United Nations to make such a request.",

vated by the desire to restrict the Court's advisory jurisdiction, nor are there any indications that the participants even discussed that the change in wording could have such an effect. The wording of Article 65 ICJ Statute was then slightly modified by a Canadian proposal.[855] This resulted in the text of Article 96 UNC, Article 65 ICJ Statute as it is today.

The verbatim records show that no delegate argued that the modification of the text constituted a narrowing of the Court's advisory jurisdiction *ratione materiae*. As Judge *Schwebel* pointed out, the new wording was adopted without any analytical discussion about the difference between the old and the new wording.[856] As such, the change in wording from "dispute or question" in Article 14 of the League's Covenant to "any legal question" in the UNC and ICJ Statute cannot be considered a deliberate attempt to curtail the Court's advisory jurisdiction or to create a sharper distinction between the Court's advisory and contentious jurisdictions. Instead, the delegates understood the wording as a continuation of the broad advisory jurisdiction of the PCIJ. The drafting history of Article 96 UNC and Article 65 ICJ Statue thus indicates that the drafters of the UNC and ICJ Statute intended the ICJ to be able to address inter-state disputes through its advisory jurisdiction irrespective of state consent.[857]

VI. Interim conclusions on state consent

A grammatical interpretation of Article 96 UNC and Article 65 ICJ Statute does not yield a clear result whether the ICJ may use its advisory procedure to address inter-state disputes without state consent. On the one hand, the provision's wording is broad. Legal questions which form the subject-matter of an inter-state dispute clearly fall within the purview of "any legal question". On the other hand, the wording "any legal question" *prima*

United Nations Conference on International Organization, Sixteenth Meeting of Committee IV/1, 31 May 1945, Doc. 714, IV/1/57, Vol. 3, 241–2.

855 The Canadian proposal substituted the word "whoever" by the words "whatever body" and added the words "or in accordance with" after the words "authorized by", United Nations Conference on International Organization, Nineteenth Meeting of Committee IV/1, 7 June 1945, Doc. 828, IV/1/67, Vol. 3, 286.

856 *S. M. Schwebel*, Was the Capacity to Request an Advisory Opinion Wider in the Permanent Court of International Justice than it is in the International Court of Justice?, in: S. M. Schwebel (ed.), Justice in International Law: Selected Writings of Judge Stephen M. Schwebel, 1994, 27 (59–60).

857 So also *M. Lando*, 61 CJTL 1 (2023), 67 (98).

facie seems narrower than the wording employed in the Covenant of the League of Nations which described the PCIJ's advisory jurisdiction which explicitly referred to disputes ("dispute or question"). Interpreting the two provisions in line with the UNC's and ICJ Statute's object and purpose supports the conclusion that the ICJ is free in answering any legal question that is referred to it by an authorized organ, even if it relates to a pending inter-state dispute. Considering the power and duty of the UNSC and UNGA to monitor and resolve any situation or dispute which could threaten international peace, legal questions at the heart of inter-state disputes are an important subject-matter for the ICJ to address within its advisory jurisdiction. While the recourse to subsequent practice in the application of the two provisions does not provide clear guidance, the provisions' drafting history argues in favor of a broad jurisdiction of the Court. In particular, the change in wording between the League's Covenant and the UNC was not intended to limit the Court's capacity to address inter-state disputes.

In sum, Article 96 UNC and Article 65 ICJ Statute do not prevent the ICJ from addressing inter-state disputes by means of its advisory procedure, irrespective of state consent.[858] Considering that the ICJ's jurisdictional framework thus does not oblige the Court to reject requests for advisory opinions on inter-state disputes, the question becomes what justifies the Court's Eastern Carelia doctrine? The answer may lie in a more abstract notion: the Court's "discretion" to refuse any request for an advisory opinion that is not in line with the Court's judicial function.

E. Admissibility of the request and the Court's "discretion"

In addition to having jurisdiction to issue a particular advisory opinion, the Court must be satisfied that the request for such an advisory opinion is *admissible*. The admissibility of a request refers to a broader category of grounds why the Court should or should not give the requested opinion.[859]

---

858 So also *K. J. Keith*, The extent of the advisory jurisdiction of the International Court of Justice, 1971, 131; *M. Lando*, 61 CJTL 1 (2023), 67 (131 et seq.); see however *R. Kolb*, The International Court of Justice, 2013, 1073.

859 *Y. Shany*, Jurisdiction and Admissibility, in: C. Romano/K. J. Alter/Y. Shany (eds.), The Oxford Handbook of International Adjudication, 2013, 779 (787); on the admissibility in the context of the ICJ's advisory procedure, see *R. Kolb*, The International Court of Justice, 2013, 1081 et seq.; *R. Kolb*, The Elgar companion to the International Court of Justice, 2014, 270 et seq.

To put it differently, admissibility concerns the *exercise* of jurisdiction.[860] While the Court must assess its jurisdiction *proprio motu*, it typically addresses questions of admissibility only if a participant in the proceeding raises an objection in this regard.[861] An exception are matters which concern the protection of the Court's judicial function, which the Court has a duty to address.[862]

The ICJ derives its power to decide matters of admissibility from Article 65 ICJ Statute. The Court thus found that Article 65 "gives the Court the power to examine whether the circumstances of the case are of such a character as should lead it to decline to answer the Request."[863] The ICJ regularly refers to its power to refuse certain requests for an advisory opinion as a matter of "discretion". The Court thus held in its *Chagos* opinion:

> "The discretion whether or not to respond to a request for an advisory opinion exists so as to protect the integrity of the Court's judicial function as the principal judicial organ of the United Nations."[864]

However, both the discretionary nature and the extent of the ICJ's power to refuse certain requests for an advisory opinion are contested. To approach this question, the study first examines the historical context of the current debate by assessing the PCIJ's power to refuse requests for an advisory opinion (*infra* I.). It then compares these findings with the ICJ's own position on its "discretion" (*infra* II.) and the scholarly debate on the matter (*infra* III.).

---

860 *Y. Shany*, Jurisdiction and Admissibility, in: C. Romano/K. J. Alter/Y. Shany (eds.), The Oxford Handbook of International Adjudication, 2013, 779 (787).

861 *R. Kolb*, The International Court of Justice, 2013, 203.

862 Ibid., 203.

863 *Interpretation of Peace Treaties with Bulgaria, Hungary and Romania (First Phase)*, Advisory Opinion, ICJ Reports 1950, 65 (72).

864 With further references *Legal Consequences of the Separation of the Chagos Archipelago from Mauritius in 1965*, Advisory Opinion, ICJ Reports 2019, 95 (113, para. 64); *Legal Consequences of the Construction of a Wall in the Occupied Palestinian Territory*, Advisory Opinion, ICJ Reports 2004, 136 (156-157, paras. 44-45); *Accordance with international law of the unilateral declaration of independence in respect of Kosovo*, Advisory Opinion, ICJ Reports 2010, 403 (415-416, para. 29).

I. "Discretion" of the PCIJ under the League's Covenant

Just like today regarding the ICJ, the question of discretion was also a point of contention regarding the PCIJ.[865] This debate was sparked by the difference in wording between the English and French versions of Article 14 sentence 3 of the Covenant of the League of Nations. The respective versions read:

> "The Court may also give an advisory opinion upon any dispute or question referred to it by the Council or by the Assembly."
> "Elle donnera aussi des avis consultatifs sur tout différend ou tout point, dont la saisira le Conseil ou l'Assemblée."

The English wording "may give" implied a discretionary character of the Court's advisory competence. In contrast, the French wording "donnera" by using the indicative future tense could be understood as denying the Court any freedom of decision when a request for an advisory opinion is made.[866] The Treaty of Versailles stipulated that the English and the French version of the Covenant were equally authentic.[867] Because of this, both versions are assumed to be equally authoritative.[868] On interpreting treaty provisions that have different authentic texts, the PCIJ found in its 1924 *Mavrommatis Palestine Concessions* case that "where two versions possessing equal authority exist one of which appears to have a wider bearing than the other, it is bound to adopt the more limited interpretation which can be made to harmonise with both versions and which, as far as it goes, is doubtless in accordance with the common intentions of the Parties."[869]

865 With further references, see *M. Giles Samson/D. Guilfoyle*, The Permanent Court of International Justice and the "Invention" of International Advisory Jurisdiction, in: C. J. Tams/M. Fitzmaurice (eds.), Legacies of the Permanent Court of International Justice, 2013, 41 (49). Most commentators at the time agreed that the Court had discretion to refuse requests for an advisory opinion, see with further references *D. Pratap*, The advisory jurisdiction of the International Court, 1972, 143.

866 Cf. *M. Giles Samson/D. Guilfoyle*, The Permanent Court of International Justice and the "Invention" of International Advisory Jurisdiction, in: C. J. Tams/M. Fitzmaurice (eds.), Legacies of the Permanent Court of International Justice, 2013, 41 (49).

867 The Annex to the Treaty of Versailles (after Art. 440) contains the following sentence: "THE PRESENT TREATY, of which the French and English texts are both authentic, shall be ratified."

868 Cf. Art. 33 para. 1 VCLT: "When a treaty has been authenticated in two or more languages, the text is equally authoritative in each language, unless the treaty provides or the parties agree that, in case of divergence, a particular text shall prevail."

The matter of discretion was addressed by Judge *Moore* in his aide-mémoire which he presented during the drafting process of the first Rules of the Court in 1922.[870] Highly critical of the idea of conferring an advisory jurisdiction on the PCIJ, he argued that Article 14 of the Covenant did not impose on the Court an unconditional obligation to give an advisory opinion.[871] Moore argued that the wording "donnera" does not imply a duty of the Court to reply, as such a duty would have been indicated much more clearly by the term "elle devra donner". Because of this, the wording "may be interpreted more liberally.[872] Moore's grammatical interpretation seems rather result-oriented for one could equally make the opposite argument saying that if the parties intended for discretion of the Court, they could have added the word "peut".

However, Moore's teleological argument merits further attention as it lies at the heart of today's arguments in favor of a discretionary power of the Court to refuse certain requests for an advisory opinion. *Moore* argued that a duty to reply regardless of the circumstances of the request would be "inconsistent with and potentially destructive of the judicial character" of the Court.[873] *Moore* highlighted the fact that the Committee of Jurists when drafting the PCIJ Statute could not agree on a provision governing the PCIJ's advisory function and proposed to leave the question of how to deal with requests for advisory opinions to the practice of the Court.[874]

The 1929 revision of the PCIJ Statute[875] introduced an Article 65 which took up the wording of Article 14 of the Covenant but aligned the English and French wording to "may give" and "peut donner", respectively. The States Parties to the PCIJ Statute seem to have taken inspiration from *Moore's* analysis of Article 14. The 1929 revision could thus be understood as emphasizing the PCIJ's discretionary power to refuse certain requests for an advisory opinion.

---

869 Mavrommatis Palestine Concessions (Greece v. United Kingdom), Judgment, 1924, PCIJ Series A, no. 2, 19.

870 *J. B. Moore*, The question of advisory opinions, 1922, PCIJ Series D. No. 2.

871 Ibid., 397.

872 Ibid., 384.

873 Ibid., 384–385.

874 Ibid., 396, 398.

875 Resolution Concerning the Revision of the Statute of the Permanent Court of International Justice, adopted by the Assembly of the League of Nations, 14 September 1929, PCIJ Series D. No. 1, Statute and Rules of the Court, fourth edition (April 1940), 8. On the drafting history of the PCIJ Statute, see §1.B.IV.

However, the 1929 revision only resolved the uncertainty surrounding the difference in wording between the English and French versions. It did not clarify the meaning of the wording "may give". The original proposal for Article 14 sentence 3 of the Covenant did not contain the wording "may give" but "shall give".[876] Similarly a proposal by the Advisory Committee of Jurists to include an Article in the PCIJ Statute on the Court's advisory jurisdiction which would have employed the wording "shall give" was not adopted by the Assembly of the League.[877] The decision not to adopt the stricter wording "shall give" indicates the intention of the parties to confer upon the Court a certain flexibility in the exercise of its advisory jurisdiction.

In contrast, *Abi-Saab* argued that the word "may" was merely inserted in Article 14 to emphasize that the PCIJ may give advisory opinions at all, an activity which was beyond the regular functions of a court of law.[878] *Abi-Saab* argued that while the settlement of disputes was a "normal function of a court of law", the advisory jurisdiction was so novel that it required an express authorization.[879] The word "may" was thus not intended to define this jurisdiction but merely to authorize it.[880]

II. The ICJ's standard of "discretion"

The ICJ summarized its standard of discretion in the 2019 *Chagos* advisory opinion:

> "The fact that the Court has jurisdiction does not mean, however, that it is obliged to exercise it: "The Court has recalled many times in the past that Article 65, paragraph 1, of its Statute, which provides that 'The

876 *D. Pratap*, The advisory jurisdiction of the International Court, 1972, 143.

877 Procès-Verbaux of the Proceedings of the Committee, June 16th-July 24th 1920, p. 567, https://www.icj-cij.org/public/files/permanent-court-of-international-justice/serie_D/D_proceedings_of_committee_annexes_16june_24july_1920.pdf.

878 *G. Abi-Saab*, On Discretion: Reflections on the nature of the consultative function of the International Court of Justice, in: L. Boisson de Chazournes/P. Sands (eds.), International law, the World Court of justice and nuclear weapons, 1999, 36 (38); see also *R. Kolb*, 12 AJICL (2000), 799; *R. Kolb*, The International Court of Justice, 2013, 1085.

879 *G. Abi-Saab*, On Discretion: Reflections on the nature of the consultative function of the International Court of Justice, in: L. Boisson de Chazournes/P. Sands (eds.), International law, the World Court of justice and nuclear weapons, 1999, 36 (38).

880 Ibid., 38.

> Court *may* give an advisory opinion ...' (emphasis added), should be interpreted to mean that the Court has a discretionary power to decline to give an advisory opinion even if the conditions of jurisdiction are met." [...] The discretion whether or not to respond to a request for an advisory opinion exists so as to protect the integrity of the Court's judicial function as the principal judicial organ of the United Nations. [...] The Court is, nevertheless, mindful of the fact that its answer to a request for an advisory opinion "represents its participation in the activities of the Organization, and, in principle, should not be refused". Thus, the consistent jurisprudence of the Court is that only "compelling reasons" may lead the Court to refuse its opinion in response to a request falling within its jurisdiction."[881]

The ICJ relies on a grammatical as well as a functional interpretation of Article 65 ICJ Statute to establish that it has discretion in the exercise of its advisory jurisdiction. According to the ICJ, the word "may" signifies discretion.

By linking the Court's discretionary power to the Court's character as the principal judicial organ of the UN (Article 92 UNC) and its judicial function, the Court bases its discretionary power on a normative foundation, one that is rooted in a functionalist understanding of the powers of the Court. The Court as an organ of the UN does not only have the powers which are expressly conferred upon it, but also all those powers which are necessary for the proper exercise of its powers and functions.[882] Situations may arise in which giving an advisory opinion conflicts with the effective exercise of the Court's judicial function. In such situations the Court needs to have the power to refuse such a request. Rooting the Court's discretion in a functionalist reading of the Court's powers does not only lead to an extension of the Court's powers, it also limits them. The Court may only use its discretionary power for the purpose of protecting its judicial

881 *Legal Consequences of the Separation of the Chagos Archipelago from Mauritius in 1965*, Advisory Opinion, ICJ Reports 2019, 95 (113, paras. 63-65) (references omitted).

882 *Reparation for Injuries Suffered in the Service of the United Nations*, Advisory Opinion, ICJ Reports 1949, 174 (182); *Legality of the Use by a State of Nuclear Weapons in Armed Conflict*, Advisory Opinion, ICJ Reports 1996, 66 (78-29, para. 25); *N. M. Blokker*, International Organizations or Institutions, Implied Powers (last updated 2021), in: A. Peters/R. Wolfrum (eds.), The Max Planck Encyclopedia of Public International Law, 2008 (3 et seq.); *M. N. Shaw*, International law, 7. ed. 2014, 946; *A. von Arnauld*, Völkerrecht, 5. ed. 2023, 50, para. 125.

function. Unless the Court's judicial function is impaired, the Court may not refuse to give a requested advisory opinion. The functionalist argument has a third consequence to which the Court alluded on another occasion: When the judicial function of the Court is at stake, the Court not only has the power but also the duty (or obligation[883]) to exercise its discretion in order to refuse a request for an advisory opinion. The Court has the "duty to satisfy itself, each time it is seised of a request for an opinion, as to the propriety of the exercise of its judicial function."[884]

It becomes apparent that the Court does not understand its "discretion" as a freedom of choice. Instead, *whether* and *to which extent* the Court may exercise its discretion is determined by the discretion's function which is the protection of the integrity of the Court's judicial function.[885] Unless the integrity of the Court's judicial function is at stake, the Court is obliged to give the requested advisory opinion as part of its duty to participate in the activities of the UN. Therefore, only "compelling reasons"[886] may lead the Court to refuse the requested advisory opinion.

Some commentators have referred to the Court's general willingness to respond to requests for advisory opinions as "sheepish contrition"[887] towards the requesting organ. However, one could also understand the Court's narrow interpretation of its discretionary power as an effort to strengthen its advisory function. By defining the exclusionary grounds narrowly, the Court gives states and other actors less room to argue for the rejection of an advisory opinion. Only if there is an unresolvable conflict between its advisory activity and its other functions may and must the

---

883 *M. Virally*, La notion de fonction dans la théorie de l'organisation internationale, in: M. Virally (ed.), Le droit international en devenir, 1990 (paras. 73-78).

884 *Legal Consequences of the Construction of a Wall in the Occupied Palestinian Territory*, Advisory Opinion, ICJ Reports 2004, 136 (157, para. 45); *Accordance with international law of the unilateral declaration of independence in respect of Kosovo*, Advisory Opinion, ICJ Reports 2010, 403 (416, para. 31); *P. d'Argent*, in: A. Zimmermann/C. J. Tams/K. Oellers-Frahm/C. Tomuschat/D. W. K. Anderson (eds.), The Statute of the International Court of Justice, 3. ed., 2019: Article 65, para. 5.

885 The Court's position on its discretionary power is an example for what M. Virally described as the three normative characteristics of functionalism which are authorization, limitation and obligation, see *M. Virally*, La notion de fonction dans la théorie de l'organisation internationale, in: M. Virally (ed.), Le droit international en devenir, 1990 (51 et seq.).

886 With further references, see *Legal Consequences of the Separation of the Chagos Archipelago from Mauritius in 1965*, Advisory Opinion, ICJ Reports 2019, 95 (113, para. 65).

887 *R. Kolb*, The International Court of Justice, 2013, 1084.

Court refuse an advisory opinion. Such a stance seems less "sheepish" and more self-assertive.

III. Views in legal doctrine on the "discretion" of the ICJ

Kolb identified three "currents of opinion" in legal doctrine regarding the Court's discretion to refuse requests for an advisory opinion: the "discretionalist school", the "eclecticist school", and the "school of denial".[888] Only the discretionalist school argues that the Court has complete freedom of choice to give or deny an advisory opinion, while the other two currents believe in some form of legal determination of the Court's power to give advisory opinions.

1. Discretionalist school

The representatives of the "discretionalist school"[889] advocate for an absolute freedom of the Court when giving advisory opinions.[890] The Court may weigh the arguments in favor and against the giving of the requested advisory opinion on a case-by-case basis, without being restricted to legal considerations alone.[891] An undercurrent of this school argues that certain arguments rank higher than others, in particular the protection of the integrity of the Court's judicial function and the Court's independence from the political organs of the UN.[892]

888 Ibid., 1086–1089.

889 Ibid., 1086.

890 *H. Kelsen*, The law of the United Nations, 2. ed. 1951, 549; *D. Pratap*, The advisory jurisdiction of the International Court, 1972, 142; cf. *K. Oellers-Frahm/E. Lagrange*, in: B. Simma/D.-E. Khan/G. Nolte/A. Paulus (eds.), The Charter of the United Nations, 4. ed., 2024: Art. 96, para. 32.

891 See *Oellers-Frahm* who argues that certain cases, which are situated between law and politics, may force the Court to find "pragmatic solutions that may be disappointing from the legal perspective", see *K. Oellers-Frahm*, in: B. Simma/D.-E. Khan/G. Nolte/A. Paulus (eds.), The Charter of the United Nations, 3. ed., 2012: Art. 96, para. 22.

892 *Kolb* refers to the Individual Opinion by Judge *Anzilotti* in the case on the *Consistency of certain Danzig legislative decrees with the Constitution of the Free City*, PCIJ Series A/B, No. 65, 61, see *R. Kolb*, The International Court of Justice, 2013, 1087; see also *M. Pomerance*, The advisory function of the International Court in the League and U.N. eras, 1973, 279 et seq.

Pratap, one of the representatives of this group, defines discretion as the "right of the Court to refuse an opinion if it considers that there are reasons which make it improper to accede to the request."[893] In contrast to other commentators, *Pratap* speaks of a "right" of the Court rather than a power or duty.

Pratap distinguishes between two types of discretion of the Court: statutory discretion under Article 65 ICJ Statute and discretion in the exercise of judicial powers or inherent powers as a Court of Justice.[894] The statutory discretion, *Partap* argues, is expressly conferred upon the Court by Article 65 ICJ Statute, according to which the Court "may give an advisory opinion" (instead of "shall give").[895] *Pratap* relies on *Kelsen* who argued that by virtue of its statutory discretion "the Court is only authorized, not obliged, to give advisory opinions. The Court may, for reasons completely within its discretion, refuse to give an advisory opinion requested in conformity with the Charter."[896]

This broad statutory discretion is contrasted in *Pratap's* writing with the Court's narrow discretion in the exercise of its judicial powers. The Court possesses this second type of discretion as an expression of its character as a court of justice.[897] The Court's discretion in the exercise of its judicial powers exists so as to allow the Court to protect the integrity of its judicial character.[898] If giving an advisory opinion contradicts the Court's judicial character, the Court must exercise its judicial power so as to refuse the requested advisory opinion.[899]

According to *Pratap,* the Court's statutory discretion goes beyond what the Court can do in the exercise of its judicial powers.[900] Under its statutory discretion, the Court may refuse requests in situations which do not affect its judicial character, for example when the Court fears that its response would adversely affect the resolution of the underlying dispute or if contentious proceedings were pending on the same matter.[901]

893 *D. Pratap*, The advisory jurisdiction of the International Court, 1972, 142.
894 Ibid., 142.
895 Ibid., 145.
896 Ibid., 145, citing *H. Kelsen*, The Law of the United Nations, 2. ed. 1951, 549.
897 Ibid., 142.
898 Ibid., 145–150.
899 Ibid., 142.
900 Ibid., 150–151.
901 Ibid., 151.

2. Eclecticist school

The representatives of the "eclecticist school"[902] argue for an objectivized discretion of the Court.[903] They accept that the Court has discretion, but they argue that this discretion finds its limits in what the Court refers to as "compelling reasons".[904] In other words, the discretion of the Court is not free but limited to the achievement of certain functions, chief among them the protection of the Court's judicial function.

Keith argues that the Court, as a principal organ of the UN is bound by the general provisions governing the work of the UN, in particular the purposes and principles of the UN as laid out in Articles 1 and 2 UNC.[905] This requires the Court to cooperate with the other UN organs and UN Member States.[906] At the same time, the UNC and the ICJ Statute – in particular in light of its drafting history – require that the Court must always – even when giving advisory opinions – act judicially.[907] To ensure that the Court can fulfill this obligation, the Court has discretion.[908] *Keith* argues that the Court's character as a court of justice determines how the Court must exercise its advisory function.[909] One consequence of this is that the Court's advisory function must follow the same procedural safeguards as the Court's contentious procedure which include requirements of notification and publicity of the proceedings, the right of interested parties to present their position, and the requirement to have a sufficient factual basis on which to base the opinion.[910]

902 *R. Kolb*, The International Court of Justice, 2013, 1087.
903 *K. J. Keith*, The extent of the advisory jurisdiction of the International Court of Justice, 1971, 142 et seq.; *H. Mosler*, in: B. Simma/H. Mosler/R. Bernhardt (eds.), Charta der Vereinten Nationen, 1991: Art. 96, para. 23; *P. d'Argent*, in: A. Zimmermann/C. J. Tams/K. Oellers-Frahm/C. Tomuschat/D. W. K. Anderson (eds.), The Statute of the International Court of Justice, 3. ed., 2019: Article 65, 41 et seq.
904 *K. J. Keith*, The extent of the advisory jurisdiction of the International Court of Justice, 1971, 142 et seq.; *H. Mosler*, in: B. Simma/H. Mosler/R. Bernhardt (eds.), Charta der Vereinten Nationen, 1991: Art. 96, para. 23; *P. d'Argent*, in: A. Zimmermann/C. J. Tams/K. Oellers-Frahm/C. Tomuschat/D. W. K. Anderson (eds.), The Statute of the International Court of Justice, 3. ed., 2019: Article 65, 42.
905 *K. J. Keith*, The extent of the advisory jurisdiction of the International Court of Justice, 1971, 146.
906 Ibid., 146.
907 Ibid., 152.
908 Ibid., 151.
909 Ibid., 155.
910 Ibid., 155–156.

Rosenne locates the Court's discretion entirely within the powers expressly conferred upon the Court by its Statute. The permissive wording of Article 65 gives the Court a general discretion, while Article 68 additionally confers upon the Court a broad discretion regarding the procedure to be applied in any given case.[911] *Rosenne* identifies two principles which "guide the Court in the exercise of its discretion":

> "The first is the principle originally laid down in the answer given to the Council of the League of Nations in the *Eastern Carelia* case that the Court, being a court of justice, cannot, even in giving advisory opinions, depart from the essential rules guiding its activity as a Court. The second, which is unique to the present Court, is that since the Court is a principal organ of the United Nations, it is under a duty to co-operate with other organs; consequently, a request for an advisory opinion should not in principle be refused, and only compelling reasons (*raisons décisives*) should lead the Court to refuse to give the requested opinion."[912]

At the same time, *Rosenne* criticizes the Court's duty to respond because it "implies three presumptions, that the resolution adopting the request was *intra vires* the requesting organ, that the question was a legal question, and that the question was not directed to the settlement of an international dispute between two international entities acting on the international level."[913] *Rosenne* therefore speaks of a rebuttable presumption in favor of giving requested opinions. Once the Court's competence is challenged, it must "adopt positive arguments to establish it, and especially that there are no compelling reasons for it to decline to render a requested opinion."[914]

911 *S. Rosenne*, The law and practice of the International Court, 1920-2005, 4th ed. 2006, 975.
912 Ibid., 976.
913 Ibid., 992.
914 Ibid., 992.

3. School of denial

The representatives of the "school of denial"[915] argue that the Court has no discretion when giving advisory opinions.[916] The core argument is that, being a judicial body, the ICJ can reject a request for an advisory opinion exclusively based on legal considerations.[917] *Kolb* therefore argues in favor of replacing the term discretion with the term 'propriety'.[918] According to *Kolb*, the term 'propriety' conveys more clearly that the Court's decision whether to give an advisory opinion is limited to an assessment of the proper course of action for a court of justice.[919]

Similarly, *H. Lauterpacht* recognized that there were certain limits to the ICJ's duty to reply to requests for an advisory opinion. However,

> "these limits are of a legal character; they are determined by the fact that the Court is the judicial organ of the United Nations and that in acting in an advisory capacity it must act in accordance with its judicial character, the requirements of its Statute, and the principles of international law. The Court has not considered itself free to decline to render an advisory opinion on account of political considerations or for reasons of its own convenience."[920]

Abi-Saab is another prominent critic of the Court's "discretion" when giving advisory opinions.[921] He argued that the Court's references to "discretion" are not meant to convey an unfettered discretion to refuse a request for an advisory opinion for reasons of convenience or opportunity.[922] Such an interpretation could not be reconciled with the remainder of the Court's *dicta* in this context.[923] *Abi-Saab* points to the *Certain Expenses* advisory opinion in

---

915 *R. Kolb*, The International Court of Justice, 2013, 1088.

916 *H. Lauterpacht*, The development of international law by the International Court, 2. ed. 1958, 250; *G. Abi-Saab*, Les exceptions préliminaires dans la procédure de la Cour internationale, 1966, 152–153; *R. Kolb*, 12 AJICL (2000), 799; with further rerefernces *R. Kolb*, The International Court of Justice, 2013, 1088–1094.

917 *R. Kolb*, The International Court of Justice, 2013, 1088–1089.

918 *R. Kolb*, The Elgar companion to the International Court of Justice, 2014, 274.

919 Ibid., 274.

920 *H. Lauterpacht*, The development of international law by the International Court, 2. ed. 1958, 250.

921 *G. Abi-Saab*, On Discretion: Reflections on the nature of the consultative function of the International Court of Justice, in: L. Boisson de Chazournes/P. Sands (eds.), International law, the World Court of justice and nuclear weapons, 1999, 36.

922 Ibid., 42–43.

923 Ibid., 42–43.

which the Court emphasized that as a principal organ the reply to a request for an advisory opinion constitutes the Court's participation in the activities of the UN and may only be refused when there are compelling reasons.[924] According to *Abi-Saab*, the word "compelling" negates any choice on the part of the Court.[925] Additionally, the Court referred to the inherent limitations of the judicial function as "imperative".[926] As the Court can only refuse requests for advisory opinions when there are "compelling" or "imperative" reasons, the Court does not enjoy unfettered discretion which would leave room for considerations of opportunity or convenience.

However, *Abi-Saab* argues, the Court has a wide margin of appreciation of the general considerations of admissibility of a request which includes the propriety of giving the requested advisory opinion.[927] Propriety, according to *Abi-Saab*, "is subject to the test of what is proper for a judicial organ to do, that is, what is compatible with the judicial function."[928] To act according to these requirements, the Court has a "special duty of vigilance" to ensure that the inherent limitations of the judicial function are not trespassed when giving advisory opinions.[929] *Abi-Saab* also highlights the fact that the Court has continuously regarded its advisory activity as part of its judicial function. The exercise of this function cannot be guided by opportunity or convenience "[f]or – unlike a right, which is a power or a faculty its holder can exercise or not exercise, keep or abandon – a function combines a power with a charge or an obligation to exercise it in the pursuit of a specific finality."[930]

Arguing along similar lines, *Kolb* proposes to distinguish between two concepts based on the degree of freedom an organ enjoys when making decisions: discretion in the proper sense of the term and a rule-based duty of

---

924 Abi-Saab cites *Certain Expenses of the United Nations (Article 17, paragraph 2, of the Charter)*, Advisory Opinion, ICJ Reports 1962, 151 (155).

925 *G. Abi-Saab*, On Discretion: Reflections on the nature of the consultative function of the International Court of Justice, in: L. Boisson de Chazournes/P. Sands (eds.), International law, the World Court of justice and nuclear weapons, 1999, 36 (49).

926 Abi-Saab cites *Northern Cameroons (Cameroon v. United Kingdom) (Preliminary Objections)*, Judgment, ICJ Reports 1963, 15 (30).

927 *G. Abi-Saab*, On Discretion: Reflections on the nature of the consultative function of the International Court of Justice, in: L. Boisson de Chazournes/P. Sands (eds.), International law, the World Court of justice and nuclear weapons, 1999, 36 (44–45).

928 Ibid., 44.

929 Ibid., 45.

930 Ibid., 44.

appreciation.[931] Discretion is the freedom to decide between two or more options without this decision depending on objective, previously defined reasons.[932] A discretionary decision is only guided by "simple opportunity" or "political reasons".[933] Discretion, according to *Kolb*, always requires a "residuum of free choice" beyond purely legal considerations.[934] A decision is not discretionary in this sense, if the outcome of the decision is determined by a rule, regardless of how broadly defined and subject to interpretation it may be.[935] Instead, the organ applying such a rule is under a rule-based duty of assessment.[936] While this duty of assessment may be subject to a wide margin of appreciation, it is not a discretionary decision.[937]

Applying these considerations to the ICJ's advisory function, *Kolb* argues that the Court's decision whether to grant a requested advisory opinion is entirely determined by a legal norm, according to which the Court must protect the integrity of its judicial function.[938] The Court's decision on the admissibility of the request is the result of a legal rather than a political assessment.[939] There is no categorical difference between this assessment and other considerations of admissibility, other than the relative vagueness of the norm to be applied (i.e., the integrity of the Court's judicial function).[940] However, *Kolb* argues that this only means that the Court has a wider margin of appreciation when making its legal assessment.[941] The Court cannot refuse an advisory opinion based on extra-legal reasons, just as the Court cannot decide *to give* an advisory opinion if this would harm the Court's judicial function.[942] As *Kolb* rightly points out, if the Court refused to give an advisory opinion and thereby refused to perform a judicial task for reasons beyond legal considerations, the Court would

931 *R. Kolb*, The International Court of Justice, 2013, 1091.

932 Ibid., 1091.

933 *R. Kolb*, The Elgar companion to the International Court of Justice, 2014, 274.

934 *R. Kolb*, The International Court of Justice, 2013, 1092.

935 Ibid., 1091.

936 Ibid., 1091.

937 Ibid., 1091.

938 Ibid., 1092.

939 Ibid., 1092.

940 Ibid., 1092–1093; *R. Kolb*, The Elgar companion to the International Court of Justice, 2014, 274.

941 *R. Kolb*, The International Court of Justice, 2013, 1092–1093; *R. Kolb*, The Elgar companion to the International Court of Justice, 2014, 274.

942 *R. Kolb*, The International Court of Justice, 2013, 1092–1093; *R. Kolb*, The Elgar companion to the International Court of Justice, 2014, 274.

act politically rather than judicially.[943] This would contradict rather than strengthen the integrity of the Court's judicial function.

IV. Interim conclusions

The Court's power to refuse requests for advisory opinions must be considered in light of its character as an organ of the UN. As an organ of the UN the ICJ exists because the UN's Member States intended for the Court to pursue certain objectives. In the case of the UN, these objectives include the maintenance of international peace and security, the development of friendly relations among states and international cooperation (Article 1 UNC). To contribute to the attainment of these objectives, the UN Member States have given the Court certain functions and equipped it with certain powers which allow the Court to exercise these functions. The powers of the Court exist solely for the purpose of exercising its functions. Article 96 UNC and Article 65 ICJ Statute confer upon the ICJ the function to assist the other UN organs in their work by issuing advisory opinions on any legal question requested by them. The Court does not have the *right* to give advisory opinions but the *function* to do so.[944] Functions, in contrast to rights, confer upon the respective organ a duty to act in accordance with the relevant function.[945] Since the organ of an international organization has the duty to perform its functions, the non-performance of a function, such as the advisory function, requires a legal justification.[946] The legal justification identified by the Court for refusing certain requests for an advisory opinion is the protection of its judicial function. All of these considerations are best encapsulated by *Kolb's* concept of a rule-based duty of appreciation. The next and decisive question is then: What is the Court's judicial function and how can the giving of an advisory opinion negatively affect the Court's judicial function?

---

943 *R. Kolb*, The International Court of Justice, 2013, 1093–1094.

944 Ibid., 1093–1094.

945 *M. Virally*, La notion de fonction dans la théorie de l'organisation internationale, in: M. Virally (ed.), Le droit international en devenir, 1990 (73–78).

946 Cf. Ibid., para. 73.

§ 6 Justification of the Eastern Carelia doctrine: the Court's judicial function

As illustrated in the previous chapters, the ICJ derives its power to refuse certain requests for advisory opinions from its duty to act in accordance with and protect its judicial function. In its *Chagos* advisory opinion, the ICJ found:

> "The discretion whether or not to respond to a request for an advisory opinion exists so as to protect the integrity of the Court's judicial function as the principal judicial organ of the United Nations."[947]

Likewise, in several earlier advisory opinions the ICJ referred to the Court's duty to "remain faithful to the requirements of its judicial character".[948]

The Eastern Carelia doctrine can be seen as a result of the dual character of the ICJ. On the one hand the Court is a principal organ of the UN.[949] As an organ of the UN, the Court has a duty to promote the activities of the organization.[950] As part of this duty, the Court renders any advisory opinion requested of it by an authorized organ in order to assist that organ in its functions within the organization.[951] On the other hand, the

---

947 *Legal Consequences of the Separation of the Chagos Archipelago from Mauritius in 1965*, Advisory Opinion, ICJ Reports 2019, 95 (113, para. 64), citing Legal Consequences of the Construction of a Wall in the Occupied Palestinian Territory, Advisory Opinion, ICJ Reports 2004, p. 136 (156-157), paras. 44-45; Accordance with International Law of the Unilateral Declaration of Independence in Respect of Kosovo, Advisory Opinion, ICJ Reports 2010, p. 403 (415-416), para. 29.

948 *Judgments of the Administrative Tribunal of the ILO upon Complaints Made against UNESCO*, Advisory Opinion, ICJ Reports 1956, 77 (84); *Constitution of the Maritime Safety Committee of the Inter-Governmental Maritime Consultative*, Advisory Opinion, ICJ Reports 1960, 150 (153); *Legal Consequences for States of the Continued Presence of South Africa in Namibia (South West Africa) notwithstanding Security Council Resolution 276 (1970)*, Advisory Opinion, ICJ Reports 1971, 16 (27, para. 41); *Western Sahara*, Advisory Opinion, ICJ Reports 1975, 12 (21, para. 23).

949 See Article 7 para. 1 UNC: "There are established as the principal organs of the United Nations: a General Assembly, a Security Council, an Economic and Social Council, a Trusteeship Council, an International Court of Justice, and a Secretariat."

950 *Interpretation of Peace Treaties with Bulgaria, Hungary and Romania (First Phase)*, Advisory Opinion, ICJ Reports 1950, 65 (71).

951 Ibid.

ICJ is also the UN's principal *judicial* organ,[952] which imposes certain limits on the ICJ's duty to participate in the activities of the UN.[953] Being a judicial organ, the Court must ensure that all of its activities comply with its "judicial character"[954] or "judicial function".[955] The Court's judicial function thus limits the Court's duty to cooperate with other UN organs. When deciding whether or not to give an advisory opinion the ICJ is thus guided by two competing duties stemming from its dual character as an organ of an international organization and as a court: a *duty to give* any advisory opinion requested by an authorized UN organ and a *duty to refuse to give* any advisory opinion that is incompatible with the Court's judicial function.

The Eastern Carelia doctrine is based on the premise that there is a tension between the Court rendering advisory opinions on inter-state disputes without the consent of the relevant states and the Court's judicial function. The Court expressed this tension in its *Western Sahara* opinion:

> "In certain circumstances, therefore, the lack of consent of an interested State may render the giving of an advisory opinion incompatible with the Court's judicial character. An instance of this would be when the circumstances disclose that to give a reply would have the effect of circumventing the principle that a State is not obliged to allow its disputes to be submitted to judicial settlement without its consent."[956]

---

952 See Article 92 UNC: "The International Court of Justice shall be the principal judicial organ of the United Nations. It shall function in accordance with the annexed Statute, which is based upon the Statute of the Permanent Court of International Justice and forms an integral part of the present Charter."

953 *Interpretation of Peace Treaties with Bulgaria, Hungary and Romania (First Phase)*, Advisory Opinion, ICJ Reports 1950, 65 (71); *S. Rosenne*, The law and practice of the International Court, 1920-2005, 4th ed. 2006, 142.

954 *Constitution of the Maritime Safety Committee of the Inter-Governmental Maritime Consultative*, Advisory Opinion, ICJ Reports 1960, 150 (153); *Legal Consequences for States of the Continued Presence of South Africa in Namibia (South West Africa) notwithstanding Security Council Resolution 276 (1970)*, Advisory Opinion, ICJ Reports 1971, 16 (27, para. 41); *Western Sahara*, Advisory Opinion, ICJ Reports 1975, 12 (25, para. 33).

955 *Legal Consequences of the Construction of a Wall in the Occupied Palestinian Territory*, Advisory Opinion, ICJ Reports 2004, 136 (156-157, paras. 44-45); *Accordance with international law of the unilateral declaration of independence in respect of Kosovo*, Advisory Opinion, ICJ Reports 2010, 403 (415-416, para. 29); *Legal Consequences of the Separation of the Chagos Archipelago from Mauritius in 1965*, Advisory Opinion, ICJ Reports 2019, 95 (113, para. 64).

956 *Western Sahara*, Advisory Opinion, ICJ Reports 1975, 12 (24-25, para. 33).

At the heart of the Eastern Carelia doctrine lies the concern that the advisory opinion procedure could be abused to circumvent the principle of consensual dispute settlement as it is codified for the Court's contentious procedure in Article 36 ICJ Statute. Judge *Donoghue* warned against such a negative relationship between the Court's advisory and contentious procedures in the *Chagos* case, when she voiced the concern that the advisory opinion procedure was becoming "a fall-back mechanism to be used to overcome the absence of consent to jurisdiction in contentious cases."[957] Judge *Donoghue* advocated in favor of strengthening the distinction between the two procedures in order to safeguard their integrity.[958] Integrity in this sense means exclusivity.

The aim of this chapter is to examine the persuasiveness of the Court's Eastern Carelia doctrine. In particular, the chapter seeks to assess the Court's claim that advisory opinions on inter-state disputes are in tension with the Court's judicial function and the principle of consensual dispute settlement. As illustrated above, the ICJ uses the terms "judicial function" and "judicial character" without defining them as if their meaning was apparent. However, considering that the Court derives from its judicial function certain limits of its advisory procedure, and thus limits of the right of the requesting UN organ to receive an answer from the Court, a clearer concept of the terms "judicial function" and "judicial character" is needed.

To approach the two terms, it may be illustrative to examine similar discussions about the role of the judiciary in domestic legal systems. ICs like the ICJ have been created long after the creation of domestic courts. Domestic concepts of courts and their function within domestic legal systems has preceded and informed the creation of ICs. While one must be careful not to blindly transfer legal concepts from municipal law to international law,[959] it nevertheless seems illustrative to start the analysis of the term "judicial function" by examining similar discussions in domestic legal systems (*infra* A.). The chapter then examines different understand-

957 *Legal Consequences of the Separation of the Chagos Archipelago from Mauritius in 1965*, Advisory Opinion, Dissenting Opinion Donoghue, ICJ Reports 2019, 95 (266, para. 23).

958 Ibid.

959 Emphasizing the difference in cogency between municipal law and international law, *H. Lauterpacht* argues that analogies to private law should be limited to "general principles of private law recognised by the main systems of jurisprudence", see *H. Lauterpacht*, Private law sources and analogies of international law, 1927, 84–85; see also *G. I. Hernández*, The International Court of Justice and the judicial function, 2014, 44.

ings of the term "judicial function" used by the ICJ (*infra* B.). Following this, the chapter turns to the question of whether the giving of advisory opinions may undermine the Court's judicial function by circumventing the principle of consensual settlement of disputes. To this end, the chapter examines the scope of the consent requirement as it applies to the Court's contentious procedure (*infra* C.). It then seeks to answer the question whether the giving of an advisory opinion on an inter-state dispute without the consent of the disputing states constitutes a circumvention of this consent requirement (*infra* D.). In order to answer this question, the chapter compares the Eastern Carelia doctrine with the Monetary Gold doctrine.

A. The role of courts under domestic legal systems

Article 92 of the German Basic Law (*Grundgesetz*) contains the central provision on the role of the judiciary in the German legal system. It stipulates:

> "The judicial power shall be vested in the judges; it shall be exercised by the Federal Constitutional Court, by the federal courts provided for in this Basic Law and by the courts of the *Länder*."[960]

The meaning of the key term "judicial power" ("*rechtsprechende Gewalt*") is contested in German scholarship and case law.[961]

I. The concept of "judicial power" in Germany

Many prominent legal commentators define the term judicial power by reference to certain characteristic features of courts. *Stern*, for example, defines judicial power "as the legal judgment of facts in specially regulated proceedings leading to the final binding decision in application of the

960 Article 92 Basic Law, translated by Professor Christian Tomuschat, Professor David P. Currie, Professor Donald P. Kommers and Raymond Kerr, in cooperation with the Language Service of the German Bundestag, https://www.gesetze-im-internet.de/englisch_gg/englisch_gg.html.

961 *A. Voßkuhle*, Rechtsschutz gegen den Richter, 1993, 69 et seq.; *C. Möllers*, Gewaltengliederung, 2005, 98; *H. Schulze-Fielitz*, in: H. Dreier (ed.), Grundgesetz Kommentar, 2018: Art. 92, para. 25; *M. Payandeh*, in: W. Kahl/C. Waldhoff/C. Walter (eds.), Bonner Kommentar zum Grundgesetz, June 2020: Art. 92, para. 121.

applicable law by an uninvolved (state) organ, the judge".[962] According to *Böckenförde*, judicial power includes "the handling of a case by an uninvolved, neutral body ("independent third party") and that its independent decisions, which are aimed at legal force, are not made according to political or other considerations of expedience, but (solely) in accordance with the applicable law (law and justice)".[963] *Schulze-Fielitz* provides an extensive definition of judicial power:

> "The exercise of judicial power presupposes (1) a special decision-making procedure regulated by law, establishes (2) specific facts on a case-by-case basis, assesses (3) this against the background of uncertain, because contested or violated law and decides (4) a dispute in a final and binding manner solely by applying the applicable law by (5) an independent (neutral) state body that is not involved in the initial dispute."[964]

In its early case law, the German Federal Constitutional Court (FCC) similarly identified a set of minimum requirements of judicial power, without, however, providing a comprehensive definition of the term.[965] Accordingly, the "judicial power" requires *inter alia* that decisions are rendered by an uninvolved third party[966], that the law is applied by an independent, legally competent body[967] and that certain requirements for the composition of the court and the procedure are respected[968].[969]

In a landmark decision in 1967, the FCC adopted the so-called "substantive" or "material" concept of judicial power.[970] Accordingly, the term judi-

---

962 *K. Stern*, Das Staatsrecht der Bundesrepublik Deutschland, 1980, vol. II, 898, translated by the author.

963 *E.-W. Böckenförde*, Verfassungsfragen der Richterwahl, 1974, 87, translated by the author.

964 *H. Schulze-Fielitz*, in: H. Dreier (ed.), Grundgesetz Kommentar, 2018: Art. 92, para. 26, translated by the author.

965 *M. Payandeh*, in: W. Kahl/C. Waldhoff/C. Walter (eds.), Bonner Kommentar zum Grundgesetz, June 2020: Art. 92, para. 126.

966 FCC, order of the first senate of 29 April 1954 – 1 BvR 328/52 – BVerfGE 3, 377 (381) – *Schwerbeschädigtenschutz*; FCC, order of the first senate of 9 November 1955 – 1 BvL 13/52, 1 BvL 21/53 – BverfGE 4, 331 (346) – *Soforthilfegesetz*.

967 FCC, order of the first senate of 21 October 1954 – 1 BvL 9/51, 1 BvL 2/53 – BverfGE 4, 74 (93) – *Ärztliches Berufsgericht*.

968 Ibid.

969 *M. Payandeh*, in: W. Kahl/C. Waldhoff/C. Walter (eds.), Bonner Kommentar zum Grundgesetz, June 2020: Art. 92, 121 et seq.

970 *C. Möllers*, Gewaltengliederung, 2005, 99; *M. Payandeh*, in: W. Kahl/C. Waldhoff/C. Walter (eds.), Bonner Kommentar zum Grundgesetz, June 2020: Art. 92, para. 125.

cial power stipulates certain substantive guarantees, in particular a constitutional guarantee that the judiciary has a certain set of core competences, irrespective of an express allocation in the Basic Law or statutes.[971] These core competences include the traditional areas of judicial activity, namely deciding civil law disputes and criminal adjudication.[972] In adopting a material concept of judicial power, the FCC emphasized the departure of the Basic Law from the formalistic approach of the Imperial Constitution of Weimar (*Weimarer Reichsverfassung*), which did not contain such substantive guarantees and did not reserve certain tasks to the judiciary.[973]

The extensive case law of the FCC on the matter, which sometimes focused on certain minimum characteristics of the judiciary, sometimes on the organizational composition of a court and sometimes emphasized the tasks allocated to a court, has led to some confusion in legal scholarship.[974] Several scholars have tried to derive from the case law of the FCC a single comprehensive definition of the term judicial function.[975] However, as *Payandeh* points out, the case law, and the ensuing debate in legal scholarship, conflate two separate, albeit related, questions under the concept of judicial power: the tasks of the judiciary on the one hand (*What do the courts do?*) and the functional elements and essential characteristics of the judiciary (*How do the Courts operate?*) on the other.[976] The "substantive" or "material" concept of judicial power focuses on the "what", while the approaches focusing on the characteristics and composition of the judiciary focus on the "*how*".[977] As *Payandeh* explains, Article 92 of the Basic Law combines both elements of the debate:

> "A meaningful distinction and separation of the judicial power from the other two powers presupposes, on the one hand, that certain state tasks and institutions must be constitutionally assigned to the third power and are barred from being exercised by the other two powers. (...) At the

971 FCC, judgment of the second senate of 7 and 8 March 1967 – 2 BvR 375, 53/60 and 18/65 – BVerfGE 22, 49 (75 et seq.) – *Verwaltungsstrafverfahren*; FCC, judgment of the second senate of 5 December 2000 – 2 BvF 1/00 – BVerfGE 103, 111 (138) – *Wahlprüfung Hessen.*

972 FCC, judgment of the second senate of 7 and 8 March 1967 – 2 BvR 375, 53/60 and 18/65 – BVerfGE 22, 49 (78) – *Verwaltungsstrafverfahren.*

973 *M. Payandeh*, in: W. Kahl/C. Waldhoff/C. Walter (eds.), Bonner Kommentar zum Grundgesetz, June 2020: Art. 92, para. 144.

974 Ibid., 137 et seq.

975 Ibid., para. 148.

976 Ibid., para. 148.

977 Ibid., para. 150.

same time, there must also be differentiation criteria between the judicial power and the other two state powers in functional terms – in terms of organization, activity, procedure and decision-making effect. For the separation of powers serves not only to divide sovereign power between different organs and officials, but is also justified by the functional characteristics of the respective powers: The judicial power is granted a special status under constitutional law and certain tasks are assigned to it, not only because it differs from the other two powers in the first place, but also and precisely because of certain essential characteristics of the judicial exercise of sovereign power."[978]

In summary, the term "judicial power" as used in Article 92 of the Basic Law refers to two related, but distinct concepts: the tasks assigned to the judiciary and the essential (functional) characteristics for fulfilling these tasks. Both shall briefly be examined below.

II. Characteristics and tasks of domestic courts

1. Characteristics of domestic courts

With *Payandeh*, the core characteristics of judicial power under the German Basic Law can be summarized as "the legally binding and final decision of an individual case by a neutral third party according to the standard of law in a special procedure."[979] This short definition entails five dimensions of judicial power: Characteristics concerning the decision-making body, the subject-matter of the decision, the standard of the decision, the decision-making procedure and the effects of the decision.[980]

a) Decision-making body

A first characteristic of judicial power is that judicial decisions are made by an uninvolved, neutral and impartial decision-making body.[981] The de-

978 Ibid., para. 154.
979 Ibid., para. 189, translated by the author.
980 Ibid., para. 169.
981 With further references, see Ibid., para. 170.

cision-making body must be independent,[982] it must not be affected by the decision and must have no personal interest in the outcome of the proceedings.[983]

b) Subject-matter of the decision

The subject-matter of judicial activity is often described as dispute-settlement.[984] However, to equate judicial activity with the settlement of disputes is both over- und under-inclusive.[985] It is over-inclusive in the sense that non-judicial forms of dispute settlement, such as political or administrative forms of dispute-settlement are included.[986] It is under-inclusive in that there are many forms of judicial activity which do not concern dispute-settlement, yet clearly fall within the purview of judicial power.[987] These include for example the administration of criminal justice, the issuing of judicial orders in criminal proceedings, or the judicial review of statutes.[988] It thus seems more persuasive to dispense with the element of dispute-settlement as an essential characteristic of the judicial power.[989] Instead, the essential characteristic of the judicial power is the decision of individual cases.[990]

982 Ibid., para. 170.
983 *A. Voßkuhle*, Rechtsschutz gegen den Richter, 1993, 105 et seq.
984 With further references, see *M. Payandeh*, in: W. Kahl/C. Waldhoff/C. Walter (eds.), Bonner Kommentar zum Grundgesetz, June 2020: Art. 92, para. 170.
985 Critical *C. Möllers*, Gewaltengliederung, 2005, 100; *M. Payandeh*, in: W. Kahl/C. Waldhoff/C. Walter (eds.), Bonner Kommentar zum Grundgesetz, June 2020: Art. 92, para. 176.
986 *C. Möllers*, Gewaltengliederung, 2005, 100.
987 Ibid., 100; *M. Payandeh*, in: W. Kahl/C. Waldhoff/C. Walter (eds.), Bonner Kommentar zum Grundgesetz, June 2020: Art. 92, para. 176.
988 *M. Payandeh*, in: W. Kahl/C. Waldhoff/C. Walter (eds.), Bonner Kommentar zum Grundgesetz, June 2020: Art. 92, para. 176.
989 With further references, see Ibid., para. 177.
990 *C. Möllers*, Gewaltengliederung, 2005, 99–100; *M. Payandeh*, in: W. Kahl/C. Waldhoff/C. Walter (eds.), Bonner Kommentar zum Grundgesetz, June 2020: Art. 92, para. 177.

c) Standard of decision-making

Another characteristic of judicial power is that the law forms the only reference point for judicial reasoning.[991] This means that courts must apply legal methods and base their decisions on legal standards.[992] A consequence of this is that courts are prohibited from deciding cases based on expediency or political considerations and from pursuing independently set purposes.[993]

d) Decision-making procedure

The decision-making of courts must follow special procedures which are established in advance and which ensure the fair administration of justice.[994] Typical procedural principles include equality of arms between the parties and the publicity of the proceedings.[995] The goal of these procedures is to ensure the neutral administration of justice.[996] As part of this neutrality, courts are typically prohibited from initiating proceedings on their own accord but rely on an application from the outside.[997]

e) Effects of the decision

A final characteristic of judicial power concerns the effects of judicial decisions. Decisions rendered by a court are binding for the parties of the individual case. This means that the parties are under an obligation to comply with the decision and, at the same time, have an obligation not

991 *C. Möllers*, Gewaltengliederung, 2005, 95; *M. Payandeh*, in: W. Kahl/C. Waldhoff/C. Walter (eds.), Bonner Kommentar zum Grundgesetz, June 2020: Art. 92, para. 181.
992 *C. Möllers*, Gewaltengliederung, 2005, 95; *M. Payandeh*, in: W. Kahl/C. Waldhoff/C. Walter (eds.), Bonner Kommentar zum Grundgesetz, June 2020: Art. 92, para. 181.
993 *A. Voßkuhle*, Rechtsschutz gegen den Richter, 1993, 79 et seq.; *M. Payandeh*, in: W. Kahl/C. Waldhoff/C. Walter (eds.), Bonner Kommentar zum Grundgesetz, June 2020: Art. 92, para. 182.
994 *M. Payandeh*, in: W. Kahl/C. Waldhoff/C. Walter (eds.), Bonner Kommentar zum Grundgesetz, June 2020: Art. 92, para. 183.
995 Ibid., para. 184.
996 Ibid., para. 183.
997 *C. Möllers*, Gewaltengliederung, 2005, 96–97; *M. Payandeh*, in: W. Kahl/C. Waldhoff/C. Walter (eds.), Bonner Kommentar zum Grundgesetz, June 2020: Art. 92, para. 184.

to deviate from it.[998] Additionally, organs of the legislative and executive branches cannot overrule or annul decisions of the judiciary.[999] Even other judicial bodies have very limited powers to amend or overturn judicial decisions.[1000] Importantly, the legal effects of court decisions are not limited to the immediate parties to a case. Instead, they exert authority beyond the individual case.[1001] The legal nature of such "judicial precedents" beyond the individual case is disputed in German legal scholarship.[1002] Some commentators argue that judicial precedents may be binding as a form of customary law,[1003] or constitute a legal source *sui generis*[1004]. A strong current in German legal scholarship ascribes judicial precedents only factual effects and deny them any normative force altogether.[1005] Another approach claims that judicial precedents possess normative force insofar, as they exert authority in legal discourse which creates an obligation to take such precedents into account.[1006]

---

998 *M. Payandeh*, in: W. Kahl/C. Waldhoff/C. Walter (eds.), Bonner Kommentar zum Grundgesetz, June 2020: Art. 92, para. 186.

999 FCC, order of the second senate of 28 November 1957 – 2 BvL 11/56 – BVerfGE 7, 183 (188) – *Zeugenvernehmung Verwaltungsverfahren; M. Payandeh*, in: W. Kahl/C. Waldhoff/C. Walter (eds.), Bonner Kommentar zum Grundgesetz, June 2020: Art. 92, para. 186; cf. *C. Möllers*, Gewaltengliederung, 2005, 95–96.

1000 *C. Möllers*, Gewaltengliederung, 2005, 186.

1001 Ibid., 188.

1002 For an analysis of the debate, see *M. Payandeh*, Judikative Rechtserzeugung, 2017, 111 et seq.; *M. Payandeh*, in: W. Kahl/C. Waldhoff/C. Walter (eds.), Bonner Kommentar zum Grundgesetz, June 2020: Art. 92, para. 188.

1003 For a legal historic account of the development of the customary law approach to precedents, see *H. Weller*, Die Bedeutung der Präjudizien im Verständnis der deutschen Rechtswissenschaft, 1979, 101 et seq.; *Röhl* argues that the separation of powers prohibits judges from creating laws, however, judicial precedents may gradually become customary law over time, see *K. F. Röhl*, Allgemeine Rechtslehre, 1995, 571 et seq.

1004 *W. Fikentscher*, Methoden des Rechts, 1977, vol. IV, 313 et seq.; *H. W. Kruse*, Das Richterrecht als Rechtsquelle des innerstaatlichen Rechts, 1971, 6 et seq. *Kruse* defines judicial precedents or *Richterrecht* as "those norms which courts have formed intra legem" (translated by the author), ibid., 10. He bases the power of judges to create such legal norms on abstract legal terms [*unbestimmte Rechtsbegriffe*] which authorize judges to develop legal standards, see ibid., 7.

1005 *J. Esser*, Richterrecht, Gerichtsgebrauch und Gewohnheitsrecht, in: J. Esser/H. Thieme (eds.), Festschrift für Fritz von Hippel zum 70. Geburtstag, 1967, 95 (113–114); *K. Larenz*, Methodenlehre der Rechtswissenschaft, 6. ed. 1991, 429 et seq.

1006 *M. Payandeh*, Judikative Rechtserzeugung, 2017, 134 et seq.; *M. Payandeh*, in: W. Kahl/C. Waldhoff/C. Walter (eds.), Bonner Kommentar zum Grundgesetz, June 2020: Art. 92, para. 188.

2. Tasks of domestic courts

As stated above, the term "judicial power" not only refers to the necessary characteristics of a court, it also entails certain tasks reserved for the judiciary.[1007] The prevailing view is that Article 92 of the Basic Law guarantees an effective judiciary that has the necessary resources and organizational structure to perform essential judicial functions.[1008] There is no fixed list of tasks that are necessarily allocated to the judiciary.[1009] This means that the tasks which a judiciary must perform may vary across different legal systems and the determination of such tasks requires an interpretation of the respective constitution and statutes.[1010] Additionally, certain tasks may be part of the catalogue of judicial tasks due to legal tradition or because the intensity of the intervention in individual rights requires an act of the judiciary.[1011] According to *Payandeh*, the tasks which the German constitution allocates exclusively to the judiciary are the final and binding decision of disputes in the area of civil law,[1012] the decision over questions of conviction or acquittal, the determination of guilt and sentencing in criminal proceedings,[1013] the assessment of the legality of acts of public authority[1014] and the preventive legal protection against unlawful legal acts[1015]. Constitutionally permissible but not mandatory tasks are, for example, judicial administration[1016] and the participation in amicable dispute resolution mechanisms[1017].

III. Advisory procedures as a challenge to the judicial function of domestic constitutional courts

Heated discussions on the compatibility of advisory procedures with the judicial function are not limited to the international level. Domestic courts have also had to grapple with the question of whether and – if so – how

1007 *M. Payandeh*, in: W. Kahl/C. Waldhoff/C. Walter (eds.), Bonner Kommentar zum Grundgesetz, June 2020: Art. 92, 208 et seq.
1008 Ibid., para. 210.
1009 Ibid., para. 212.
1010 Cf. Ibid., para. 213.
1011 Ibid., para. 213.
1012 Ibid., para. 239.
1013 Ibid., para. 245.
1014 Ibid., para. 248.
1015 Ibid., para. 249.
1016 Ibid., para. 251.
1017 Ibid., para. 250.

to reconcile the function of rendering binding judgments with the function of providing non-binding advisory opinions. Examples of two domestic courts which have had to navigate this challenge and which have reached different conclusions are the Supreme Court of the United States of America (SCOTUS) and the Federal Constitutional Court of Germany (FCC).

1. US Supreme Court

The opposition towards judicial advisory opinions in the United States dates back to the country's founding, in particular to an exchange of correspondences between Thomas Jefferson, then Secretary of State under President Washington and Supreme Court of the United States (SCOTUS) Chief Justice Jay.[1018] On 18 July 1793, Jefferson wrote a letter to the SCOTUS asking for advice on a number of legal questions concerning the rights and obligations of the United States under the Franco-American Treaty of 1778 in the context of the recent Franco-British war.[1019] The US President's cabinet followed up with a list of 29 questions which it sent to the SCOTUS.[1020] On 8 August 1793, Chief Justice Jay responded on behalf of the SCOTUS in a consequential and famous letter to US President Washington. The letter reads in relevant part:

> "The lines of separation drawn by the Constitution between the three departments of the government – their being in certain respects checks upon each other – and our being judges of a court in the last resort – are considerations which afford strong arguments against the propriety of our extrajudicially deciding the questions alluded to; especially as the power given by the Constitution to the President calling on the heads of departments for opinions, seems to have been purposely as well as expressly limited to the executive departments."[1021]

1018 *E. A. Young*, The Supreme Court and the constitutional structure, 2012, 80–81; *C. Burset*, 74 Vanderbilt Law Review 3 (2021), 621 (628 et seq.).

1019 The letter by Thomas Jefferson is printed in *E. A. Young*, The Supreme Court and the constitutional structure, 2012, 80–81.

1020 Ibid., 81.

1021 The response letter by the US SC is printed in Ibid., 82.

The categorical rejection by Chief Justicy Jay to give advisory opinions has become a precedent which (barring certain exceptions) the SCOTUS Justices have observed to this day.[1022]

Jay's letter contains several constitutional arguments for why the SCOTUS refused to give the requested advisory opinion.[1023] The reference to the "extrajudicial" nature of the requested legal opinion may be read as a reference to Article III Section 2 of the US Constitution which limits the powers of the federal judiciary to adjudicate "cases" and "controversies".[1024] In later judgments, the SCOTUS interpreted this passage restrictively to only mean actual disputes which involve competing parties.[1025] The purpose of Article III Section 2 is to limit the possibility of judicial law-making to the necessary extent and thus create a clear distinction between the judiciary and the legislative branch.[1026] It seems that the SCOTUS in its letter to the US President considered advisory opinions to constitute neither cases, nor controversies in the sense of Article III Section 2.[1027] The letter's reference to the SCOTUS being "a court in the last resort" may be a reference to the principle that federal court judgments must be final and non-reversible by any other branch.[1028] If the SCOTUS were to issue non-binding advisory opinions, the US President could review and even ignore the opinions. This – it could be argued – would effectively make the SCOTUS a subordinate officer of the executive branch which would constitute a breach of the separation of powers.[1029] While the precedent is still being observed as good

---

1022 *D. P. Currie*, The Constitution in the Supreme Court, 1985, 12.

1023 *Currie* identified six different constitutional arguments, see Ibid., 13; for an overview of the constituional law debate over the correspondence, see *C. Burset*, 74 Vanderbilt Law Review 3 (2021), 621 (628 et seq.).

1024 *D. P. Currie*, The Constitution in the Supreme Court, 1985, 12–13; *L. Yackle*, Advisory Opinions, in: D. S. Tanenhaus (ed.), Encyclopedia of the Supreme Court of the United States, 2008, 34 (34).

1025 *L. Yackle*, Advisory Opinions, in: D. S. Tanenhaus (ed.), Encyclopedia of the Supreme Court of the United States, 2008, 34 (34).

1026 Ibid., 34.

1027 Cf. *D. P. Currie*, The Constitution in the Supreme Court, 1985, 12.

1028 Ibid., 13; Cf. *L. Yackle*, Advisory Opinions, in: D. S. Tanenhaus (ed.), Encyclopedia of the Supreme Court of the United States, 2008, 34 (34).

1029 *D. P. Currie*, The Constitution in the Supreme Court, 1985, 13; Cf. *L. Yackle*, Advisory Opinions, in: D. S. Tanenhaus (ed.), Encyclopedia of the Supreme Court of the United States, 2008, 34 (34); *Burset* argues that the rejection must be seen in a broader context of many different Common Law countries rejecting the institution of judicial advisory proceedings, see *C. Burset*, 74 Vanderbilt Law Review 3 (2021), 621 (630 et seq.).

law, several SCOTUS Justices have nonetheless given unofficial advice to the federal government over the years.[1030]

If one transferred the terminology used above to describe "judicial power" to the advisory procedure of the SCOTUS, one could say that the SCOTUS mostly focused on the (alleged) incompatibility of an advisory procedure with the characteristics of a court. The letter referred to the necessary finality of court decisions and the independence from the executive, both of which concern the characteristics of the court rather than its tasks.

2. Federal Constitutional Court of Germany

In contrast to the SCOTUS, the FCC was initially expressly given an advisory function by the federal law: Section 97 Federal Constitutional Court Act. Under the FCC's advisory procedure, the Federal President and, by joint submission, the Bundestag, the Bundesrat and the Federal Government could request an advisory opinion from the FCC "on a specific constitutional question".[1031] Like the ICJ, the FCC has had to deal with challenges to its advisory procedure on the grounds that the procedure was alien to its nature ("*wesensfremd*") as a court.[1032] The FCC's second advisory opinion presented an opportunity for the court to address these challenges.

a) The FCC's advisory opinion in the context of German rearmament

The FCC's second advisory opinion is set in the context of one of the most controversial projects of post-war German politics: German rearmament

1030 *D. P. Currie*, The Constitution in the Supreme Court, 1985, 12; *J. R. Gundersen*, Advisory Opinions, in: K. L. Hall (ed.), The Oxford Companion to the Supreme Court of the United States, 2, 2005, 21 (21).

1031 Section 97 Federal Constitutional Court Act old version read:
"(1) The Bundestag, the Bundesrat and the Federal Government may, by joint submission, request the Federal Constitutional Court to issue a legal opinion on a specific constitutional question.
(2) The Federal President has the same right.
(3) The legal opinion is issued by the plenary session of the Federal Constitutional Court." (translated by the author).

1032 Cf. *M. Hilf*, 30 Zeitschrift für Rechtspolitik 7 (1997), 270 (270).

and the creation of the European Defence Community (EDC).[1033] In 1952, in an effort to combine German rearmament and Western integration, the German Federal Republic pursued plans to create the EDC consisting of Germany, the Benelux countries, France and Italy. The FCC found itself in the midst of this controversy when both the opposition and the government factions in the Bundestag as well as the Federal President initiated a total of three judicial proceedings: On 31 January 1952, the opposition in the German Bundestag, the social-democratic faction, seized the first senate of the FCC with an abstract judicial review (*abstrakte Normenkontrolle*) of a hypothetical federal law which would allow the participation of Germans in an armed force, or obligate Germans to perform military service. Being opposed to German rearmament, the social-democratic faction intended to use the FCC to block any law by which the Bundestag consents to the creation of the EDC.[1034] However, on 30 July 1952 the FCC ruled the request inadmissible, as the abstract judicial review procedure does not apply to hypothetical federal laws or legislative drafts.[1035] With the opposition being intent on resubmitting its application once a law has been passed in the Bundestag, the Chancelor Adenauer feared that the first senate of the FCC, which was mostly made up of left-leaning judges and thus mistrusted by Adenauer, could veto this "key element"[1036] of his agenda.[1037] Chancelor Adenauer and his Minister of Justice Dehler therefore convinced the German Federal President Theodor Heuss to request an advisory opinion from the plenary session.[1038] On 10 June 1952, after the German Federal Government had signed the "Treaty establishing the European Defence Community", alongside several other supplementary treaties, President Heuss requested an advisory opinion by the plenary session of the FCC on the compatibility of these treaties with the German Basic Law. To make matters even more complicated, on 6 December 1952, the governing factions in the Bundestag filed a constitutional complaint between government bodies (*Organstreitverfahren*) before the second senate of the

1033 On the debates surrounding the EDC and the conflict it created between the Adenauer government and the FCC, see *O. W. Lembcke*, Hüter der Verfassung, 2007, 175 et seq.

1034 Ibid., 176.

1035 FCC, judgment of the first senate of 30 July 1952 – 1 BvF 1/52 – BVerfGE 1, 396 – *Deutschlandvertrag*.

1036 *O. W. Lembcke*, Hüter der Verfassung, 2007, 180.

1037 Ibid., 176.

1038 *F. Burmeister*, Gutachten des Bundesverfassungsgerichts zu völkerrechtlichen Verträgen, 1998, 169.

FCC. The second senate was largely made up of conservative judges at the time and Chancelor Adenauer thus hoped for an outcome in his favor.[1039] The request asked the second senate to declare that the Bundestag minority violated the rights of the Bundestag and the Bundestag majority by denying that the EDC treaty laws can be passed by a simple majority.[1040]

The FCC found itself in a complicated situation: on the one hand it had to prevent its procedures from being instrumentalized for political gains, on the other hand it had to ensure that an advisory opinion rendered by the plenary session would not be ignored by the second senate in a later decision.[1041] On 8 December 1952, the FCC therefore decided to move forward with the advisory procedure before the plenary session. It also ruled that any advisory opinion rendered by the plenary session binds both senates in any future proceedings. Because of this order and after being asked to do so by Chancelor Adenauer,[1042] President Heuss withdrew his request for an advisory opinion on 10 December 1952 stating that "the character of an advisory opinion and its fundamental essence seems to me to be nullified by this decision of the Federal Constitutional Court."[1043] Despite the withdrawal, the FCC decided to continue the proceeding, finding that the request raised questions which were of fundamental importance beyond the case at hand.[1044]

b) Content of the advisory opinion

The FCC addressed the incompatibility of an advisory procedure with the judicial function of a court. In addressing this issue, the FCC distinguished between ordinary courts and constitutional courts. The FCC conceded that, in general, it is the function of a court to decide legal disputes between disputing parties and as such the issuing of advisory opinions

1039 *O. W. Lembcke*, Hüter der Verfassung, 2007, 176.

1040 This request was later ruled inadmissible by the FCC, see FCC, judgment of the second senate of 7 March 1953 – 2 BvE 4/52 – BverfGE 2, 143 – *EVG-Vertrag*.

1041 *F. Burmeister*, Gutachten des Bundesverfassungsgerichts zu völkerrechtlichen Verträgen, 1998, 170.

1042 *O. W. Lembcke*, Hüter der Verfassung, 2007, 187.

1043 FCC, order of the plenary session of 8 December 1952 – 1 PBvV 1/52 – BVerfGE 2, 79 (83) – *Plenargutachten Heuß*.

1044 Ibid., 98.

is fundamentally alien to the judicial function.[1045] However, a constitutional court, which exclusively adjudicates constitutional law, cannot be judged by the same yardstick as an ordinary civil or criminal court.[1046] The FCC found that this was not only true when the proceeding concerned abstract questions of constitutional law:

> "Even where it [the FCC] decides on violated rights or alleged obligations, it is less in the service of enforcing subjective rights than in the service of the objective preservation of constitutional law."[1047]

Based on the fundamental difference in the function of constitutional courts and ordinary courts, the FCC found that the issuing of advisory opinions is not incompatible with the judicial function of the FCC.[1048] Because it is the FCC's function to uphold the constitutional law, the FCC recognized a duty to issue a requested advisory opinion if the jurisdictional requirements are fulfilled.[1049] The FCC further held that it may not reject a request for an advisory opinion merely because the same matter may arise before the court by means of its contentious procedures.[1050]

The second important question addressed by the FCC concerned the legal nature of FCC advisory opinions. The FCC held in its order of 8 December 1952 that advisory opinions issued by the plenary session bind the two senates in future proceedings. The FCC based its power to develop a rule on the relationship between its advisory opinion procedure and its judgment procedures on the implied powers doctrine: The FCC held that the legislator, when creating the rules governing the procedures of the FCC, could not envision all potential scenarios.[1051] As a consequence, the procedural rules enshrined in the Basic Law and the Federal Constitutional Court Act are necessarily incomplete.[1052] In order to function properly, the

1045 The FCC referred to the decision of the US Supreme Court to reject a request for an advisory opinion made by the US President, see ibid., 86.

1046 Ibid.

1047 Ibid. Translated by the author, the German original reads: "Auch da, wo es über verletzte Rechte oder behauptete Pflichten entscheidet, steht es weniger im Dienste subjektiver Rechtsverfolgung als im Dienste objektiver Bewahrung des Verfassungsrechts."

1048 Ibid., 87. So also *F. Giese*, 78 Archiv des öffentlichen Rechts 3/4 (1952/1953), 389 (394–395).

1049 FCC, order of the plenary session of 8 December 1952 – 1 PBvV 1/52 – BVerfGE 2, 79 (87) – *Plenargutachten Heuß*.

1050 Ibid.

1051 Ibid., 84.

1052 Ibid.

FCC must fill these gaps.[1053] One of these gaps concerned the relationship between the FCC's advisory procedure and its contentious procedures.

In assessing the legal nature of its advisory opinions, the FCC distinguished between the "external" and "internal" binding force of its advisory opinions. Externally, FCC advisory opinions are not binding on their addressees and they lack enforceability.[1054] Internally, however, the FCC held that they bind the two senates of the FCC.[1055] The FCC based its finding *inter alia* on the opinions' authority. An FCC advisory opinion "is not a mere summary of the opinions of the individual judges".[1056] Instead, such an opinion "emanates from the court as such and has its authority".[1057] While advisory opinions lack binding force, their "material content" is the same as that of FCC judgments.[1058] Consequently, no organ of the state (including the FCC itself) can afford to act in contradiction to an advisory opinion of the FCC.[1059] This "internal" binding force can become "external"

1053 Ibid.

1054 Only "decisions" in accordance with Section 31 para. 1 Federal Constitutional Court Act have external binding force, ibid., 88.

1055 Ibid., 91.

1056 Ibid., 87, translation by the author.

1057 Ibid., translation by the author.

1058 Ibid., 89. The FCC derived the "internal" binding force of its advisory opinion also from a teleological interpretation of Section 16 para. 1 Act on the Federal Constitutional Court, according to which the plenary session can decide over divergences in interpretation between the two senates and acts as a "tie-breaker" when a senate wishes to deviate from the legal opinion contained in a decision of the other senate, see ibid., 90. Approving of the FCC's argumentation, see *F. Giese*, 78 Archiv des öffentlichen Rechts 3/4 (1952/1953), 389 (397–398). See however the dissenting opinion by Judge Willi Geiger in which he criticizes the teleological interpretation and argues that Section 16 Act on the Federal Constitutional Court only applies to resolve controversies that have already arisen between the two senates and not to prevent such controversies, see *W. Geiger*, Abweichende Meinungen zu Entscheidungen des Bundesverfassungsgerichts, 1989, 9–10. On the dissenting opinion of Judge Geiger, see *F. Burmeister*, Gutachten des Bundesverfassungsgerichts zu völkerrechtlichen Verträgen, 1998, 173.

1059 FCC, order of the plenary session of 8 December 1952 – 1 PBvV 1/52 – BVerfGE 2, 79 (89) – *Plenargutachten Heuß*. See, however, Judge Willi Geiger who argued in his dissenting opinion that advisory opinions – by definition – can only persuade and not bind the court or any other addressee. To ascribe any more legal effects to advisory opinions would change their legal nature from an opinion to a judgment, see *W. Geiger*, Abweichende Meinungen zu Entscheidungen des Bundesverfassungsgerichts, 1989, 10–11.

binding force, if an applicant initiates a judgment procedure on a question already dealt with by the advisory procedure.[1060]

c) Removal of the FCC advisory procedure

After the FCC issued its second advisory opinion in December of 1954, the relationship between the FCC and the federal government came under severe pressure, with government officials calling the opinion "a legal *nullum*".[1061] The FCC received no more requests for advisory opinions,[1062] and a larger debate arose concerning the need for reforming the FCC.[1063] Important commentators called for the FCC advisory procedure to be abandoned, arguing that such a procedure was alien to the judicial function and lead to bias among the judges which could create "problematic prejudicial ties".[1064] Even the judges of the FCC eventually joined the call to discontinue its advisory procedure, arguing that the advisory procedure was "a task alien to the nature of the constitutional court".[1065] The FCC also feared that the non-binding nature of its advisory opinions could prove detrimental to the reputation of the court, if state organs or other

1060 This point was raised by the FCC as well, see FCC, order of the plenary session of 8 December 1952 - 1 PBvV 1/52 - BVerfGE 2, 79 (91) - *Plenargutachten Heuß*. Based on this, *Burmeister* called the distinction between "internal" and "external" binding force "bloße Makulatur" (i.e., mere paper waste), see *F. Burmeister*, Gutachten des Bundesverfassungsgerichts zu völkerrechtlichen Verträgen, 1998, 174.

1061 See on this Ibid., 172–175; *O. W. Lembcke*, Hüter der Verfassung, 2007, 186–192.

1062 The FCC issued its last advisory opinion on 16 June 1954, however, the request had been made prior to the publication of the second advisory opinion, see FCC, order of the plenary session of 16 June 1954 - 1 PBvV 2/52 - BVerfGE 3, 407 - *Baugutachten*.

1063 Discussions focused mainly on the division of jurisdiction between the two senates, the constitutional complaint procedure (Verfassungsbeschwerde) and the election of judges, however, the advisory procedure was also subject of the broader discussion, see *F. Burmeister*, Gutachten des Bundesverfassungsgerichts zu völkerrechtlichen Verträgen, 1998, 175.

1064 *R. Thoma*, 6 (new series) Jahrbuch des öffentlichen Rechts (1957), 161 (185).

1065 Unpublished memorandum of the FCC to the Federal Ministry of Justice, cited in *W. Geiger*, Zur Reform des Bundesverfassungsgesetzes, in: T. Maunz (ed.), Vom Bonner Grundgesetz zur gesamtdeutschen Verfassung, 1956, 211 (216), translated by the author.

courts decided to ignore them.[1066] The advisory opinion procedure was thus eventually abolished without replacement in 1956.[1067]

d) Relevance for the ICJ's advisory procedure

The FCC's advisory opinion raises several interesting aspects worth considering when analyzing the ICJ's advisory function. The FCC initially rejected claims about the incompatibility of its advisory procedure with its judicial function by emphasizing the different task which a constitutional court (like the FCC) and ordinary civil and criminal courts perform. The FCC held that it was not the FCC's task to settle bilateral disputes, but to answer questions of constitutional law.[1068] As will be elaborated in more detail, the ICJ could be said to combine the functions of ordinary courts and constitutional courts. Its functions include the settlement of bilateral disputes (see Art. 38 para. 1 ICJ Statute), but also the stabilization of normative expectations and the development of international law.[1069] The FCC also focused on the "authority" of its pronouncements, thus a question of the characteristics of the court. The FCC based the "internal" binding force of its advisory opinion *inter alia* on the institutional authority of the court, not the reception or acceptance of the advisory opinion itself.[1070] FCC advisory opinions derive their authority from the fact that they are issued by the full court in plenary session and as such represent not the individual opinions of the judges involved, but that of the entire court. As will be elaborated below, this content-independent "institutional authority" is also of critical importance for ascribing authority to ICJ advisory opinions. They, just like FCC advisory opinions, are expressly given by the full court and

1066 Ibid.

1067 Art. 1 No. 19 Act amending the Act on the Federal Constitutional Court of 21 July 1956 (*Gesetz zur Änderung des Gesetzes über das Bundesverfassungsgericht*), Federal Law Gazette 1956, Part I, p. 662. Various state constitutional courts also had advisory opinion procedures. However, these were gradually abolished over the following decades, see on this *F. Burmeister*, Gutachten des Bundesverfassungsgerichts zu völkerrechtlichen Verträgen, 1998, 177, footnote 90.

1068 This is why the FCC famously held that it is not the highest court of appeal ("*Superrevisionsgericht*"), see FCC, order of the first senate of 14 March 1967 – 1 BvR 334/61 – BverfGE 21, 209 (216) – *Auslegung einfachen Rechts*; FCC, order of the first senate of 20 December 1978 – 1 BvR 385/77 – BVerfGE 53, 30 (53) – *Mülheim-Kärlich*.

1069 See *infra* in this Chapter Section B.II.

1070 So also *O. W. Lembcke*, Hüter der Verfassung, 2007, 186.

likewise represent the opinion of the Court. It is the particular authority of ICJ advisory opinions which raises the challenges of the Eastern Carelia doctrine to begin with.

IV. Interim conclusions

The discussions about the "judicial power" in Article 92 Basic Law have shown that one must carefully distinguish between two related, yet separate concepts: the characteristics of courts (i.e., which qualities do courts possess and how do courts operate?) and the tasks of courts (i.e., what is it that (only) courts may do?). Clearly, the two questions influence each other. Courts possess certain characteristics in order to fulfil the tasks which they have been allocated. Characteristics and tasks can thus be understood as two sides of the same coin. Nevertheless, one must be careful to distinguish between the two questions so as not to risk conceptual confusion. The distinction between characteristics and tasks may also help to understand the concept of "judicial function" used by the ICJ. As will be shown below, different commentators have understood the term "judicial function" along these two dimensions: characteristics which the ICJ as a court of justice must possess and must adhere to (in particular procedural requirements) and certain tasks which the ICJ must perform and must not undermine (in particular its dispute-settlement function).

B. The ICJ's judicial function

The way in which legal scholarship has defined the term "judicial function" is similar to the two dimensions of the term "judicial power" examined above. The term "judicial function" was similarly understood in two ways: first, to denote certain judicial characteristics which an IC as a court of justice must possess and adhere to (*infra* I.), and secondly, to describe the tasks assigned to an IC (*infra* II.).

Keith and *Amerasinghe* focus on the characteristics of the ICJ as a court of justice.[1071] *Keith* defined the Court's judicial character from a procedu-

1071 *K. J. Keith*, The extent of the advisory jurisdiction of the International Court of Justice, 1971, 153 et seq.; *C. F. Amerasinghe*, Reflections on the Judicial Function in International Law, in: T. M. Ndiaye/R. Wolfrum/C. Kojima (eds.), Law of the sea, environmental law, and settlement of disputes, 2007, 119 (122 et seq.).

ral perspective.[1072] In order to safeguard the Court's judicial character, the Court must act in accordance with certain judicial procedures. These procedures apply equally to the Court's contentious and advisory opinion procedure.[1073] *Amerasinghe* equated the Court's judicial function with certain necessary characteristics of a court of justice like impartiality and independence.[1074]

Other writers like *Tomuschat*,[1075] *Wittich*,[1076] *Ebobrah*,[1077] as well as *von Bogdandy* and *Venzke*[1078] focus on the tasks of the judicial organ to define that organ's judicial function.

Finally, *Hernández* examines both the characteristics of the ICJ as a court of justice and its tasks when referring to the Court's judicial function.[1079]

I. Defining "judicial function" as judicial characteristics

Keith approached the Court's judicial character by reference to the rules applicable to the Court's contentious procedure.[1080] According to *Keith*, to act judicially in advisory proceedings means that the ICJ must substantially follow the same procedures which the ICJ Statute has established for its contentious procedure.[1081] A statement by the PCIJ in its *Eastern Carelia* opinion can be read in this way:

1072 *K. J. Keith*, The extent of the advisory jurisdiction of the International Court of Justice, 1971, 153 et seq.

1073 Ibid., 153 et seq.

1074 *C. F. Amerasinghe*, Reflections on the Judicial Function in International Law, in: T. M. Ndiaye/R. Wolfrum/C. Kojima (eds.), Law of the sea, environmental law, and settlement of disputes, 2007, 119 (122 et seq.).

1075 Cf. *C. Tomuschat*, International Courts and Tribunals (last updated 2019), in: A. Peters/R. Wolfrum (eds.), The Max Planck Encyclopedia of Public International Law, 2008 (35).

1076 *S. Wittich*, The Judicial Functions of the International Court of Justice, in: I. Buffard/J. Crawford/A. Pellet/S. Wittich (eds.), International law between universalism and fragmentation, 2008, 981 (985–986)

1077 *S. T. Ebobrah*, International Human Rights Courts, in: C. Romano/K. J. Alter/Y. Shany (eds.), The Oxford Handbook of International Adjudication, 2013, 225.

1078 *A. v. Bogdandy/I. Venzke*, 26 LJIL 1 (2013), 49 (52).

1079 *G. I. Hernández*, The International Court of Justice and the judicial function, 2014, 41 et seq.

1080 *K. J. Keith*, The extent of the advisory jurisdiction of the International Court of Justice, 1971, 153 et seq.

1081 Ibid., 154–155.

> "The Court, being a Court of Justice, cannot, even in giving advisory opinions, depart from the essential rules guiding their activity as a Court."[1082]

By comparing the Court's advisory practice with its contentious practice, *Keith* highlights three core characteristics of any judicial procedure: publicity of the proceedings, equality of the parties, and sufficient access to information by the Court.[1083] To ensure that the ICJ's advisory opinion procedure conforms to these characteristics, the Court has progressively assimilated its advisory opinion procedure with its contentious procedure.[1084]

Such an assimilation between the Court's contentious and advisory opinion procedure is also envisioned by Article 68 ICJ Statute which stipulates:

> "In the exercise of its advisory functions the Court shall further be guided by the provisions of the present Statute which apply in contentious cases to the extent to which it recognizes them to be applicable."

However, as *Keith* points out, the assimilation of the two procedure predates the creation of Article 68 which is why Article 68 recognized rather than caused the practice of the Court.[1085] The Court has assimilated the two procedures in relation to all three characteristics identified by *Keith* (publicity, equality of the parties, and access to information). The Court first passed rules on the publicity of the advisory proceedings in 1926 when it amended its Rules of the Court which were later incorporated into the PCIJ Statute.[1086] The position of interested states which are affected by an underlying dispute on which the Court is asked to give an advisory opinion was also assimilated to the position of States Parties to contentious proceedings.[1087] States are informed by the Registrar of the Court of the initiation of advisory proceedings, they can under certain circumstances appoint a judge *ad hoc* and can participate in the proceedings by submitting written and oral statements, which the Court has to take into account

---

1082 *Status of Eastern Carelia*, Advisory Opinion, PCIJ Series B 1923, 7 (29).

1083 *K. J. Keith*, The extent of the advisory jurisdiction of the International Court of Justice, 1971, 155 et seq.

1084 Ibid., 157, 181.

1085 With further references, see Ibid., 191.

1086 Ibid., 156–157.

1087 Ibid., 157–185.

before issuing the advisory opinion.[1088] *Keith* identifies certain remaining differences between the two procedures including the number of rounds of written and oral statements.[1089] Whereas in contentious proceedings states usually present several rounds of memorials and counter-memorials and address the Court on several occasions during oral proceedings, in advisory proceedings states usually submit one written statement, sometimes followed by a written comment and have one occasion to present oral arguments.[1090]

The Court has not yet assimilated how it deals with preliminary objections to its jurisdiction. In contentious proceedings, the Court holds separate proceedings in which it decides upon preliminary objections, thereby protecting the right of the parties to the dispute not to plead on the merits of the case until the Court has established its jurisdiction.[1091] In advisory proceedings, the Court decides upon preliminary matters and the merits of a case jointly. In situations when advisory proceedings concern actual disputes between states, a similar approach to contentious proceedings may be appropriate. Some states have tried to assert their right not to plead on the merits until the jurisdiction of the Court is established by limiting their written statement to matters of jurisdiction and admissibility.[1092] However, even where particularly affected states did not make submissions on the

1088 Ibid., 157–185; *M. Giles Samson/D. Guilfoyle*, The Permanent Court of International Justice and the "Invention" of International Advisory Jurisdiction, in: C. J. Tams/M. Fitzmaurice (eds.), Legacies of the Permanent Court of International Justice, 2013, 41 (50–51).

1089 *K. J. Keith*, The extent of the advisory jurisdiction of the International Court of Justice, 1971, 181.

1090 Ibid., 181. See, however, Art. 66 para. 4 ICJ Statute which provides for a second round of written submissions in which states and organizations may comment on previous submissions. The Court often fixes the time-limits for the first and second round of written submissions within the same order, see for example *Accordance with International Law of the Unilateral Declaration of Independence by the Provisional Institutions of Self-Government of Kosovo*, Order of 17 October 2008, ICJ Reports 2008, p. 409 (410); *Judgment No. 2867 of the Administrative Tribunal of the International Labour Organization upon a Complaint Filed against the International Fund for Agricultural Development*, Order of 29 April 2010, ICJ Reports 2010, p. 298 (301); *Legal Consequences of the Separation of the Chagos Archipelago from Mauritius in 1965*, Order of 14 July 2017, ICJ Reports 2017, p. 282 (283).

1091 Ibid., 193.

1092 See for example ICJ Pleadings, *Legal Consequences of the Construction of a Wall in the Occupied Palestinian Territory*, Written Statement of Israel, para. 1.2. However, Israel has prefaced its arguments on the jurisdiction and admissibility of the request for an advisory opinion with extensive factual information on which the merits of the advisory proceeding, the Court always decided the substantive questions. These attempts therefore merely meant that those states forgoe on their opportunity to present their written statements on the merits.

As *Keith* pointed out, the Court's practice shows that it has "constantly and consistently assimilated nearly every facet of its advisory procedure to its contentious procedure."[1093] When critics invoke the potential incompatibility of the Court's advisory activity with its judicial function, their criticism is thus likely not directed at the way the advisory procedure is structured. It is a more fundamental critique which concerns the relationship between the Court's advisory procedure and its contentious procedure. The critique may thus relate to the second meaning of the term judicial function which refers to the different tasks the Court performs by means of the two procedures.

II. Defining "judicial function" as judicial tasks

Writers like *Tomuschat*[1094], *Wittich*[1095], *Ebobrah*[1096], *von Bogdandy* and *Venzke*[1097] define the concept of judicial function by reference to the tasks which ICs perform or are designed to perform.

Court relied in its deliberation of the merits of the case. In 2023, Israel similarly refused to make a statement on the merits in the *Legal Consequences arising from the Policies and Practices of Israel in the Occupied Palestinian Territory, including East Jerusalem* case. Instead, Israel gave a short written statement in which it criticized the framing of the submitted question and emphasized that it did not give its consent to the proceedings, see ICJ Pleadings, *Legal Consequences arising from the Policies and Practices of Israel in the Occupied Palestinian Territory, including East Jerusalem*, Written Statement of Israel. Nevertheless, Israel provided the Court with 170 pages of material on the admissibility of the request and on the merits of the case.

1093 *K. J. Keith*, The extent of the advisory jurisdiction of the International Court of Justice, 1971, 195.

1094 Cf. *C. Tomuschat*, International Courts and Tribunals (last updated 2019), in: A. Peters/R. Wolfrum (eds.), The Max Planck Encyclopedia of Public International Law, 2008 (35).

1095 *S. Wittich*, The Judicial Functions of the International Court of Justice, in: I. Buffard/J. Crawford/A. Pellet/S. Wittich (eds.), International law between universalism and fragmentation, 2008, 981 (985–986).

1096 *S. T. Ebobrah*, International Human Rights Courts, in: C. Romano/K. J. Alter/Y. Shany (eds.), The Oxford Handbook of International Adjudication, 2013, 225.

1097 *A. v. Bogdandy/I. Venzke*, 26 LJIL 1 (2013), 49 (52).

Wittich identifies three different meanings of the term judicial function:[1098] First, the professional or official position of a person, i.e. the capacity in which the person acts. Secondly, the performance of a particular task or activity for which an institution is particularly suited, used, or created. Thirdly, a series of interrelated actions that contribute to a larger action and thus serve a higher purpose. Function thus encompasses the powers, competences and specific tasks of the judiciary as distinguished from the executive and the legislature.[1099] In particular, the first and second definition indicate a consideration that not only takes into account the *ex ante* attribution of tasks, for example in the Court's constituent instrument, but also the actual practice of the court.

Approaches like the ones by *Ebobrah*[1100] as well as *von Bogdandy* and *Venzke*[1101] similarly take into consideration the tasks the respective court actually performs. According to these approaches, not only those tasks that are defined in advance are relevant when considering the functions of a judicial organ, but also the tasks actually performed by the court as well as other contributions of the respective institution.[1102] Consequently, a court may fulfil a number of different functions.[1103]

In her dissenting opinion to the *Chagos* advisory opinion, Judge *Donoghue* applied a formalistic approach to the functions of the ICJ and distinguished between two functions: an advisory function and a contentious function.[1104] However, the Court majority has not limited the Court's judicial function to its contentious function. The Court has pointed out on several occasions that it exercises a uniform judicial function regardless of the type of procedure. For example, in its *Northern Cameroons* decision the ICJ held:

1098 *Wittich* derives his definition from the use of the term "function" in the Vienna Convention on Diplomatic Relations (VCDR), see *S. Wittich*, The Judicial Functions of the International Court of Justice, in: I. Buffard/J. Crawford/A. Pellet/S. Wittich (eds.), International law between universalism and fragmentation, 2008, 981 (985–986).

1099 Ibid., 986.

1100 *S. T. Ebobrah*, International Human Rights Courts, in: C. Romano/K. J. Alter/Y. Shany (eds.), The Oxford Handbook of International Adjudication, 2013, 225.

1101 *A. v. Bogdandy/I. Venzke*, 26 LJIL 1 (2013), 49 (52).

1102 Ibid., 52.

1103 Ibid., 52.

1104 *Legal Consequences of the Separation of the Chagos Archipelago from Mauritius in 1965*, Advisory Opinion, Dissenting Opinion Donoghue, ICJ Reports 2019, 95 (266, para. 23).

> "[B]oth the Permanent Court of International Justice and this Court have emphasized the fact that the Court's authority to give advisory opinions must be exercised as a judicial function. [...] in both situations [i.e., advisory opinion and contentious procedures], the Court is exercising a judicial function."[1105]

When the ICJ uses the term "judicial function", it thus refers to more than its contentious function. Rather, it refers to the entirety of its "judicial tasks" which it fulfills through both procedures. By exercising its powers in connection with its advisory procedure and its contentious procedure, the Court performs various different tasks. These include settling disputes, stabilizing normative expectations, developing the law, and controlling the exercise of powers of other actors.[1106]

1. Primary judicial task: Dispute settlement

The settlement of international legal disputes is one of the principal functions of the ICJ.[1107] It is the only function expressly enshrined in the ICJ Statute. Article 38 para. 1 ICJ Statute states that the Court's "function is to decide in accordance with international law such disputes as are submitted to it". Article 33 UNC names the judicial settlement of disputes as one means of settling a "dispute, the continuance of which is likely to endanger the maintenance of international peace and security". Article 33 UNC emphasizes, judicial dispute settlement in the UN system is functionally linked to the maintenance of international peace and security. This connection il-

1105 *Northern Cameroons (Cameroon v. United Kingdom) (Preliminary Objections)*, Judgment, ICJ Reports 1963, 15 (30); see also *Conditions of Admission of a State to Membership in the United Nations (Article 4 of the Charter)*, Advisory Opinion, ICJ Reports 1948, 57 (61); *Legal Consequences for States of the Continued Presence of South Africa in Namibia (South West Africa) notwithstanding Security Council Resolution 276 (1970)*, Advisory Opinion, Dissenting Opinion Gros, ICJ Reports 1971, 16 (331, para. 17).

1106 For an overview of the different functions, see *J. E. Alvarez*, What are International Judges for?: The Main Functions of International Adjudication, in: C. Romano/K. J. Alter/Y. Shany (eds.), The Oxford Handbook of International Adjudication, 2013, 158.

1107 *LaGrand (Germany v. United States of America)*, Provisional Measures, Order of 3 March 1999, ICJ Reports 1999, p. 9 (15, para. 25); *Application of the Convention on the Prevention and Punishment of the Crime of Genocide (Bosnia and Herzegovina v. Serbia and Montenegro)*, Judgment, ICJ Reports 2007, 43 (90, para. 116).

lustrates the special importance of the ICJ's dispute settlement function,[1108] which the Court's predecessor, the PCIJ, has even described as the "true function of the Court".[1109]

While Article 33 UNC places judicial dispute settlement alongside other methods of dispute resolution, Article 36 para. 3 UNC states that "legal disputes should as a general rule be referred by the parties to the International Court of Justice".

The ICJ's dispute settlement function rests on two supporting functions, the Court's law-finding function and its fact-finding function.[1110] Since these supporting functions are necessary for the Court to exercise its primary, expressly conferred dispute settlement function, the supporting functions can be understood as an expression of the implied powers doctrine.

a) First supporting task: law-finding task

According to Article 38 para. 1 ICJ Statute, the Court's function is to settle disputes "in accordance with international law". To apply international law, the ICJ must first identify the applicable law. The ICJ emphasized its law-finding function in the *Northern Cameroons* case by stating that its function was "to state the law".[1111] The law-finding function is of decisive importance, particularly in the area of customary international law, but also regarding the clarification of oftentimes vague treaty provisions.[1112]

However, the ICJ also found that finding the law is not an end in itself. The overall task remains the settlement of the inter-state disputes. In the *Northern Cameroons* case the ICJ thus found that its decision "must have some practical consequence in the sense that it can affect existing legal

---

1108 So also *S. Wittich*, The Judicial Functions of the International Court of Justice, in: I. Buffard/J. Crawford/A. Pellet/S. Wittich (eds.), International law between universalism and fragmentation, 2008, 981 (990).

1109 Case Concerning the Payment of Various Serbian Loans Issued in France, Judgment, PCIJ Series A, 1929, 19.

1110 *J. E. Alvarez*, What are International Judges for?: The Main Functions of International Adjudication, in: C. Romano/K. J. Alter/Y. Shany (eds.), The Oxford Handbook of International Adjudication, 2013, 158 (166 et seq.).

1111 *Northern Cameroons (Cameroon v. United Kingdom) (Preliminary Objections)*, Judgment, ICJ Reports 1963, 15 (33); see also *Legality of the Threat or Use of Nuclear Weapons*, Advisory Opinion, ICJ Reports 1996, 226 (237, para. 18).

1112 *S. Wittich*, The Judicial Functions of the International Court of Justice, in: I. Buffard/J. Crawford/A. Pellet/S. Wittich (eds.), International law between universalism and fragmentation, 2008, 981 (991–992).

rights or obligations of the parties, thus removing uncertainty from their legal relations."[1113]

b) Second supporting task: Fact-finding task

The process of judicial decision making depends on the establishment of facts to which the Court then applies the law. The Court's Statute, Rules, and Practice Directions contain different modes of gathering factual evidence to establish the facts of a case.

First and foremost, the Court relies on the participating states to provide relevant information. In contentious proceedings, the parties to the proceedings are responsible to produce the necessary factual evidence.[1114] When contentious proceedings are commenced, the ICJ makes an order (Article 48 ICJ Statute) to fix the time limit within which the parties may produce documents in support of their submissions (Article 43 para. 3 ICJ Statute). Beyond this time limit, the Court may refuse to accept any further oral or written evidence unless all parties consent to the introduction of the evidence (Article 52 ICJ Statute). After written proceedings are closed, the Court will only authorize the production of new documents by a party if the other parties consent or if the Court considers the production necessary and justified (Article 56 Rules of the Court, Practice Directions IX). The parties may not only produce documents to support their claims, they may also call upon experts and witnesses (Article 63 Rules of the Court) which are examined by the parties and questioned by the Court (Article 65 Rules of the Court). Apart from the parties to the dispute, other states that have a legal interest which may be affected by the decision in the case (Article 62 Statute) and, if the case concerns the construction of a multilateral treaty, the States Parties to that treaty (Article 63 ICJ Statute), may also produce evidence before the Court. The ICJ may also on its own accord entrust an individual, body, bureau, commission, or organization to make

---

1113 *Northern Cameroons (Cameroon v. United Kingdom) (Preliminary Objections)*, Judgment, ICJ Reports 1963, 15 (34), emphasis added. Because its decision could not bring about such practical effects, the Court could not decide the merits of the case, see Ibid. (38).

1114 Critical of the ICJ's dependence on the parties to the dispute to provide the relevant facts and the Court's tendency to circumvent this problem by finding that the particular facts are not decisive for a decision on the legal questions at hand, see *T. M. Franck*, Fact-Finding in the I.C.J., in: R. B. Lillich (ed.), Fact-finding before international tribunals, 1992, 21 (31).

an inquiry or produce an expert opinion on a specific subject (Article 50 ICJ Statute, Article 67 Rules of the Court)[1115] as well as make site visits to obtain evidence (Article 66 Rules of the Court).[1116]

In advisory opinion proceedings, states may similarly participate by submitting written and oral statements. To this effect, the Registrar will notify all states entitled to appear before the Court[1117] of the request for an advisory opinion (Article 66 para. 1 ICJ Statute). The Registrar further notifies all such states and international organizations which the Court considers to be likely to furnish information on the question that the ICJ received. They may submit written and oral statements on the matter within a certain time limit fixed by the Court (Article 66 para. 2 ICJ Statute).[1118] International non-governmental organizations may also submit written statements. However, such statements do not become part of the case file but are treated like publications in the public domain (Practice Direction XII).

There is, however, a crucial difference between the ICJ's capacity to ascertain the facts of a case in contentious proceedings and in advisory proceedings. The difference boils down to the burden of proof.[1119] For contentious proceedings, the ICJ has held that "it is the duty of the party

---

1115 On the distinction between inquiry and expert opinion, see *C. J. Tams/J. Devaney*, in: A. Zimmermann/C. J. Tams/K. Oellers-Frahm/C. Tomuschat/D. W. K. Anderson (eds.), The Statute of the International Court of Justice, 3. ed., 2019: Art. 50, para. 4.

1116 The Court made use of its power to order site visits only once thus far: In the *Gabčíkovo-Nagymaros* case the Members of the Court visited a number of locations along the Danube river and received technical explanations on the project, see *Gabčíkovo-Nagymaros Project (Hungary v. Slovakia)*, Judgment, ICJ Reports 1998, 7 (14, para. 10). On the topic of site visits by the ICJ, see *S. Rosenne*, Visit to the Site by the International Court, in: E. Yakpo/T. Boumedra (eds.), Liber amicorum Judge Mohammed Bedjaoui, 1999, 461.

1117 These include all UN Member States and states falling under Article 35 para. 2 UNC.

1118 Often these two notifications occur at the same time, see *A. Paulus*, in: A. Zimmermann/C. J. Tams/K. Oellers-Frahm/C. Tomuschat/D. W. K. Anderson (eds.), The Statute of the International Court of Justice, 3. ed., 2019: Art. 66, para. 20.

1119 Emphasizing this difference between contentious and advisory proceedings, see *C. Greenwood*, Judicial Integrity and the Advisory Jurisdiction of the International Court of Justice, in: J. Grote Stoutenburg/G. Gaja (eds.), Enhancing the rule of law through the International Court of Justice, 2014, 63 (68–70); see also *Legal Consequences arising from the Policies and Practices of Israel in the Occupied Palestinian Territory, including East Jerusalem*, Advisory Opinion, Separate Opinion Nolte, Publication pending in ICJ Reports 2024, 1 (2, para. 5).

which assert certain facts to establish the existence of such facts."[1120] This principle has been consistently upheld by the Court[1121] and applies to the assertions of facts both by the Applicant and the Respondent state. If a party asserts a fact but fails to prove it, the ICJ can render a judgment based on the burden of proof.

Advisory proceedings have no parties and consequently the Court cannot rely on the burden of proof to facilitate the determination of the facts of a case.[1122] Nevertheless, the ICJ must ensure that it has in each case sufficient information to issue an advisory opinion lest the Court acts in contradiction to its judicial function.[1123] Considering that the Court cannot recur on the burden of proof in advisory proceedings, in theory the Court should be much more likely to render a *non liquet* decision in advisory proceedings than in contentious proceedings. However, as the Court held in its *Wall* opinion, the Court does not rely exclusively on the interested states for information.[1124] Instead, the Court may also rely on reports by international organizations (oftentimes the UNSG provides the Court with detailed studies of the submitted questions) and special rapporteurs, or the submissions of other states.[1125] The reason why the ICJ may have a more liberal recourse to other sources of information to establish the facts of a case lies in the different function of advisory proceedings in contrast to contentious proceedings.[1126] Advisory proceedings seek not to settle international disputes, but to provide legal guidance to the requesting UN organ

---

1120 Pulp Mills on the River Uruguay (Argentina v. Uruguay), Judgment, ICJ Reports 2010, 14 (71, para. 162).

1121 Military and Paramilitary Activities in and against Nicaragua (Nicaragua v. United States of America), Jurisdiction and Admissibility, Judgment, ICJ Reports 1984, 392 (437, para. 101); Application of the Convention on the Prevention and Punishment of the Crime of Genocide (Bosnia and Herzegovina v. Serbia and Montenegro), Judgment, ICJ Reports 2007, 43 (128, para. 204); Sovereignty over Pedra Branca/Pulau Batu Puteh, Middle Rocks and South Ledge (Malaysia v. Singapore), Judgment, ICJ Reports 2008, 12 (31, para. 45); Maritime Delimitation in the Black Sea (Romania v. Ukraine), Judgment, ICJ Reports 2009, 61 (86, para. 68).

1122 *C. Greenwood*, Judicial Integrity and the Advisory Jurisdiction of the International Court of Justice, in: J. Grote Stoutenburg/G. Gaja (eds.), Enhancing the rule of law through the International Court of Justice, 2014, 63 (69).

1123 *Legal Consequences of the Construction of a Wall in the Occupied Palestinian Territory*, Advisory Opinion, ICJ Reports 2004, 136 (161, para. 56).

1124 Ibid. (161-162, para. 57).

1125 Ibid.

1126 *Legal Consequences arising from the Policies and Practices of Israel in the Occupied Palestinian Territory, including East Jerusalem*, Advisory Opinion, Separate Opinion Nolte, Publication pending in ICJ Reports 2024, 1 (1-2, paras. 4-5).

on the legal questions submitted to the Court. As such, the Court needs to establish the facts of the case only to the extent as is necessary for answering the submitted question. As Judge *Nolte* stated in his Separate Opinion in the recent *Policies and Practices of Israel in the Occupied Palestinian Territories* case:

> "In contentious proceedings, the Court "decide[s] ... disputes" in a binding and final manner. These proceedings are retrospective: their contribution to the peaceful settlement of disputes consists in ending a dispute by making a binding determination that is endowed with legal certainty and finality, the *res judicata* effect. In contrast, advisory proceedings are consultative and prospective: the Court gives an advisory opinion on a legal question to provide guidance for the requesting organ's future conduct. The conclusions of the Court in advisory opinions are not the end but the beginning of a process that seeks to establish and maintain peace through law. (...) The particular purpose of advisory proceedings explains why the factual assessment in this Advisory Opinion has a different focus and depth than factual determinations made in contentious proceedings. This does not mean that the standard of proof in advisory proceedings is lower. However, it is different from that in contentious proceedings, where the burden of adducing evidence lies with the parties. In advisory proceedings the Court will examine the facts only to the extent necessary for its response to the legal question posed, and it will draw legal conclusions only to the extent permitted by those facts."[1127]

The difference in function between advisory proceedings (consultative and prospective) and contentious proceedings (determinative and retrospective) also means that the Court's factual findings in advisory proceedings cannot be considered to be as conclusive as factual assessments in contentious proceedings. As Judge *Nolte* stated:

> "In cases involving very broad requests, such as the present one, the function of advisory opinions to provide guidance to the requesting organ justifies a particularly broad and merely illustrative approach to the factual assessment. However, this broad focus, together with the principle of consent to jurisdiction, precludes such assessment from having the conclusive effect attributed to factual assessments for the purpose of determining State responsibility in contentious proceedings."[1128]

1127 Ibid. (2, para. 5).
1128 Ibid.

Judge *Nolte* limits his claim about the non-conclusiveness of factual assessments in advisory proceedings to "cases involving very broad requests". However, the fact that the Court cannot invoke the burden of proof seems in itself to justify the claim that the Court's factual assessments in advisory proceedings are less conclusive than in contentious proceedings.

2. Other judicial tasks

a) Stabilizing normative expectations

The ICJ fulfils another (closely related) function by clarifying the factual and legal parameters of a case: the stabilization of normative expectations.[1129] When states bring their international dispute before the ICJ, this can be seen as an expression of the parties' dissent regarding their mutually applicable obligations and rights. At least one party questions the validity or applicability of a certain obligation under international law or the existence of exceptions in a specific case. Because of this expression of doubt, the respective legal obligation may dilute. Does the state claim that the obligation does not apply because its legal or factual conditions are not fulfilled? Or because the state can invoke a ground for justification? Or does the obligation simply have a different legal consequence than the opposing party claims? It is the ICJ's task to remove this legal uncertainty.[1130] By clarifying the legal and factual situation and reducing the uncertainty between the parties, the ICJ puts the parties in a position to form a strengthened expectation about their bilaterally applicable legal rights and obligations.[1131] Overall, the ICJ thus achieves a stabilization of the normative expectations

1129 On this, see *S. Wittich*, The Judicial Functions of the International Court of Justice, in: I. Buffard/J. Crawford/A. Pellet/S. Wittich (eds.), International law between universalism and fragmentation, 2008, 981 (992–993); *A. v. Bogdandy/I. Venzke*, 26 LJIL 1 (2013), 49 (54–55).

1130 The ICJ describes the reduction of legal uncertainty as an essential element of its judicial function, see *Northern Cameroons (Cameroon v. United Kingdom) (Preliminary Objections)*, Judgment, ICJ Reports 1963, 15 (34); *Application of the Convention on the Prevention and Punishment of the Crime of Genocide (Bosnia and Herzegovina v. Serbia and Montenegro)*, Judgment, ICJ Reports 2007, 43 (101, para. 139).

1131 *S. Wittich*, The Judicial Functions of the International Court of Justice, in: I. Buffard/J. Crawford/A. Pellet/S. Wittich (eds.), International law between universalism and fragmentation, 2008, 981 (992).

of the parties.[1132] The stabilizing effect even extends beyond the parties of a case.[1133] Third states can derive from a decision of the ICJ the permissible conduct in a given circumstance.[1134] They know that they would likely receive a similar judgment by the ICJ (or by another IC) if they act in an identical fashion.[1135] The judgments of the ICJ may also influence other ICs. While there is no hierarchy between courts, the ICJ enjoys a considerable authority which is why other ICs need to consider the ICJ's dicta lest they risk losing authority themselves.[1136]

In the *Application for Review* advisory opinion, the ICJ indicated that it fulfils its function of stabilizing normative expectations not only in contentious proceedings but also in advisory proceedings. The Court emphasized the importance of its advisory opinions for guiding the activities of international organizations such as the UN.[1137] By clarifying the legal relations between the UNGA and a subsidiary body of the UNGA, the ICJ assisted the UN in placing its activities on a secure legal footing.[1138] Advisory opinions of the Court can be a particularly helpful tool to fill gaps in the constituent instruments of international organizations.[1139]

b) Law-making

The Court's law-making function counts among its more controversial, but nonetheless essential functions.[1140] While the dispute settlement function

1132 Ibid., 992.

1133 *S. D. Murphy*, International Judicial Bodies for Resolving Disputes Between States, in: C. Romano/K. J. Alter/Y. Shany (eds.), The Oxford Handbook of International Adjudication, 2013, 182 (197).

1134 Ibid., 197.

1135 Ibid., 197.

1136 *M. N. Shaw*, Rosenne's Law and Practice of the International Court: 1920-2015, 5th ed 2016, Vol. 3, Ch. 27, § 377A.

1137 *Application for Review of Judgment No. 273 of the United Nations Administrative Tribunal*, Advisory Opinion, ICJ Reports 1982, 325 (347, para. 45).

1138 Ibid.

1139 Cf. *S. D. Murphy*, International Judicial Bodies for Resolving Disputes Between States, in: C. Romano/K. J. Alter/Y. Shany (eds.), The Oxford Handbook of International Adjudication, 2013, 182 (199–200).

1140 On the law-making functions of ICs, see *M. Cappelletti*, 8 MULR 1 (1981), 15; *C. G. Weeramantry*, 10 LJIL 2 (1997), 309; *A. E. Boyle/C. Chinkin*, The making of international law, 2007, 263 et seq.; *S. Wittich*, The Judicial Functions of the International Court of Justice, in: I. Buffard/J. Crawford/A. Pellet/S. Wittich (eds.), International law between universalism and fragmentation, 2008, 981 (994 et seq.);

is expressly conferred upon the ICJ by Article 38 para. 1 ICJ Statute, the law-making function lacks a clear legal foundations. What is more, the states signatories to the Court's constituent instrument did not intend to confer upon the ICJ a legislative function.[1141] It is thus not surprising that the ICJ explicitly denied that it even had such a law-making function in its *Nuclear Weapons* advisory opinion. The ICJ found:

> "Finally, it has been contended by some States that in answering the question posed, the Court would be going beyond its judicial role and would be taking upon itself a law-making capacity. It is clear that the Court cannot legislate [...] [The Court] states the existing law and does not legislate."[1142]

Nevertheless, the ICJ implicitly acknowledged its law-making function immediately afterwards:

> "This is so even if, in stating and applying the law, the Court necessarily has to specify its scope and sometimes note its general trend."[1143]

Part of the legal literature interpreted the passage "note its general trend" as an implicit recognition of the function of the ICJ to further develop the law.[1144] Individual judges of the ICJ were much more explicit. Judge *Alvarez*, for example, stated in the 1950 *Admissions* case:

> "the Court was entrusted with a mission which was not conferred – at any rate not in express terms – on the Permanent Court of International Justice, namely the *development* and consequently the *creation* of law. [...] The common view that international law must be created solely by States is, therefore, not valid to-day – nor indeed has it ever been. In truth, alongside of conventional law there is customary law, and above

---

A. v. Bogdandy/I. Venzke, 26 LJIL 1 (2013), 49 (55 et seq.); *A. v. Bogdandy/I. Venzke*, In wessen Namen?, 2nd ed. 2014, 25 et seq.; *Christian J Tams*, The ICJ as a 'Law-Formative Agency': Summary and Synthesis, in: C. J. Tams/J. Sloan (eds.), The development of international law by the International Court of Justice, 2014.

1141 *J. E. Alvarez*, What are International Judges for?: The Main Functions of International Adjudication, in: C. Romano/K. J. Alter/Y. Shany (eds.), The Oxford Handbook of International Adjudication, 2013, 158 (159–160).

1142 *Legality of the Threat or Use of Nuclear Weapons*, Advisory Opinion, ICJ Reports 1996, 226 (237, para. 18).

1143 Ibid.

1144 *S. Wittich*, The Judicial Functions of the International Court of Justice, in: I. Buffard/J. Crawford/A. Pellet/S. Wittich (eds.), International law between universalism and fragmentation, 2008, 981 (995).

> all the doctrines of jurists, who not only have the opportunity of establishing custom, but have formulated rules which have been respected by States. In future, it is to the General Assembly of the United Nations, to the International Court of Justice and to the jurists that we shall look, more than to anyone, for the creation of the new international law."[1145]

In the same vein, Judge *Tanaka* stated in the 1964 *Barcelona Traction* case:

> "The more important function of the Court as the principal judicial organ of the United Nations is to be found not only in the settlement of concrete disputes, but also in its reasoning, through which it may contribute to the *development of international law*."[1146]

Numerous commentators argue that the ICJ is not only engaged in "law-finding", but also in "law-making".[1147] The ICJ acts as a law-maker primarily by shaping the international legal discourse.[1148] Due to its singular reputation among states, international organizations, other ICs, and international lawyers, the ICJ's pronouncements have enormous persuasive power.[1149] The decisions of the ICJ do not formally bind the ICJ nor other ICs in later proceedings.[1150] Nevertheless, the ICJ, other ICs, states, and international legal scholars rely on *dicta* of the Court to prove or disprove legal arguments.[1151]

1145 *Competence of the General Assembly for the Admission of a State to the United Nations*, Advisory Opinion, Dissenting Opinion Alvarez, ICJ Reports 1950, 4 (12–13), emphasis in original.

1146 *Barcelona Traction, Light and Power Company, Limited (Belgium v. Spain) (Preliminary Objections)*, Judgment, Separate Opinion Tanaka, ICJ Reports 1964, 6 (65), emphasis added.

1147 *C. G. Weeramantry*, 10 LJIL 2 (1997), 309 (312); *S. Wittich*, The Judicial Functions of the International Court of Justice, in: I. Buffard/J. Crawford/A. Pellet/S. Wittich (eds.), International law between universalism and fragmentation, 2008, 981 (995); *A. v. Bogdandy/I. Venzke*, 26 LJIL 1 (2013), 49 (56); *A. v. Bogdandy/I. Venzke*, In wessen Namen?, 2nd ed. 2014, 25; *A. Kulick*, 27 Int. Community Law Rev. 1-2 (2025), 33 (41).

1148 *C. G. Weeramantry*, 10 LJIL 2 (1997), 309 (309 et seq.); *A. v. Bogdandy/I. Venzke*, 26 LJIL 1 (2013), 49 (56).

1149 Cf. *C. G. Weeramantry*, 10 LJIL 2 (1997), 309 (311); *A. v. Bogdandy/I. Venzke*, 26 LJIL 1 (2013), 49 (57).

1150 See Article 59 ICJ Statute: "The decision of the Court has no binding force except between the parties and in respect of that particular case."

1151 Cf. *C. G. Weeramantry*, 10 LJIL 2 (1997), 309 (311); *A. v. Bogdandy/I. Venzke*, 26 LJIL 1 (2013), 49 (57). On the authority of the ICJ, see *infra* in this Chapter Section D.II.2. and 3.

It is important to note that *judicial* law-making is different from *legislative* law-making.[1152] Judicial law-making is a process in which ICs, in the course of their judicial proceedings, fill gaps within existing rules of international law and thereby develop the law.[1153] In contrast, an organ engaged in legislative law-making creates new legal rules within their law-making capacity.[1154] The scope of judicial law-making in contrast to legislative law-making is thus significantly narrower. Additionally, judicial law-makers cannot act on their own accord and in pursuance of their own agenda. The ICJ can thus only act as a judicial law-maker after it has been seized by the parties to a dispute or – in the case of an advisory opinion – by an authorized organ and it must act impartially and in the interest of the law without any political agenda.[1155] The Court's dictum in the *Nuclear Weapons* opinion, in which it emphasized that it was not a legislator while accepting to a certain extent its law-making capacity,[1156] can be read as emphasizing exactly this difference between legislative and judicial law-making.

The Court's Registry expressly recognized in a recent publication that the ICJ is actively involved in the development of international law:

> "A judgment of the Court does not simply decide a particular dispute, but inevitably also contributes to the development of international law. Fully aware of this, the Court takes account of these two objectives in preparing and drafting its judgments."[1157]

The ICJ contributes to the development of the law in different ways.[1158] One important area of this concerns rules on procedure.[1159] Because the UNC and the ICJ Statute govern the Court's procedure only fragmentedly,

---

1152 *M. Cappelletti*, 8 MULR 1 (1981), 15.

1153 *D. Akande*, 9 EJIL 3 (1998), 437 (465).

1154 Ibid., 465.

1155 *M. Cappelletti*, 8 MULR 1 (1981), 15 (31–32); *D. Akande*, 9 EJIL 3 (1998), 437 (465).

1156 *Legality of the Threat or Use of Nuclear Weapons*, Advisory Opinion, ICJ Reports 1996, 226 (237, para. 18).

1157 Handbook of the International Court of Justice, 6th edition 2018, pp. 77–78, accessible under https://www.icj-cij.org/public/files/publications/handbook-of-the-court-en.pdf.

1158 *Weeramantry* distinguishes between 12 different ways in which the ICJ contributes to the development of the law, see *C. G. Weeramantry*, 10 LJIL 2 (1997), 309 (313 et seq.).

1159 According to *Amerasinghe*, this power to establish procedural rules is inherent in the judicial function of a court and thus not strictly a question of law making, see *C. F. Amerasinghe*, Reflections on the Judicial Function in International Law, in: T.

the Court must fill these gaps through legal interpretation.[1160] One way the Court does this is by deducing concrete rules from general principles of law. The Court for example found that in a case in which the facts continue to develop, general principles of judicial process require the Court to consider all facts that occur until the end of the oral proceedings on the merits.[1161] Although the ICJ claims that it merely applies general principles, in applying these principles the Court clarifies and develops their precise scope.

In principle, the Court's potential for judicial law-making is wider under its advisory jurisdiction than under its contentious jurisdiction. An authorized organ could ask the ICJ for an advisory opinion on any legal question. However, the Court has been reluctant to make broad findings on the law in its advisory capacity as the *Nuclear Weapons* advisory opinion demonstrated.

c) Control

One may add another function: the Court's function to control compliance with international law.[1162] Whereas the dispute resolution function focuses on the relationship between certain parties, the control function focuses on the objective interest of the international community in the compliance with international law.[1163] However, the Court's procedures are far from an ideal compliance control mechanism, in particular when it comes to the conduct of organs of international organizations.[1164] The Court cannot act on its own accord but always requires proceedings to be initiated by some other actor. International organizations cannot be parties to contentious

M. Ndiaye/R. Wolfrum/C. Kojima (eds.), Law of the sea, environmental law, and settlement of disputes, 2007, 119 (127).

1160 According to C. F. Amerasinghe, this power to establish procedural rules is inherent in the judicial function of a court and thus not strictly a question of law making, see Ibid., 127.

1161 *Case Concerning Military and Paramilitary Activities in and against Nicaragua (Nicaragua v. United States of America) (Merits)*, Judgment, ICJ Reports 1986, 14 (39, para. 58).

1162 *S. Wittich*, The Judicial Functions of the International Court of Justice, in: I. Buffard/J. Crawford/A. Pellet/S. Wittich (eds.), International law between universalism and fragmentation, 2008, 981 (996).

1163 Ibid., 996.

1164 *S. Schmahl*, Die Internationalen und die Supranationalen Organisationen, in: W. Vitzthum/A. Proelß (eds.), Law of Nations, 8th ed., 2019, 319 (para. 179).

proceedings and states cannot initiate advisory proceedings concerning the conduct of international organizations.[1165] The organs themselves will most likely only request an advisory opinion from the Court when they are convinced that their conduct is lawful.[1166] Nevertheless, the ICJ has demonstrated its willingness to judicially review the lawfulness of the actions taken by other UN organs.[1167]

III. Interim conclusions

The ICJ's judicial function can be understood to refer to both the Court's characteristics as a court of justice as well as the tasks which are assigned to it and which it must fulfil. The Court and legal commentators often refer to the Court's "dispute-settlement function", i.e., its task to settle international disputes, as the element of the Court's judicial function which stands most at odds with the Court's advisory jurisdiction. The following sections examine the argument that giving an advisory opinion on a matter that is the subject of an international dispute without the consent of the disputing states undermines the Court's dispute settlement function by circumventing the consent requirement of the contentious procedure. To this end, it is necessary to first define the scope of the consent requirement.

C. Scope of the consent requirement in contentious procedures

According to Article 36 ICJ Statute, the "jurisdiction of the Court" in contentious proceedings is subject to the consent of the parties to the case. The consent requirement thus protects states against the exercise of jurisdiction by the ICJ without their consent. To determine the scope of the consent

1165 Ibid., para. 179.
1166 Ibid., para. 179.
1167 With respect to the UNGA, see *Certain Expenses of the United Nations (Article 17, paragraph 2, of the Charter)*, Advisory Opinion, ICJ Reports 1962, 151; with respect to the UNSC, see *Questions of Interpretation and Application of the 1971 Montreal Convention arising from the Aerial Incident at Lockerbie (Libyan Arab Jamahiriya v. United States of America)*, Preliminary Objections, Judgment, ICJ Reports 1998, 115; on the relationship between the ICJ and the UNSC, see *R. J. St. MacDonald*, 31 Canadian Yearbook of International Law/Annuaire canadien de droit international (1994), 3; *V. Gowlland-Debbas*, 88 Am. j. int. law 4 (1994), 643; *J. E. Alvarez*, 90 Am. j. int. law 1 (1996), 1.

requirement, it is thus necessary to determine what the ICJ Statute means when it states that the "jurisdiction of the Court" is subject to consent.

I. Defining the term jurisdiction

The term "jurisdiction" has different meanings depending on the context in which it is used. In particular, one can distinguish between jurisdiction of states (1.), jurisdiction clauses in human rights instruments (2.) and jurisdiction of ICs (3.).

1. Jurisdiction of states

The traditional context in which the term "jurisdiction" was used concerns the jurisdiction of states. States have the sovereign power to create rules to regulate the behavior of persons.[1168] This power entails two different dimensions: the power to create rules (jurisdiction to prescribe) and the power to enforce such rules (jurisdiction to enforce).[1169] A state exercises these powers through its executive, legislative, and judicial bodies.[1170] These powers both result from and are limited by the sovereign equality of states.[1171] The sovereign equality of states dictates that a state may not exercise its jurisdiction over matters which lie in the exclusive jurisdiction of another state.[1172] The term jurisdiction therefore not only refers to the power of a state but also to the delimitation of powers *between* states.[1173] The distinction between a state's *jurisdiction to prescribe* and its *jurisdiction to enforce* is essential for this delimitation. A state's *jurisdiction to enforce* is strictly territorial in the sense that a state may not enforce its laws on

1168 *M. Milanović*, 8 HRLR 3 (2008), 411 (420); *M. N. Shaw*, International law, 7. ed. 2014, 469; *C. Ryngaert*, Jurisdiction in international law, 2. ed. 2015, 5; *M. N. Shaw*, International law, 8th ed. 2017, 469; *C. Staker*, Jurisdiction, in: M. D. Evans (ed.), International law, 5th ed., 2018 (289).

1169 *M. N. Shaw*, International law, 8th ed. 2017, 469; M Milanović names the adjudicatory jurisdiction as a third dimension, *M. Milanović*, 8 HRLR 3 (2008), 411 (420).

1170 *M. N. Shaw*, International law, 7. ed. 2014, 469.

1171 Cf. *C. Ryngaert*, Jurisdiction in international law, 2. ed. 2015, 6, 37.

1172 Cf. *M. N. Shaw*, International law, 8th ed. 2017, 471.

1173 *A. Peters*, 48 AVR 1 (2010), 1 (3); this is why *Ryngaert* refers to the rules governing jurisdiction as "do not obligations", see *C. Ryngaert*, Jurisdiction in international law, 2. ed. 2015, 22.

the territory of another state without that state's consent.[1174] Whether such a territorial limitation also exists for a state's *jurisdiction to prescribe* is disputed.[1175] In its landmark decision in the *Lotus* case, the PCIJ held that a state may enact laws that extend to matters outside its territory and enforce such laws within its territory.[1176] Restrictions on the jurisdiction to prescribe could only result from a prohibitive rule of international law, which did not exist for the subject-matter of the *Lotus* case.[1177] The debate between an extensive, extraterritorial understanding of the jurisdiction to prescribe and the "permissive principles approach", which places the power to exercise jurisdiction under a reservation of prior permission, continue to dominate discussions about the extent of a state's jurisdiction to prescribe until today.[1178] The ICJ has yet to decide this question.[1179]

2. Jurisdiction clauses in human rights treaties

In inter-state relations, the term jurisdiction is thus used to delimit the exercise of sovereign powers between states. In contrast, jurisdiction clauses in human rights treaties concern the applicability of human rights obligations under a treaty *vis-à-vis* the respective treaty party.[1180] Jurisdiction in this sense is used to determine when human rights obligations are triggered.[1181] A fundamental condition for the exercise of jurisdiction over persons is the factual (rather than legal) exercise of power over persons. As *Milanović* put it:

1174 *M. Milanović*, 8 HRLR 3 (2008), 411 (420).

1175 *C. Ryngaert*, Jurisdiction in international law, 2. ed. 2015, 29 et seq.

1176 *S.S. "Lotus" (France v. Turkey)*, Judgment, PCIJ Series A 1927, 4 (18–19). The *Lotus* case concerned a legal dispute between France and Turkey over the legality of Turkey's prosecuting the French officer of the watch in Turkish courts after the French mail steamer "Lotus" collided with a Turkish collier on the high seas, resulting in the deaths of eight Turkish seamen and passengers. A key question in the case was whether Turkey needed a positive permission under international law to exercise criminal jurisdiction over the French officer (France's position) or whether it could exercise its criminal jurisdiction unless there was a conflicting prohibitive rule under international law (Turkey's position), see ibid., 18.

1177 Ibid. (19).

1178 *C. Ryngaert*, Jurisdiction in international law, 2. ed. 2015, 29-30, 34-38.

1179 Ibid., 30.

1180 *M. Milanović*, 8 HRLR 3 (2008), 411; *C. Ryngaert*, Jurisdiction in international law, 2. ed. 2015, 22 et seq.

1181 *M. Milanović*, 8 HRLR 3 (2008), 411 (416).

> "[...] [T]he notion of jurisdiction in human rights treaties relates essentially to a question of fact, of actual authority and control that a state has over a given territory or person. 'Jurisdiction', in this context, simply means actual power, whether exercised lawfully or not – nothing more, and nothing less."[1182]

Jurisdiction clauses in human rights treaties also allocate responsibilities between different addresses of human rights obligations.[1183]

3. Jurisdiction of international courts and tribunals

The first two notions of jurisdiction focus on the state, either regarding the delimitation of its powers vis-à-vis other states or regarding the applicability of human rights obligations. There are relevant connections between the jurisdiction of states and the jurisdiction of ICs. For example, if certain treaty obligations under IHRL do not apply to a state because the matter falls outside a treaty's jurisdictional scope, the IC that has jurisdiction to interpret that treaty will also lack jurisdiction *ratione materiae* over the matter.[1184] At the same time, there are also important differences. One concerns procedure: Questions of jurisdiction of ICs are dealt with in advance before dealing with the substance of a dispute. Questions of jurisdiction of states, however, concern the substance or merits of the case.[1185] Another difference concerns the conceptual basis of jurisdiction: states have jurisdiction to act because they are sovereign.[1186] ICs, on the other hand, can only act insofar as they have been authorized by a subject of international law.[1187]

1182 Ibid., 435–436.

1183 Particularly in the context of the extraterritorial application of human rights obligations, questions of delimitating responsibilities arise, see *W. Vandenhole*, The 'J' Word, in: S. Allen/D. Costelloe/M. Fitzmaurice/P. Gragl/E. Guntrip (eds.), The Oxford handbook of jurisdiction in international law, 2019, 413.

1184 *M. Milanović*, 8 HRLR 3 (2008), 411 (416).

1185 Ibid., 416–417.

1186 *R. Kolb*, Le Droit International Comme Corps de «Droit Privé» et de «Droit Public» (Volume 419), Collected Courses of the Hague Academy of International Law, 2021 (270, para. 245).

1187 *R. Kolb*, The International Court of Justice, 2013, 200; with respect to the similar status of international organizations, *Kolb* refers to an "inverted Lotus principle": "le principe de spécialité tend à corseter les compétences de l'Orginsation en un principe du Lotus inversé: ce qui n'est pas permis est interdit; ce qui n'est pas conféré n'est pas acquis.", see *R. Kolb*, Le Droit International Comme Corps de

Any power they exercise must be attributed to them in an act of voluntary and collective self-restraint of states.[1188] It is this attribution of powers that is entailed by the term "jurisdiction of ICs". Jurisdiction, in other words, is what enables ICs to operate in the first place. Consequently, *Balasko* defined jurisdiction of ICs as "the legal capacity, conferred by the explicit common will of two or more States, of an international jurisdictional body, regularly constituted, to investigate and judge disputes arisen or arising between these States."[1189]

Some authors define jurisdiction of ICs more narrowly as the judicial power to decide a matter with final and binding force.[1190] However, this definition can be criticized for excluding the advisory jurisdiction,[1191] which the ICJ regularly includes when referring to the term 'jurisdiction'.[1192]

The ICJ has so far decided not to expand on the general meaning of the word "jurisdiction".[1193] However, the Court has elucidated the concept to some extent when it described the ILO Administrative Tribunal's jurisdiction as its power "to examine the complaints submitted to it and to

---

«Droit Privé» et de «Droit Public» (Volume 419), Collected Courses of the Hague Academy of International Law, 2021 (273, para. 248).

1188 *M. N. Shaw*, Rosenne's Law and Practice of the International Court: 1920-2015, 5th ed 2016, Vol. 2, Ch. 9, § 148.

1189 *A. Balasko*, Causes de nullité de la sentence arbitrale en droit international public, 1938, 139 (cited in: G. Abi-Saab, Les exceptions préliminaires dans la procédure de la Cour internationale, 58; translated from the French original: "l'aptitude juridique légale, attribuée par la volonté explicite commune de deux ou plusieurs Etats [sic], d'un organe international d'ordre juridictionnel, régulièrement constitué, pour instruire et pour juger des litiges nés ou à naître entre ces mêmes Etats [sic]").

1190 *M. N. Shaw*, Rosenne's Law and Practice of the International Court: 1920-2015, 5th ed 2016, Vol. 2, Ch. 9, § 148; similarly defined by Black's Law Dictionary as the "legal power and authority of a court to make a decision that binds the parties to any matter properly brought before the court", H. C. Black, B. A. Garner (eds.), Black's law dictionary, 2007.

1191 With further references *G. Abi-Saab*, Les exceptions préliminaires dans la procédure de la Cour internationale, 1966, 55–57.

1192 See for example *Legal Consequences of the Construction of a Wall in the Occupied Palestinian Territory*, Advisory Opinion, ICJ Reports 2004, 136 (148-156, §§ 24-42); *Accordance with international law of the unilateral declaration of independence in respect of Kosovo*, Advisory Opinion, ICJ Reports 2010, 403 (412-415, §§ 18-28); *Legal Consequences of the Separation of the Chagos Archipelago from Mauritius in 1965*, Advisory Opinion, ICJ Reports 2019, 95 (112-113, §§ 55-62).

1193 *Nottebohm (Liechtenstein v. Guatemala)*, Preliminary Objections, Judgment, ICJ Reports 1953, 111 (121).

adjudicate on the merits of the claims set out therein".[1194] The jurisdiction of an IC can thus be defined as the legal power, attributed by states, to be seised of a matter, examine it and make judicial pronouncements on it.

While the ICJ has used the terms 'jurisdiction' and 'competence' interchangeably,[1195] some authors argue in favor of a distinction between the two terms. *Balasko* and *Fitzmaurice* differentiate between the abstract and the concrete, with 'jurisdiction' describing the entirety of powers given to an IC and 'competence' describing the powers regarding a particular case.[1196] *Abi-Saab* uses the term jurisdiction to describe the judicial activity and the judicial powers, and the term competence to describe the scope of application of this activity and of these powers.[1197] The majority of legal doctrine, however, does not ascribe great importance to the distinction between the terms jurisdiction and competence.[1198]

II. Jurisdictional regime of the ICJ Statute

The ICJ Statue refers to the term jurisdiction only in Articles 36 and 37 in connection with the Court's contentious procedure.[1199] Jurisdiction thus refers to the power of the ICJ to decide inter-state legal disputes in a manner that is binding on the parties by means of the contentious proce-

1194 *Judgments of the Administrative Tribunal of the ILO upon Complaints Made against UNESCO*, Advisory Opinion, ICJ Reports 1956, 77 (87).

1195 See for example *Case of the monetary gold removed from Rome in 1943 (Italy v. France, United Kingdom and United States) (Preliminary Question)*, Judgment, ICJ Reports 1954, 19 (28); with further references *G. Abi-Saab*, Les exceptions préliminaires dans la procédure de la Cour internationale, 1966, 58.

1196 *A. Balasko*, Causes de nullité de la sentence arbitrale en droit international public, 1938, 139 (cited in: G. Abi-Saab, Les exceptions préliminaires dans la procédure de la Cour internationale, 58-59); *G. G. Fitzmaurice*, 29 British Yearbook of International Law (BYIL) 1 (1952), 1 (41–42).

1197 *G. Abi-Saab*, Les exceptions préliminaires dans la procédure de la Cour internationale, 1966, 60–61.

1198 *R. Kolb*, The International Court of Justice, 2013, 211; *M. N. Shaw*, Rosenne's Law and Practice of the International Court: 1920-2015, 5th ed 2016, Vol. 2, Ch. 9, § 149; *M. M. Aljaghoub*, The Advisory Function of the International Court of Justice 1946 - 2005, 2006, 36–37.

1199 The Statute uses the word jurisdiction exclusively in Art. 36 and Art. 54, which in turn refers to Art. 36 and 37. The French term *compétence* is also used in Art. 2, but this does not refer to the powers of the Court, but to the qualifications of the judges.

dure.[1200] Legal doctrine distinguishes between several overlapping layers of the ICJ's jurisdiction. Firstly, one can distinguish between general and special jurisdiction. Secondly, one can distinguish between abstract and concrete jurisdiction. Lastly, one can distinguish along the parameters of personal, material, temporal, and spatial jurisdiction.

1. General and special jurisdiction

The general jurisdiction of the ICJ refers to the fundamental limits of the Court's activity.[1201] It states what the Court can and cannot do.[1202] These limits are drawn by the UNC, the ICJ Statute and the Rules of the Court. The limitation of the Court's powers is an expression of the collective will of the Member States of the Court's constituent instrument and cannot be modified by the parties to the proceedings.[1203] Examples of these basic jurisdictional limits include that only states have access to the Court's contentious procedure (Article 34 para. 1 ICJ Statute) and that these states must either be Member States of the ICJ Statute (Article 35 para. 1 ICJ Statute) or must fulfil special requirements determined by the UNSC (Article 35 para. 2 ICJ Statute).[1204] Another example of the general jurisdiction of the Court is that judgments of the ICJ are final and unappealable (Article 60 ICJ Statute). General jurisdiction in contentious proceedings thus regulates the outer limits of the ICJ's dispute settlement function.

However, the general jurisdiction does not regulate which specific disputes the Court may decide. The power of the Court to decide a specific dispute between two or more parties in a binding manner is referred to

1200 *C. Tomuschat*, in: A. Zimmermann/C. J. Tams/K. Oellers-Frahm/C. Tomuschat/D. W. K. Anderson (eds.), The Statute of the International Court of Justice, 3. ed., 2019: Art. 36 ICJ Statute, para. 7.

1201 *T. Thienel*, Drittstaaten und die Jurisdiktion des Internationalen Gerichtshofs. Die Monetary Gold-Doktrin, 2016, 59–60; *H. W. Thirlway*, The international court of justice, in: M. D. Evans (ed.), International law, 5th ed., 2018 (579).

1202 *T. Thienel*, Drittstaaten und die Jurisdiktion des Internationalen Gerichtshofs. Die Monetary Gold-Doktrin, 2016, 59–60; *H. W. Thirlway*, The international court of justice, in: M. D. Evans (ed.), International law, 5th ed., 2018 (579).

1203 *T. Thienel*, Drittstaaten und die Jurisdiktion des Internationalen Gerichtshofs. Die Monetary Gold-Doktrin, 2016, 59–60; *H. W. Thirlway*, The international court of justice, in: M. D. Evans (ed.), International law, 5th ed., 2018 (579).

1204 *H. W. Thirlway*, The international court of justice, in: M. D. Evans (ed.), International law, 5th ed., 2018 (579–580).

as the Court's special jurisdiction.[1205] It is only through the attribution of special jurisdiction that the ICJ acquires the power to adjudicate on the legal position of a state. This attribution of power is dependent on prior consent of the state that is subject to the Court's decision.[1206] The special jurisdiction consists of two elements, the abstract and the concrete jurisdiction.[1207]

2. Abstract and concrete jurisdiction

The abstract and the concrete jurisdiction are sub-categories of the Court's special jurisdiction. One can thus also speak of the abstract-special and the concrete-special jurisdiction. The abstract-special jurisdiction governs which disputes (*ratione materiae* and *ratione tempore*) between which states (*ratione personae*) the ICJ may decide.[1208] The scope of abstract-special jurisdiction is determined by the relevant jurisdictional title.[1209] Article 36 ICJ Statute names three types of jurisdictional titles: first, the submission of a dispute by special agreement of the parties (*compromis*) (Article 36 para. 1 Alt. 1 ICJ Statute), secondly, compromissory clauses in international treaties[1210] or treaties for the peaceful settlement of disputes (Article 36 para. 1 Alt. 2, 37 ICJ Statute) and thirdly, the optional clause (or compulsory jurisdiction) (Article 36 para. 2 ICJ Statute). The third of these titles was supposed to create a network among all states so that on a voluntary basis a system of compulsory international jurisdiction would be

1205 *T. Thienel*, Drittstaaten und die Jurisdiktion des Internationalen Gerichtshofs. Die Monetary Gold-Doktrin, 2016, 59–60.

1206 Ibid., 65.

1207 Ibid., 66.

1208 Cf. Ibid., 66.

1209 Ibid., 66; *H. W. Thirlway*, The international court of justice, in: M. D. Evans (ed.), International law, 5th ed., 2018 (579).

1210 An example of a treaty-based abstract special jurisdiction title of the ICJ can be found in Art. XXI para. 2 of the Treaty of Amity, Economic Relations, and Consular Rights between the United States and Iran, according to which the ICJ has the power to decide any dispute between the US and Iran over the interpretation or application of the Treaty, see *United States Diplomatic and Consular Staff in Tehran (United States of America v. Iran)*, Judgment, ICJ Reports 1980, 3 (26 et seq., paras. 50 et seq.).

established.[1211] However, this expectation was dampened by the reluctance of states to submit declarations under Article 36 para. 2 ICJ Statute and the widespread use of reservations.[1212] A fourth jurisdictional title can be found in Article 38 para. 5 of the Rules of the Court: *forum prorogatum.* According to the principle of *forum prorogatum*, an otherwise lacking abstract-special jurisdiction of the ICJ is established if the respondent state agrees to continue the proceedings by performing procedural acts.[1213] While the jurisdictional titles in Article 36 ICJ Statute require prior consent of both parties, *forum prorogatum* is characterized by prior consent of the Applicant state and consent of the Respondent state only after the initiation of proceedings.[1214]

Yet, the ICJ cannot act based on its abstract-special jurisdiction alone. While the abstract-special jurisdiction indicates who the parties of potential proceedings are and which generally defined dispute they could bring before the Court, it does not authorize the Court to act in specific proceedings. The abstract-special jurisdiction must therefore be concretized. This is the domain of the concrete-special jurisdiction.[1215] The concrete-special jurisdiction is the focalization of the Court's powers to a concrete case with concrete parties which bring before the Court a concrete dispute.[1216] This focalization occurs by way of seisin the Court, i.e., by the initiation of

1211 *C. Tomuschat*, in: A. Zimmermann/C. J. Tams/K. Oellers-Frahm/C. Tomuschat/D. W. K. Anderson (eds.), The Statute of the International Court of Justice, 3. ed., 2019: Art. 36 ICJ Statute, 71.

1212 Ibid., 72.

1213 *Y. Ronen*, Forum Prorogatum (last updated 2020), in: A. Peters/R. Wolfrum (eds.), The Max Planck Encyclopedia of Public International Law, 2008 (1, 9); see also *Certain Questions of Mutual Assistance in Criminal Matters (Djibouti v. France)*, Judgment, ICJ Reports, 177 (203-206, paras. 60-64); *Armed Activities on the Territory of the Congo (New Application: 2002) (Democratic Republic of the Congo v. Rwanda)*, Jurisdiction and Admissibility, Judgment, ICJ Reports 2006, 6 (18-19, paras. 19-22).

1214 *Y. Ronen*, Forum Prorogatum (last updated 2020), in: A. Peters/R. Wolfrum (eds.), The Max Planck Encyclopedia of Public International Law, 2008 (5, 9); see also Art. 38 para. 5 Rules of the Court.

1215 *T. Thienel*, Drittstaaten und die Jurisdiktion des Internationalen Gerichtshofs. Die Monetary Gold-Doktrin, 2016, 66; cf. *H. W. Thirlway*, The international court of justice, in: M. D. Evans (ed.), International law, 5th ed., 2018 (581).

1216 *T. Thienel*, Drittstaaten und die Jurisdiktion des Internationalen Gerichtshofs. Die Monetary Gold-Doktrin, 2016, 66; cf. *H. W. Thirlway*, The international court of justice, in: M. D. Evans (ed.), International law, 5th ed., 2018 (581).

the proceedings by both or one of the parties.[1217] The seisin occurs in one of two ways: by submission of a joint special agreement or by unilateral written application (Article 40 para. 1 ICJ Statute).[1218] According to the first variant, the establishment of the abstract-special jurisdiction and the establishment of the concrete-special jurisdiction take place in a single step. The disputing states conclude a special agreement after the dispute has arisen, in which they agree on the subject matter of the dispute and agree to accept a judgment of the Court as binding.[1219] The proceedings are then initiated by the transmission of this special agreement to the Court's Registrar.[1220] Whether the transmission is to be made by all parties jointly or unilaterally is determined by the special agreement. Under this variant, the parties have more extensive control over their proceedings, but at the same time it presupposes a high degree of inter-state cooperation, which is why only few proceedings have been initiated so far under Article 40 para. 1 variant 1 ICJ Statute have been initiated so far.[1221] Proceedings are therefore much more frequently initiated by means of a written application under Article 40 para. 1 variant 2 ICJ Statute. In this case, the subject-matter of the proceedings is unilaterally determined by the Applicant and can only be extended but not restricted by the Respondent by submitting a counter-claim (Article 80 Rules of Court) or an extension of the claim by the Applicant.[1222]

1217 *T. Thienel*, Drittstaaten und die Jurisdiktion des Internationalen Gerichtshofs. Die Monetary Gold-Doktrin, 2016, 66; cf. *H. W. Thirlway*, The international court of justice, in: M. D. Evans (ed.), International law, 5th ed., 2018 (581).

1218 *S. Yee*, in: A. Zimmermann/C. J. Tams/K. Oellers-Frahm/C. Tomuschat/D. W. K. Anderson (eds.), The Statute of the International Court of Justice, 3. ed., 2019: Art. 40, paras. 18–19.

1219 *H. W. Thirlway*, The international court of justice, in: M. D. Evans (ed.), International law, 5th ed., 2018 (581).

1220 Ibid., 581.

1221 *S. Yee*, in: A. Zimmermann/C. J. Tams/K. Oellers-Frahm/C. Tomuschat/D. W. K. Anderson (eds.), The Statute of the International Court of Justice, 3. ed., 2019: Art. 40, para. 22.

1222 *T. Thienel*, Drittstaaten und die Jurisdiktion des Internationalen Gerichtshofs. Die Monetary Gold-Doktrin, 2016, 66–67.

3. Personal, material, temporal, and spatial jurisdiction

Another categorization concerns the personal, material, temporal, and spatial jurisdiction of the ICJ.[1223] These categories cut across the categories of general and special, as well as abstract and concrete jurisdiction.[1224]

The personal jurisdiction (*jurisdiction ratione personae*) determines who may be a party in proceedings before the Court.[1225] At the level of general jurisdiction, the Court's jurisdiction *ratione personae* is limited to states that are either members of the ICJ Statute or fulfil the requirements of Article 35 para. 2 ICJ Statute (*general jurisdiction ratione personae*). At the level of special jurisdiction, the jurisdictional title must extend to the parties of the proceedings (*abstract-special jurisdiction ratione personae*), and it must be these parties that initiate proceedings before the Court (*concrete-special jurisdiction ratione personae*).

The material jurisdiction (*jurisdiction ratione materiae*) determines what the subject of the proceedings may be.[1226] At the level of general jurisdiction, material jurisdiction requires that the proceedings have as their object the resolution of a dispute (*general jurisdiction ratione materiae*). At the level of special jurisdiction, the questions to be decided by the ICJ must be covered by the jurisdictional title (*abstract-special jurisdiction ratione materiae*) and must have been requested by the parties in the context of the initiation of proceedings (*concrete-special jurisdiction ratione materiae*).

The temporal jurisdiction (*jurisdiction ratione temporis*) determines when certain acts must have occurred, i.e., it relates to the temporal scope of the Court's jurisdiction.[1227] One reading of the temporal jurisdiction of the Court concerns the rule that all jurisdictional prerequisites must have existed at the relevant point in time and must continue to exist.[1228] This reading, however, does not add any analytical clarity as it is already an intrinsic characteristic of the respective jurisdictional prerequisite (or any prerequisite for that matter) that it must be fulfilled at the relevant point

1223 Ibid., 81 et seq.; *R. Kolb*, The International Court of Justice, 2013, 214–215.

1224 *T. Thienel*, Drittstaaten und die Jurisdiktion des Internationalen Gerichtshofs. Die Monetary Gold-Doktrin, 2016, 81.

1225 *R. Kolb*, The International Court of Justice, 2013, 214.

1226 Ibid., 214.

1227 Ibid., 214.

1228 *T. Thienel*, Drittstaaten und die Jurisdiktion des Internationalen Gerichtshofs. Die Monetary Gold-Doktrin, 2016, 83–84.

in time.[1229] Instead, the jurisdiction *ratione temporis* concerns a potential limitation of the Court's jurisdiction to disputes, facts, events, etc. that have occurred before or after a certain point in time.[1230] These limitations may only extend to the Court's special jurisdiction and not to the Court's general jurisdiction as the UNC and the Statute of the Court do not limit the Court's temporal jurisdiction in any way.[1231]

The spatial jurisdiction (*jurisdiction ratione loci*) determines where certain acts must have occurred.[1232] Just like for the Court's temporal jurisdiction, there are no general limits to the Court's spatial jurisdiction,[1233] but there may be limits to the Court's special spatial jurisdiction. The jurisdictional title attributing abstract-special jurisdiction may exclude or be limited to certain geographical areas (*abstract-special jurisdiction ratione loci*). Likewise, the parties may limit the concrete dispute they bring before the Court to certain areas (*concrete-special jurisdiction ratione loci*).

Germany's declaration of compulsory jurisdiction under Article 36 para. 2 ICJ Statute illustrates how states may limit all four jurisdictional sub-categories.[1234] First, Germany limited the Court's *temporal* jurisdiction to "all disputes arising after the present declaration, with regard to situations or facts subsequent to this date". Secondly, Germany limited the Court's *material* jurisdiction by excluding "any dispute which relates to, arises from or is connected with the deployment of armed forces abroad, involvement in such deployments or decisions thereon". Thirdly, Germany limited the Court's *spatial* jurisdiction by excluding any disputes which "relates to, arises from or is connected with the use for military purposes of the territory of the Federal Republic of Germany, including its airspace, as well as maritime areas subject to German sovereign rights and jurisdiction". Finally, Germany limited the Court's *personal* jurisdiction by excluding "any dispute in respect of which any other Party to the dispute has accepted the compulsory jurisdiction of the International Court of Justice only in

1229 Cf. Ibid., 84.

1230 *Jurisdictional Immunities of the State (Germany v. Italy: Greece intervening)*, Judgment, ICJ Reports 2012, 99 (118-119, paras. 42-44); *T. Thienel*, Drittstaaten und die Jurisdiktion des Internationalen Gerichtshofs. Die Monetary Gold-Doktrin, 2016, 84.

1231 *R. Kolb*, The International Court of Justice, 2013, 214.

1232 Ibid., 214.

1233 Ibid., 214. *Kolb* argues that the ICJ's jurisdiction could therefore extend to disputes with states on other planets if they fulfilled the conditions of Art. 35 UNC.

1234 For the text of Germany's declaration recognizing the jurisdiction of the Court as compulsory, see https://www.icj-cij.org/en/declarations/de, last accessed on 6 May 2024.

relation to or for the purpose of the dispute or where the acceptance of the Court's compulsory jurisdiction on behalf of any other Party to the dispute was deposited or ratified less than twelve months prior to the filing of the application bringing the dispute before the Court".

III. Exercise of jurisdiction limited to binding decisions

Having laid out the jurisdictional parameters of the ICJ Statute, the question arises in which cases the ICJ exercises its jurisdiction over a state. The crucial question is whether only the rendering of a binding decisions constitutes an exercise of jurisdiction over a state which requires that state's consent[1235] or whether any consideration of and judicial pronouncements on the rights and obligations of a state by the Court constitutes an exercise of jurisdiction.[1236] The distinction between binding decisions and other judicial pronouncements is of little relevance in the context of the ICJ's contentious proceedings: The ICJ may only deal with a case in the context of contentious proceedings, if it can conclude the proceedings by rendering a binding decision.[1237] However, this distinction is crucial in the context of advisory proceedings.[1238]

1235 *A. Orakhelashvili*, 3 The Law and Practice of International Courts and Tribunals (2003), 501 (503); *S. Rosenne*, The law and practice of the International Court, 1920-2005, 4th ed. 2006, 524; *T. Thienel*, Drittstaaten und die Jurisdiktion des Internationalen Gerichtshofs. Die Monetary Gold-Doktrin, 2016, 112, 127.

1236 Raising this distinction, see *T. Thienel*, Drittstaaten und die Jurisdiktion des Internationalen Gerichtshofs. Die Monetary Gold-Doktrin, 2016, 105.

1237 Ibid., 105; see also *Northern Cameroons (Cameroon v. United Kingdom) (Preliminary Objections)*, Judgment, ICJ Reports 1963, 15 (33–34): "The function of the Court is to state the law, but it may pronounce judgment only in connection with concrete cases where there exists at the time of the adjudication an actual controversy involving a conflict of legal interests between the parties. The Court's judgment must have some practical consequence in the sense that it can affect existing legal rights or obligations of the parties, thus removing uncertainty from their legal relations. No judgment on the merits in this case could satisfy these essentials of the judicial function."

1238 A similar question arises in cases where judicial decisions concern third parties, especially in the context of the so-called Monetary Gold doctrine. On the Monetary Gold doctrine, see *T. Thienel*, Drittstaaten und die Jurisdiktion des Internationalen Gerichtshofs. Die Monetary Gold-Doktrin, 2016, 105 et seq.

1. Binding decisions as an exercise of jurisdiction

The ICJ has consistently emphasized that the jurisdiction of the Court to issue advisory opinions is not subject to state consent.[1239] The ICJ explained its position with the non-binding nature of its advisory opinions:

> "The consent of States, parties to a dispute, is the basis of the Court's jurisdiction in contentious cases. The situation is different in regard to advisory proceedings even where the Request for an Opinion relates to a legal question actually pending between States. The Court's reply is only of an advisory character: as such, it has no binding force. It follows that no State, whether a Member of the United Nations or not, can prevent the giving of an Advisory Opinion which the United Nations considers to be desirable in order to obtain enlightenment as to the course of action it should take."[1240]

Thus, according to the ICJ, the Court exercises jurisdiction over a state only if it issues a binding decision. As advisory opinions are not binding, they do not constitute an exercise of jurisdiction over a state regardless of the content of the advisory opinion and thus do not depend on prior consent.

2. The elements of a binding decision: Binding force and res judicata

Finding that only binding decisions are subject to state consent, the question arises what constitutes a binding decision. The binding nature of ICJ decisions can be separated into two related concepts: the decision's binding force and its *res judicata* effect.[1241] Binding force and *res judicata*, which constitute general principles of law,[1242] serve two overarching pur-

1239 *Interpretation of Peace Treaties with Bulgaria, Hungary and Romania (First Phase)*, Advisory Opinion, ICJ Reports 1950, 65 (71); *Western Sahara*, Advisory Opinion, ICJ Reports 1975, 12 (20, para. 21); *Applicability of Article VI, Section 22, of the Convention on the Privileges and Immunities*, Advisory Opinion, ICJ Reports 1989, 177 (189-190, para. 33); *Legal Consequences of the Construction of a Wall in the Occupied Palestinian Territory*, Advisory Opinion, ICJ Reports 2004, 136 (157-158, para. 47).

1240 *Interpretation of Peace Treaties with Bulgaria, Hungary and Romania (First Phase)*, Advisory Opinion, ICJ Reports 1950, 65 (71).

1241 For a detailed account of the principles of binding force and res judicata, see *R. Kolb*, The International Court of Justice, 2013, 760–775.

1242 Ibid., 762.

poses: justice and legal security.[1243] The peaceful resolution of a dispute not only lies in the interest of the parties, but also of the broader international community which has an interest in keeping the peace.[1244] The settlement of disputes can therefore be considered a "public good".[1245] Neither a final and peaceful end to the dispute nor any certainty in the legal relations between the disputing States could be achieved if the decisions of the Court were subject to constant review by the parties.

a) Binding force

For the ICJ, the binding force of its decisions follows from Article 94 UNC and Article 59 ICJ Statute.[1246]

Article 94 UNC states:

> "Each Member of the United Nations undertakes to comply with the decision of the International Court of Justice in any case to which it is a party."

Article 59 ICJ Statute stipulates:

> "The decision of the Court has no binding force except between the parties and in respect of that particular case."

The negative formulation of Article 59 ICJ Statute, which originates from the wording of Article 84 para. 1 of the 1907 Hague Convention,[1247] emphasizes three aspects of the binding force: the limitation of the binding force of the decision to the parties to the case, the inapplicability of the common law doctrine of *stare decisis* in international law, and the fact that the Court does not perform a legislative function.[1248] The ICJ rephrased Article 59 in positive terms in its *Bosnian Genocide* case:

1243 Ibid., 762–763.

1244 *C. P. Romano/K. J. Alter/Y. Shany*, Mapping International Adjudicative Bodies, the Issues, and Players, in: C. Romano/K. J. Alter/Y. Shany (eds.), The Oxford Handbook of International Adjudication, 2013 (5).

1245 Ibid., 5.

1246 On the concept of binding force see *C. Brown*, in: A. Zimmermann/C. J. Tams/K. Oellers-Frahm/C. Tomuschat/D. W. K. Anderson (eds.), The Statute of the International Court of Justice, 3. ed., 2019: Article 59 ICJ Statute, 30 et seq.; *R. Kolb*, The International Court of Justice, 2013, 761 et seq.

1247 *R. Kolb*, The International Court of Justice, 2013, 763.

1248 Ibid., 763–764.

> "Article 59 of the Statute, notwithstanding its negative wording, has at its core the positive statement that the parties are bound by the decision of the Court in respect of the particular case."[1249]

The term 'decision of the Court' as used in Article 59 ICJ Statute is understood broadly and includes several different kinds of judicial pronouncements.[1250] These include final decisions on the merits of a case, decisions on preliminary objections,[1251] and orders (such as provisional measures).[1252] Article 59 ICJ Statute and Article 94 UNC deliberately use the term 'decision' rather than 'judgment'. The term 'judgment' is used in Article 95 of the Rules of the Court to describe the entirety of the judicial pronouncement which is delivered in contentious proceedings. 'Judgment', in other words, refers to the judicial document, which includes all the elements listed in Article 95 of the Rules.

The term 'decision' as employed by Article 59 ICJ Statute and Article 94 UNC, on the other hand, refers to a narrower sub-set of the judgment or order which contains the obligations of the parties.[1253] This sub-set includes only the operative provisions of the judgment (also known as *dispositif*) and to a limited extent the reasons supporting the operative provisions.[1254] The operative provisions of a judgment are relatively short and succinct

1249 *Application of the Convention on the Prevention and Punishment of the Crime of Genocide (Bosnia and Herzegovina v. Serbia and Montenegro)*, Judgment, ICJ Reports 2007, 43 (90, para. 115).

1250 See *C. Brown*, in: A. Zimmermann/C. J. Tams/K. Oellers-Frahm/C. Tomuschat/D. W. K. Anderson (eds.), The Statute of the International Court of Justice, 3. ed., 2019: Article 59 ICJ Statute, paras. 35–40.

1251 *South-West Africa (Liberia v. South Africa)*, Judgment, ICJ Reports 1966 (36–37); *Application of the Convention on the Prevention and Punishment of the Crime of Genocide (Bosnia and Herzegovina v. Serbia and Montenegro)*, Judgment, ICJ Reports 2007, 43 (101, para. 138).

1252 *LaGrand (Germany v. United States of America)*, Judgment, ICJ Reports 2001, 466 (502-503, para. 102); *Jadhav (India v. Pakistan)*, Provisional Measures, Order, ICJ Reports 2017, 231 (245, para. 59); while provisional measures are binding, they do not become res judicata, see *C. Brown*, in: A. Zimmermann/C. J. Tams/K. Oellers-Frahm/C. Tomuschat/D. W. K. Anderson (eds.), The Statute of the International Court of Justice, 3. ed., 2019: Article 59 ICJ Statute, para. 40.

1253 *R. Kolb*, The International Court of Justice, 2013, 768.

1254 *Judgments of the Administrative Tribunal of the ILO upon Complaints Made against UNESCO*, Advisory Opinion, ICJ Reports 1956, 77 (87); *Interhandel (Switzerland v. United States of America)*, Judgment, ICJ Reports 1959, 6 (28); *Right of Passage over Indian Territory (Portugal v. India) (Merits)*, Judgment, ICJ Reports 1960, 6 (32); *Arrest Warrant of 11 April 2000 (Democratic Republic of the Congo v. Belgium)*, Judgment, ICJ Reports 2002, 3 (18, para. 43); *S. Rosenne*, The law and determinations of the existence of claims, rights, and duties of the parties. The judges vote on each operative provision individually and the outcome of the vote is listed in the judgment in accordance with Article 95 Rules of the Court.[1255]

While the operative provisions are binding, the underlying reasoning of the Court is only binding to the extent that it is necessary for the understanding or implementation of the operative provisions.[1256] Excluded from the binding force of the decision is thus any part of the reasoning which is not necessary for the understanding or implementation of the operative provisions, that is "peripheral or subsidiary matters"[1257] as well as *obiter dicta* which have no direct bearing on the operative provisions at all.[1258]

According to Article 59 ICJ Statute, the decision of the Court is only binding on the parties of the case (*inter partes* effect of ICJ decisions). Only states may be parties to the contentious proceedings before the ICJ, Article 34 para. 1 ICJ Statute. This excludes all international organizations and their organs (including the UN), as well as private individuals, companies, and NGOs.[1259] States that are not parties to the case as well as international organizations are not bound by a decision of the Court. They may, however, agree to be bound by the decision on their own accord. The binding force

practice of the International Court, 1920-2005, 4th ed. 2006, 1536; *R. Kolb*, The International Court of Justice, 2013, 767.

1255 Cf. *C. Brown*, in: A. Zimmermann/C. J. Tams/K. Oellers-Frahm/C. Tomuschat/D. W. K. Anderson (eds.), The Statute of the International Court of Justice, 3. ed., 2019: Article 59 ICJ Statute, para. 41.

1256 *Polish Postal Service in Danzig*, Advisory Opinion, PCIJ Series B 1925, 6 (29–30); *Application of the Convention on the Prevention and Punishment of the Crime of Genocide (Bosnia and Herzegovina v. Serbia and Montenegro)*, Judgment, ICJ Reports 2007, 43 (95, para. 126); *R. Kolb*, The International Court of Justice, 2013, 767; *C. Brown*, in: A. Zimmermann/C. J. Tams/K. Oellers-Frahm/C. Tomuschat/D. W. K. Anderson (eds.), The Statute of the International Court of Justice, 3. ed., 2019: Article 59 ICJ Statute, para. 41.

1257 *Application of the Convention on the Prevention and Punishment of the Crime of Genocide (Bosnia and Herzegovina v. Serbia and Montenegro)*, Judgment, ICJ Reports 2007, 43 (95, para. 126).

1258 *R. Kolb*, The International Court of Justice, 2013, 767; *C. Brown*, in: A. Zimmermann/C. J. Tams/K. Oellers-Frahm/C. Tomuschat/D. W. K. Anderson (eds.), The Statute of the International Court of Justice, 3. ed., 2019: Article 59 ICJ Statute, para. 42.

1259 *C. Brown*, in: A. Zimmermann/C. J. Tams/K. Oellers-Frahm/C. Tomuschat/D. W. K. Anderson (eds.), The Statute of the International Court of Justice, 3. ed., 2019: Article 59 ICJ Statute, para. 50.

in such a case results not from the ICJ Statute or the UNC but from the separately concluded agreement.[1260]

The *inter partes* effect of ICJ decisions as enshrined in Article 59 ICJ Statute protects third states from being bound by a decision which they have neither initiated nor otherwise contributed to. There are, however, several exceptions to the strict *inter partes* effect of ICJ decisions.[1261] Certain decisions on treaty interpretation and territorial or maritime delimitation create 'objective results' which third parties may not ignore.[1262] Another exception to the *inter partes* effect concerns the intervention of third states in line with Articles 62 and 63 ICJ Statute.[1263] A third potential context in which the protection provided by Article 59 ICJ Statute is insufficient concerns cases in which the subject-matter of the proceedings before the Court necessarily relates to the rights of a third state not party to the proceedings.[1264] Although not bound by the judgment, the third state's legal interests may be particularly affected. This situation has entered the jurisprudence of the Court under the name of the *Monetary Gold doctrine*[1265] and will be examined more closely and compared to advisory opinions on pending bilateral disputes in the next section.

According to Article 59 ICJ Statute, a decision of the ICJ has binding force only "in respect of that particular case". This means that the Court can only decide the case that is presented to it by the parties and not render decisions on the legal relations of the parties merely on occasion of the case. What constitutes the "case" in the sense of Article 59 ICJ Statute is

1260 *C. Brown*, in: A. Zimmermann/C. J. Tams/K. Oellers-Frahm/C. Tomuschat/D. W. K. Anderson (eds.), The Statute of the International Court of Justice, 3. ed., 2019: Article 59 ICJ Statute, para. 50; *R. Kolb*, The International Court of Justice, 2013, 764.

1261 See *C. Brown*, in: A. Zimmermann/C. J. Tams/K. Oellers-Frahm/C. Tomuschat/D. W. K. Anderson (eds.), The Statute of the International Court of Justice, 3. ed., 2019: Article 59 ICJ Statute, 52 et seq.

1262 Ibid., para. 59.

1263 Ibid., paras. 60–63.

1264 Ibid., paras. 64–66.

1265 *Case of the monetary gold removed from Rome in 1943 (Italy v. France, United Kingdom and United States) (Preliminary Question)*, Judgment, ICJ Reports 1954, 19 (32–33); for an extensive analysis of the Monetary Gold doctrine, see *T. Thienel*, Drittstaaten und die Jurisdiktion des Internationalen Gerichtshofs. Die Monetary Gold-Doktrin, 2016.

determined by the claims and potential counter-claims of the parties.[1266] In other words, *stare decisis* does not apply to ICJ decisions.[1267]

b) Res judicata

While *res judicata* is not identical with the concept of binding force, it is closely related to it.[1268] Whereas the decision's binding force describes the obligations which follow from the decisions for the parties of the case, *res judicata* concerns the fate of the decision itself.[1269] *Res judicata*, as enshrined in Articles 59, 60, and 61 ICJ Statute, means that decisions of the Court are 'final'. This entails two things[1270]: first, the decision may no longer be overturned, modified or suspended by the parties to the proceedings (*res judicata* in the formal sense).[1271] In general, a decision becomes *res judicata* in the formal sense either immediately after the decisions of the Court has been rendered if there is no legal remedy available to the parties or once the time limit to exercise a legal remedy has lapsed.[1272] In the case of the ICJ, there is no appeals procedure (Article 60 ICJ Statute), however, there is a revision procedure in case decisive, previously unknown facts emerge (Article 61 para. 1 ICJ Statute). The application for revision must be made within six months of the discovery of the new fact (Article 61 para. 4 ICJ Statute). After ten years, a decision may no longer be revised (Article 61 para. 5 ICJ Statute). Secondly, the decision which is *res judicata* cannot form the subject-matter in subsequent proceedings between the same parties (*res judicata* in the material sense).[1273]

1266 *C. Brown*, in: A. Zimmermann/C. J. Tams/K. Oellers-Frahm/C. Tomuschat/D. W. K. Anderson (eds.), The Statute of the International Court of Justice, 3. ed., 2019: Article 59 ICJ Statute, para. 68.

1267 *R. Kolb*, The International Court of Justice, 2013, 763.

1268 On the difference between binding force and res judicata see Ibid., 761–762; *C. Brown*, in: A. Zimmermann/C. J. Tams/K. Oellers-Frahm/C. Tomuschat/D. W. K. Anderson (eds.), The Statute of the International Court of Justice, 3. ed., 2019: Article 59 ICJ Statute, para. 40.

1269 *R. Kolb*, The International Court of Justice, 2013, 761.

1270 See Ibid., 761.

1271 Cf. *Application of the Convention on the Prevention and Punishment of the Crime of Genocide (Bosnia and Herzegovina v. Serbia and Montenegro)*, Judgment, ICJ Reports 2007, 43 (90, para. 115).

1272 *R. Kolb*, The International Court of Justice, 2013, 761.

1273 Cf. *Application of the Convention on the Prevention and Punishment of the Crime of Genocide (Bosnia and Herzegovina v. Serbia and Montenegro)*, Judgment, ICJ

The extent of the application of *res judicata* is determined by the "triple identity test".[1274] *Res judicata* thus only prevents the Court from being seised in subsequent proceedings if the subsequent proceedings are identical to the previous ones in terms of the parties, the relief sought, and the cause of action.[1275]

3. Advisory opinions on inter-state disputes as an intervention in domestic matters?

One could argue that by requesting an advisory opinion on an inter-state dispute as well as by rendering the requested opinion, the requesting UN organ and the ICJ "intervene in matters which are essentially within the domestic jurisdiction" of the affected states or "require the Members to submit such matters to settlement under the present Charter" in the sense of Article 2 para. 7 UNC.[1276] Article 2 para. 7 UNC codifies the customary[1277] principle of non-intervention as it concerns the activities of the UN *vis-à-vis* its Member States.[1278] To successfully base a consent requirement

Reports 2007, 43 (90, para. 115); *R. Kolb*, The International Court of Justice, 2013, 761.

1274 *Interpretation of Judgments Nos. 7 and 8 (Factory at Chorzów)*, Judgment, Dissenting Opinion Anzilotti, PCIJ Series A, 1927, 23; *C. Brown*, in: A. Zimmermann/C. J. Tams/K. Oellers-Frahm/C. Tomuschat/D. W. K. Anderson (eds.), The Statute of the International Court of Justice, 3. ed., 2019: Article 59 ICJ Statute, para. 31; *J. H. Fahner*, Two Takes on Chagos: Reconciling the Advisory Opinion with the Res Judicata Effect of the UNCLOS Arbitral Award, in: T. Burri/J. Trinidad (eds.), The International Court of Justice and decolonisation, 2021, 71 (79).

1275 Or as *Anzilotti* put it "persona, petitum, causa petendi", see *Interpretation of Judgments Nos. 7 and 8 (Factory at Chorzów)*, Judgment, Dissenting Opinion Anzilotti, PCIJ Series A, 1927, 23; see also *Trail Smelter Arbitration (United States of America v. Canada)*, Award, UNRIAA, Vol. III (1941), 1905 (1952).

1276 Art. 2 para. 7 UNC stipulates:
"Nothing contained in the present Charter shall authorize the United Nations to intervene in matters which are essentially within the domestic jurisdiction of any state or shall require the Members to submit such matters to settlement under the present Charter; but this principle shall not prejudice the application of enforcement measures under Chapter VII."

1277 See *Case Concerning Military and Paramilitary Activities in and against Nicaragua (Nicaragua v. United States of America) (Merits)*, Judgment, ICJ Reports 1986, 14 (106, para. 202).

1278 The principle of non-intervention is "part and parcel of customary international law", see Ibid. The principle of non-intervention between states is enshrined in Art. 2 para. 1 UNC, see *A. von Arnauld*, Völkerrecht, 5. ed. 2023, 150, para. 357.

on Article 2 para. 7 UNC, the request for an advisory opinion and/or the ensuing rendering of the opinion would thus need to qualify as an intervention in matters which are essentially within the domestic jurisdiction of the affected Member States.

a) Intervention

It is contested which actions qualify as an intervention in the sense of Article 2 para. 7 UNC.[1279] One may generally distinguish between a narrow and a wide interpretation of the term "intervention".[1280] According to the narrow interpretation of Article 2 para. 7 UNC, only "dictatorial interferences" such as the use of force or similar forms of "imperative pressure" qualify as an intervention.[1281] Taken to an extreme, this view excludes any discussions, studies, enquiries and recommendations from the purview of Article 2 para. 7 UNC.[1282] This view has attracted criticism as it would leave almost no scope of application for Article 2 para. 7 UNC since most UN organs may only make recommendations.[1283] *H. Lauterpacht* therefore adhered to a modified version of this view arguing that only a certain kind of recommendation may qualify as an intervention which is "calculated to exercise direct pressure, likely to be followed by measures of enforcement, upon a State in a matter which is essentially within the domestic jurisdiction of a State".[1284]

A wide interpretation of the term "intervention" includes all actions by which the UN exerts pressure on states and restricts their choice of a political, economic, social and cultural system and the formulation of foreign policy.[1285] According to this view, any substantive discussion and recom-

1279 *G. Nolte*, in: B. Simma/D.-E. Khan/G. Nolte/A. Paulus (eds.), The Charter of the United Nations, 4. ed., 2024: Art. 2(7), 10 et seq.

1280 Ibid., para. 10.

1281 *H. Kelsen*, The law of the United Nations, 2. ed. 1951, 770.

1282 *H. Lauterpacht*, The international protection of human rights, 1947, 19.

1283 With further references, see *G. Nolte*, in: B. Simma/D.-E. Khan/G. Nolte/A. Paulus (eds.), The Charter of the United Nations, 4. ed., 2024: Art. 2(7), para. 10.

1284 *L. Oppenheim/H. Lauterpacht*, International Law, 7. ed. 1948, 378.

1285 *G. Nolte*, in: B. Simma/D.-E. Khan/G. Nolte/A. Paulus (eds.), The Charter of the United Nations, 4. ed., 2024: Art. 2(7), para. 20 citing *Case Concerning Military and Paramilitary Activities in and against Nicaragua (Nicaragua v. United States of America) (Merits)*, Judgment, ICJ Reports 1986, 14 (108).

mendation can amount to an intervention.[1286] This wide interpretation of Article 2 para. 7 UNC is guided by developments regarding the customary principle of non-intervention as it concerns inter-state relations.[1287]

The ICJ has found in its 1986 *Nicaragua* judgment that the "element of coercion (...) defines, and indeed forms the very essence of, prohibited intervention". However, similarly to the discussions on the term "to intervene" in Article 2 para. 7 UNC, the exact definition of coercion is contested.[1288] The most extreme example of coercion is the threat or use of force.[1289] However, conduct below the threshold of force may also constitute coercion, since otherwise the principle of non-intervention would have no scope of application distinct from the prohibition of the threat or use of force. The UNGA defined the element of coercion in its 1970 "Friendly Relations Declaration" broadly:

> "No State or group of States has the right to intervene, directly or indirectly, for any reason whatsoever, in the internal or external affairs of another State. (...) No State may use or encourage the use of economic, political or any other type of measure to coerce another State in order to obtain from it the subordination of the exercise of its sovereign rights and to secure from it advantages of any kind."[1290]

The UNGA used similarly broad terms in its 1974 "Charter of Economic Rights and Duties of States":

> "No State may use or encourage the use of economic, political or any other type of measures to coerce another State in order to obtain from it the subordination of the exercise of its sovereign rights."[1291]

1286 Ibid., para. 21.

1287 Ibid., para. 19.

1288 See on this *W. Heintschel von Heinegg*, § 55. Vom ius ad bellum zum ius contra bellum, in: V. Epping/W. Heintschel von Heinegg (eds.), Völkerrecht, 7th edition, 2018 (paras. 48-51); *A. von Arnauld*, Völkerrecht, 5. ed. 2023, 151-157, paras. 363-379.

1289 *Case Concerning Military and Paramilitary Activities in and against Nicaragua (Nicaragua v. United States of America) (Merits)*, Judgment, ICJ Reports 1986, 14 (107-107, para. 205).

1290 UNGA resolution 2625(XXV) of 24 October 1970, UN doc. A/RES/2625(XXV) (Friendly Relations Declaration).

1291 UNGA resolution 3281 (XXIX) of 12 December 1974, UN doc. A/RES/3281(XXIX) (Charter of Economic Rights and Duties of States), Art. 32.

Examples of activities which fall below the threshold of force but which are sufficiently coercive to constitute a prohibited intervention include actions directed at regime change such as the financing, training and provision of weapons to insurgents,[1292] the violation of a state's territorial integrity,[1293] and economic coercion[1294].

Recent developments thus point towards a more flexible understanding of the term "intervention".[1295] In particular discussions and recommendations on a matter may in principle amount to a prohibited intervention.[1296] However, such discussions and recommendations only constitute a prohibited intervention if they concern matters which are essentially within the domestic jurisdiction of the state in question.

b) In matters essentially within the domestic jurisdiction

The term "domestic jurisdiction" is not an absolute concept. It does not refer to certain matters which are *per se* beyond the reach of international law.[1297] Instead, "domestic jurisdiction" is a relative term which refers to those matters which – considering the law at the time – are not governed by rules of international law.[1298] As the PCIJ held in its *Nationality Decrees* advisory opinion:

> "The question whether a certain matter is or is not solely within the jurisdiction of a State is an essentially relative question; it depends on the development of international relations."[1299]

1292 *Case Concerning Military and Paramilitary Activities in and against Nicaragua (Nicaragua v. United States of America) (Merits)*, Judgment, ICJ Reports 1986, 14 (124, para. 242); *A. von Arnauld*, Völkerrecht, 5. ed. 2023, 152-154, paras. 366-369.

1293 *A. von Arnauld*, Völkerrecht, 5. ed. 2023, 154-155, paras. 371-375.

1294 Ibid., 156-157, para. 378.

1295 *G. Nolte*, in: B. Simma/D.-E. Khan/G. Nolte/A. Paulus (eds.), The Charter of the United Nations, 4. ed., 2024: Art. 2(7), 21 et seq.

1296 Ibid., para. 22.

1297 *J. Crawford*, Brownlie's Principles of Public International Law, 9. ed. 2019, 439; *G. Nolte*, in: B. Simma/D.-E. Khan/G. Nolte/A. Paulus (eds.), The Charter of the United Nations, 4. ed., 2024: Art. 2(7), para. 30.

1298 *J. Crawford*, Brownlie's Principles of Public International Law, 9. ed. 2019, 439; *G. Nolte*, in: B. Simma/D.-E. Khan/G. Nolte/A. Paulus (eds.), The Charter of the United Nations, 4. ed., 2024: Art. 2(7), para. 30.

1299 *Nationality Decrees Issued in Tunis and Morocco*, Advisory Opinion, PCIJ Rep Ser. B No. 4 (1923), 7 (24).

Advisory opinions may only be requested on questions of international law which arise within the requesting organ's scope of activities.[1300] As such, their subject-matter is inherently international in nature and thus not "essentially within the domestic jurisdiction" of affected states. Therefore, while the request for an advisory opinion may in general be an action which could constitute an intervention, this intervention can by definition not occur within a state's domestic jurisdiction. Non-binding judicial pronouncements on a state's international obligations, such as advisory opinions, are thus not subject to any consent requirement.[1301]

4. Sovereign equality of states

Some critics of the Court's application of its advisory procedure to inter-state disputes have based their criticism not on Article 2 para. 7 UNC, but on the principle of sovereign equality of states.[1302] This raises the question what, if anything at all, can one derive from the principle of sovereign equality of states for the question at hand. Before the creation of the UNC, legal discourse focused on the principle of "sovereignty" which initially entailed a defensive right of states vis-à-vis other states. In this vein, Arbitrator *Huber* stated in the 1928 *Island of Palmas* case that

> "[s]overeignty in the relations between states signifies independence. Independence in regard to a portion of the globe which is the right to exercise therein, to the exclusion of any other state, the functions of a state."[1303]

Sovereignty in this sense operates as a shield which protects a state's internal order from outside interference.[1304] Influential concepts such as

1300 See *supra*: § 5 Section C.I.2.

1301 So also *M. M. Aljaghoub*, 24 ALQ 2 (2010), 191 (199 et seq.).

1302 See *Interpretation of Peace Treaties with Bulgaria, Hungary and Romania (First Phase)*, Advisory Opinion, Separate Opinion Azevedo, ICJ Reports 1950, 79 (84); *Interpretation of Peace Treaties with Bulgaria, Hungary and Romania (First Phase)*, Advisory Opinion, Dissenting Opinion Zoričić, ICJ Reports 1950, 98 (99 et seq.); *Interpretation of Peace Treaties with Bulgaria, Hungary and Romania (First Phase)*, Advisory Opinion, Dissenting Opinion Krylov, ICJ Reports 1950, 105 (109).

1303 *Island of Palmas (Netherlands v. United States of America)*, Award, UNRIAA, 1928, Vol. II, 829 (838).

1304 *B. Fassbender*, in: B. Simma/D.-E. Khan/G. Nolte/A. Paulus (eds.), The Charter of the United Nations, 4. ed., 2024: Art. 2(1), para. 11.

Triepel's separation between domestic and international law[1305] built on this understanding of sovereignty.[1306] Under contemporary international law, the principle of sovereignty is inextricably linked with the principle of equality of states.[1307] In relation to domestic court proceedings, the principle of equality entails that

> "the courts of one State are not competent to question the validity of the acts of another State insofar as those acts purport to take effect within the sphere of validity of the latter State's national legal order."[1308]

It becomes immediately apparent that this notion is not easily transferred to the question at hand. The ICJ is not a domestic court and the legal questions presented to it do not concern a state's national legal order but exclusively its international obligations.

Through the creation of the UNC, the principles of sovereignty and equality of states merged to form the principle of sovereign equality as enshrined in Article 2 para. 1 UNC. The principle of sovereign equality has experienced its most important concretization through the 1970 UNGA *Friendly Relations Declaration*,[1309] which is treated as an authoritative statement on the content of the principle of sovereign equality of states.[1310] It states on the principle of sovereign equality:

> "All States enjoy sovereign equality. They have equal rights and duties and are equal members of the international community, notwithstanding differences of an economic, social, political or other nature.
>
> In particular, sovereign equality includes the following elements:
>
> (a) States are judicially equal;
> (b) Each State enjoys the rights inherent in full sovereignty;
> (c) Each State has the duty to respect the personality of other States;

1305 See *Heinrich Triepel*, Völkerrecht und Landesrecht, 1899.

1306 *B. Fassbender*, in: B. Simma/D.-E. Khan/G. Nolte/A. Paulus (eds.), The Charter of the United Nations, 4. ed., 2024: Art. 2(1), para. 11.

1307 On the emergence of the notion of sovereign equality in the 1943 Moscow Declaration, see *H. Kelsen*, 53 Yale Law Journal 2 (1944), 207; on the principle of equality of states, see *B. Fassbender*, in: B. Simma/D.-E. Khan/G. Nolte/A. Paulus (eds.), The Charter of the United Nations, 4. ed., 2024: Art. 2(1), 15 et seq.

1308 *H. Kelsen*, 53 Yale Law Journal 2 (1944), 207 (209).

1309 UNGA resolution 2625(XXV) of 15 December 1970, UN doc. A/RES/2625(XXV).

1310 *B. Fassbender*, in: B. Simma/D.-E. Khan/G. Nolte/A. Paulus (eds.), The Charter of the United Nations, 4. ed., 2024: Art. 2(1), para. 35.

(d) The territorial integrity and political independence of the State are inviolable;
(e) Each State has the right freely to choose and develop its political, social, economic and cultural systems;
(f) Each State has the duty to comply fully and in good faith with its international obligations and to live in peace with other States."[1311]

While certain elements of this definition seem relatively clear like the concept of "territorial integrity", other elements such as "the rights inherent in full sovereignty" are just as indeterminate as the original term. What becomes apparent, however, is that sovereign equality entails a balance between rights and duties. On the one hand, states are judicially equal. This could support the argument for an extensive understanding of consent requirements in international judicial proceedings involving the rights and obligations of states. On the other hand, each state, as part of its sovereign equality, "has the duty to comply fully and in good faith with its international obligations". An advisory opinion which clarifies the international obligations of a state may arguably help a state fulfil this element of its sovereign equality of states.

Kelsen argued that the only purpose of the principle of sovereign equality is to prevent "the possibility that new obligations might be imposed upon an unwilling State".[1312] *Kelsen's* understanding of the principle of sovereign equality helps illustrate the reason for the existence of consent requirements in contentious proceedings, as the parties to the proceedings are legally bound by the outcome of the proceedings. The situation is, of course, drastically different for advisory proceedings, in which no "new obligations", as *Kelsen* put it, are created.

IV. Interim conclusions

The principle of consensual dispute settlement protects states against the exercise of jurisdiction by an IC against their will. The term jurisdiction of ICs refers to a multitude of related concepts which describe the parameters of how ICs may operate. However, the ICJ only exercises jurisdiction over a state if it decides over the legal rights and obligations of the respective state in a binding manner, i.e., with binding force and *res judicata* effect.

1311 UNGA resolution 2625(XXV) of 15 December 1970, UN doc. A/RES/2625(XXV).
1312 *H. Kelsen*, 53 Yale Law Journal 2 (1944), 207 (213).

Considering that the consent principle protects states against the exercise of jurisdiction against their will and considering that only binding judicial decisions constitute an exercise of jurisdiction over a state, the question arises how the issuing of a non-binding advisory opinion on an inter-state dispute can be considered a circumvention of the consent requirement to judicial dispute settlement. This is the subject of the next section.

D. *Advisory opinions as a circumvention of the contentious procedure's consent requirement*

The ICJ has continuously reaffirmed that the exercise of its advisory jurisdiction does not depend on the consent of states.[1313] The advisory opinion is given to the requesting organ and as such a state's lack of consent does not *per se* hinder the Court from exercising its advisory jurisdiction.[1314] At the same time, the ICJ has also emphasized that the giving of an advisory opinion on the subject-matter of a pending dispute without the consent of the disputing states may constitute a circumvention of the principle of consensual dispute settlement. While being non-binding, could advisory opinions have other legal or non-legal effects which may affect the States Parties to a dispute in a similar manner as a binding Court decision? It is conceivable that they have such important effects that the issuing of an advisory opinion on a pending bilateral dispute without the consent of one of the parties to the dispute could be seen as a circumvention of the contentious procedure's strict jurisdictional requirements. This would deplete the contentious procedure's consent requirement of its protective function thereby harming the integrity of the contentious procedure.[1315] The idea that an advisory opinion while not binding for the disputing states could nevertheless negatively affect their legal interests resembles

1313 *Interpretation of Peace Treaties with Bulgaria, Hungary and Romania (First Phase)*, Advisory Opinion, ICJ Reports 1950, 65 (71); *Western Sahara*, Advisory Opinion, ICJ Reports 1975, 12 (20, para. 21); *Legal Consequences of the Construction of a Wall in the Occupied Palestinian Territory*, Advisory Opinion, ICJ Reports 2004, 136 (157-158, para. 47).

1314 *Interpretation of Peace Treaties with Bulgaria, Hungary and Romania (First Phase)*, Advisory Opinion, ICJ Reports 1950, 65 (71).

1315 This idea builds on Thienel's explanation of the Monetary Gold doctrine's legal basis, see *T. Thienel*, Drittstaaten und die Jurisdiktion des Internationalen Gerichtshofs. Die Monetary-Gold-Doktrin, 2017, 207.

another important (yet often criticized[1316]) ICJ doctrine: the *Monetary Gold doctrine*.[1317]

I. Circumvention of state consent in contentious matters: The Monetary Gold doctrine

According to the Monetary Gold doctrine, the ICJ will not decide an inter-state dispute, despite having jurisdiction to do so, if deciding the dispute would necessarily require the Court to make a judicial pronouncement on the rights and obligations of a third state that has neither participated in nor consented to the proceedings.[1318] Even though the Monetary Gold doctrine concerns the Court's contentious procedure, it may provide a useful comparison to the Eastern Carelia doctrine.[1319] In both contexts, the Court hesitates to issue a judicial pronouncement on the rights and obligations of a state without its consent despite the fact that the respective judicial pronouncement would have no binding force for the state in question: due to the *inter partes* effect of decisions in contentious matters and the non-binding nature of advisory opinions. This section examines the Monetary Gold doctrine as it has evolved in the ICJ's case law and assesses its underlying rationale. The aim is to assess whether the Court's reasoning in the context of the Monetary Gold doctrine also applies to the Eastern Carelia doctrine.

1316 Arguing that the Monetary Gold doctrine should be abandoned because it conflicts with the Court's obligation to decide cases brought before it by the parties, see *Z. Mollengarden/N. Zamir*, 115 Am. j. int. law 1 (2021), 41.

1317 See for example *Kolb*, who argues that the Eastern Carelia doctrine is an application of the Monetary Gold doctrine to advisory proceedings, see *R. Kolb*, The International Court of Justice, 2013, 1073.

1318 For a detailed study of the Monetary Gold doctrine, see *T. Thienel*, Drittstaaten und die Jurisdiktion des Internationalen Gerichtshofs. Die Monetary Gold-Doktrin, 2016; see also *C. M. Chinkin*, Third parties in international law, 1993, 199 et seq.; *A. Orakhelashvili*, 2 Journal of International Dispute Settlement 2 (2011), 373.

1319 Cf. *C. F. Amerasinghe*, Jurisdiction of International Tribunals, 2003, 528, although *Amerasinghe* regards the Eastern Carelia doctrine as a matter of jurisdiction (or competence) rather than admissibility, see Ibid., 529.

1. Content of the Monetary Gold doctrine

The case which lends its name to the Monetary Gold doctrine is the *Monetary Gold removed from Rome in 1943* case.[1320] In that case, the ICJ was asked to decide upon the rightful ownership of 2.4 tons of gold which were seized in Germany after World War II, and which previously belonged to the Albanian national bank in Rome. After the war, all the gold which was stolen by Nazi Germany was pooled and managed by the United States, the United Kingdom and France. The three states established a "Tripartite Commission for the Restitution of Monetary Gold" to decide upon the use of seized gold to satisfy claims for restitution.[1321] When Italy and Albania were in dispute about the rightful ownership of the 2.4 tons of gold previously owned by the Albanian national bank, the Tripartite Commission declared that it lacked jurisdiction to decide upon the matter. Instead, the Commission asked an arbitrator to decide the dispute, who then sided with Albania.[1322] However, at the time Albania owed damages to the United Kingdom following the *Corfu Channel* case.[1323] The arbitrator therefore decided that the gold had to be paid out directly to the United Kingdom as payment for the damages Albania owed to the United Kingdom.[1324]

Following the arbitrator's decision, Italy initiated proceedings against the UK, the USA and France before the ICJ. Italy argued that the gold belonged to Italy as reparation for the nationalization of the Albanian national bank which predominantly belonged to Italian investors. Despite bringing the case before the ICJ, Italy argued that the Court lacked jurisdiction as it was asked to decide upon the international responsibility of Albania without Albania's consent.[1325] The United Kingdom argued that Italy could not make

1320 *Case of the monetary gold removed from Rome in 1943 (Italy v. France, United Kingdom and United States) (Preliminary Question)*, Judgment, ICJ Reports 1954, 19.

1321 See ICJ Pleadings, *Case of the monetary gold removed from Rome in 1943 (Italy v. France, United Kingdom and United States)*, Written statement of the United States of America, 86.

1322 Ibid., 86–87.

1323 *Corfu Channel (United Kingdom v. Albania)*, Merits, Judgment, ICJ Reports 1949, 4.

1324 See ICJ Pleadings, *Case of the monetary gold removed from Rome in 1943 (Italy v. France, United Kingdom and United States)*, Written statement of the United States of America, 86 (87).

1325 ICJ Pleadings, *Case of the monetary gold removed from Rome in 1943 (Italy v. France, United Kingdom and United States)*, Written statement of Italy, 16 (20–21).

preliminary objections if it was the one that initiated the proceedings.[1326] The United States argued that Albania's legal interests were sufficiently protected by the *inter partes* effect of the Court's decisions under Article 59 ICJ Statute and that the right of third states to intervene (Article 62 ICJ Statute) showed that the ICJ Statute in principle allowed proceedings which affect third states.[1327] The Court sided with Italy, finding that deciding the case at hand was tantamount to deciding the dispute between Italy and Albania. The ICJ found that the right to intervene under Article 62 ICJ Statute provided insufficient protection in situations in which "Albania's legal interests would not only be affected by a decision, but would form the very subject-matter of the decision."[1328]

Similarly, while Article 59 ICJ ensured that the decision would only bind the parties to the proceedings, it did not sufficiently protect Albania's legal interests. The Court held:

> "Where, as in the present case, the vital issue to be settled concerns the international responsibility of a third State, the Court cannot, without the consent of that third State, give a decision on that issue binding upon any State, either the third State, or any of the parties before it."[1329]

Although the US had previously rejected Italy's arguments in the *Monetary Gold* case, it adopted them in the *Nicaragua* case in 1984.[1330] The case concerned allegations by Nicaragua against the United States of violating *inter alia* the principle of non-intervention and the prohibition of the threat or use of force.

At the Preliminary Objections stage of the proceedings, the USA argued that the Court could not rule on its international responsibility for its activities in Nicaragua because the decision would also affect the legal

1326 ICJ Pleadings, *Case of the monetary gold removed from Rome in 1943 (Italy v. France, United Kingdom and United States)*, Written statement of the United Kingdom, 77 (80–81).

1327 ICJ Pleadings, *Case of the monetary gold removed from Rome in 1943 (Italy v. France, United Kingdom and United States)*, Written statement of the United States of America, 86 (92, 94).

1328 *Case of the monetary gold removed from Rome in 1943 (Italy v. France, United Kingdom and United States) (Preliminary Question)*, Judgment, ICJ Reports 1954, 19 (32).

1329 Ibid. (33).

1330 *Case Concerning Military and Paramilitary Activities in and against Nicaragua (Nicaragua v. United States of America) (Jurisdiction and Admissibility)*, Judgment, ICJ Reports, 392.

interests of Honduras, Costa Rica and El Salvador.[1331] These countries were not parties to the case, but Nicaragua claimed the US operated from their territories.[1332] While the United States' argument was similar to Italy's arguments thirty years earlier, the Court rejected it. In doing so, the Court specified its earlier judgment and decided that it will only decline to exercise its jurisdiction

> "where the legal interests of a third State would not only be affected by a decision, but would form the very subject-matter of the decision. Where however claims of a legal nature are made by an Applicant against a Respondent in proceedings before the Court, and made the subject of submissions, the Court has in principle merely to decide upon those submissions, with binding force for the parties only, and no other State, in accordance with Article 59 of the Statute."[1333]

In essence, the Court decided that the rights and obligations of Honduras, Costa Rica, and El Salvador did not form the subject-matter of the proceedings between Nicaragua and the United States.

This "subject-matter test" was further fleshed out in the 1992 *Phosphates in Nauru* case.[1334] The case concerned a dispute between Nauru and Australia over Australia's exploitation of phosphate deposits in Nauru between 1919 and 1967. During this time, Nauru was administered by Australia, New Zealand and the United Kingdom first as a mandate territory under the League of Nations, then as a trust territory under the United Nations. The three administering powers jointly exploited the island's phosphate resources through an "Administering Authority". Australia argued that the Court could not rule on its international responsibility because to do so would require the Court to also rule on the international responsibility of New Zealand and the United Kingdom, since all three states acted jointly

---

1331 ICJ Pleadings, *Case Concerning Military and Paramilitary Activities in and against Nicaragua (Nicaragua v. United States of America)*, Counter-Memorial of the United States of America, 86–90.

1332 Ibid.

1333 *Case Concerning Military and Paramilitary Activities in and against Nicaragua (Nicaragua v. United States of America) (Jurisdiction and Admissibility)*, Judgment, ICJ Reports, 392 (431).

1334 *Certain Phosphate Lands in Nauru (Nauru v. Australia)*, Preliminary Objections, Judgment, ICJ Reports 1992, 240; on the Phosphates in Nauru case, see *I. Scobbie*, 42 ICLQ 3 (1993), 705 (710–718).

through the Administering Authority.[1335] The ICJ rejected Australia's argument and decided that the legal rights and obligations of New Zealand and the United Kingdom were not the subject-matter of the case. The Court distinguished the *Phosphates in Nauru* case from the *Monetary Gold* case.[1336] In the *Monetary Gold* case, the Court could only decide upon Italy's claims if it first decided upon the international responsibility of Albania. In contrast, in the *Phosphates in Nauru* case, the Court could decide upon the international responsibility of Australia without also deciding about the international responsibility of New Zealand and the UK. The Court could assess Australia's conduct separately and without considering the conduct of the other two states. Of course, since all three states acted jointly through the Administering Authority, the Court's decision on the lawfulness of Australia's conduct could have implications for the lawfulness of the conduct of New Zealand and the United Kingdom. However, such necessary implications were not a sufficient reason for the Court to decline to exercise its jurisdiction.[1337] This makes sense, given that such implications are by no means conclusive, as there could be other reasons why the conduct of the third states had to be assessed differently (e.g., the existence of a bilateral treaty permitting the conduct). In sum, the rights and obligations of third states only form the subject-matter of a decision if the Court necessarily has to rule on them to decide the matter before it. Or, as the ICJ put it, if the link between the decision about the rights and obligations of third states and the decision at hand is "not purely temporal but also logical".[1338]

The 1995 *East Timor* case[1339] marks another important stage of the development of the Monetary Gold doctrine by the ICJ. Australia and Indonesia had concluded a treaty on the joint exploration and exploitation of the continental shelf of East Timor. In response to this, Portugal brought proceedings against Australia before the ICJ. Portugal argued that the conclusion of the treaty violated the right of self-determination of the people of East Timor as well as Portugal's rights as administering power under Chapter XI UNC. In contrast, Australia argued that a decision of the ICJ would

1335 ICJ Pleadings, *Certain Phosphate Lands in Nauru (Nauru v. Australia)*, Preliminary Objections of Australia, 135–138.

1336 *Certain Phosphate Lands in Nauru (Nauru v. Australia)*, Preliminary Objections, Judgment, ICJ Reports 1992, 240 (261, para. 55).

1337 Ibid.

1338 Ibid.

1339 *East Timor (Portugal v. Australia)*, Judgment, ICJ Reports 1995, 90; *C. Chinkin*, 45 ICLQ 3 (1996), 712.

require the Court to decide upon the lawfulness of the invasion of East Timor by Indonesia and the legal validity of the treaty between Australia and Indonesia. As Indonesia was not a party to the case, the Court could not decide upon the matter.[1340]

The Court agreed with Australia. The Court held that the request of Portugal

> "would amount to a determination that Indonesia's entry into and continued presence in East Timor are unlawful and that, as a consequence, it does not have the treaty-making power in matters relating to the continental shelf resources of East Timor. Indonesia's rights and obligations would thus constitute the very subject-matter of such a judgment made in the absence of that State's consent. Such a judgment would run directly counter to the well-established principle of international law embodied in the Court's Statute, namely, that the Court can only exercise jurisdiction over a State with its consent."[1341]

The Court found itself unable to examine Australia's conduct separately from the conduct of Indonesia.

In summary, the Monetary Gold doctrine as applied by the ICJ prevents the Court, in the course of its contentious procedure, from making any judicial pronouncement directly concerning the rights and obligations of third states which are not parties to the proceedings. However, the doctrine does not prevent the Court from ruling on the rights and obligations of the parties to the case, even if the ruling may have implications for the rights and obligations of third states.[1342]

2. Doctrinal justification of the Monetary Gold doctrine

Thienel argues that there are three potential doctrinal justifications for the *Monetary Gold doctrine.*[1343]

According to the first justification for the Monetary Gold doctrine, the Court lacks jurisdiction to decide the case because deciding the case would amount to an exercise of jurisdiction over a third state without that state's

1340 *East Timor (Portugal v. Australia)*, Judgment, ICJ Reports 1995, 90 (99–106).

1341 Ibid. (105), references omitted.

1342 So also *T. Thienel*, Drittstaaten und die Jurisdiktion des Internationalen Gerichtshofs. Die Monetary Gold-Doktrin, 2016, 47–48.

1343 Ibid., 52 et seq., 144 et seq.

consent.[1344] In the *Monetary Gold case*, the Court implied that deciding the case would constitute an exercise of jurisdiction over the third state when it stated that "[t]o adjudicate upon the international responsibility of Albania without her consent would run counter to a well-established principle of international law [...] that the Court can only exercise jurisdiction over a State with its consent."[1345]

The first justification assumes that the Court exercises jurisdiction over a state when making judicial pronouncements on the legal rights and obligations of a third state and that this exercise of jurisdiction requires the consent of that state.[1346] This, of course, raises the question what constitutes an exercise of jurisdiction of an IC over a state.[1347] The decisions of the ICJ become binding only on the parties to the case (Article 59 ICJ Statute) and it is only between these parties that the decisions become *res judicata* (Articles 59–60 ICJ Statute).[1348] The binding force and the effect of *res judicata* result from the procedural relationship which is created between the parties on the one hand and between the parties and the Court on the other hand through the consent of the parties and the *seisin* of the Court.[1349] Such a relationship does not exist *vis-à-vis* the third state. For the third state the decision cannot be binding or become *res judicata*.[1350]

According to the second justification for the Monetary Gold doctrine, the Court lacks jurisdiction because there is no real dispute between the parties to the proceedings because the real dispute exists between the applicant and the non-participating third state.[1351] This justification is also echoed in the ICJ's case law. In the *Monetary Gold* case, the Court implied that the real dispute was not between Italy on the one hand and France, the United States and the United Kingdom on the other, but between Italy and Albania:

1344 Ibid., 52 et seq.

1345 *Case of the monetary gold removed from Rome in 1943 (Italy v. France, United Kingdom and United States) (Preliminary Question)*, Judgment, ICJ Reports 1954, 19 (32).

1346 See for example, *C. Brown*, in: A. Zimmermann/C. J. Tams/K. Oellers-Frahm/C. Tomuschat/D. W. K. Anderson (eds.), The Statute of the International Court of Justice, 3. ed., 2019: Article 59 ICJ Statute, para. 66.

1347 Extensively on this question, see *T. Thienel*, Drittstaaten und die Jurisdiktion des Internationalen Gerichtshofs. Die Monetary Gold-Doktrin, 2016, 105 et seq.

1348 Ibid., 128. See on this *supra*: § 6 Section C.III.

1349 Ibid., 130 et seq.

1350 Ibid., 132.

1351 Ibid., 148.

"To go into the merits of such questions would be to decide a dispute between Italy and Albania."[1352]

However, this second justification stretches the function of the requirement of a dispute, which is primarily to ensure that the Court is not seised of purely abstract questions of law which have no relevance to the legal relations between the parties.[1353]

According to the third justification for the Monetary Gold doctrine, the Court has jurisdiction but it declines to exercise it in order to protect the integrity of the ICJ Statute's jurisdictional regime.[1354] This also finds expression in the Court's case law. In the *Nicaragua case*, the ICJ raised the question if the situation required the Court to "*decline* [...] *to exercise* the jurisdiction conferred upon it".[1355]

The Court could only decide to decline to exercise its jurisdiction, if the conditions for its jurisdiction are fulfilled in the first place. The ICJ thus expressed the view that it did not lack jurisdiction but that it may decline to exercise it.

Thienel argues that the *Monetary Gold doctrine* protects the integrity of the jurisdictional scheme of the Court's contentious procedure by complementing the protective function of the consent requirement.[1356] The contentious procedure's consent requirement would lose its protective function and become ineffective, if the legal rights and obligations of a non-consenting state could be similarly affected by the Court through the initiation of contentious proceedings between other states.[1357] As stated before, the *inter partes* effect of ICJ decisions means that decisions of the Court are binding only for the parties to a case before the Court and only in respect of the particular case.[1358] The consent requirement to ICJ contentious proceedings protects the third state from being bound by ICJ decisions against its will.

1352 *Case of the monetary gold removed from Rome in 1943 (Italy v. France, United Kingdom and United States) (Preliminary Question)*, Judgment, ICJ Reports 1954, 19 (32).

1353 *T. Thienel*, Drittstaaten und die Jurisdiktion des Internationalen Gerichtshofs. Die Monetary Gold-Doktrin, 2016, 148.

1354 Ibid., 196 et seq.

1355 *Case Concerning Military and Paramilitary Activities in and against Nicaragua (Nicaragua v. United States of America) (Jurisdiction and Admissibility)*, Judgment, ICJ Reports, 392 (431), emphasis added.

1356 *T. Thienel*, Drittstaaten und die Jurisdiktion des Internationalen Gerichtshofs. Die Monetary Gold-Doktrin, 2016, 208–209.

1357 Ibid., 235

1358 See Article 59 ICJ Statute.

The Monetary Gold doctrine complements this protection in situations where the third state, although not directly bound by the ICJ decision, is similarly affected in its legal position.[1359] In other words, the Monetary Gold doctrine provides an additional layer of protection for the third state in a situation in which reliance on the *inter partes* effect of ICJ decisions proves insufficient to protect its legal position.[1360] Such a situation may arise indirectly for a third state because of the legal effect the Court's decision has for the parties to the dispute. As the decision becomes binding for the parties to the dispute, they may be confronted with two conflicting legal obligations: on the one hand they have the obligation to respect the rights of the third state. On the other hand they have the obligation to obey the decision of the Court which may oblige them to act in a manner which is detrimental to these rights of the third state.[1361] The two legal obligations are of the same rank, but the disputing states may feel more obliged to follow the authoritative decision of the Court than to respect the rights of the third state.[1362]

An example may help to illustrate this dilemma: State A and State B have entered into trade relations with one another according to which both states have agreed to remove any trade barriers for goods. State C believes that the agreement between State A and State B violates the rights of State C as it also applies to goods produced on the territory of State C which is currently illegally occupied by State B. State C therefore initiates proceedings against State A. The Court decides that State A must cease all conduct which recognizes the sovereignty of State B over the territory of State C including importing products from State B that have been produced on illegally occupied territory of State C. State A is thus under conflicting obligations following from its treaty with State B on the one hand and the decision in the case between States A and C.

Other actors may also adapt their behavior *vis-à-vis* the non-consenting third state in accordance with the Court's decision.[1363] If the Court decided

1359 *T. Thienel*, Drittstaaten und die Jurisdiktion des Internationalen Gerichtshofs. Die Monetary Gold-Doktrin, 2016, 207–208.

1360 Ibid., 208–209.

1361 In the case of the ICJ, see Article 94 para. 1 UNC: "Each Member of the United Nations undertakes to comply with the decision of the International Court of Justice in any case to which it is a party."

1362 On the authority of ICs, see *infra* in this Chapter Section C.II.

1363 *T. Thienel*, Drittstaaten und die Jurisdiktion des Internationalen Gerichtshofs. Die Monetary Gold-Doktrin, 2016, 235.

that the third state violated its international obligations, other states may adopt countermeasures and rely on the Court's judgment as justification. The moral authority of the Court's decision may convince these states to act in such a manner. What is more, the Court may be more likely to find that these countermeasures are lawful if it had already found that the third state's actions were illegal. While the Court is not bound to by previous decisions,[1364] it is likely to follow its previous determinations regarding the content[1365] and the application of the law[1366]. As *H. Lauterpacht* observed:

> "The Court follows its own decisions for the same reasons for which all courts—whether bound by the doctrine of precedent or not—do so, namely, because such decisions are a repository of legal experience to which it is convenient to adhere; because they embody what the Court has considered in the past to be good law; because respect for decisions given in the past makes for certainty and stability, which are of the essence of the orderly administration of justice; and (a minor and not invariably accurate consideration) because judges are naturally reluctant, in the absence of compelling reasons to the contrary, to admit that they were previously in the wrong."[1367]

The Court may thus be inclined to decide other cases involving the third state in a similar manner. The *Monetary Gold doctrine* seeks to prevent the third state from being prejudged in such a manner.

1364 *R. Kolb*, The International Court of Justice, 2013, 765.

1365 *Continental Shelf (Libyan Arab Jamahiriya v. Malta)*, Application to Intervene, Judgment, Dissenting Opinion Jennings, ICJ Reports 1984, 148 (157 et seq., paras. 27 et seq.); cf. *M. Payandeh*, Internationales Gemeinschaftsrecht, 2010, 464; *A. v. Bogdandy/I. Venzke*, 23 European Journal of International Law 1 (2012), 7 (18–19); *T. Thienel*, Drittstaaten und die Jurisdiktion des Internationalen Gerichtshofs. Die Monetary Gold-Doktrin, 2016, 198; *A. Pellet*, in: A. Zimmermann/C. J. Tams/K. Oellers-Frahm/C. Tomuschat/D. W. K. Anderson (eds.), The Statute of the International Court of Justice, 3. ed., 2019: Art. 38, 308 et seq.

1366 *Legality of Use of Force (Serbia and Montenegro v. Belgium)*, Preliminary Objections, Joint Declaration of Vice-President Ranjeva, Judges Guillaume, Higgins, Kooijmans, Al-Khasawneh, Buergenthal, Elaraby, ICJ Reports 2004, 330 (332–333); *T. Thienel*, Drittstaaten und die Jurisdiktion des Internationalen Gerichtshofs. Die Monetary Gold-Doktrin, 2016, 198; *A. Pellet*, in: A. Zimmermann/C. J. Tams/K. Oellers-Frahm/C. Tomuschat/D. W. K. Anderson (eds.), The Statute of the International Court of Justice, 3. ed., 2019: Art. 38, para. 314.

1367 *H. Lauterpacht*, The development of international law by the International Court, 2. ed. 1958, 14.

3. Applying the rationale of the Monetary Gold doctrine to advisory proceedings

The Eastern Carelia doctrine and the Monetary Gold doctrine share certain features which may indicate that both doctrines follow the same logic:

For a start, both doctrines have been developed as a response to the same problem: How should the Court deal with the non-consent and non-participation by a state in the proceedings if that state's rights and legal interests may be affected by the outcome of the proceedings? Both doctrines flow from the Court's presumption that the Court may not directly render a judicial decision on the rights and interest of a state without that state's consent. In the context of the Monetary Gold doctrine, the Court referred to the "well-established principle of international law embodied in the Court's Statute, namely, that the Court can only exercise jurisdiction over a State with its consent."[1368] In the Eastern Carelia context, the same notion is referred to by the Court as the "principle that a State is not obliged to allow its disputes to be submitted to judicial settlement without its consent."[1369]

Does the justification of the Monetary Gold doctrine thus also justify the Eastern Carelia doctrine?[1370] In other words, does the Eastern Carelia doctrine like the Monetary Gold doctrine aim to protect the jurisdictional structure of the Court's contentious procedure from being circumvented?

At first sight, the situation with which the Court is faced in both contexts appears similar. The Court is asked to make a judicial pronouncement on the rights and obligations of a state without the consent or participation of that state. In both scenarios, the judicial pronouncements – while legally persuasive and morally authoritative – are not binding on that (third) state. The judicial pronouncements cannot alter the rights and obligations of the non-participating state, in one case because of the *inter partes* effect of ICJ decisions (Article 59 ICJ Statute), in the other because ICJ advisory opin-

---

1368 *Case of the monetary gold removed from Rome in 1943 (Italy v. France, United Kingdom and United States) (Preliminary Question)*, Judgment, ICJ Reports 1954, 19 (32); *East Timor (Portugal v. Australia)*, Judgment, ICJ Reports 1995, 90 (105, para. 34).

1369 *Western Sahara*, Advisory Opinion, ICJ Reports 1975, 12 (25, para. 33).

1370 On this point, see also *Lando* who distinguishes the two doctrines based on the fact that consent is a jurisdictional requirement only for contentious proceedings, *M. Lando*, 61 CJTL 1 (2023), 67 (107–108); *Kolb* argues that the Eastern Carelia doctrine (or "non-circumvention rule") is an application of the Monetary Gold doctrine to advisory proceedings, see *R. Kolb*, The International Court of Justice, 2013, 1073.

ions are generally not binding. In both scenarios, therefore, the legal rights and obligations of the non-participating state formally remain unaltered by the outcome of the proceedings.

Nevertheless, the ICJ is still concerned that rendering a decision or issuing an advisory opinion in such a case may circumvent the non-consent of the state in question. Since the state's legal rights and obligations are not directly affected by the outcome of the proceedings, the reason for the existence of the respective doctrines seems not to be to protect the non-participating state from the *legal* effects of the proceedings, but from their *factual* effects.

The question is therefore whether advisory opinions are capable of factually affecting the state in question in a manner similar to the decisions in the context of the Monetary Gold doctrine, so as to warrant a similar response from the Court.

When comparing the effects of ICJ decisions on third states and ICJ advisory opinions on interested states, there appears to be one striking difference: the binding force of ICJ judgments.

The ICJ Statute and the UNC explicitly limit the binding force of ICJ pronouncements to "decisions" of the Court. Advisory opinions do not qualify as decisions in the sense of Article 59 ICJ Statute, Article 94 para. 1 UNC and are thus not binding.[1371] Only the operative provisions (or *dispositif*) of a judgment are binding.[1372] The reasons which underly a decision are generally non-binding, unless they are indispensable to understand

1371 *Interpretation of Peace Treaties with Bulgaria, Hungary and Romania (First Phase)*, Advisory Opinion, ICJ Reports 1950, 65 (71); *Judgments of the Administrative Tribunal of the ILO upon Complaints Made against UNESCO*, Advisory Opinion, ICJ Reports 1956, 77 (84); *G. G. Fitzmaurice*, 29 British Yearbook of International Law (BYIL) 1 (1952), 1 (45); *E. Hambro*, 3 ICLQ 1 (1954), 2 (5–6); *K. J. Keith*, The extent of the advisory jurisdiction of the International Court of Justice, 1971, 195; *M. Shahabuddeen*, Precedent in the World Court, 1996, 165 et seq.; *S. Rosenne*, The law and practice of the International Court, 1920-2005, 4th ed. 2006, 304; *P. d'Argent*, in: A. Zimmermann/C. J. Tams/K. Oellers-Frahm/C. Tomuschat/D. W. K. Anderson (eds.), The Statute of the International Court of Justice, 3. ed., 2019: Article 65, para. 48.

1372 *Application of the Convention on the Prevention and Punishment of the Crime of Genocide (Bosnia and Herzegovina v. Serbia and Montenegro)*, Judgment, ICJ Reports 2007, 43 (94, para. 123); *C. Brown*, in: A. Zimmermann/C. J. Tams/K. Oellers-Frahm/C. Tomuschat/D. W. K. Anderson (eds.), The Statute of the International Court of Justice, 3. ed., 2019: Article 59 ICJ Statute, para. 41.

and implement the operative provisions.[1373] Advisory opinions lack such operative provisions. The Rules of the Court differentiate on this point between judgments and advisory opinions. While judgments shall contain "the operative provisions of the judgment" (Article 95), advisory opinions contain "the reply to the question put to the Court" (Article 107). As such, advisory opinions are not binding for states in the sense described above.[1374]

Nevertheless, advisory opinions may create certain legal obligations for the requesting UN organ.[1375] According to *Abi-Saab*, the requesting organ has the duty to recognize the advisory opinion of the Court as the legal view of the UN on the particular legal question and it may not replace the Court's legal assessment with its own.[1376] Others argue that the requesting organ has a duty to take the opinion into account.[1377] However, this does not mean that the requesting organ has a legal obligation to also *implement* this legal view.[1378] Instead, the requesting organ remains free to adopt a different (political) solution than the (legal) solution proposed by the Court.[1379] Advisory opinions also lack the effect of *res judicata* with

1373 *C. Brown*, in: A. Zimmermann/C. J. Tams/K. Oellers-Frahm/C. Tomuschat/D. W. K. Anderson (eds.), The Statute of the International Court of Justice, 3. ed., 2019: Article 59 ICJ Statute, para. 41.

1374 *Interpretation of Peace Treaties with Bulgaria, Hungary and Romania (First Phase)*, Advisory Opinion, ICJ Reports 1950, 65 (71); *Judgments of the Administrative Tribunal of the ILO upon Complaints Made against UNESCO*, Advisory Opinion, ICJ Reports 1956, 77 (84); *G. G. Fitzmaurice*, 29 British Yearbook of International Law (BYIL) 1 (1952), 1 (45); *E. Hambro*, 3 ICLQ 1 (1954), 2 (5–6); *K. J. Keith*, The extent of the advisory jurisdiction of the International Court of Justice, 1971, 195; *M. Shahabuddeen*, Precedent in the World Court, 1996, 165 et seq.; *S. Rosenne*, The law and practice of the International Court, 1920-2005, 4th ed. 2006, 304; *P. d'Argent*, in: A. Zimmermann/C. J. Tams/K. Oellers-Frahm/C. Tomuschat/D. W. K. Anderson (eds.), The Statute of the International Court of Justice, 3. ed., 2019: Article 65, para. 48.

1375 *G. Abi-Saab*, Les exceptions préliminaires dans la procédure de la Cour internationale, 1966, 82–84.

1376 Ibid., 82–84; so also *R. Kolb*, The International Court of Justice, 2013, 1097; cf. *D. Négulesco*, 57 Recueil des cours d'Académie de Droit International de La Haye (1936), 5 (64).

1377 *K. Oellers-Frahm/E. Lagrange*, in: B. Simma/D.-E. Khan/G. Nolte/A. Paulus (eds.), The Charter of the United Nations, 4. ed., 2024: Art. 96, para. 43.

1378 *G. Abi-Saab*, Les exceptions préliminaires dans la procédure de la Cour internationale, 1966, 82–84; cf. *D. Négulesco*, 57 Recueil des cours d'Académie de Droit International de La Haye (1936), 5 (64).

1379 *G. Abi-Saab*, Les exceptions préliminaires dans la procédure de la Cour internationale, 1966, 82–84; *K. Oellers-Frahm/E. Lagrange*, in: B. Simma/D.-E. Khan/G.

regard to subsequent judicial proceedings. The ICJ could give an advisory opinion or render a judgment on the same matter on which it has already given an advisory opinion.[1380] The ICJ is further not bound by its own advisory opinions. However, this is also true for judgments as the ICJ does not follow any *stare decisis* principle.[1381]

The non-binding nature of advisory opinions reflects the different function of advisory opinions as opposed to judgments. Advisory opinions – in contrast to judgments – do not settle international disputes, but guide the requesting UN organ in its future activities with respect to a certain issue by clarifying the underlying legal questions. As Judge *Nolte* held in his Separate Opinion in the recent *Policies and Practices of Israel in the Occupied Palestinian Territory* case:

> "In contentious proceedings, the Court "decide[s] ... disputes" in a binding and final manner. These proceedings are retrospective: their contribution to the peaceful settlement of disputes consists in ending a dispute by making a binding determination that is endowed with legal certainty and finality, the *res judicata* effect. In contrast, advisory proceedings are consultative and prospective: the Court gives an advisory opinion on a legal question to provide guidance for the requesting organ's future conduct. The conclusions of the Court in advisory opinions are not the end but the beginning of a process that seeks to establish and maintain peace through law."[1382]

There may exceptionally be instances where a state or an international organization has a legal obligation to comply with an advisory opinion. However, such 'compulsive'[1383] or 'binding'[1384] advisory opinions are the re-

---

Nolte/A. Paulus (eds.), The Charter of the United Nations, 4. ed., 2024: Art. 96, para. 42; *Legal Consequences arising from the Policies and Practices of Israel in the Occupied Palestinian Territory, including East Jerusalem*, Advisory Opinion, Separate Opinion Nolte, Publication pending in ICJ Reports 2024, 1 (1-2, para. 4).

1380 *D. Pratap*, The advisory jurisdiction of the International Court, 1972, 227 et seq.; *P. d'Argent*, in: A. Zimmermann/C. J. Tams/K. Oellers-Frahm/C. Tomuschat/D. W. K. Anderson (eds.), The Statute of the International Court of Justice, 3. ed., 2019: Article 65, para. 50.

1381 *D. Pratap*, The advisory jurisdiction of the International Court, 1972, 228; *R. Kolb*, The International Court of Justice, 2013, 763.

1382 *Legal Consequences arising from the Policies and Practices of Israel in the Occupied Palestinian Territory, including East Jerusalem*, Advisory Opinion, Separate Opinion Nolte, Publication pending in ICJ Reports 2024, 1 (1-2, para. 4).

1383 *D. Pratap*, The advisory jurisdiction of the International Court, 1972, 228.

1384 *R. Ago*, 85 AJIL 3 (1991), 439.

sult of separate agreements concluded between states and/or international organizations in which they agree to comply with the advisory opinion.[1385] Referring to such opinions as 'binding advisory opinions' is therefore somewhat misleading as it is not the advisory opinion that is compulsive or binding but the separate agreement. The agreement refers to the advisory opinion and adopts its content as binding. The binding force, therefore, does not originate from the advisory opinion but from the agreement.[1386] The example of 'binding advisory opinions' thus supports rather than contradicts the rule that advisory opinions have no binding force.

While ICJ decisions are similarly non-binding for third parties,[1387] they differ from advisory opinions insofar as they create not only a moral but a legal obligation for the states parties to the case to act in a certain way.[1388] Article 94 para. 1 UNC obliges UNC Member States to comply with all ICJ decisions in cases to which they are parties.[1389] "Decisions" in the sense of Article 94 para. 1 UNC include not only final judgments in contentious cases but also non-procedural binding orders such as orders indicating provisional measures.[1390] Such ICJ decisions can create different

1385 See for example the Convention on the Privileges and Immunities of the United Nations, 1 UNTS 15, Section 30: "All differences arising out of the interpretation or application of the present convention shall be referred to the International Court of Justice, unless in any case it is agreed by the parties to have recourse to another mode of settlement. If a difference arises between the United Nations on the one hand and a Member on the other hand, a request shall be made for an advisory opinion on any legal question involved in accordance with Article 96 of the Charter and Article 65 of the Statute of the Court. The opinion given by the Court shall be accepted as decisive by the parties." See also ILOAT Statute, Article XII, para. 2.

1386 *M. N. Shaw*, Rosenne's Law and Practice of the International Court: 1920-2015, 5th ed 2016, Vol. 3, Ch. 30, § 415; *C. Brown*, in: A. Zimmermann/C. J. Tams/K. Oellers-Frahm/C. Tomuschat/D. W. K. Anderson (eds.), The Statute of the International Court of Justice, 3. ed., 2019: Article 59 ICJ Statute, para. 51; *R. Ago*, 85 AJIL 3 (1991), 439 (439–451).

1387 See Art. 59 ICJ Statute: "The decision of the Court has no binding force except between the parties and in respect of that particular case."

1388 See, however, *Thirlway* who argues that the "nature of an international judicial act would suggest that the law as declared by the Court is binding on the parties to the same extent after the judgment as it was before", see *H. W. Thirlway*, 60 British Yearbook of International Law (BYIL) 1 (1989), 1 (103).

1389 Art. 94 UNC reads: "Each Member of the United Nations undertakes to comply with the decision of the International Court of Justice in any case to which it is a party."

1390 *K. Oellers-Frahm*, in: B. Simma/D.-E. Khan/G. Nolte/A. Paulus (eds.), The Charter of the United Nations, 3. ed., 2012: Art. 94, paras. 4–5; *R. Kolb*, The Internatypes of obligations. Typically, the ICJ will make a declaratory judgment declaring that one or multiple parties have breached international law.[1391] Such declaratory judgments create an obligation on the parties to recognize the unlawfulness of the conduct. The ICJ will usually accompany such a decision with a decision that the State Party in violation of international law has a duty to immediately cease a certain unlawful act and refrain from such acts in the future.[1392] As the Court held:

> "This obligation to cease wrongful conduct derives both from the general obligation of each State to conduct itself in accordance with international law and from the specific obligation upon States parties to disputes before the Court to comply with its judgments, pursuant to Article 59 of its Statute."[1393]

Such decisions give rise to an obligation to refrain from a certain conduct. Occasionally, the Court will also order the violating state to give assurances and guarantees of non-repetition.[1394] However, the Court will only do so in exceptional circumstances as it must be assumed that the state will act in good faith.[1395] The ICJ will also usually combine such declaratory decisions on the unlawfulness of a certain conduct with a judgment on reparations and either indicate a general obligation to make reparation[1396] or indicate a specific type of reparation that is owed, i.e. restitution, the

tional Court of Justice, 2013, 835–836; for the opposite view, arguing that Art. 94 UNC only applies to judgments of the Court, see *A. Pillepich*, in: J.-P. Cot/A. Pellet (eds.), La Charte des Nations Unies, 3. ed., 2005: Art. 94, paras. 15–16. In *LaGrand*, the ICJ raised the question but decided not to answer it, limiting itself to stating that orders indicating provisional measures have "binding effect" on the parties to the case, see *LaGrand (Germany v. United States of America)*, Judgment, ICJ Reports 2001, 466 (505-506, paras. 108-109).

1391 *M. N. Shaw*, International law, 7. ed. 2014, 798.

1392 See for example *Case Concerning Military and Paramilitary Activities in and against Nicaragua (Nicaragua v. United States of America) (Merits)*, Judgment, ICJ Reports 1986, 14 (149); *Dispute regarding Navigational and Related Rights (Costa Rica v. Nicaragua)*, Judgment, ICJ Reports 2009, 213 (267, para. 148).

1393 *Dispute regarding Navigational and Related Rights (Costa Rica v. Nicaragua)*, Judgment, ICJ Reports 2009, 213 (267, para. 148).

1394 Ibid. (267, para. 150); *M. N. Shaw*, International law, 7. ed. 2014, 800.

1395 *Nuclear Tests (Australia v. France)*, Judgment, ICJ Reports 1974, 253 (272, para. 60); *Dispute regarding Navigational and Related Rights (Costa Rica v. Nicaragua)*, Judgment, ICJ Reports 2009, 213 (267, para. 150).

1396 See for example *Case Concerning Military and Paramilitary Activities in and against Nicaragua (Nicaragua v. United States of America) (Merits)*, Judgment, ICJ Reports 1986, 14 (149).

payment of damages or satisfaction.[1397] Such decisions create an obligation of conduct for the parties to the dispute to make reparation. The ICJ may also prescribe a certain conduct as it did in the *LaGrand* case, in which the Court found that the USA committed itself to allow the review and reconsideration of convictions and sentencing whenever foreign nationals are arrested in future cases.[1398]

To illustrate the difference between ICJ decisions and advisory opinions, let us return to the *Chagos* case. The ICJ found that the continuous administration of the Chagos Archipelago by the United Kingdom constituted an internationally wrongful act and that the United Kingdom was therefore under an obligation to return the archipelago to Mauritius.[1399] Furthermore, the Court derived from the right to self-determination an *erga omnes* obligation on all UN Member States to cooperate with the UN to facilitate the return of the Chagos Archipelago to Mauritius.[1400] The advisory opinion thus directly concerned the rights and obligations of the United Kingdom, Mauritius, and of all UN Member States. However, the opinion merely recognized the legal rights and obligations of the parties at the time the Court rendered the advisory opinion. The opinion itself did not alter any existing rights or obligations or create any additional legal obligation that did not exist before the opinion was issued. The issuance of the advisory opinion thus did not create any independent legal incentives for any of the involved states to act in a certain manner. Instead it only created an additional *moral* incentive by presenting a persuasive account of the law by a highly authoritative IC.

We will now consider a hypothetical scenario in which the case would have been heard by the ICJ under its contentious procedure without the participation of the United Kingdom. Let us suppose that Mauritius and

1397 *The Factory at Chorzow (Germany* v. *Poland)*, Merits, PCIJ Series A No. 17, 1928, 47; *Corfu Channel (United Kingdom v. Albania)*, Judgment on Compensation, ICJ Reports 1949, 244; *Gabčíkovo-Nagymaros Project (Hungary v. Slovakia)*, Judgment, ICJ Reports 1998, 7 (80 et seq., paras. 148 et seq.); *M. N. Shaw*, International law, 7. ed. 2014, 798–799; *C. Brown*, in: A. Zimmermann/C. J. Tams/K. Oellers-Frahm/C. Tomuschat/D. W. K. Anderson (eds.), The Statute of the International Court of Justice, 3. ed., 2019: Article 59 ICJ Statute, para. 41.

1398 *LaGrand (Germany v. United States of America)*, Judgment, ICJ Reports 2001, 466 (516, para. 128); see also *Avena and Other Mexican Nationals (Mexico v. United States of America)*, Judgment, ICJ Reports 2004, 12 (73, para. 153).

1399 *Legal Consequences of the Separation of the Chagos Archipelago from Mauritius in 1965*, Advisory Opinion, ICJ Reports 2019, 95 (138-139, paras. 175-179).

1400 Ibid. (139-140, paras. 180-182).

the Maldives requested the Court to settle their dispute over the territorial sovereignty of the Chagos Archipelago and the United Kingdom refused to consent to the proceedings and to participate in them.[1401] In the event that the ICJ had rendered a decision in such a scenario (which the Court would invariably have refused to do in line with the Monetary Gold doctrine), it would have to decide over the territorial sovereignty over the Chagos Archipelago with binding force for Mauritius and the Maldives. Both states would not only be bound by the law as it was recognized by the Court, but the decision itself would create a legal obligation incumbent upon both states not to recognize the territorial sovereignty of the United Kingdom. In a hypothetical scenario in which one of the parties had concluded a treaty with the United Kingdom which recognized British sovereignty over the archipelago, that state would even be under contradictory international law obligations as a consequence of the ICJ judgment.

In brief, one major difference between ICJ judgments in the Monetary Gold scenario and advisory opinions in the Eastern Carelia scenario is that ICJ decisions create independent legal obligations for the States Parties to the proceedings, while advisory opinions merely recognize the law as it stood at the time of the rendering of the opinion without creating additional legal obligations.

The Monetary Gold doctrine aims to ensure that the *inter partes* effect (or relativity) of ICJ decisions does not only exist in theory but also in practice. This alone makes it difficult to transfer the rationale of the Monetary Gold doctrine to the Eastern Carelia doctrine. Advisory opinions have no binding force which needs to be contained to the disputing parties. As such there is no need to provide "collateral protection"[1402] of the *inter partes* effect. However, one notion may be transferred to the discussion of the Eastern Carelia doctrine: the idea that ICJ pronouncements may have effects beyond binding force and *res judicata* for the state in question. It is therefore necessary to examine such other legal effects of advisory opinions for interested states as a potential reason for the Eastern Carelia doctrine.

1401 This is the backdrop to the recent proceeding before ITLOS between Mauritius and the Maldives, see *Dispute concerning delimitation of the maritime boundary between Mauritius and Maldives in the Indian Ocean (Mauritius v. Maldives)*, Preliminary Objections, Judgment, ITLOS Reports 2021, 17.

1402 *T. Thienel*, Drittstaaten und die Jurisdiktion des Internationalen Gerichtshofs. Die Monetary Gold-Doktrin, 2016, 208–209.

II. Legal effects analogous to binding force: The authority of ICJ advisory opinions

As laid out above, ICJ advisory opinions differ from decisions in contentious cases in their lack of binding force and *res judicata* effect.[1403] However, they may have certain legal effects that are analogous to the legal effects of ICJ decisions which justify the Court's caution in rendering advisory opinions on inter-state disputes. The idea that advisory opinions possess certain qualities that set them apart from mere legal advice is not new.[1404] Advisory opinions are described by legal commentators and ICs as more than "mere utterances having no real importance in respect of their [i.e., states'] rights and interests",[1405] they are "an authoritative statement of the law",[1406] they have "legal value and a moral authority",[1407] they "carry with them the prestige and the authority of the Court",[1408] they exert "precedential influence",[1409] or simply have "legal effects".[1410] Others claim that the Court's advisory opinions carry the same authority as ICJ decisions in contentious proceedings.[1411]

1403 Instead of many, see *S. Rosenne*, The law and practice of the International Court, 1920-2005, 4th ed. 2006, 304.

1404 *G. Abi-Saab*, Les exceptions préliminaires dans la procédure de la Cour internationale, 1966, 75–76.

1405 *Interpretation of Peace Treaties with Bulgaria, Hungary and Romania (First Phase)*, Advisory Opinion, Dissenting Opinion Winiarski, ICJ Reports 1950, 65 (91–92).

1406 *South-West Africa (Liberia v. South Africa)*, Second Phase, Judgment, Dissenting Opinion Tanaka, ICJ Reports 1966, 250 (260); *Dispute concerning delimitation of the maritime boundary between Mauritius and Maldives in the Indian Ocean (Mauritius v. Maldives)*, Preliminary Objections, Judgment, ITLOS Reports 2021, 17 (77, para. 202); *M. Shahabuddeen*, Precedent in the World Court, 1996, 168.

1407 *Interpretation of Peace Treaties with Bulgaria, Hungary and Romania (First Phase)*, Advisory Opinion, Dissenting Opinion Winiarski, ICJ Reports 1950, 65 (91–92).

1408 *P. d'Argent*, in: A. Zimmermann/C. J. Tams/K. Oellers-Frahm/C. Tomuschat/D. W. K. Anderson (eds.), The Statute of the International Court of Justice, 3. ed., 2019: Article 65, para. 49.

1409 *M. Shahabuddeen*, Precedent in the World Court, 1996, 167.

1410 *Dispute concerning delimitation of the maritime boundary between Mauritius and Maldives in the Indian Ocean (Mauritius v. Maldives)*, Preliminary Objections, Judgment, ITLOS Reports 2021, 17 (78, para. 205).

1411 *Legal Consequences for States of the Continued Presence of South Africa in Namibia (South West Africa) notwithstanding Security Council Resolution 276 (1970)*, Advisory Opinion, Separate opinion de Castro, ICJ Reports 1971, 170 (173, para. 4); *M. Shahabuddeen*, Precedent in the World Court, 1996, 171.

The ITLOS Special Chamber in the *Maritime Delimitations case*[1412] between Mauritius and the Maldives emphasized the authority of ICJ advisory opinions when it found:

> "An advisory opinion is not binding because even the requesting entity is not obligated to comply with it in the same way as parties to contentious proceedings are obligated to comply with a judgment. However, judicial determinations made in advisory opinions carry no less weight and authority than those in judgments because they are made with the same rigour and scrutiny by the "principal judicial organ" of the United Nations with competence in matters of international law."[1413]

The frequent references to the authority of advisory opinions beg the question what "authority" means in the context of ICs in general and ICJ advisory opinions in particular and whether the authority of ICJ advisory opinions may justify the Eastern Carelia doctrine.

1. Authority of international courts and tribunals

There are different approaches on how to define the authority of ICs.[1414] In a broad sense, authority can be defined as the power to "induce change in behavior".[1415] In an authoritative relationship, the change in one's behavior is not the result of certain substantive reasons but of the authoritative relationship itself.[1416] The authority provides a content-independent reason for the change in behavior.[1417] Authority can be distinguished from coercion by the fact that an authoritative relationship leaves the other side a residue of freedom of choice.[1418] In other word, authority persuades, whereas coercion

1412 *Dispute concerning delimitation of the maritime boundary between Mauritius and Maldives in the Indian Ocean (Mauritius v. Maldives)*, Preliminary Objections, Judgment, ITLOS Reports 2021, 17.

1413 Ibid. (77, para. 203).

1414 For an overview of the debate on the authority of ICs, see K. J. Alter, L. R. Helfer, M. R. Madsen (eds.), International court authority, 2018.

1415 *K. J. Alter/L. R. Helfer/M. R. Madsen*, International Court Authority in a Complex World, in: K. J. Alter/L. R. Helfer/M. R. Madsen (eds.), International court authority, First edition, 2018, 3 (6).

1416 *B. Çalı*, Authority, in: J. d' Aspremont/S. Singh (eds.), Concepts for international law, 1. ed., 2019, 39 (41).

1417 Ibid., 41.

1418 Ibid., 41.

forces. In a legal context, authority can be defined as the "legal capacity to determine others and to influence their freedom, i.e., to shape their legal or factual situation".[1419]

The field of legal scholarship has devoted a significant amount of attention to the subject of authority,[1420] particularly in relation to ICs.[1421] *Alter, Helfer* and *Madsen* identified four dominant approaches to studying the authority of international institutions: legal formalist approaches, normative approaches, sociological legitimacy theories, and compliance and performative approaches.[1422] They also propose a fifth perspective, which focuses on the practice of key audiences including (potential) litigants, government, and judges.[1423] The present study will apply this fifth approach, which focuses on the practice of key audiences (practice-based approach). However, let us first briefly examine the different approaches.

a) Legal formalist approaches

From a formalist perspective, authority of ICs is always delegated and delimited.[1424] Authority is delegated in the sense that authority originates

1419 *A. v. Bogdandy/I. Venzke*, 23 European Journal of International Law 1 (2012), 7 (18).

1420 For a succinct overview of the concept of authority and how it relates to in international law, see *B. Çalı*, Authority, in: J. d' Aspremont/S. Singh (eds.), Concepts for international law, 1. ed., 2019, 39; on the concept of authority more generally, see *J. Raz*, The authority of law, 1979; *S. Shapiro*, Authority, in: J. L. Coleman/S. Shapiro (eds.), The Oxford Handbook of Jurisprudence and Philosophy of Law, 2004, 382.

1421 For a general overview, see *K. J. Alter/L. R. Helfer/M. R. Madsen*, International Court Authority in a Complex World, in: K. J. Alter/L. R. Helfer/M. R. Madsen (eds.), International court authority, First edition, 2018, 3; *N. Lanzoni*, 2 Ital. Rev. Int. Comp. Law 2 (2022), 296.

1422 *K. J. Alter/L. R. Helfer/M. R. Madsen*, International Court Authority in a Complex World, in: K. J. Alter/L. R. Helfer/M. R. Madsen (eds.), International court authority, First edition, 2018, 3 (6–14); focusing on formalist and normative approaches, see *N. Lanzoni*, 2 Ital. Rev. Int. Comp. Law 2 (2022), 296.

1423 See *K. J. Alter/L. R. Helfer/M. R. Madsen*, International Court Authority in a Complex World, in: K. J. Alter/L. R. Helfer/M. R. Madsen (eds.), International court authority, First edition, 2018, 3; *K. J. Alter/L. R. Helfer/M. R. Madsen*, How Context Shapes the Authority of International Courts, in: K. J. Alter/L. R. Helfer/M. R. Madsen (eds.), International court authority, First edition, 2018, 24.

1424 *K. J. Alter/L. R. Helfer/M. R. Madsen*, International Court Authority in a Complex World, in: K. J. Alter/L. R. Helfer/M. R. Madsen (eds.), International court authority, First edition, 2018, 3 (6); on the delegation of adjudicative powers, see *C. Bradley/J. Kelley*, 71 Law and Contemporary Problems 1 (2008), 1 (11 et seq.).

from states and is then delegated to the IC by means of some formal source of law, often in the form of the IC's constituent instrument.[1425] In the case of the ICJ, these formal sources are the UNC and the ICJ Statute which give authority to the Court to decide contentious cases in a binding[1426] and final[1427] manner and to render (non-binding) advisory opinions at the request of an authorized organ.[1428] Authority is delimited in the sense that the extent to which an IC can exert authority is predetermined by its delegated competences.[1429] Important discussions within legal formalist debates concern the extent of delegated powers and whether these powers can be extended by means of subsequent practice.[1430]

The type of authority that is bestowed by a formal source of law is called formal or *de jure* authority.[1431] While this type of authority is a necessary starting point for any kind of authority an IC can exercise,[1432] it seems clear that formal authority alone cannot explain the effects which judicial decisions have on their addressees. The insufficiency of a purely formalist-legalist perspective becomes apparent if one considers that even the most competent IC would be irrelevant if it was not given any cases to decide or its decisions were ignored.[1433] The fundamental challenge every IC thus faces is how to transform its delegated formal authority into *de*

1425 *K. J. Alter/L. R. Helfer/M. R. Madsen*, International Court Authority in a Complex World, in: K. J. Alter/L. R. Helfer/M. R. Madsen (eds.), International court authority, First edition, 2018, 3 (6); *N. Lanzoni*, 2 Ital. Rev. Int. Comp. Law 2 (2022), 296 (300).

1426 Art. 59 ICJ Statute, Art. 94 UNC.

1427 Art. 60 ICJ Statute

1428 Art. 65 ICJ Statute, Art. 96 UNC.

1429 *K. J. Alter/L. R. Helfer/M. R. Madsen*, International Court Authority in a Complex World, in: K. J. Alter/L. R. Helfer/M. R. Madsen (eds.), International court authority, First edition, 2018, 3 (6).

1430 See *G. Nolte*, Treaties and subsequent practice, 2013; *G. Nolte*, Third report on subsequent agreements and subsequent practice in relation to the interpretation of treaties, 7. April 2015, UN Docs A/CN.4/683.

1431 *K. J. Alter/L. R. Helfer/M. R. Madsen*, International Court Authority in a Complex World, in: K. J. Alter/L. R. Helfer/M. R. Madsen (eds.), International court authority, First edition, 2018, 3 (6); *N. Lanzoni*, 2 Ital. Rev. Int. Comp. Law 2 (2022), 296 (300).

1432 *K. J. Alter/L. R. Helfer/M. R. Madsen*, How Context Shapes the Authority of International Courts, in: K. J. Alter/L. R. Helfer/M. R. Madsen (eds.), International court authority, First edition, 2018, 24 (33).

1433 Ibid., 26.

facto authority.[1434] Other approaches to IC authority help answering this question.

b) Normative approaches

For scholars who apply a normative approach, the authority of an IC is tantamount to its legitimacy.[1435] According to this approach, to be able to induce behavioral changes, ICs must fulfil certain abstract legal criteria of legitimacy.[1436] *Franck* argued that the legitimacy of an IC directly influences the degree to which states comply with their legal obligations.[1437] According to *Franck*, the compliance-pull of a legal norm depends to a large extent on the norm's determinacy.[1438] ICs in turn play a crucial role in the process of increasing norm-determinacy. Whether an IC is successful in this, *Franck* argues, depends largely on its legitimacy:

> "Whether the clarifying process is successful in transforming rule indeterminacy into determinacy depends on the legitimacy that the members of the international system ascribe to the specific process. This implicates such factors of legitimacy as *who* is doing the interpreting, their *pedigree* or authority to interpret and the *coherence* of the principles the interpreters apply."[1439]

ICs possess normative authority not because of certain legal sources but because of their aspiration to meet the characteristics of an ideal judicial institution.[1440] Many scholars have developed theories of what the charac-

1434 Cf. Ibid., 26.

1435 *K. J. Alter/L. R. Helfer/M. R. Madsen*, International Court Authority in a Complex World, in: K. J. Alter/L. R. Helfer/M. R. Madsen (eds.), International court authority, First edition, 2018, 3 (7); *N. Lanzoni*, 2 Ital. Rev. Int. Comp. Law 2 (2022), 296 (300).

1436 *K. J. Alter/L. R. Helfer/M. R. Madsen*, International Court Authority in a Complex World, in: K. J. Alter/L. R. Helfer/M. R. Madsen (eds.), International court authority, First edition, 2018, 3 (7).

1437 *T. M. Franck*, The power of legitimacy among nations, 1990.

1438 Apart from a rule's determinacy, *Franck* identified three other factors which contribute to rule-compliance: symbolic validation, coherence, and adherence, see *T. M. Franck*, 82 Am. j. int. law 4 (1988), 705 (712); *T. M. Franck*, The power of legitimacy among nations, 1990, 49.

1439 *T. M. Franck*, The power of legitimacy among nations, 1990, 61.

1440 *K. J. Alter/L. R. Helfer/M. R. Madsen*, International Court Authority in a Complex World, in: K. J. Alter/L. R. Helfer/M. R. Madsen (eds.), International court authorteristics of an ideal legal institution could look like. Famous examples include *Fuller*'s eight principles of legality which form an "internal morality of the law"[1441] and *Raz*'s service-conception of authority, according to which law derives its legitimacy from the fact that it provides a service to its addressees.[1442] Other normative approaches focus on the processes of making and applying the law and use normative criteria such as transparency, proportionality, accessibility, accountability, and representativeness to determine the legitimacy of legal rules and institutions.[1443] Finally, some scholars derive the authority of an institution from the authority of its creator, i.e., from the actor that has delegated certain powers to the institution.[1444]

When considering the normative authority of a judicial body like the ICJ, one can distinguish between the authority of the institution itself (or its *strictu sensu* authority) and the authority of its judicial pronouncements (also called its persuasive authority).[1445] *Strictu sensu* authority is the authority an institution claims because of certain intrinsic qualities.[1446] In other words, *strictu sensu* authority describes a content-independent authority that the institution itself possesses.[1447] Persuasive authority describes the degree to which a judicial decision is able to persuade its recipients (its direct addressees as well as the broader international community) of

ity, First edition, 2018, 3 (7); Cf. *N. Lanzoni*, 2 Ital. Rev. Int. Comp. Law 2 (2022), 296 (300).

1441 *Fuller* claimed that compliance with the law is only possible if law-makers comply with certain principles of legality. Accordingly, laws must be general, publicized, non-retroactive, clear, consistent, possible to obey, stable, and congruent, see *L. L. Fuller*, The morality of law, Revised edition 1969, 33 et seq. Building on Fuller's account, see for example *J. Brunnée/S. J. Toope*, Legitimacy and legality in international law, 2010.

1442 *Raz* argued that law provides the service of replacing complex primary reasons for acting in a certain manner (i.e., moral reasons) with more easily comprehensible secondary reasons for action (i.e., legal obligations), thereby solving complex collective action problems, see *J. Raz*, The authority of law, 1979.

1443 *K. J. Alter/L. R. Helfer/M. R. Madsen*, International Court Authority in a Complex World, in: K. J. Alter/L. R. Helfer/M. R. Madsen (eds.), International court authority, First edition, 2018, 3 (7). See for example *A. Nollkaemper*, 23 Eur J Int Law 3 (2012), 769; *A. v. Bogdandy/I. Venzke*, 23 European Journal of International Law 1 (2012), 7.

1444 See for example *A. Cassese*, 25 Leiden Journal of International Law 2 (2012), 491.

1445 *N. Lanzoni*, 2 Ital. Rev. Int. Comp. Law 2 (2022), 296 (301).

1446 Ibid., 301.

1447 Ibid., 301.

the "correctness" of its pronouncements.[1448] In contrast to the *strictu sensu* authority, persuasive authority is content-dependent.[1449] In other words, the authority derives not from the judicial body rendering the decision but from the content of the decision.

There are different factors which bestow persuasive authority upon a judicial decision. The first factor of persuasive authority is the decision's relationship to previous decisions (also called *per relationem* authority).[1450] A decision is perceived as more authoritative if it is consistent with previous decisions of the same court or other ICs, as this consistency increases the predictability of the application of the law.[1451] As several ICJ judges stated in the *Legality of Use of Force* case:

> "[The ICJ] must ensure consistency with its own past case law in order to provide predictability. Consistency is the essence of judicial reasoning. This is especially true in different phases of the same case or with regard to closely connected cases."[1452]

ICs are keen on highlighting the *per relationem* authority of their decisions by referencing their own case law or the case law of other ICs.[1453]

A second source of a judicial decision's persuasive authority is its form and content.[1454] This is also called a judicial decision's "autonomous persuasive authority" as the authority emanates from the decision itself.[1455] A decision can claim a high degree of authority of content if it contains a sound interpretation and application of the law.[1456] The authority of form concerns the decision's rhetoric.[1457] Elements of this include the decision's

1448 Ibid., 302.
1449 Ibid., 302.
1450 Ibid., 303.
1451 Ibid., 303.
1452 *Legality of Use of Force (Serbia and Montenegro v. Belgium)*, Preliminary objections, Joint declaration of Vice-President Ranjeva, Judges Guillaume, Higgins, Kooijmans, Al Khasawneh, Buergenthal and Elaraby, ICJ Reports 2004, 330 (330, para. 3).
1453 *H. Lauterpacht*, The development of international law by the International Court, 2. ed. 1958, 14 Member of the ILC Bimal Patel recently referred to an "uncodified rule" of maintaining consistency and stated that ICs followed a kind of horizontal stare decisis in practice, see ILC, Provisional summary record of the 3633rd meeting held at the Palais des Nations, Geneva, 26 May 2023, A/CN.4/SR.3633, 9.
1454 *N. Lanzoni*, 2 Ital. Rev. Int. Comp. Law 2 (2022), 296 (304).
1455 Ibid., 304.
1456 Ibid., 304.
1457 Ibid., 304.

logical structure, the consistency of the argumentation and the use of clear and unambiguous language.[1458]

In 2023, the ILC published its draft conclusions on subsidiary means for the determination of rules of international law. The ILC listed six criteria for assessing the weight of subsidiary means. These criteria reflect both legal formalist and normative approaches.[1459]

c) Sociological approaches

Sociological approaches to the study of institutional authority build on the work of *Max Weber*.[1460] Like normative theories, most sociological theories define authority as legitimated power.[1461] However, unlike normative approaches, sociological approaches do not measure an institution's legitimacy against some objective normative criteria but instead focus on *perceived* legitimacy.[1462] An example of this is the concept of "semantic authority", as developed by *Venzke*.[1463] Semantic authority refers to the ability of an actor

---

1458 Ibid., 304.

1459 ILC, Seventy-fourth session, Subsidiary means for the determination of rules of international law, Geneva, 2 June 2023, A/CN.4/L.985., draft conclusion 3:
"When assessing the weight of subsidiary means for the determination of rules of international law, regard should be had to, inter alia:
(a) their degree of representativeness;
(b) the quality of the reasoning;
(c) the expertise of those involved;
(d) the level of agreement among those involved;
(e) the reception by States and other entities;
(f) where applicable, the mandate conferred on the body."

1460 See *M. R. Madsen*, Sociological Approaches to International Courts, in: C. Romano/K. J. Alter/Y. Shany (eds.), The Oxford Handbook of International Adjudication, 2013, 388.

1461 *K. J. Alter/L. R. Helfer/M. R. Madsen*, International Court Authority in a Complex World, in: K. J. Alter/L. R. Helfer/M. R. Madsen (eds.), International court authority, First edition, 2018, 3 (9–10). Applying a sociological approach to international law, see *D. Beetham*, The legitimation of power, 1991; *G. A. Caldeira/J. L. Gibson*, 89 The American Political Science Review 2 (1995), 356; *B. Çalı/A. Koch/N. Bruch*, 35 Human Rights Quarterly 4 (2013), 955.

1462 *K. J. Alter/L. R. Helfer/M. R. Madsen*, International Court Authority in a Complex World, in: K. J. Alter/L. R. Helfer/M. R. Madsen (eds.), International court authority, First edition, 2018, 3 (9); On the "social legitimacy" of the ECtHR, see *B. Çalı/A. Koch/N. Bruch*, 35 Human Rights Quarterly 4 (2013), 955.

1463 *I. Venzke*, How interpretation makes international law, 2012; *I. Venzke*, 14 Theoretical Inquiries in Law 2 (2013), 381; *I. Venzke*, 4 Transnational Legal Theory 3 (2013), such as an IC to create reference points about the law, which other actors cannot ignore when engaging in legal discourse irrespective of whether they agree or disagree with the assessment of the law.[1464] The notion of semantic authority premises on the idea that the formal sources of international law do not adequately represent the nature of international law. Instead, international law is a "communicative practice".[1465] In contrast to normative approaches, semantic authority is not premised on persuasion.[1466] While persuasiveness may increase an actors authority, the constitutive feature of semantic authority is that it looks at an actor's capacity to bring others to engage with its legal reasoning irrespective of agreement on the merits of the argument.[1467] The concept of semantic authority also makes no statement about the legitimacy of the exercise of authority.[1468]

d) Compliance studies and performance-based approaches

Compliance studies regard the degree to which litigants comply with an IC's decisions as the principal benchmark for the authority of an IC.[1469] Performance-based approaches move the perspective further and examine

354; *I. Venzke*, Semantic authority, legal change and the dynamics of international law, in: P. Capps/H. P. Olsen (eds.), Legal authority beyond the state, 2018, 102; *I. Venzke*, Semantic Authority, in: J. d' Aspremont/S. Singh (eds.), Concepts for international law, 1. ed., 2019, 815.

1464 *I. Venzke*, Semantic Authority, in: J. d' Aspremont/S. Singh (eds.), Concepts for international law, 1. ed., 2019, 815 (815).

1465 The concept of semantic authority traces its roots to the German free law movement (*Freirechtsschule*) and US American legal realism, in particular the New Haven School, see Ibid., 817–820.

1466 Ibid., 820.

1467 Ibid., 821; cf. *S. Shapiro*, Authority, in: J. L. Coleman/S. Shapiro (eds.), The Oxford Handbook of Jurisprudence and Philosophy of Law, 2004, 382 (383).

1468 *I. Venzke*, Semantic Authority, in: J. d' Aspremont/S. Singh (eds.), Concepts for international law, 1. ed., 2019, 815 (822).

1469 *K. J. Alter/L. R. Helfer/M. R. Madsen*, International Court Authority in a Complex World, in: K. J. Alter/L. R. Helfer/M. R. Madsen (eds.), International court authority, First edition, 2018, 3 (11–12). Examples of such compliance studies include *H. Keller/A. Stone Sweet*, A Europe of rights, 2008; *M. Wind*, 48 J of Common Market Studies 4 (2010), 1039; *A. Nollkaemper*, National courts and the international rule of law, 2012.

the cumulative impact of IC decisions beyond individual proceedings.[1470] An example of the latter is *Shany's* approach to evaluate the effectiveness of an IC by comparing the IC's cumulative output with its objectives.[1471] Using an IC's objectives as a reference point and the degree to which it fulfils these objectives as a benchmark for authority has the advantage of providing a clear metric. However, it ignores the possible impact of an IC's activities beyond its pre-defined objectives.[1472]

e) Practice-based approaches

The practice-based approach developed by *Alter, Helfer* and *Madsen* intends to accommodate for this shortcoming of the performance-based approach by extending the scope of the perspective beyond an IC's pre-determined goals and towards other effects on the actions of its addressees.[1473] The core idea of the practice-based approach is to measure the authority of IC's by reference to the practice of its key audiences.[1474] *Alter et al.* argue that *de facto* authority exists when judgments of an IC are reflected in the practices of its audiences:

> "The capacity of an IC to exercise authority is, therefore, its ability to influence practices in law, politics, and society. More specifically, IC authority is a court's ability to project its ideas and values about the law and to have these projections reflected by, or even internalized in, the actions of individuals, groups, and organizations within society."[1475]

In this framework, it is irrelevant why a particular actor does or does not comply with an IC's judgment.[1476] What matters is whether the key audiences recognize their obligation to comply with the decision and take

1470 *K. J. Alter/L. R. Helfer/M. R. Madsen*, International Court Authority in a Complex World, in: K. J. Alter/L. R. Helfer/M. R. Madsen (eds.), International court authority, First edition, 2018, 3 (12).

1471 *Y. Shany*, 106 American Journal of International Law 2 (2012), 225.

1472 Cf. *K. J. Alter/L. R. Helfer/M. R. Madsen*, International Court Authority in a Complex World, in: K. J. Alter/L. R. Helfer/M. R. Madsen (eds.), International court authority, First edition, 2018, 3 (12).

1473 Ibid., 12.

1474 Ibid., 13.

1475 Ibid., 13.

1476 Ibid., 11.

meaningful action toward giving effect to the decision.[1477] Importantly, according to this approach, authority is not binary.[1478] *Alter et al.* paint a differentiated picture of authority which accounts for the fact that reactions to IC decisions may vary significantly among audiences with some actors rejecting a decision while others adhere to it.[1479] The practice-based approach also accounts for the fact that *de facto* authority is susceptible to change and erosion and is shared between institutions operating at international and national levels.

Importantly and unlike the normative and the sociological approaches, the practice-based approach separates the question of authority from the question of legitimacy.[1480] The authority of an IC, according to the practice-based approach, depends on how its decisions are accepted, not on the institution's legitimacy. Separating authority from legitimacy has the advantage of evading the problematic amalgamation of two often correlating but not identical concepts. As *Peters* and *Schaffer* highlight, the idea that authority derives from legitimacy would mean that every particularly authoritative institution is also particularly legitimate, an idea which runs counter the empirically observable fact of illegitimate institutions with great authority.[1481]

2. Formal and normative authority of ICJ advisory opinions

From a formalist perspective, the degree to which the ICJ exerts authority by issuing advisory opinions is determined by the Court's constituent instrument. The power to give advisory opinions is bestowed upon the ICJ by virtue of Article 96 UNC and Article 65 ICJ Statute. The ICJ Statute distinguishes between "decisions" and "judgments" on the one hand, which are

1477 *K. J. Alter/L. R. Helfer/M. R. Madsen*, How Context Shapes the Authority of International Courts, in: K. J. Alter/L. R. Helfer/M. R. Madsen (eds.), International court authority, First edition, 2018, 24 (29).

1478 *K. J. Alter/L. R. Helfer/M. R. Madsen*, International Court Authority in a Complex World, in: K. J. Alter/L. R. Helfer/M. R. Madsen (eds.), International court authority, First edition, 2018, 3 (5).

1479 Ibid., 5, 11. See the five-level metric of factual authority developed by *Alter et al.* referenced in the case study below.

1480 Ibid., 4, 9; *K. J. Alter/L. R. Helfer/M. R. Madsen*, How Context Shapes the Authority of International Courts, in: K. J. Alter/L. R. Helfer/M. R. Madsen (eds.), International court authority, First edition, 2018, 24 (28–29).

1481 See *B. Peters/J. K. Schaffer*, 4 Transnational Legal Theory 3 (2013), 315 (334).

binding under the Articles 59 and 60 ICJ Statute, and "advisory opinions" on the other which lack such binding force.[1482] Lacking binding force, the formal authority of ICJ advisory opinions is significantly lower than that of ICJ decisions.

Article 38 para. 1 lit. d ICJ Statute stipulates that the Court shall apply "subject to the provisions of Article 59, judicial decisions (...) as subsidiary means for the determination of rules of law."

The reference to "decisions" seems to exclude ICJ advisory opinions.[1483] This reading of the provision's scope is supported by the drafting history of the PCIJ Statute.[1484] However, the Court has used both decisions and advisory opinions in the same manner as subsidiary means for the determination of the law.[1485] Thus, as *H. Lauterpacht* put it, an ICJ advisory opinion "is as authoritative a statement of the law as a judgment rendered in contentious proceedings".[1486]

Special Rapporteur on subsidiary means for the determination of rules of international law *Jalloh* therefore argued that the term "decisions" in Article 38 para. 1 lit. d ICJ Statute also extends to advisory opinions,[1487] a view that was shared by "virtually all members" of the ILC when he proposed it during the ILC's 74th session.[1488]

Judge *Moore* was one of the first to comment on the relationship between the authority of judicial decisions and their binding force. In his 1922 memorandum on the PCIJ, Judge *Moore* stated:

> "Human experience, especially as exemplified in legislation, justifies the belief that the moral authority of judicial decisions is derived chiefly from the fact that they have the authority of law and legally bind the parties to the dispute. If deprived of this effect their so-called moral authority would promptly vanish."[1489]

1482 On the non-binding nature of advisory opinions, see *supra*: § 6 Section D.I.3.

1483 *H. Lauterpacht*, 10 British Yearbook of International Law (1929), 65 (65).

1484 *C. C. Jalloh*, First Report on Subsidiary Means for the Determination of Rules of International Law, Second reissue 16 May 2023, A/CN.4/760, para. 277.

1485 Ibid., para. 277.

1486 *H. Lauterpacht*, 10 British Yearbook of International Law (1929), 65 (185).

1487 *C. C. Jalloh*, First Report on Subsidiary Means for the Determination of Rules of International Law, Second reissue 16 May 2023, A/CN.4/760, para. 280.

1488 ILC, Provisional summary record of the 3633rd meeting held at the Palais des Nations, Geneva, 26 May 2023, A/CN.4/SR.3633, 6.

1489 *J. B. Moore*, The question of advisory opinions, 1922, PCIJ Series D. No. 2, 392.

Yet, contrary to *Moore's* prediction in 1922 and despite their lack of binding force, the (normative) authority of advisory opinions did not "promptly vanish" but instead rose steadily over the decades. Scholars and practitioners have identified three primary reasons for the authority of ICJ advisory opinions: The intrinsic merit or persuasiveness of the advisory opinions,[1490] the (*strictu sensu*) authority of the institution rendering the advisory opinions[1491] and the judicial process of rendering the opinions[1492].

Hambro dismissed the reliance on the Court's *strictu sensu* authority and argued that the authority of advisory opinions depended exclusively on their intrinsic merit or persuasive authority:

> "Advisory Opinions, even more than the judgments of the Court, will be judged on their intrinsic merits. A judgment of the Court, even if it is not perfect and even if the reasoning can be criticised, can serve a useful purpose because it will put an end to a dispute between two or more States. An Advisory Opinion, on the other hand, does not serve this purpose. It stands or falls with the legal arguments that can be deduced from the reasoning of the majority and it is very much to be feared that a Court seriously split on any legal question submitted to it for Advisory Opinion will not contribute anything useful to the solution of that question."[1493]

Hambro voiced this as a critique of allowing separate and dissenting opinions in advisory proceedings and he is not the first one to do so. Judge *Moore* in his 1922 Memorandum voiced a similar concern arguing that an advisory opinion which is rendered by a small majority against a strong minority opinion "might not prove to be either convincing or conspicuously weighty."[1494]

Moore and *Hambro* point to an important aspect. ICJ decisions have binding force and as such enjoy a high degree of formal authority irrespective of whether the decision has been rendered unanimously or only by a

1490 *Interpretation of Peace Treaties with Bulgaria, Hungary and Romania (First Phase)*, Advisory Opinion, Dissenting Opinion Winiarski, ICJ Reports 1950, 65 (91–92); *E. Hambro*, 3 ICLQ 1 (1954), 2 (21); *D. Pratap*, The advisory jurisdiction of the International Court, 1972, 231; *M. Shahabuddeen*, Precedent in the World Court, 1996, 167.

1491 *D. Pratap*, The advisory jurisdiction of the International Court, 1972, 231.

1492 *Interpretation of Peace Treaties with Bulgaria, Hungary and Romania (First Phase)*, Advisory Opinion, Dissenting Opinion Zoričić, ICJ Reports 1950, 98 (101–102).

1493 *E. Hambro*, 3 ICLQ 1 (1954), 2 (21).

1494 *J. B. Moore*, The question of advisory opinions, 1922, PCIJ Series D. No. 2, 392.

small majority. In contrast, advisory opinions have no binding force and as such their authority may be significantly lower if they are issued by a small majority instead of unanimously. This critique is a legal formalist critique, as it primarily makes a distinction on the basis of the formal authority bestowed upon decisions by virtue of them being binding. If one were to focus exclusively on the question of persuasiveness, the fact that a decision is delivered by a small majority against a powerful minority would lead to a reduction in the authority of the decision in question.[1495] In this respect, there is no difference between decisions and advisory opinions. The institution of separate and dissenting opinions in advisory proceedings has not led to a reduction in normative authority (neither *strictu sensu* authority regarding the institution nor persuasive authority). If scholars, practitioners or the Court itself cite ICJ advisory opinions on a point of law, they refer to them in the same manner as they refer to ICJ decisions.[1496] As Judge *Zoričić* stated:

> "[T]he Court's advisory opinions enjoy the same authority as its judgments, and are cited by jurists who attribute the same importance to them as to judgments. The Court itself refers to its previous advisory opinions in the same way as to its judgments."[1497]

1495 This is reflected in the Draft conclusion 3 lit. d of the ILC Draft conclusions on Subsidiary means for the determination of rules of international law passed during the 74th session, in which the ILC lists as one of the criteria for assessing the weight of a subsidiary means for determining the rules of international law "the level of agreement among those involved", see A/CN.4/L.985 Subsidiary means for the determination of rules of international law Titles and texts of draft conclusions 1 to 3 provisionally adopted by the Drafting Committee, Geneva, 2 June 2023.

1496 In the May 2023 session on Subsidiary means for the determination of rules of international law, all members of the ILC shared the view that advisory opinions could have the same authority as judicial decisions. This position was expressed in light of the fact that the ICJ and other ICs, such as the ITLOS and the IACtHR, refer to their previous judgments and advisory opinions without distinguishing between the two, see ILC, Provisional summary record of the 3633rd meeting held at the Palais des Nations, Geneva, 26 May 2023, A/CN.4/SR.3633. On the practice of the ICJ in this regard, see *D. Pratap*, The advisory jurisdiction of the International Court, 1972, 257–259; *M. Shahabuddeen*, Precedent in the World Court, 1996, 168.

1497 *Interpretation of Peace Treaties with Bulgaria, Hungary and Romania (First Phase)*, Advisory Opinion, Dissenting Opinion Zoričić, ICJ Reports 1950, 98 (101).

However, the authority of an advisory opinion is not limited to the merit of its legal reasoning.[1498] Otherwise, there would be no difference between an advisory opinion of the ICJ and the opinion of a group of particularly capable legal scholars. The claim to authority of ICJ advisory opinions goes further. When the ICJ issues an advisory opinion, it does not merely give legal advice.[1499] It makes a judicial pronouncement following a pre-defined legal procedure and thus performs a judicial function.[1500] The drafters of the League's Covenant already intended to underscore the distinction between "advice" and an "advisory opinion" by choosing the wording "give an advisory opinion" instead of "to advise" as was proposed by the Committee of Jurists.[1501] In 1971, Judge *de Castro* referred to this distinction when he stated that the ICJ's "constitutional status and independence" meant that its "authority may never be compared to that of a legal consultant or advisor".[1502]

Advisory opinions are rendered by the ICJ in full plenum. As such, they represent the legal opinion of the Court[1503] and carry the same authority and prestige as the institution of the Court, increasing the opinions' *strictu sensu* authority.[1504] It was a deliberate decision during the drafting process of the PCIJ Statute to give the power to issue advisory opinions to the full

1498 See however E. Hambro, who bases the authority of ICJ advisory opinions primarily on their 'intrinsic merits', that is the legal reasoning, *E. Hambro*, 3 ICLQ 1 (1954), 2 (21).

1499 See however Judge Jennings, who stated "The advice is simply advice and is not a binding decision of the Court", *R. Y. Jennings*, Advisory Opinions of the International Court of Justice, in: B. Boutros-Ghali (ed.), Amicorum Discipulorumque Liber, 1998, 531 (532).

1500 *Judgments of the Administrative Tribunal of the ILO upon Complaints Made against UNESCO*, Advisory Opinion, ICJ Reports 1956, 77 (84); *M. O. Hudson*, 42 AJIL 3 (1948), 630 (630); *D. Pratap*, The advisory jurisdiction of the International Court, 1972, 230.

1501 *D. Négulesco*, 57 Recueil des cours d'Académie de Droit International de La Haye (1936), 5 (66).

1502 *Legal Consequences for States of the Continued Presence of South Africa in Namibia (South West Africa) notwithstanding Security Council Resolution 276 (1970)*, Advisory Opinion, Separate opinion de Castro, ICJ Reports 1971, 170 (173, para. 4).

1503 *Hudson* contrasts this with the practice of US State Supreme Courts in which the advisory opinions represent the opinions of individual judges, *M. O. Hudson*, 37 Harvard Law Review 8 (1924), 970 (1000).

1504 In contrast, separate and dissenting opinions are the opinions of the individual judges and as such only attributable to the named judge and not the Court, see *C. C. Jalloh*, First Report on Subsidiary Means for the Determination of Rules of International Law, Second reissue 16 May 2023, A/CN.4/760, para. 282.

Court and not to an advisory chamber. The Advisory Committee of Jurists, in drafting the PCIJ Statute, proposed the creation of such an advisory chamber composed of three to five members of the Court.[1505] The idea was meant to give the PCIJ greater flexibility when the same matter came before the plenary in contentious proceedings. It was believed that the Court could more easily overturn a position taken in an advisory opinion if the opinion was issued by a smaller chamber rather than by the full Court. However, this idea was rejected by the Committee of the Assembly of the League of Nations.[1506]

There are various provisions in the UNC and the ICJ Statute which are formulated to underscore the ICJ's *strictu sensu* authority. The ICJ is the "principal judicial organ of the United Nations" (Article 92 UNC), and it "shall be composed of a body of independent judges, elected (...) from among persons of high moral character, who (...) are jurisconsults of recognized competence in international law" (Article 2 ICJ Statute). Collectively, the Court shall be a "representation of the main forms of civilization and of the principal legal systems of the world" (Article 9 ICJ Statute).

During a meeting on subsidiary means for the determination of rules of international law, several ILC members emphasized the Court's status as the principal judicial organ of the United Nations and as the only IC with general jurisdiction over inter-state disputes, arguing that this status gives its decisions greater weight than those of other ICs.[1507] Others pointed to the Court's long history of outstanding jurisprudence and its standard-setting decision-making process as further elements conferring intrinsic or *strictu sensu* authority on the ICJ.[1508]

Another important factor bestowing a high degree of authority on the Court's advisory opinions is the fact that the Court's advisory procedure closely resembles the Court's contentious procedure. Judge *Zoričić* argued

1505 *J. B. Moore*, The question of advisory opinions, 1922, PCIJ Series D. No. 2, 391, citing the Report of the Advisory Committee of Jurists.

1506 On the drafting history of the PCIJ Statute, see *supra*: § 1 Section B.II.

1507 See ILC, Provisional summary record of the 3633rd meeting held at the Palais des Nations, Geneva, 26 May 2023, A/CN.4/SR.3633, 4–5; others including Special Rapporteur Jalloh emphasized the decentralized nature of the international judicial system and that there was no hierarchy among the different ICs, see in the same Provisional summary record, 6.

1508 *N. Lanzoni*, 2 Ital. Rev. Int. Comp. Law 2 (2022), 296 (302).

that the judicial procedure applied in advisory proceedings on inter-state disputes made them into "unenforceable judgments".[1509] *Zoričić* found that:

> "in such a case, the procedure normally follows the same course as in an actual contentious case. The States parties to the dispute submit written and oral statements, the case is argued in open Court, the full Court deliberates, the national judges take part in the deliberations of the Court and in the voting and, finally, the opinion is read out at a public sitting and printed in the Court's publications exactly in the same way as a judgment."[1510]

Keith argued that there was an interaction between the authority of the advisory opinion and the judicial procedure to be followed:

> "The more authoritative the opinions, the more likely the Court is to insist on a judicial procedure and conversely the more "judicial" the procedure the more authoritative the opinions are likely to be."[1511]

Similarly, *Hambro* argued that because advisory proceedings follow essentially the same procedural safeguards as contentious proceedings, "the legal reasons behind the Opinions carry the same weight and are invested with the same high authority as in the case of judgments."[1512] *Hambro* gives the example of the Court's practice of allowing *ad hoc* judges to participate in advisory proceedings, which he sees as an indication that advisory opinions "are, in effect, much more than advisory".[1513]

3. De-facto authority of ICJ advisory opinions

In terms of the de-facto authority of advisory opinions, it seems useful to first consider the different questions which have been brought before the ICJ in advisory proceedings thus far. The submitted questions have broadly

---

1509 *Interpretation of Peace Treaties with Bulgaria, Hungary and Romania (First Phase)*, Advisory Opinion, Dissenting Opinion Zoričić, ICJ Reports 1950, 98 (101).

1510 *Interpretation of Peace Treaties with Bulgaria, Hungary and Romania (First Phase)*, Advisory Opinion, Dissenting Opinion Zoričić, ICJ Reports 1950, 98 (101).

1511 *K. J. Keith*, The extent of the advisory jurisdiction of the International Court of Justice, 1971, 151.

1512 *E. Hambro*, 3 ICLQ 1 (1954), 2 (5).

1513 Ibid., 6.

concerned four subject-areas:[1514] The first category concerned requests concerning institutional matters arising from the activities of the requesting organ.[1515] The second category concerned abstract questions of international law on which differing views exist among states and international organizations but which do not relate to a specific controversy.[1516] A third category concerned questions of law concerning a specific legal controversy between two or more states (inter-state disputes).[1517] A fourth type of requests related to the now discontinued appeals procedure against decisions of UN administrative tribunals in employment disputes between UN agencies and staff members.[1518] ICJ advisory opinions have had significant effects in clarifying institutional matters of the UN and other organizations and in answering

1514 *D. Akande*, 7 J Int. Disp. Settlement 2 (2016), 320 (339–340); *N. Lanzoni*, 2 Ital. Rev. Int. Comp. Law 2 (2022), 296 (307–308).

1515 Examples include: *Conditions of Admission of a State to Membership in the United Nations (Article 4 of the Charter)*, Advisory Opinion, ICJ Reports 1948, 57; *Reparation for Injuries Suffered in the Service of the United Nations*, Advisory Opinion, ICJ Reports 1949, 174; *Competence of the General Assembly for the Admission of a State to the United Nations*, Advisory Opinion, ICJ Reports 1950, 4; *Certain Expenses of the United Nations (Article 17, paragraph 2, of the Charter)*, Advisory Opinion, ICJ Reports 1962, 151; *Interpretation of the Agreement of 25 March 1951 between the WHO and Egypt*, Advisory Opinion, ICJ Reports 1980, 73; *Difference Relating to Immunity from Legal Process of a Special Rapporteur of the HRC*, Advisory Opinion, ICJ Reports 1999, 62.

1516 Examples include *Legality of the Use by a State of Nuclear Weapons in Armed Conflict*, Advisory Opinion, ICJ Reports 1996, 66; *Legality of the Threat or Use of Nuclear Weapons*, Advisory Opinion, ICJ Reports 1996, 226.

1517 Examples include *Legal Consequences for States of the Continued Presence of South Africa in Namibia (South West Africa) notwithstanding Security Council Resolution 276 (1970)*, Advisory Opinion, ICJ Reports 1971, 16; *Legal Consequences of the Construction of a Wall in the Occupied Palestinian Territory*, Advisory Opinion, ICJ Reports 2004, 136; *Accordance with international law of the unilateral declaration of independence in respect of Kosovo*, Advisory Opinion, ICJ Reports 2010, 403; *Legal Consequences of the Separation of the Chagos Archipelago from Mauritius in 1965*, Advisory Opinion, ICJ Reports 2019, 95.

1518 See *Effect of Awards of Compensation Made by the United Nations Administrative Tribunal*, Advisory Opinion, ICJ Reports 1954, 47; *Judgments of the Administrative Tribunal of the ILO upon Complaints Made against UNESCO*, Advisory Opinion, ICJ Reports 1956, 77; *Application for Review of Judgment No. 158 of the United Nations Administrative Tribunal*, Advisory Opinion, ICJ Reports 1973, 166; *Application for Review of Judgment No. 273 of the United Nations Administrative Tribunal*, Advisory Opinion, ICJ Reports 1982, 325; *Application for Review of Judgment No. 333 of the United Nations Administrative Tribunal*, Advisory Opinion, ICJ Reports, 18; *Judgment No. 2867 of the Administrative Tribunal of the ILO*, Advisory Opinion, ICJ Reports 2012, 10.

abstract questions of law.[1519] However, have they also been successful in bringing about change in behavior in the context of specific inter-state disputes? *Alter et al.'s* practice-based approach provides a useful framework for studying such practical effects.[1520]

a) A practice-based approach to studying the authority of ICJ advisory opinions

The practice-based approach asks whether "one or more audience recognizes by their words, actions, or both, that IC rulings are legally binding and engage in actions that push toward giving full effect to those rulings."[1521]

What is required is an element of "*recognition*" accompanied by "*meaningful action*" to implement the relevant obligation.[1522] Since ICJ advisory opinions are not binding, the criteria of the practice-based approach need to be adapted. Accordingly, the focus is on whether the relevant audiences, by their words, actions, or both, recognize as legally binding the legal obligation not *created by*, but *referenced in* the advisory opinion, and take meaningful action to comply with that obligation. In line with the practice-

1519 See on this *K. Oellers-Frahm*, 12 GLJ 5 (2011), 1033 (1040 et seq.); *Lanzoni* refers to the "obvious normative authority" of ICJ advisory opinions and notes that in the context of institutional questions they "produce substantially binding effects vis-à-vis the requesting organ and other UN bodies", see *N. Lanzoni*, 2 Ital. Rev. Int. Comp. Law 2 (2022), 296 (308–309).

1520 Other commentators, such as *Lando,* also support a practice-based approach, arguing that the legal effects of advisory opinions "cannot be determined a priori" and as such they should be "assessed depending on whether States and international organisations have acted on, and consistent with, the judicial determinations in those opinions", see *M. Lando*, Binding Advisory Opinions, in: R. Buchan/D. Franchini/N. Tsagourias (eds.), The Changing Character of International Dispute Settlement: Challenges and Prospects, 2023, 106 (120).

1521 *K. J. Alter/L. R. Helfer/M. R. Madsen*, How Context Shapes the Authority of International Courts, in: K. J. Alter/L. R. Helfer/M. R. Madsen (eds.), International court authority, First edition, 2018, 24 (28).

1522 Ibid., 29; others like *Huneeus* focus only on the actions of a state, not on its recognition of the ruling as binding, see *A. Huneeus*, Compliance with Judgments and Decisions, in: C. Romano/K. J. Alter/Y. Shany (eds.), The Oxford Handbook of International Adjudication, 2013, 437 (442).

based approach, this section is agnostic as to the reasons for compliance or non-compliance with the relevant obligations.[1523]

In applying a practice-based approach to ICJ advisory opinions, the section applies the five-level metric developed by *Alter et al.* to describe the different types of factual authority an IC can acquire:[1524]

On the most basic level, an IC's judicial pronouncements could have no factual authority.[1525] This describes a situation in which an IC is either inactive despite apparent infringements of international law, which it is competent to adjudicate upon, or its decisions are widely ignored.[1526]

The second level of de-facto authority *Alter et al.* call "narrow authority".[1527] Narrow authority exists when only the parties to the dispute accept the decision as legally binding and take meaningful steps towards implementation while others do not take notice of it.[1528] ICJ advisory opinions have no parties in the formal sense.[1529] As the ICJ held:

> "The Court's Opinion is given not to the States, but to the organ which is entitled to request it".[1530]

Nevertheless, there are several immediate audiences of ICJ advisory opinions, first and foremost the requesting organ. The requesting organ has a duty to consider, potentially even a duty to comply with the advisory opinion.[1531] Other immediate audiences of advisory opinions are the states that

---

1523 Cf. *K. J. Alter/L. R. Helfer/M. R. Madsen*, How Context Shapes the Authority of International Courts, in: K. J. Alter/L. R. Helfer/M. R. Madsen (eds.), International court authority, First edition, 2018, 24 (28).

1524 See in detail, Ibid., 31–33.

1525 Ibid., 31.

1526 Ibid., 31.

1527 Ibid., 31.

1528 Ibid., 31.

1529 *M. Benzing*, in: A. Zimmermann/C. J. Tams/K. Oellers-Frahm/C. Tomuschat/D. W. K. Anderson (eds.), The Statute of the International Court of Justice, 3. ed., 2019: Evidentiary Issues, 1412; On the audiences of ICJ advisory opinions, see *J. Salmon*, Who are the addressees of the Opinions?, in: L. Boisson de Chazournes/P. Sands (eds.), International law, the World Court of justice and nuclear weapons, 1999.

1530 *Interpretation of Peace Treaties with Bulgaria, Hungary and Romania (First Phase)*, Advisory Opinion, Dissenting Opinion Winiarski, ICJ Reports 1950, 65 (71).

1531 *Lanzoni* argues that ICJ advisory opinions produce "substantially binding effects vis-à-vis the requesting organ and other UN bodies", see *N. Lanzoni*, 2 Ital. Rev. Int. Comp. Law 2 (2022), 296 (309); on this see also *G. Abi-Saab*, Les exceptions préliminaires dans la procédure de la Cour internationale, 1966, 82–84; so also *R. Kolb*, The International Court of Justice, 2013, 1097; cf. *D. Négulesco*, 57 Recueil des are particularly affected by the underlying dispute[1532], i.e., the states whose legal rights and obligations form the subject-matter of the proceedings. In the *Wall* case this is Israel, in the *Chagos* case these are the United Kingdom and Mauritius. Although these states are not directly bound by the advisory opinion itself, the respective opinion addresses their legal obligations and calls upon them to act in a certain way. In this respect, the disputing states, which have a particular interest in the outcome of the advisory proceedings, take the position of the parties to the proceedings in the narrow authority sense.

The third level of factual authority *Alter et al.* call "intermediate authority."[1533] In contentious proceedings, intermediate authority refers to a situation in which the judgment is recognized and acted upon by actors for whom the judgment is not directly binding but who nevertheless adapt their actions accordingly.[1534] These actors include potential future litigants, governments and domestic courts,[1535] as well as the Member States of the requesting organization, other organs and specialized agencies which may be in a similar situation to the requesting organ, as well as other states, particularly those that have participated in the proceedings.[1536] In the context of advisory proceedings, this group consists of those states and organizations whose conduct is not the subject-matter of the proceedings but which nevertheless have an interest in the outcome of the proceeding.

The fourth level of legal authority is called "extensive authority" and it describes a situation in which judgments are recognized and acted upon by a wider audience within the legal profession, including legal practitioners, scholars and NGO lawyers.[1537]

---

cours d'Académie de Droit International de La Haye (1936), 5 (64). On "binding" advisory opinions, see *supra*: § 6 Section D.I.3.

1532 Cf. *J. Salmon*, Who are the addressees of the Opinions?, in: L. Boisson de Chazournes/P. Sands (eds.), International law, the World Court of justice and nuclear weapons, 1999 (31–32).

1533 *K. J. Alter/L. R. Helfer/M. R. Madsen*, How Context Shapes the Authority of International Courts, in: K. J. Alter/L. R. Helfer/M. R. Madsen (eds.), International court authority, First edition, 2018, 24 (31–32).

1534 Ibid., 31–32.

1535 Ibid., 31–32.

1536 Cf. *J. Salmon*, Who are the addressees of the Opinions?, in: L. Boisson de Chazournes/P. Sands (eds.), International law, the World Court of justice and nuclear weapons, 1999 (29–32).

1537 *K. J. Alter/L. R. Helfer/M. R. Madsen*, How Context Shapes the Authority of International Courts, in: K. J. Alter/L. R. Helfer/M. R. Madsen (eds.), International court authority, First edition, 2018, 24 (32); cf. *J. Salmon*, Who are the addressees

Lastly, an IC reaches "popular authority", the fifth level of authority, when its judgments, or in the case of advisory opinions the obligations referenced to therein, are considered binding by the general public.[1538]

It is important to note that these types of de-facto authority relate to different audiences and are independent of each other.[1539] This means that the different types of de-facto authority are not structured in some kind of hierarchy, where an IC that achieves a "higher" level of authority (e.g., intermediate authority) automatically has "more" authority than one whose authority is at a "lower" level (e.g., narrow authority).[1540] An IC may influence the behavior of potential future litigants and thus exert intermediate authority, while it may not be able to conduce change in the behavior of the parties to a case before it and thus lacks narrow authority.[1541] In particular, the advisory opinions of the ICJ regularly influence the international legal discourse at large and the behavior of many states not directly involved, without creating sufficient compliance pull on the states whose legal obligations are the subject-matter of the proceedings.

Having set out the parameters of the practice-based approach, let us now revisit two of the most recent advisory opinions relating to inter-state disputes: the *Wall* and the *Chagos* advisory opinions. Before doing so, one point should be emphasized: *Alter et al.* have developed the practice-based approach to assess the authority of ICs, not the authority of individual decisions.[1542] Nevertheless, the practice-based approach may still provide a useful framework for assessing the authority of individual ICJ advisory opinions.

---

of the Opinions?, in: L. Boisson de Chazournes/P. Sands (eds.), International law, the World Court of justice and nuclear weapons, 1999 (34–35).

1538 *K. J. Alter/L. R. Helfer/M. R. Madsen*, How Context Shapes the Authority of International Courts, in: K. J. Alter/L. R. Helfer/M. R. Madsen (eds.), International court authority, First edition, 2018, 24 (32–33); cf. *J. Salmon*, Who are the addressees of the Opinions?, in: L. Boisson de Chazournes/P. Sands (eds.), International law, the World Court of justice and nuclear weapons, 1999 (35).

1539 *K. J. Alter/L. R. Helfer/M. R. Madsen*, International Court Authority in a Complex World, in: K. J. Alter/L. R. Helfer/M. R. Madsen (eds.), International court authority, First edition, 2018, 3 (4).

1540 Cf. Ibid., 4.

1541 Ibid., 4.

1542 Cf. *K. J. Alter/L. R. Helfer/M. R. Madsen*, How Context Shapes the Authority of International Courts, in: K. J. Alter/L. R. Helfer/M. R. Madsen (eds.), International court authority, First edition, 2018, 24 (28 et seq.).

b) De-facto authority of the Wall advisory opinion

In 2004, the ICJ rendered its *Wall* advisory opinion[1543] addressing the construction of a wall (or fence) by Israel extending into large swaths of the Palestinian territory within the West Bank, including East Jerusalem, thus leading to a fragmentation of Palestinian communities and destruction of Palestinian property. The ICJ held that Israel committed an internationally wrongful act by constructing the wall on Palestinian territory.[1544] In particular, Israel violated its obligation to respect the Palestinian people's right to self-determination, Israel's obligations under international humanitarian law[1545] as well as Israel's obligations under international human rights law.[1546] The Court found that Israel's conduct could not be justified as an act of self-defense under Article 51 UNC or UNSC resolutions 1368 (2001) and 1373 (2001) since Israel's actions are not directed against another state.[1547] The ICJ further found that the situation did not meet the strict requirements of the customary law exception of necessity.[1548]

As a consequence of Israel's breaches of international law, the Court found that Israel was under an obligation to stop its construction of the wall, dismantle any parts that were located on Palestinian territory, repeal any legislative acts that have been adopted in relation to the construction of the wall and make reparations for any damage caused by the construction of the wall to all natural or legal persons, including – where possible –

1543 *Legal Consequences of the Construction of a Wall in the Occupied Palestinian Territory*, Advisory Opinion, ICJ Reports 2004, 136.

1544 Ibid. (197, para. 149); on the legal consequences of the *Wall* opinion, see *R. J. Araujo*, 22 BUILJ 2 (2004), 349 (382 et seq.); on the legal consequences of the *Wall* opinion for the UN and its Member States, see *I. Scobbie*, 16 EJIL 5 (2005), 941; for a general overview of the Israeli-Palestinian conflict, see *V. Kattan*, The Palestine question in international law, 2008; *Dinstein*, The International Law of Belligerent Occupation, 2009.

1545 The Court held that the construction of the Wall led to the destruction or requisition of properties in violation of Art. 46 and 52 of the Hague Regulations and Art. 53 of the fourth Geneva Convention.

1546 *Legal Consequences of the Construction of a Wall in the Occupied Palestinian Territory*, Advisory Opinion, ICJ Reports 2004, 136 (197, para. 149).

1547 Ibid. (194, para. 139); criticizing the Court's interpretation of Art. 51 UNC, see *S. D. Murphy*, 99 AJIL 1 (2005), 62; in defence of the Court's interpretation of Art. 51 UNC, see *I. Scobbie*, 99 AJIL 1 (2005), 76.

1548 *Legal Consequences of the Construction of a Wall in the Occupied Palestinian Territory*, Advisory Opinion, ICJ Reports 2004, 136 (194-195, para. 140).

by returning the land used for the construction of the wall.[1549] The ICJ further found that since Israel's construction of the wall violated *erga omnes* obligations (including the Palestinians' right to self-determination), all states had the obligation "not to recognize the illegal situation resulting from the construction of the wall in the Occupied Palestinian Territory" and "not to render aid or assistance in maintaining the situation created by such construction".[1550]

The Court also asked the UNGA and the UNSC to "consider what further action is required to bring to an end the illegal situation resulting from the construction of the wall and the associated régime, taking due account of the present Advisory Opinion".[1551]

The ICJ finally considered that "it has a duty to draw the attention of the General Assembly, to which the present Opinion is addressed, to the need for these efforts to be encouraged with a view to achieving as soon as possible, on the basis of international law, a negotiated solution to the outstanding problems and the establishment of a Palestinian State, existing side by side with Israel and its other neighbours, with peace and security for all in the region."[1552]

While shying away from recognizing specific obligations incumbent upon the UNGA, the Court emphasized that the opinion is addressed to the UNGA and that there was a need for the UNGA to intensify efforts to facilitate negotiations on a two-state-solution.

When assessing the effects of the *Wall* advisory opinion, one must bear in mind that the opinion is but one link in a long chain of efforts to resolve the Israeli-Palestinian conflict such as negotiations, UN resolutions and court proceedings. The conflict has already been the subject of numerous UN resolutions and Israel's illegal settlement activities in the occupied ter-

1549 Ibid. (197-198, paras. 150-152).

1550 Ibid. (200, para. 159); on the question whether violations of erga omnes obligations can create obligations for other states, see *I. Scobbie*, 16 EJIL 5 (2005), 941 (949–952).

1551 *Legal Consequences of the Construction of a Wall in the Occupied Palestinian Territory*, Advisory Opinion, ICJ Reports 2004, 136 (200, para. 160).

1552 Ibid. (201, para. 162).

ritory have been criticized by the UNSC[1553] and the UNGA[1554] on numerous occasions prior to the *Wall* opinion. Recent efforts to resolve the conflict by means of negotiation include the "Road Map for Peace" initiative which was launched in 2002 and overseen by the so-called "Quartet"[1555]. The *Wall* opinion has to be seen against this backdrop and its impact is therefore inevitably limited. What is more, the recurring escalations of violence between Israel and Palestinians in 2008, 2012, 2014, 2021, and since October 2023 as well as the continued settlement activities in the West Bank conducted by Israeli settlers and encouraged and legalized by the Israeli government already seem to indicate that the *Wall* opinion had a limited effect. However, it may still be worth examining whether the *Wall* opinion and the obligations of Israel and other states recognized therein find resonance in meaningful action taken thereafter.

aa) Narrow de-facto authority: Reactions by the UNGA and Israel

Let us therefore start by examining whether the two primary addressees of the opinion – Israel and the UNGA – took specific action in reaction to the findings of the Court. To do so we shall look at Israel's obligation to cease and dismantle the construction of the wall and make reparation for the damage caused by its construction.

(1) Reactions by Israel

The most apparent way in which the *Wall* advisory opinion failed to bring about practical change concerns the physical topography of the region. Instead of ceasing further and dismantling existing parts of the wall on Palestinian territory, Israel continued to build its "security fence" which in

1553 See for example UNSC resolutions 242 (1967) of 22 November 1967, 338 (1973) of 22 October 1973, 446 (1979) of 22 March 1979, 1322 (2000) of 7 October 2000, 1397 (2002) of 12 March 2002, 1402 (2002) of 30 March 2002, 1403 (2002) of 4 April 2002, 1405 (2002) of 19 April 2002, 1435 (2002) of 24 September 2002, 1515 (2003) of 19 November 2003, and 1544 (2004) of 19 May 2004.

1554 See for example UNGA resolutions ES-10/9 of 24 December 2001, ES-10/10 of 14 May 2002, ES-10/11 of 10 September 2003, ES-10/12 of 25 September 2003, ES-10/13 of 27 October 2003, and ES-10/14 of 12 December 2003.

1555 The "Quartet on the Middle East" is made up of the EU, the UN, Russia and the United States.

2020 already extended to 525 km in length with another 200 km being planned.[1556] It is worth noting that the Israeli Supreme Court rendered several decisions in which it obliged the Israeli government to alter the route of the Wall.[1557] However, Israel's Supreme Court did not base its decisions on the ICJ's findings that the Wall in its entirety violated international law. The Supreme Court held in the *Alfei Menashe* case:

> "[T]he ICJ's conclusion, based upon a factual basis different than the one before us, is not res judicata, and does not obligate the Supreme Court of Israel to rule that each and every segment of the fence violates international law."[1558]

While the Israeli Supreme Court recognized the ICJ advisory opinion, it expressly rejected any binding effect for the Supreme Court. Instead, the Supreme Court merely found that specific segments of the Wall did not strike an appropriate balance between Israel's reasonable security interests and the rights of the Palestinian inhabitants of the area.[1559]

(2) Reactions by the UNGA and other UN organs

Shortly after the ICJ rendered its *Wall* opinion, the UNGA passed resolution ES-10/15 in which it endorsed the *Wall* advisory opinion and demanded from Israel and all other UN Member States to comply with their legal obligations as recognized in the advisory opinion.[1560] The *Wall* advisory opinion was subsequently referred to *inter alia* in a resolution by the UNSC in which it condemned Israel's illegal settlement activities in the West Bank,[1561] in the application of Palestine for admission to full membership

1556 *A. Watts/R. Jorritsma*, Israeli Wall Advisory Opinion (last updated 2019), in: A. Peters/R. Wolfrum (eds.), The Max Planck Encyclopedia of Public International Law, 2008 (47).

1557 Beit Sourik Village Council v. The Government of Israel et. al., HCJ 2056/04, Supreme Court of Israel, 20 June 2004; Mara'abe et al. v Prime Minister of Israel et al. (Alfei Menashe), HCJ 7957/04, Supreme Court of Israel, 15 September 2005, para. 116.

1558 *Mara'abe et al. v Prime Minister of Israel et al. (Alfei Menashe)*, HCJ 7957/04, Supreme Court of Israel, 15 September 2005, paras. 76, 116.

1559 Ibid, para. 116.

1560 UNGA resolution ES-10/15 of 20 July 2004, UN doc. A/RES/ES-10/15, para. 2. On the discussion in the General Assembly in the aftermath of the advisory opinion, see *R. J. Araujo*, 22 BUILJ 2 (2004), 349 (387 et seq.)

1561 UNSC resolution 2334 (2016), UN doc. S/RES/2334(2016).

in the UN,[1562] the UNGA's decision to grant non-member observer status to Palestine in the UN,[1563] as well as numerous other UNGA resolutions like the annual resolution entitled "*Peaceful settlement of the question of Palestine*"[1564].

To facilitate the fulfillment of Israel's obligation to make reparations, the UNGA requested the UNSG to draft a proposal for a register of damage which collects and documents all damages caused to natural or legal persons by the construction of the Wall.[1565] In doing so, the UNGA expressly referred to paras. 152 and 153 of the Court's *Wall* opinion.[1566] The *United Nations Register of Damage Caused by the Construction of the Wall in the Occupied Palestinian Territory* (UNRoD) was established two years later as a subsidiary body of the UNGA under the administration of the UNSG.[1567] Its function is to "serve as a record, in documentary form, of the damage caused to all natural and legal persons concerned as a result of the construction of the wall by Israel, the occupying Power, in the Occupied Palestinian Territory, including in and around East Jerusalem."[1568]

UNRoD's function is strictly preparatory in nature. UNRoD is only competent to conduct fact-finding missions and collect claims, not, however, to

---

1562 Application of Palestine for admission to membership in the United Nations, submitted on 23 September 2011, Annex II, Letter dated 23 September 2011 from the President of Palestine to the Secretary-General.

1563 UNGA resolution 67/19 of 29 November 2012, UN doc. A/RES/67/19.

1564 UNGA resolutions 59/31 (2004), 60/39 (2005), 61/25 (2006), 62/83 (2007), 63/29 (2008), 64/19 (2009), 65/16 (2010), 66/17 (2011), 67/23 (2012), 68/15 (2013), 69/23 (2014), 70/15 (2015), 71/23 (2016), 72/14 (2017), 73/19 (2018), 74/11 (2019), 75/22 (2020), 76/10 (2021), 77/25 (2022).

1565 UNGA resolution ES-10/15 of 20 July 2004, UN doc. A/RES/ES-10/15, para. 4.

1566 The resolution reads in relevant part: "*Requests* the Secretary-General to establish a register of damage caused to all natural or legal persons concerned in connection with paragraphs 152 and 153 of the advisory opinion", UNGA resolution ES-10/15 of 20 July 2004, UN doc. A/RES/ES-10/15 para. 4.

1567 UNGA resolution ES-10/17 of 15 December 2006, UN doc. A/RES/ES-10/17, para. 3(a). The first UNRoD Board was appointed on 10 May 2007 and UNRod started registering claims in 2008. By 2020, UNRoD collected 71,547 damage registration application forms in the West Bank, of which 36,023 were included in the register, see Progress report of the Board of the United Nations Register of Damage Caused by the Construction of the Wall in the Occupied Palestinian Territory, A/ES-10/839, paras. 4–5. On the UNRoD, see *R. C. Williams*, 49 ILM 2 (2010), 620.

1568 UNGA resolution ES-10/17 of 15 December 2006, UN doc. A/RES/ES-10/17, para. 3(a).

decide about these claims.[1569] Any potential mechanism to decide about the claims collected by UNRoD has yet to be established.[1570]

The installation of the UNRoD was welcomed by many states particularly by the Member States of the Organization of the Islamic Conference and the Non-Aligned Movement. Israel, on the other hand, strongly criticized the establishment of UNRoD, claiming it would damage the legitimacy of the UN and undermine the prospects of resolving the dispute by bilateral negotiations.[1571] Israel's Permanent Representative to the UNGA Gillermann stated in no uncertain terms:

> "This Register, despite the perception of its being yet another achievement for the Palestinian observer, (...) cannot help the Palestinian people. Let me make it very clear: no Palestinian impacted by the security fence will be helped or assisted by this mechanism."[1572]

Despite its apparent disapproval, Israel has cooperated with UNRoD by providing relevant material and granting visas to UNRoD employees who collect claims in the West Bank.[1573] However, Israel rejected the idea that damages can be claimed through any kind of international mechanism. Instead, Gillerman referred to the possibility for Palestinians to register their damages with an Israeli registry, which, according to Gillerman, had already paid out more than $1.5 million to Palestinian complainants by 2006.[1574]

On the one hand, UNRoD and the *Wall* advisory opinion have hardly had any impact on the matter of compensation. They have failed to bring about any reparations being paid to legal or natural persons affected by the construction of the Wall. On the other hand, regarding a potential negotiated solution in the future, the preparatory work done by the UNRoD may become invaluable in facilitating a fact-based solution. In a sense,

---

1569 *A. Watts/R. Jorritsma*, Israeli Wall Advisory Opinion (last updated 2019), in: A. Peters/R. Wolfrum (eds.), The Max Planck Encyclopedia of Public International Law, 2008 (49).

1570 Ibid., para. 49.

1571 UNGA, Tenth Emergency Special Session, 30th meeting, 15 December 2006, Verbatim record.

1572 Ibid.

1573 Progress report of the Board of the United Nations Register of Damage Caused by the Construction of the Wall in the Occupied Palestinian Territory, A/ES-10/839, para. 17.

1574 UNGA, Tenth Emergency Special Session, 30th meeting, 15 December 2006, Verbatim record.

UNRoD's limited scope thus gives greater room for such a negotiated, political solution to the conflict. Against this background, it is worrying that the financial crisis of the UN also affects the work of UNRoD. In 2020, its Board expressed the concern that UNRoD's claim collection program may need to be suspended if no further funding can be secured.[1575]

The idea of a register of damage was subsequently taken up by another international organizations. In 2023, the Council of Europe established the Register of Damage Caused by the Aggression of the Russian Federation against Ukraine.[1576]

bb) Intermediate authority: Reactions by other states and organizations

Let us now turn to the reactions of other states and organizations, particularly in light of the obligations the Court recognized as being incumbent upon all UN Member States as a consequence of Israel's internationally wrongful act.[1577]

(1) Obligations of third states not to recognize and support the Wall regime

Regarding third states, the ICJ held in its *Wall* opinion that

> "all States are under an obligation not to recognize the illegal situation resulting from the construction of the wall in the Occupied Palestinian

---

1575 Progress report of the Board of the United Nations Register of Damage Caused by the Construction of the Wall in the Occupied Palestinian Territory, A/ES-10/839, para. 16.

1576 According to Art. 2(1) of the Register's Statute, the "Register shall receive and process information on claims of damage and evidence; categorise, classify and organise such claims, assess and determine the eligibility of claims for inclusion in the Register and record the eligible claims for the purposes of their future examination and adjudication. The Register shall not have any adjudication functions with respect to such claims, including determination of responsibility and allocation of any payments or compensation.", Appendix to resolution CM/Res(2023)3 establishing the Enlarged Partial Agreement on the Register of Damage Caused by the Aggression of the Russian Federation against Ukraine, adopted by the Committee of Ministers on 12 May 2023 at the 1466th meeting of the Ministers' Deputies.

1577 For more a detailed discussion of the obligations of third states regarding Israeli settlements in the West Bank, see *J. Crawford*, Opinion: Third Party Obligations with respect to Israeli Settlements in the Occupied Palestinian Territories, 2012.

Territory, including in and around East Jerusalem. They are also under an obligation not to render aid or assistance in maintaining the situation created by such construction. It is also for all States, while respecting the United Nations Charter and international law, to see to it that any impediment, resulting from the construction of the wall, to the exercise by the Palestinian people of its right to self-determination is brought to an end. In addition, all the States parties to the Geneva Convention relative to the Protection of Civilian Persons in Time of War of 12 August 1949 are under an obligation, while respecting the United Nations Charter and international law, to ensure compliance by Israel with international humanitarian law as embodied in that Convention."[1578]

The Court referred to three obligations all states have as a consequence of Israel's breach of international law: the obligation of non-recognition, the obligation of non-support, and the obligation to ensure compliance by Israel with international humanitarian law. The ICJ derived these obligations from the *erga omnes* nature of the obligations breached by Israel, namely the right of the Palestinian people to self-determination and certain obligations under international humanitarian law.[1579] *Erga omnes* obligations have been described by the Court in its *Barcelona Tractions* judgment as a "concern of all States".[1580] Because of their importance "all States can be held to have a legal interest in their protection".[1581]

Since *erga omnes* obligations are obligations owed to the international community as a whole, any state can invoke the international responsibility of the state that violates *erga omnes* obligations, regardless of any harm directly suffered. This right of non-injured states is also enshrined in Article 48 para. 1 lit. b of the ILC Articles on State Responsibility:

"Any State other than an injured State is entitled to invoke the responsibility of another State in accordance with paragraph 2 if: (...) (b) the obligation breached is owed to the international community as a whole."

1578 *Legal Consequences of the Construction of a Wall in the Occupied Palestinian Territory*, Advisory Opinion, ICJ Reports 2004, 136 (200, para. 159); on the question whether violations of erga omnes obligations can create obligations for other states, see *I. Scobbie*, 16 EJIL 5 (2005), 941 (949–952).

1579 *Legal Consequences of the Construction of a Wall in the Occupied Palestinian Territory*, Advisory Opinion, ICJ Reports 2004, 136 (199, para. 155).

1580 *Barcelona Traction, Light and Power Company, Limited*, Second Phase, Judgment, ICJ Reports 1970, 3 (32, para. 33).

1581 Ibid.

However, the ICJ deduced something further from the *erga omnes* nature of the obligations breached by Israel. Third states not only have the *right* (or standing) to invoke the international responsibility of Israel, they also have the *obligation* not to recognize or support the illegal situation created by Israel and to ensure Israel's compliance with international humanitarian law.[1582] To support this view, the Court cited the 1970 Friendly Relations Declaration in which the UNGA stated:

> "Every State has the duty to promote, through joint and separate action, realization of the principle of equal rights and self-determination of peoples, in accordance with the provisions of the Charter, and to render assistance to the United Nations in carrying out the responsibilities entrusted to it by the Charter regarding the implementation of the principle (...)."[1583]

Regarding the *erga omnes* nature of the humanitarian obligations in question, the ICJ referred to the *Nuclear Weapons (UNGA)* opinion in which it held that "a great many rules of humanitarian law applicable in armed conflict are so fundamental to the respect of the human person and "elementary considerations of humanity" (...), that the Hague and Geneva Conventions have enjoyed a broad accession. Further these fundamental rules are to be observed by all States whether or not they have ratified the conventions that contain them, because they constitute intransgressible principles of international customary law."[1584]

The dictum from the *Nuclear Weapons (UNGA)* advisory opinion concerns the *ius cogens* nature of certain humanitarian law obligations. The ICJ thus equates the *ius cogens* nature of an obligation with its *erga omnes* nature.

The Court's finding that states have an obligation to ensure Israel's compliance with international humanitarian law is controversial. *Crawford* criticized the Court's dictum, stating:

1582 See however, *Orakhelashvili*: "It is not the erga omnes nature of an obligation that confers an imperative character on that rule or itself determines any of the consequences of its breaches.", *A. Orakhelashvili*, 11 Journal of Conflict and Security Law 1 (2006), 119 (131).

1583 UNGA resolution 2625 (XXV) of 24 October 1970, UN doc. A/RES/2625(XXV) (Friendly Relations Declaration).

1584 *Legality of the Threat or Use of Nuclear Weapons*, Advisory Opinion, ICJ Reports 1996, 226 (257, para. 79).

> "While Article 49(6) of the Fourth Geneva Convention is arguably an obligation *erga omnes*, owed to the community of States as a whole, and as such any State is *entitled* to invoke the responsibility of Israel for its breach, there is no *obligation* on States to do so stemming either from its status as *erga omnes* or otherwise. Law does not compel those concerned to seek a remedy, even if they are entitled to do so. Article 16 of the ILC Articles on State Responsibility makes it clear that a State only breaches international law when it directly aids or assists the commission of an internationally wrongful act. By inference there is no responsibility for simple neglect."[1585]

In contrast, the obligation of non-recognition[1586] and the obligation of non-support[1587] are widely recognized. The obligation of non-recognition finds its legal basis in the principle of *ex injuria ius non oritur.*[1588] As *Crawford* put it:

> "As territory cannot be acquired by the unlawful use of force nor where that purported territorial acquisition violates the right to self-determination, States are obliged to not give legal credence - recognition of authority over the territory - to the unlawful acquisition."[1589]

Both obligations also find expression in the ILC Articles on State Responsibility. The obligation of non-recognition is codified in Article 41 para. 2 of the ILC Articles which stipulates:

> "No State shall recognize as lawful a situation created by a serious breach within the meaning of article 40, nor render aid or assistance in maintaining that situation."

1585 *J. Crawford*, Opinion: Third Party Obligations with respect to Israeli Settlements in the Occupied Palestinian Territories, 2012, paras. 41–42.

1586 See UNGA resolution 2625 (XXV) of 24 October 1970, UN doc. A/RES/2625(XXV) (Friendly Relations Declaration); Human Rights Committee, ICCPR General Comment No. 12: The right to self-determination of peoples (Art. 1), 13 March 1984, paras 5–6. See also *M. Dawidowicz*, The Obligation of Non-Recognition of an Unlawful Situation, in: J. Crawford/A. Pellet/S. Olleson/K. Parlett (eds.), The law of international responsibility, 2010, 677.

1587 See *N. H. Jørgensen*, The Obligation of Non-Assistance of the Responsible State, in: J. Crawford/A. Pellet/S. Olleson/K. Parlett (eds.), The law of international responsibility, 2010, 687.

1588 *J. Crawford*, Opinion: Third Party Obligations with respect to Israeli Settlements in the Occupied Palestinian Territories, 2012, para. 46.

1589 Ibid., para. 46.

The ICJ has clarified the content of the obligation of non-recognition in its *Namibia* advisory opinion. Accordingly, states must refrain from engaging in treaty relations, invoking existing bilateral treaties, sending diplomatic missions, or establishing economic relations with an unrecognized regime regarding illegally acquired territory, as these actions may strengthen the regime's authority over the territory.[1590] However, third states are not completely barred from interacting with an occupied territory. As the ICJ held in the *Namibia* case:

> "In general, the non-recognition of South Africa's administration of the Territory should not result in depriving the people of Namibia of any advantages derived from international co-operation. In particular, while official acts performed by the Government of South Africa on behalf of or concerning Namibia after the termination of the Mandate are illegal and invalid, this invalidity cannot be extended to those acts, such as, for instance, the registration of births, deaths and marriages, the effects of which can be ignored only to the detriment of the inhabitants of the Territory."[1591]

Thus, certain economic or other dealings which are beneficial to the local population and which do not entrench the illegal authority over the territory are permitted.[1592]

The non-support obligation is likewise codified in Article 16 of the ILC Articles on State Responsibility:

> "A State which aids or assists another State in the commission of an internationally wrongful act by the latter is internationally responsible for doing so if:
> (a) That State does so with knowledge of the circumstances of the internationally wrongful act; and
> (b) The act would be internationally wrongful if committed by that State."

1590 *Legal Consequences for States of the Continued Presence of South Africa in Namibia (South West Africa) notwithstanding Security Council Resolution 276 (1970)*, Advisory Opinion, Dissenting Opinion Gros, ICJ Reports 1971, 16 (55, para. 120-122); *J. Crawford*, Opinion: Third Party Obligations with respect to Israeli Settlements in the Occupied Palestinian Territories, 2012, para. 48.

1591 *Legal Consequences for States of the Continued Presence of South Africa in Namibia (South West Africa) notwithstanding Security Council Resolution 276 (1970)*, Advisory Opinion, Dissenting Opinion Gros, ICJ Reports 1971, 16 (56, para. 125).

1592 *J. Crawford*, Opinion: Third Party Obligations with respect to Israeli Settlements in the Occupied Palestinian Territories, 2012, paras. 49–51.

As the wording indicates, the obligation of non-support has strict requirements. Third states only violate their obligation of non-support if they have actual knowledge of the circumstances and the assistance contributes significantly to the wrongful act.[1593]

Regarding violations of peremptory norms of international law, Article 41 para. 2 of the ILC Articles stipulates a specific obligation not to recognize as lawful a situation created by a serious breach against such a norm, nor render aid or assistance in maintaining that situation.

The ICJ's statements in its *Wall* advisory opinion on the obligations of third states have influenced subsequent action by the UNGA. Taking the annual "Peaceful settlement of the question of Palestine" resolutions as an example: While the UNGA had already stated in previous resolutions that Israel's occupation of the West Bank and its settlement activities therein were illegal,[1594] after the Court rendered its *Wall* opinion, the UNGA also called "upon all States Members of the United Nations to comply with their legal obligations as mentioned in the advisory opinion".[1595] The UNGA later formulated more specific obligations of third states *vis-à-vis* the Israel-Palestine conflict.[1596]

(2) Reactions by EU institutions

The non-recognition and non-support obligations recognized by the ICJ are particularly pertinent to the field of economic and commercial cooperation. By entering into or continuing certain commercial relations, third states may breach the obligations of non-recognition and non-support and

1593 Ibid., para. 77 See also ILC, Articles on Responsibility of States for Internationally Wrongful Acts, with commentaries, 2001, Art. 16(4–5).

1594 See for example UNGA resolution 58/21 of 3 December 2003, UN doc. A/RES/58/21.

1595 UNGA resolution 59/31 of 1 December 2004, UN doc. A/RES/59/31, para. 7.

1596 "*Calls* upon all States, consistent with their obligations under the Charter of the United Nations and relevant Security Council resolutions, inter alia: (a) Not to recognize any changes to the pre-1967 borders, including with regard to Jerusalem, other than those agreed by the parties through negotiations; (b) To distinguish, in their relevant dealings, between the territory of the State of Israel and the territories occupied since 1967; (c) Not to render aid or assistance to illegal settlement activities, including not to provide Israel with any assistance to be used specifically in connection with settlements in the occupied territories, in line with Security Council resolution 465 (1980) of 1 March 1980;", see UNGA resolution 73/19 of 30 Nov 2018, UN doc. A/RES/73/19, para. 14.

thereby commit an internationally wrongful act themselves.[1597] Such a situation may arise when a state enters into treaty relations with Israel in which it explicitly or implicitly recognizes Israel's sovereignty over the occupied territories. This matter arose in two cases before the Court of Justice of the European Union (CJEU): The *Brita* case[1598] and the *Organisation juive européenne* case[1599].

(a) The Brita case

The *Brita* case concerned the application of preferential treatment to goods under the trade agreements between the EU and Israel (EC-Israel Association Agreement[1600]) and the EU and Palestine (EC-PLO Association Agreement[1601]). The German company Brita imported drink-makers for sparkling water from a supplier operating in the West Bank. Brita contacted German customs authorities and applied for preferential treatment for the imported goods under the EC-Israel Association Agreement. Brita claimed the products originated in Israel and are thus eligible for preferential treatment under the EC-Israel Association Agreement. Israeli customs authorities informed German customs authorities that the goods in question originated in an area under Israeli Customs responsibility and, as such, Brita argued that the goods qualified for preferential treatment under the EC-Israel Association Agreement. However, the German customs authorities denied Brita's application on the ground that it could not conclusively establish whether the products fell within the scope of the EC-Israel Association Agreement. Brita challenged this decision before a German fiscal court which referred the question to the CJEU by means of the preliminary ruling procedure. The CJEU confirmed that the customs authorities of an import-

1597 *A. Watts/R. Jorritsma*, Israeli Wall Advisory Opinion (last updated 2019), in: A. Peters/R. Wolfrum (eds.), The Max Planck Encyclopedia of Public International Law, 2008 (51).

1598 Case C-386/08, judgment of 25 February 2010, ECLI:EU:C:2010:91 – *Brita*.

1599 Case C-363/18, judgment of 12 November 2019, ECLI:EU:C:2019:954 – *Organisation juive européenne*.

1600 Euro-Mediterranean Agreement establishing an association between the European Communities and their Member States, of the one part, and the State of Israel, of the other part (Euro-Mediterranean Agreement), OJ L 147, 21.6.2000, 3.

1601 Euro-Mediterranean Interim Association Agreement on trade and cooperation between the European Community, of the one part, and the Palestine Liberation Organization (PLO) for the benefit of the Palestinian Authority of the West Bank and the Gaza Strip, of the other part, OJ L 187 16.7.1997, 3.

ing Member State may refuse to grant preferential treatment provided for under the EC-Israel-Association Agreement if the goods originate in the West Bank.[1602] The CJEU found that the EC-Israel Association Agreement cannot grant Israeli customs authority jurisdiction over products originating in the West Bank:

> "Each of those two association agreements has its own territorial scope. Under Article 83 thereof, the EC-Israel Association Agreement applies to the 'territory of the State of Israel'. Under Article 73 thereof, the EC-PLO Association Agreement applies to the 'territories of the West Bank and the Gaza Strip'. (...) Accordingly, to interpret Article 83 of the EC-Israel Association Agreement as meaning that the Israeli customs authorities enjoy competence in respect of products originating in the West Bank would be tantamount to imposing on the Palestinian customs authorities an obligation to refrain from exercising the competence conferred upon them by virtue of the abovementioned provisions of the EC-PLO Protocol. Such an interpretation, the effect of which would be to create an obligation for a third party without its consent, would thus be contrary to the principle of general international law, '*pacta tertiis nec nocent nec prosunt*', as consolidated in Article 34 of the Vienna Convention."[1603]

While the CJEU thus decided in line with the obligation of third states not to recognize and support Israel's illegal occupation of Palestinian territoriy recognized by the ICJ, the CJEU did not base its decision on this obligation or on the ICJ's advisory opinion. Instead, the CJEU based its decision on the principle of *pacta tertiis nec nocent nec prosunt.*[1604] One reason for this may be that the focus of the Court's *Wall* opinion was not on the illegal Israeli settlements within Palestinian territories,[1605] but on the construction

---

1602 Case C-386/08, judgment of 25 February 2010, ECLI:EU:C:2010:91 – *Brita*, para. 58.

1603 Ibid., paras. 47, 52.

1604 This was highlighted by *A. Watts/R. Jorritsma*, Israeli Wall Advisory Opinion (last updated 2019), in: A. Peters/R. Wolfrum (eds.), The Max Planck Encyclopedia of Public International Law, 2008 (51).

1605 See however para. 120 of the opinion in which the Court held: "As regards these settlements, the Court notes that Article 49, paragraph 6, of the Fourth Geneva Convention provides: 'The Occupying Power shall not deport or transfer parts of its own civilian population into the territory it occupies.' That provision prohibits not only deportations or forced transfers of population such as those carried out during the Second World War, but also any measures taken by an occupying Power in order to organize or encourage transfers of parts of its own population into the occupied territory. In this respect, the information provided to the Court shows of the Wall and the legal regime surrounding that construction.[1606] Regardless of the reasons, the CJEU decided not to rely on the *Wall* opinion in the *Brita* case.

(b) The Organisation juive européenne case

In the *Organisation juive européenne* case, the CJEU held that under EU law, products originating in a territory occupied by Israel must bear not only the indication of that territory but also – where applicable – the indication that the product originates from an Israeli settlement within the occupied territory.[1607] The CJEU based its decision on Article 9 para. 1 lit. i and Article 26 para. 2 lit. a of the Regulation (EU) No 1169/2011 on the provision of food information to consumers.[1608] According to the two provisions, food products must contain an indication of the country or place of origin where an omission of this may mislead the costumer about the true country or place of origin. Based on this, the CJEU found the indication of Israel as the country of origin for products originating in the occupied territories misleading. The CJEU found:

> "displaying, on foodstuffs (...) the indication that the State of Israel is their 'country of origin', when those foodstuffs actually originate in one of the [occupied] territories (...), would be liable to deceive consumers. In addition, in order to prevent consumers being misled as to the fact that the State of Israel is present in those territories as an occupying

---

that, since 1977, Israel has conducted a policy and developed practices involving the establishment of Settlements in the Occupied Palestinian Territory, contrary to the terms of Article 49, paragraph 6, just cited...The Court concludes that the Israeli settlements in the Occupied Palestinian Territory (including East Jerusalem) have been established in breach of international law.", see *Legal Consequences of the Construction of a Wall in the Occupied Palestinian Territory*, Advisory Opinion, ICJ Reports 2004, 136 (183, para. 120).

1606 Pointing this out, *J. Crawford*, Opinion: Third Party Obligations with respect to Israeli Settlements in the Occupied Palestinian Territories, 2012, para. 16.

1607 Case C-363/18, judgment of 12 November 2019, ECLI:EU:C:2019:954 – *Organisation juive européenne*, para. 58.

1608 Regulation (EU) No 1169/2011 of the European Parliament and of the Council of 25 October 2011 on the provision of food information to consumers, OJ L 304, 22/11/2011, p. 18.

> power and not as a sovereign entity (...), it appears necessary to inform them that those foodstuffs do not originate in that State."[1609]

An informed consumer decision further required that relevant food products must bear an indication that they originate from an Israeli settlement. The Court found that the omission of the words "Israeli settlement" on the product would mislead consumers into believing that the foodstuffs came from a Palestinian (West Bank) or Syrian (Golan Heights) producer, rather than an Israeli producer.[1610]

Once again, the CJEU did not base its decision on the non-recognition and non-support obligation recognized by the ICJ in the *Wall* opinion, but on EU law. However, the CJEU referred to the ICJ's *Wall* advisory opinion on several occasions in its decision to support the point that the Palestinian people have the right to self-determination (para. 35), to demonstrate the illegality of the Israeli settlements in the West Bank (para. 48) and to emphasize the fundamental importance of the rules of international humanitarian law (para. 56). The CJEU found that the illegality of the settlements as well as the relevance of the violated rules of international law are important factors impacting consumer choices.[1611] The ICJ's *Wall* opinion thus constituted an important foundation for the CJEU's decision in the *Organisation juive européenne* case.

cc) Conclusions on the Wall advisory opinion

The unequivocal rejection by Israel indicates that the ICJ's *Wall* advisory opinion did not reach the level of narrow authority. Israel neither acknowledged any of its legal obligations recognized in the *Wall* opinion, nor took meaningful action towards complying with them. In fact, in recent years Israel has extended the wall as well as its settlement activities in the West Bank. The two CJEU cases referenced above also demonstrate a considerable hesitancy by other courts to rely on the ICJ's advisory opinion as an authoritative statement of the law. The CJEU decided to evade questions of international law which the ICJ answered in its advisory opinion and decided its cases entirely based on EU law.

1609 Case C-363/18, judgment of 12 November 2019, ECLI:EU:C:2019:954 – *Organisation juive européenne*, paras. 35–36.

1610 Ibid., paras. 49–51.

1611 Ibid., para. 55.

c) De-facto authority of the Chagos advisory opinion

In the *Chagos* advisory opinion[1612], the ICJ found that the United Kingdom's continued administration of the Chagos Archipelago rendered the decolonization process of Mauritius incomplete and constituted an internationally wrongful act. The Court further found that the United Kingdom was under an obligation to end its administration of the Chagos Archipelago as soon as possible, and that all UN Member States were under an obligation to co-operate with the UN to complete the decolonization of Mauritius.

aa) Narrow authority: Reactions by the UK, Mauritius and the UN

Shortly after the ICJ rendered its *Chagos* advisory opinion, the United Kingdom issued a statement in which it rejected the Court's findings and reaffirmed its claim to sovereignty over the Chagos Archipelago:

> "[W]e have no doubt about our sovereignty over the Chagos Archipelago, which has been under continuous British sovereignty since 1814. Mauritius has never held sovereignty over the Archipelago and we do not recognise its claim. We have, however, made a long-standing commitment since 1965 to cede sovereignty of the territory to Mauritius when it is no longer required for defence purposes. We stand by that commitment."[1613]

In contrast, the UNGA endorsed the Court's opinion on 22 May 2019 by passing resolution 73/295 in which it demanded from the United Kingdom to "withdraw its colonial administration from the Chagos Archipelago unconditionally within (...) six months".[1614]

The UNGA emphasized that the Chagos Archipelago formed an integral part of Mauritius[1615] and that the United Kingdom's ongoing administration

---

1612 *Legal Consequences of the Separation of the Chagos Archipelago from Mauritius in 1965*, Advisory Opinion, ICJ Reports 2019, 95.

1613 United Kingdom Minister of State for Europe and the Americas, Statement made on 30 April 2019, https://questions-statements.parliament.uk/written-statements/detail/2019-04-30/HCWS1528.

1614 UNGA resolution 73/295 of 22 May 2019, UN doc. A/RES/73/295, paras. 1, 3.

1615 Ibid., para. 6.

constituted an internationally wrongful act.[1616] The UNGA also urged the United Kingdom to cooperate with Mauritius in facilitating the resettlement of Mauritian nationals to the Chagos Archipelago.[1617] The resolution was passed almost unanimously with only six states voting against it. These six states included the United Kingdom, the Maldives,[1618] and the United States, the latter of which operates a military base on Diego Garcia, the largest island in the Chagos Archipelago.[1619]

The United Kingdom ignored the six-month deadline set by the UNGA and took no steps to hand over the Chagos Archipelago to Mauritius. Instead, it repeated its previous statements on the matter.[1620] However, three years later, in October of 2022, UK Foreign Secretary *Cleverly* announced that the UK had agreed to negotiate with Mauritius over the handover of the Chagos Archipelago.[1621] This shift followed early discussions between then UK Prime Minister *Truss* and Mauritian representatives in New York.[1622] On 13 June 2023, *Cleverly* was asked by Parliament about the progress of these negotiations and whether "negotiations are going on in the spirit of the International Court of Justice advisory opinion and the decision of the UN General Assembly in 2019 on the reunification of the

1616 Ibid., para. 2.

1617 Ibid., para. 4

1618 The Maldives opposed the resolution because it feared that it could negatively affect its interests in the region in particular regarding its submissions to the Commission on the Limits of the Continental Shelf, see the statement of the representative of the Maldives during the 83rd plenary meeting, A/73/PV.83, Official records.

1619 See the statement of the representative of the United States during the 83rd plenary meeting, A/73/PV.83, Official records.

1620 Alan Duncan, British Indian Ocean Territory, Statement made on 30 April 2019, HCWS1528, https://questions-statements.parliament.uk/written-statements/detail/2019-04-30/hcws1528; Christopher Pincher, British Indian Ocean Territory, Written Statement made on 5 November 2019, HCWS 90, https://questions-statements.parliament.uk/written-statements/detail/2019-11-05/hcws90. See also the statement of the representative of Mauritius during the 77th meeting of the UNGA Fourth Committee, 15 October 2019, GA/SPD/696.

1621 The Guardian, UK agrees to negotiate with Mauritius over handover of Chagos Islands, 11.04.2022, https://www.theguardian.com/world/2022/nov/03/uk-agrees-to-negotiate-with-mauritius-over-handover-of-chagos-islands.

1622 Negotiations between the United Kingdom and Mauritius have commenced amidst criticism that Chagos Islanders have been excluded from the negotiations, see The Guardian, Negotiations on Chagos Islands' sovereignty face legal challenge, 09.01.2023, https://www.theguardian.com/world/2023/jan/09/negotiations-chagos-islands-sovereignty-legal-challenge-talks-uk-mauritius.

Chagos islands with Mauritius."[1623] *Cleverly* responded that four rounds of negotiations had taken place but no concrete settlement was in sight. However, he lowered expectations of a swift settlement by emphasizing that the United Kingdom's "primary objective is to ensure the continued effective operation of our defence facility on Diego Garcia".[1624] In early October 2024, it became public that a political agreement has been reached between the UK and Mauritius concerning the Chagos Archipelago.[1625] Accordingly, the UK agreed to return the territorial sovereignty over the Chagos Archipelago to Mauritius. However, the UK is to retain sovereignty over the archipelago's largest island, Diego Garcia, for a period of 99 years "to ensure the continued operation of the base well into the next century".[1626] On 22 May 2025, the United Kingdom published the finalized agreement signed by the Prime Ministers of the UK and Mauritius.[1627] According to the treaty, the United Kingdom recognizes Mauritius's sovereignty over the Chagos Archipelago in its entirety, including Diego Garcia (Article 1) and Mauritius authorizes the United Kingdom to "exercise the rights and authorities of Mauritius with respect to Diego Garcia" (Article 2 para. 1). During the duration of the agreement, Mauritius receives an annual payment from the United Kingdom (Article 11 para. 1), which amounts to £3.4bn over the 99-year span of the treaty. Notably, the preamble of the agreement references the ICJ's Chagos advisory opinion:

> "Having regard to the decisions of international courts and tribunals, including the International Court of Justice, relating to the Chagos Archipelago;"

1623 United Kingdom House of Commons, Chagos Islands: Resettlement and Sovereignty Volume 734: debated on Tuesday 13 June 2023, https://hansard.parliament.uk/commons/2023-06-13/debates/554A9F25-BD9B-4B9B-860D-89E550C6D601/ChagosIslandsResettlementAndSovereignty.

1624 Ibid.

1625 The Guardian, Britain to return Chagos Islands to Mauritius ending years of dispute, 03.10.2024, https://www.theguardian.com/world/2024/oct/03/britain-to-return-chagos-islands-to-mauritius-ending-years-of-dispute.

1626 Joint statement between the governments of the Republic of Mauritius and the United Kingdom of Great Britain and Northern Ireland concerning the Chagos Archipelago, including Diego Garcia, 3 October 2024, https://www.gov.uk/government/news/joint-statement-between-uk-and-mauritius-3-october-2024.

1627 Agreement between the Government of the United Kingdom of Great Britain and Northern Ireland and the Government of the Republic of Mauritius concerning the Chagos Archipelago including Diego Garcia, London and Port Louis, 22 May 2025, https://assets.publishing.service.gov.uk/media/682f25afc054883884bff42a/CS_Mauritius_1.2025_Agreement_Chagos_Diego_Garcia.pdf.

The *Chagos* advisory opinion thus helped initiate negotiations which culminated in an agreement on the handing over of control over the Chagos Archipelago.

The Chagos advisory opinion was likely not the only reason for the United Kingdom to act. Another contributing factor might have been the 2021 judgment of the ITLOS Special Chamber in the *Dispute concerning delimitation of the maritime boundary between Mauritius and Maldives in the Indian Ocean (Mauritius v. Maldives)* case.[1628] In its judgment on preliminary objections, the Special Chamber dealt a major blow to the United Kingdom's claim of sovereignty over the Chagos Archipelago. The Special Chamber decided that the *Chagos* advisory opinion and the subsequent UNGA resolutions resolved the territorial dispute between the United Kingdom and Mauritius over the Chagos Archipelago and as such the United Kingdom was not an indispensable party to the proceedings between Mauritius and the Maldives.[1629] The use of the *Chagos* opinion as a quasi-precedent by Special Chamber provides an interesting example of how ICJ advisory opinions can affect pending disputes. The Special Chamber's judgment has been dubbed a "landmark judgment",[1630] with some commentators even going so far as to predict that the decision marks "the beginning of a new era where international courts and tribunals recognise ICJ advisory opinions as having the (normative) authority to resolve a dispute".[1631]

Let us therefore turn to the 2021 ruling of the ITLOS Special Chamber on preliminary objections in the case between Mauritius and the Maldives.

bb) Intermediate authority: The Maritime Delimitation case between Mauritius and the Maldives case

In 2001, Mauritius invited the Maldives to enter into negotiations about the delimitation of their respective continental shelfs around the Chagos

1628 *Dispute concerning delimitation of the maritime boundary between Mauritius and Maldives in the Indian Ocean (Mauritius v. Maldives)*, Preliminary Objections, Judgment, ITLOS Reports 2021, 17; for an analysis of the Special Chamber's decision, see *F. S. Eichberger*, 22 Melbourne Journal of International Law 2 (2021), 1.

1629 *Dispute concerning delimitation of the maritime boundary between Mauritius and Maldives in the Indian Ocean (Mauritius v. Maldives)*, Written Preliminary Objections of the Republic of Maldives, ITLOS Reports 2021 (114).

1630 *F. S. Eichberger*, 22 Melbourne Journal of International Law 2 (2021), 1 (11).

1631 *N. Lanzoni*, 2 Ital. Rev. Int. Comp. Law 2 (2022), 296 (299).

Archipelago.[1632] The Maldives rejected this offer claiming that Mauritius did not exercise jurisdiction over the archipelago:

> "As jurisdiction over the Chagos Archipelago is not exercised by the Government of Mauritius, the Government of Maldives feels that it would be inappropriate to initiate any discussions between the Government of Maldives and the Government of Mauritius regarding the delimitation of the boundary between the Maldives and the Chagos Archipelago."[1633]

Ten years later, the Maldives made submissions to the Commission on the Limits of the Continental Shelf (CLCS) on its extended continental shelf. Mauritius regarded these submissions as affecting its claims in the region. Following these submissions, a first meeting between the Maldives and Mauritius took place in October of 2010 for negotiations on the delimitation of their respective exclusive economic zones (EEZ). However, the Maldives declined to negotiate any further on a maritime boundary as it was concerned that it could be drawn into a dispute between Mauritius and the United Kingdom over the territorial sovereignty over the Chagos Archipelago. In September of 2019, after negotiations between Mauritius and the Maldives reached an impasse and following consultations with the President of the ITLOS, the two states submitted their dispute to a special chamber of the ITLOS.[1634] The Special Chamber was asked to delimit the maritime boundary between Mauritius and the Maldives in the Indian Ocean, in the EEZ, and 'the continental shelf, and to decide whether the Maldives had taken actions contrary to its obligation not to jeopardize the reaching of a final agreement on the question of delimitation.[1635]

1632 *Dispute concerning delimitation of the maritime boundary between Mauritius and Maldives in the Indian Ocean (Mauritius v. Maldives)*, Preliminary Objections, Judgment, ITLOS Reports 2021, 17 (37, para. 62).

1633 Ibid. (37-38, para. 62).

1634 Ibid. (23, para. 2); on the use of ad hoc chambers under the ITLOS Statute, see *R. Wolfrum*, Ad Hoc Chambers, in: J. M. van Dyke/S. P. Broder/S. Yi/C. Paek (eds.), Governing ocean resources, 2013, 275; for a commentary on the case, see *F. S. Eichberger*, 22 Melbourne Journal of International Law 2 (2021), 1; *T. Burri/J. Trinidad*, 60 Int. leg. mater. 6 (2021), 969; *C. D. Gaver*, 115 Am. j. int. law 3 (2021), 519.

1635 *Dispute concerning delimitation of the maritime boundary between Mauritius and Maldives in the Indian Ocean (Mauritius v. Maldives)*, Preliminary Objections, Judgment, ITLOS Reports 2021, 17 (51-52, para. 112).

(1) ITLOS Special Chamber judgment

Mauritius' claim rested on the premise that the Chagos Archipelago rightfully belonged to Mauritius, making Mauritius the opposite coastal state of the Maldives in accordance with Articles 74 and 83 UNCLOS. The validity of this premise was contested between the Maldives and Mauritius: While the Maldives claimed that the territorial sovereignty over the Chagos Archipelago remained in dispute between Mauritius and the United Kingdom, Mauritius argued that the *Chagos* advisory opinion had resolved this dispute in Mauritius' favor by finding that the Chagos Archipelago was an integral part of Mauritius.[1636]

The question of territorial sovereignty over the Chagos Archipelago was at the heart of – and in fact the reason for – the proceedings before the Special Chamber. As Judge ad hoc *Oxman* noted:

> "It is accordingly apparent (...) that this case is not before the Special Chamber because of a difference between the Parties regarding how overlapping entitlements should be delimited. It is here because one of the Parties has declined to proceed with delimitation negotiations. The reasons for doing so help to define the nature and scope of the dispute between the Parties."[1637]

The Maldives raised five preliminary objections to the jurisdiction of the Special Chamber and the admissibility of Mauritius' claims, the first two of which concerned the question of territorial sovereignty over the Chagos Archipelago.[1638] In its first preliminary objection, the Maldives argued that "the United Kingdom is an indispensable third party to the present proceedings, and, as the United Kingdom is not a party to these proceedings, the Special Chamber does not have jurisdiction over the alleged dispute".[1639]

In its second preliminary objection, the Maldives argued that "the Special Chamber has no jurisdiction to determine the disputed issue of

1636 Ibid. (36, para. 114).

1637 *Dispute concerning delimitation of the maritime boundary between Mauritius and Maldives in the Indian Ocean (Mauritius v. Maldives)*, Preliminary Objections, Separate and Dissenting Opinion Oxman, ITLOS Reports 2021 (para. 24).

1638 *Dispute concerning delimitation of the maritime boundary between Mauritius and Maldives in the Indian Ocean (Mauritius v. Maldives)*, Preliminary Objections, Judgment, ITLOS Reports 2021, 17 (43, para. 79).

1639 Ibid. (43, para. 79).

sovereignty over the Chagos Archipelago, which it would necessarily have to do if it were to determine Mauritius' claims".[1640]

This objection is premised on the principle that maritime rights are derived from the coastal state's sovereignty over the land ("the land dominates the sea"[1641]). Accordingly, sovereignty over the respective islands needs to be determined prior to and independently from maritime delimitation.

The Special Chamber decided to respond to the Maldives' first two preliminary objections jointly, finding that both objections center on the question if the territorial dispute between Mauritius and the United Kingdom had been resolved:

> "[T]he Parties' disagreement boils down to the question as to whether a sovereignty dispute between Mauritius and the United Kingdom over the Chagos Archipelago still exists or has been resolved. Accordingly, if a sovereignty dispute over the Chagos Archipelago exists, the United Kingdom may be regarded as an indispensable party and the Monetary Gold principle would prevent the Special Chamber from exercising its jurisdiction. On the other hand, if such sovereignty dispute has been resolved in favour of Mauritius, the United Kingdom may not be regarded as an indispensable party and the Monetary Gold principle would not apply."[1642]

The Special Chamber first rejected the Maldives' claim that the existence of a dispute between Mauritius and the United Kingdom was determined by the award rendered in the *Chagos Marine Protected Area Arbitration.*[1643] Finding the award had no *res judicata* effect for the matter at hand, the Special Chamber proceeded to examine the content and legal effects of the ICJ's *Chagos* advisory opinion.[1644]

1640 Ibid.

1641 *Territorial and Maritime Dispute between Nicaragua and Honduras in the Caribbean Sea (Nicaragua v. Honduras)*, Judgment, ICJ Reports 2007, 659 (699, para. 126).

1642 *Dispute concerning delimitation of the maritime boundary between Mauritius and Maldives in the Indian Ocean (Mauritius v. Maldives)*, Preliminary Objections, Judgment, ITLOS Reports 2021, 17 (48, paras. 98-99).

1643 Chagos Marine Protected Area Arbitration (Mauritius v. United Kingdom), Award, UNRIAA, Vol. XXXI (2015), 359.

1644 *Dispute concerning delimitation of the maritime boundary between Mauritius and Maldives in the Indian Ocean (Mauritius v. Maldives)*, Preliminary Objections, Judgment, ITLOS Reports 2021, 17 (53-59, paras. 120-139).

The Maldives argued that the *Chagos* opinion did not and could not resolve the territorial sovereignty dispute between Mauritius and the United Kingdom because the UNGA did not ask the Court to settle any bilateral dispute over territorial sovereignty but to give its opinion on the process of decolonization of Mauritius.[1645] The ICJ expressly stated so when it held:

> "In Question (a), the General Assembly asks the Court to examine certain events which occurred between 1965 and 1968, and which fall within the framework of the process of decolonization of Mauritius as a non-self-governing territory. It did not submit to the Court a bilateral dispute over sovereignty which might exist between the United Kingdom and Mauritius."[1646]

In fact, the Maldives pointed out, the ICJ justified the exercise of its advisory jurisdiction in the *Chagos* case on the grounds that it had not been asked to resolve the sovereignty dispute.[1647] According to the Maldives, the resolution of the sovereignty dispute was not only not intended by the ICJ, it is also not "an implied or necessary consequence" of the *Chagos* advisory opinion.[1648] This can be seen, the Maldives argued, by the fact that there was an ongoing dispute between Mauritius and the United Kingdom over the consequences of the advisory opinion for the sovereignty dispute between them.[1649] The Maldives further argued that there was no rule under international law that "an administering State which bears an obligation to complete the process of decolonisation in respect of a given territory is immediately stripped of sovereignty over that territory".[1650]

Accordingly, while the United Kingdom may be obliged to return the Chagos Archipelago to Mauritius, it still has territorial sovereignty over the archipelago. Finally, the Maldives referred to the non-binding nature of ICJ advisory opinions arguing that "even if the Court had purported to advise on the sovereignty dispute, its opinion did not have binding force on the UNGA or any State (including the United Kingdom and the Maldives)".[1651]

1645 Ibid. (60-61, para. 145).

1646 *Legal Consequences of the Separation of the Chagos Archipelago from Mauritius in 1965*, Advisory Opinion, ICJ Reports 2019, 95 (129, para. 136).

1647 *Dispute concerning delimitation of the maritime boundary between Mauritius and Maldives in the Indian Ocean (Mauritius v. Maldives)*, Preliminary Objections, Judgment, ITLOS Reports 2021, 17 (61, para. 146).

1648 Ibid. (70 et seq., paras. 176 et seq.).

1649 Ibid. (71, para. 178).

1650 Ibid. (71, para. 179).

1651 Ibid. (59, para. 195).

In contrast, Mauritius argued that the *Chagos* advisory opinion had resolved the territorial dispute between it and the United Kingdom over the Chagos Archipelago in favor of Mauritius. The *Chagos* advisory opinion thus confirmed that the archipelago "is, and always has been, a part of the territory of Mauritius".[1652]

Mauritius agreed with the Maldives that the UNGA asked the ICJ to give an opinion on the decolonization of Mauritius, however, according to Mauritius, "the underlying sovereignty dispute could not be separated from the question of decolonization, and that by answering the UNGA's questions on decolonization (...) the sovereignty issue would inevitably be resolved."[1653]

According to Mauritius, several passages in the *Chagos* opinion demonstrate that the ICJ was aware that it would have to decide the territorial sovereignty dispute between the United Kingdom and Mauritius. In particular, the ICJ referred to the United Kingdom's "obligation to bring an end to its administration of the Chagos Archipelago as rapidly as possible, thereby enabling Mauritius to complete the decolonization of its territory in a manner consistent with the right of peoples to self- determination."[1654]

Likewise the ICJ had found that "obligations arising under international law and reflected in the resolutions adopted by the General Assembly during the process of decolonization of Mauritius require the United Kingdom, as the administering Power, to respect the territorial integrity of that country, including the Chagos Archipelago."[1655]

The references to "its territory" and the "territorial integrity of that country, including the Chagos Archipelago", Mauritius argued, indicate that the ICJ considered the Chagos Archipelago to already be part of the territory of Mauritius, despite the fact that the decolonization process was

---

1652 ITLOS Pleadings, Dispute concerning delimitation of the maritime boundary between Mauritius and Maldives in the Indian Ocean (Mauritius v. Maldives), Preliminary Objections, Written Statement of the Maldives, para. 3.13.

1653 *Dispute concerning delimitation of the maritime boundary between Mauritius and Maldives in the Indian Ocean (Mauritius v. Maldives)*, Preliminary Objections, Judgment, ITLOS Reports 2021, 17 (64, para. 156).

1654 *Legal Consequences of the Separation of the Chagos Archipelago from Mauritius in 1965*, Advisory Opinion, Dissenting Opinion Donoghue, ICJ Reports 2019, 95 (139, para. 179).

1655 Ibid. (137, para. 173).

not complete.[1656] Regarding the legal effects of the *Chagos* advisory opinion, Mauritius maintained that "while an advisory opinion is not binding as such, this does not mean that it is devoid of legal effects. (...) when the ICJ gives an advisory opinion, it provides an authoritative statement of the law in relation to the issues to which the advisory proceedings give rise. (...) although compliance may not be obligatory in respect of an opinion itself, States are bound and obliged to comply with the law, as declared and defined by the ICJ, whether in contentious cases or advisory opinions."[1657]

Mauritius thus did not ask the Special Chamber to decide the territorial dispute between it and the United Kingdom but to simply recognize that the dispute had already been resolved by the ICJ in the *Chagos* advisory opinion and the ensuing UNGA resolution. As Judge ad hoc *Oxon* put it:

> "Mauritius thereby invites the Special Chamber to avoid the question of the existence of jurisdiction to determine disputed rights to land territory by attributing conclusive prescriptive and, in practical effect, *res judicata* consequences to the advisory opinion and the ensuing General Assembly resolution 73/295 of 22 May 2019. In doing so, Mauritius attempts to avoid the distinction between the authoritative nature of an advisory opinion of the ICJ and its legally binding effect, and the distinction between the competence of the General Assembly to deal with a matter and the legally binding effect of its conclusions."[1658]

The Special Chamber agreed with the Maldives that the *Chagos* advisory opinion was not directed at settling the territorial dispute between the United Kingdom and Mauritius, however, it may have important implications for it. Accordingly, the Special Chamber found:

> "It would be contrary to the principle of consent to accept the proposition that international courts or tribunals, through contentious or advisory proceedings, can resolve a bilateral dispute without the consent of a

1656 *Dispute concerning delimitation of the maritime boundary between Mauritius and Maldives in the Indian Ocean (Mauritius v. Maldives)*, Preliminary Objections, Judgment, ITLOS Reports 2021, 17 (65, paras. 160–161).

1657 Ibid. (76, paras. 197-198).

1658 *Dispute concerning delimitation of the maritime boundary between Mauritius and Maldives in the Indian Ocean (Mauritius v. Maldives)*, Preliminary Objections, Separate and Dissenting Opinion Oxman, ITLOS Reports 2021 (para. 27).

> party to the dispute. However, this does not mean that the advisory opinion could not entail implications for the disputed issue of sovereignty."[1659]

The Special Chamber found that the Court's findings in the *Chagos* advisory opinion had

> "unmistakable implications for the United Kingdom's claim to sovereignty over the Chagos Archipelago. (...) such claim is contrary to the determinations made by the ICJ that the detachment of the Chagos Archipelago was unlawful and that the United Kingdom's continued administration of the Chagos Archipelago constitutes an unlawful act of a continuing character."[1660]

The Special Chamber further found that the ICJ's findings "may also entail considerable implications for the sovereignty claim of Mauritius".[1661]

The Special Chamber highlighted two passages in the Chagos advisory opinion in which the ICJ refers to Mauritius "territorial integrity (...), including the Chagos Archipelago" as well as "the decolonization of its territory".[1662] The Special Chamber interpreted these statements as suggesting that Mauritius has sovereignty over the Chagos Archipelago.[1663] The Special Chamber further agreed with Mauritius that "the decolonization and sovereignty of Mauritius, including the Chagos Archipelago, are in-separably related".[1664]

Having found that the *Chagos* opinion contained relevant findings on the territorial sovereignty over the archipelago, the Special Chamber went on to assess the legal effects of the opinion for the dispute between the United Kingdom and Mauritius. This is arguably the most interesting, yet also the most controversial part of the judgment. The Special Chamber drew a distinction between the binding character and the authoritative nature of ICJ advisory opinions. While ICJ advisory opinions "cannot be considered legally binding", they entail "an authoritative statement of international law on the questions with which it deals".[1665] The Special Chamber found:

1659 *Dispute concerning delimitation of the maritime boundary between Mauritius and Maldives in the Indian Ocean (Mauritius v. Maldives)*, Preliminary Objections, Judgment, ITLOS Reports 2021, 17 (67, para. 168).
1660 Ibid. (69-70, para. 173).
1661 Ibid. (70, para. 174).
1662 Ibid.
1663 Ibid.
1664 Ibid. (74, para. 189).
1665 Ibid. (77, para. 202).

> "An advisory opinion is not binding because even the requesting entity is not obligated to comply with it in the same way as parties to contentious proceedings are obligated to comply with a judgment. However, judicial determinations made in advisory opinions carry no less weight and authority than those in judgments because they are made with the same rigour and scrutiny by the "principal judicial organ" of the United Nations with competence in matters of international law."[1666]

The Special Chamber found that the ICJ's findings in its *Chagos* advisory opinion had "legal effect"[1667] and that it therefore "takes them into consideration in assessing the legal status of the Chagos Archipelago".[1668] The Special Chamber found that the *Chagos* opinion authoritatively determined the question of sovereignty over the Chagos Archipelago stating that the main difference between the case at hand and the *Coastal State Rights* case, upon which the Maldives relied, was that

> "[i]n the latter case, the Annex VII Arbitral Tribunal did not have the benefit of prior authoritative determination of the main issues relating to sovereignty claims to Crimea by any judicial body. However, that does not seem to be the case in the present proceedings."[1669]

The Special Chamber consequently found that the

> "determinations made by the ICJ with respect to the issues of the decolonization of Mauritius in the Chagos advisory opinion have legal effect and clear implications for the legal status of the Chagos Archipelago. The United Kingdom's continued claim to sovereignty over the Chagos Archipelago is contrary to those determinations. While the process of decolonization has yet to be completed, Mauritius' sovereignty over the Chagos Archipelago can be inferred from the ICJ's determinations."[1670]

As a consequence of this, the Special Chamber decided that the United Kingdom had no legal interests relating to the maritime zones around the Chagos Archipelago[1671] and that Mauritius was the coastal state in respect of

1666 Ibid. (77, para. 203).
1667 Ibid. (78, para. 205).
1668 Ibid. (78, para. 206).
1669 Ibid. (87, para. 244).
1670 Ibid. (87-88, para. 246).
1671 Ibid. (88, para. 247).

the Chagos Archipelago for the purpose of the delimitation of a maritime boundary.[1672]

(2) Analysis

The ITLOS Special Chamber relied on the *Chagos* advisory opinion to make two important findings: first, that the United Kingdom had no legal interests that could be affected by the Special Chamber proceedings in the sense of the *Monetary Gold* doctrine and, secondly, that Mauritius holds territorial sovereignty over the Chagos Archipelago making Mauritius the coastal state of the archipelago for the purposes of maritime delimitation. In doing so, the Special Chamber held that the territorial dispute between the United Kingdom and Mauritius had been authoritatively resolved by the *Chagos* advisory opinion. The Special Chamber recognized that the United Kingdom continued to claim sovereignty over the Chagos Archipelago. However, the Special Chamber found that such claims were irrelevant since the ICJ had determined that the Chagos Archipelago was part of the territory of Mauritius.[1673] By deciding that the *Chagos* advisory opinion settled the dispute between the United Kingdom and Mauritius, the ITLOS Special Chamber judgment undermined the premise of the *Chagos* advisory opinion which was that the ICJ would exercise its advisory jurisdiction precisely because its opinion was not directed at settling the underlying territorial dispute and would thus not circumvent the consent requirement to judicial dispute settlement. As pointed out by the Maldives, this premise was expressly stated by the ICJ.

The Special Chamber explained its use of the *Chagos* advisory opinion by referring to the "authority" and "legal effects" of ICJ advisory opinions, without however, expanding on these concepts any further. While the Special Chamber reaffirmed the conventional position that ICJ advisory opinions had no binding force, it claimed that "judicial determinations made in advisory opinions carry no less weight and authority than those in judgments", the reason for this being that they are "made with the same rigour and scrutiny by the "principal judicial organ" of the United Nations with competence in matters of international law".[1674] This distinction between binding force and authority is not new, nor is the idea that advisory

1672 Ibid. (89, para. 250).
1673 Ibid. (86-87, paras. 243-245).
1674 Ibid. (77, para. 203).

opinions have the same authority as judgments of the ICJ.[1675] However, the way the Special Chamber relied on the advisory opinion's authority to reject the preliminary objections raised by the Maldives is highly controversial as it gives *de facto* precedential effect to the advisory opinion.[1676]

As illustrated above, ICs regularly rely on decisions of other ICs as guidance on the interpretation and application of the law.[1677] However, the Special Chamber relied on the advisory opinion not as authoritative guidance for its *own* determination of the applicable law or the facts of the case. Instead, the Special Chamber found that the advisory opinion *had already determined* the question before the Special Chamber in an authoritative manner. In doing so, the Special Chamber effectively attributed *res judicata* effect to the advisory opinion and the ensuing UNGA resolution 73/295. It is important to note that in doing so, the Special Chamber went beyond the usual reference to the advisory opinion as a secondary source of international law under Article 38 para. 1 lit. d ICJ Statute. The reliance on judicial decisions as secondary sources of international law does not relieve the deciding IC from making its own determination, albeit informed by the secondary source in question. However, the Special Chamber's subject-matter jurisdiction under Article 288 para. 1 UNCLOS did not allow the Special Chamber to make a decision about the territorial sovereignty over the Chagos Archipelago since such a determination would not constitute a "dispute concerning the interpretation or application" of UNCLOS as commonly understood in the case law.[1678]

The Special Chamber tried to "avoid the question of the existence of jurisdiction to determine disputed rights to land territory by attributing conclusive prescriptive and, in practical effect, *res judicata* consequences to the advisory opinion and the ensuing General Assembly resolution 73/295

1675 *P. d'Argent*, in: A. Zimmermann/C. J. Tams/K. Oellers-Frahm/C. Tomuschat/D. W. K. Anderson (eds.), The Statute of the International Court of Justice, 3. ed., 2019: Article 65, para. 49.

1676 See on this Special Rapporteur Jalloh who points out that "[t]his view stands in tension with their technically non-binding nature, the subsidiary character of Article 38 (1) (d) of the ICJ Statute and the formal lack of precedent in international law.", *C. C. Jalloh*, First Report on Subsidiary Means for the Determination of Rules of International Law, Second reissue 16 May 2023, A/CN.4/760, para. 279.

1677 With further references, see *N. Lanzoni*, 2 Ital. Rev. Int. Comp. Law 2 (2022), 296.

1678 See Dispute Concerning Coastal State Rights in the Black Sea, Sea of Azov, and Kerch Strait (Ukraine v. the Russian Federation), Award on Preliminary Objections, PCA Case No. 2017-06, 54–55 para. 176.

of 22 May 2019."[1679] In doing so, the Special Chamber negated the difference between the authoritative nature of ICJ advisory opinions and their legally binding effect as well as the difference between the power of the UNGA to pass a resolution on a matter and its legal effects.[1680] In sum, while the Special Chamber claimed to recognize that ICJ advisory opinions had no binding force, by relying on the opinion's "legal effects" to dispose of the United Kingdom as a necessary third party in the sense of the Monetary Gold doctrine, the Special Chamber effectively treated the *Chagos* advisory opinion as if it had binding force.[1681]

One could even argue that the quasi-precedential effect, which the Special Chamber ascribed to ICJ advisory opinions, is even more far-reaching than the binding force of ICJ decisions.[1682] While Article 59 of the ICJ Statute limits the binding force of ICJ judgments in contentious proceedings to the parties to a particular case, advisory opinions are given on questions of law and may extend beyond the scope of the bilateral dispute.[1683] Additionally, while the binding force and *res judicata* effect of judgments in contentious cases is limited to the operative provisions of the judgment, advisory opinions have no operative provisions allowing a much more flexible recourse to the findings of the Court.

cc) Conclusions on the Chagos advisory opinion

Taking stock of the practice of key audiences of the *Chagos* advisory opinion leaves a mixed picture. In terms of the Court's *narrow authority*, it is apparent that of the two states whose legal rights and obligations form the subject-matter of the Chagos advisory proceedings, Mauritius and the United Kingdom, only Mauritius recognized the authority of the opinion. It did so through public statements as well as in the proceedings before the ITLOS Special Chamber against the Maldives in which it relied on the ICJ's findings in the *Chagos* opinion. In contrast, the United Kingdom initially

1679 *Dispute concerning delimitation of the maritime boundary between Mauritius and Maldives in the Indian Ocean (Mauritius v. Maldives)*, Preliminary Objections, Separate and Dissenting Opinion Oxman, ITLOS Reports 2021 (para. 27).

1680 Cf. Ibid.

1681 So also *M. Lando*, Binding Advisory Opinions, in: R. Buchan/D. Franchini/N. Tsagourias (eds.), The Changing Character of International Dispute Settlement: Challenges and Prospects, 2023, 106 (127).

1682 See *F. S. Eichberger*, 22 Melbourne Journal of International Law 2 (2021), 1 (18).

1683 Ibid.

neither recognized the Court's advisory opinion as authoritative nor took meaningful action towards complying with it. Instead, the United Kingdom rejected the *Chagos* opinion and reasserted its claim of sovereignty over the Chagos Archipelago. Subsequently, the United Kingdom adopted a more conciliatory stance, initiating preliminary negotiations with Mauritius in 2023 regarding the transfer of the Chagos Archipelago. While negotiations initially stalled, with the UK even considering withdrawing from the talks altogether,[1684] the UK finally agreed to return sovereignty over the archipelago back to Mauritius in 2024.[1685] However, not without a big caveat: the UK will continue to exercise territorial sovereignty over the archipelago's largest island for another 99 years. One can thus not conclude that the United Kingdom acknowledged its obligation to immediately end its administration of the Chagos Archipelago in line with the *Chagos* opinion. The recognition element as one of the two key components of measuring *de facto* authority is thus lacking.

Moving to the ICJ's *intermediate authority*, i.e., the Court's power to affect the position of similarly situated actors, the position of the Maldives is particularly illustrative. The Maldives invoked the Monetary Gold doctrine and the *Chagos* opinion's lack of binding force to challenge the admissibility of the proceedings Mauritius had launched before the ITLOS Special Chamber. The Maldives argued that the *Chagos* opinion could not settle the dispute between Mauritius and the United Kingdom thus denying the opinion's capacity to exert narrow authority.

Broadening the scope further to the Court's *extensive authority*, the position of the ITLOS Special Chamber in the proceedings between Mauritius and the Maldives significantly strengthened the Court's *de facto* authority. The *Chagos* opinion is being treated as a quasi-contentious judgment in the dispute between the United Kingdom and Mauritius containing an authoritative statement on the law and facts of the case. Similarly, civil society groups like Human Rights Watch have endorsed the ICJ's *Chagos* advisory opinion and called upon the United Kingdom to make reparations

1684 The Telegraph, UK to drop plan to hand Chagos Islands back to Mauritius, 15.12.2023, https://www.telegraph.co.uk/world-news/2023/12/01/uk-drop-plan-to-hand-chagos-islands-back-mauritius/.

1685 Joint statement between the governments of the Republic of Mauritius and the United Kingdom of Great Britain and Northern Ireland concerning the Chagos Archipelago, including Diego Garcia, 3 October 2024, https://www.gov.uk/government/news/joint-statement-between-uk-and-mauritius-3-october-2024.

and "comply with the findings and recommendations of UN bodies and human rights mechanisms".[1686]

E. Conclusions on the justifications for the Eastern Carelia doctrine

The core justification for the ICJ's Eastern Carelia doctrine lies in the protection of the integrity of the Court's judicial function. The ICJ may refuse certain requests for an advisory opinion if the issuing of the advisory opinion would be incompatible with the Court's judicial function. However, herein already lies the first ambiguity of the doctrine. There is not one clearly identifiable judicial function of the ICJ. Instead, the term judicial function refers to a plethora of aims and activities the Court pursues, such as the stabilization of normative expectations, the control of the compatibility of the conduct of international actors with international law, the concretization and development of legal norms, the support of the other UN organs in their activities (especially by means of the advisory procedure), and the settlement of international disputes. Each of these functions raises different problems with respect to the Court's advisory procedure.

The function most often invoked as being at odds with requests for advisory opinions on inter-state disputes is the Court's dispute settlement function. The idea is that the issuing of advisory opinions on legal questions which form the subject-matter of an inter-state dispute constitutes a form of dispute settlement which circumvents the respective state's consent to dispute settlement and thereby undermines the contentious procedure's jurisdictional regime established by the ICJ Statute. However, the principle of consent pursues a specific function which is to prevent the exercise of judicial jurisdiction over a state without that state's consent. An IC exercises jurisdiction over a state only if it decides over that state's legal rights and obligations with binding force. Since advisory opinions lack binding force, the issuing of advisory opinions on a legal question which lies at the heart of an inter-state dispute does not constitute an exercise of judicial jurisdiction over the respective states.

Even if one broadens the perspective and asks whether the Eastern Carelia doctrine is justified as a form of complementary or auxiliary protection

1686 *C. Baldwin*, "That's When the Nightmare Started", Human Rights Watch, 2023, https://www.hrw.org/report/2023/02/15/thats-when-nightmare-started/uk-and-us-forced-displacement-chagossians-and.

of the jurisdictional system of the ICJ Statute, no other conclusion can be drawn. This was illustrated by a comparison to the Monetary Gold doctrine. In contrast to contentious cases, which form the backdrop of the Monetary Gold doctrine, advisory opinions on inter-state disputes do not create any additional legal obligations which may be at odds with the existing rights and obligations of non-participating states. An advisory opinion can only provide an additional authoritative *moral* reason to act in a certain way, but it cannot provide an additional *legal* reason to act.

ICJ advisory opinions exert significant authority. Particularly the normative authority of ICJ advisory opinions may be the principal reason for states to invoke the Eastern Carelia doctrine as a defense against advisory opinions on legal matters close to them. However, this normative authority – even if it may have practical effects for the state in question – does not mean that the ICJ exercises jurisdiction over the affected states when issuing an advisory opinion. Instead, we are left with a much more vague interest of states not to be confronted with an authoritative but non-binding legal pronouncement. Considering that the ICJ as an organ of the UN has a legal duty to assist the other UN organs in their activities, it seems unjustifiable to refuse a request merely based on such vague notions. Thus, it is asserted that there is no justification for the Eastern Carelia doctrine. Judge *Donoghue* warned in her dissenting opinion to the *Chagos* advisory opinion "that the advisory opinion procedure is available as a fall-back mechanism to be used to overcome the absence of consent to jurisdiction in contentious cases".[1687] However, it seems that as long as an authorized UN organ has expressed its need for an advisory opinion on a matter, the Court has little room to deny such a request.

1687 *Legal Consequences of the Separation of the Chagos Archipelago from Mauritius in 1965*, Advisory Opinion, Dissenting Opinion Donoghue, ICJ Reports 2019, 95 (266, para. 23).

§ 7 Conclusion and Summary

A. Conclusion

The survey of the ICJ's advisory practice and the analysis of the Court's jurisdictional framework has shown that the ICJ can use its advisory procedure to address legal questions which form the subject-matter of inter-state disputes and thus, contribute to the legal settlement of inter-state disputes by means of its advisory procedure. The Court has continuously adapted its Eastern Carelia doctrine to a point at which it has become increasingly harder to imagine any situation which would lead the Court to reject a request for an advisory opinion from an authorized organ.

Advisory opinions exert significant authority and thus greatly influence the international legal discourse on the legal questions which they address. However, they do not jeopardize the legal position of the states which they address. There is thus no need for a de-facto consent requirement as a strict application of the Eastern Carelia doctrine would establish. Additionally, the ICJ, as a UN organ, has a duty to support the other UN organs in their activities by providing legal advice in the form of advisory opinions. It is asserted that the ICJ should therefore discard the Eastern Carelia doctrine and in doing so invite more requests for advisory opinions on important matters disputed among states.

Since the Court cannot act on its own accord and relies on requests made by authorized organs, the future of the Court's advisory practice regarding inter-state disputes significantly depends on whether these organs regard the Court's advisory procedure as a legitimate means to settle inter-state disputes. The UNGA emphasized the potential of requesting advisory opinions from the Court for the settlement of inter-state disputes in its resolution 43/51 entitled "Declaration on the Prevention and Removal of Disputes and Situations Which May Threaten International Peace and Security and on the Role of the United Nations in this Field". In the resolution, the UNGA "solemnly declares" that both the UNSC and the UNGA should consider requesting advisory opinions from the Court, "if it is appropriate for promoting the prevention and removal of disputes or situations".[1688]

In his speech to the UNSC on 18 December 2020, President *Yusuf* drew attention to this resolution and invited the UNSC to make more frequent use of its power to request advisory opinions from the Court on legal questions relating to inter-state disputes:

> "The General Assembly was of the view that a request for an advisory opinion from the Court could play an important role in the Council's work to prevent situations or disputes from becoming a threat to international peace and security. I share that view, and I believe that the Council could consider that possibility more often."[1689]

President *Yusuf* indicated a willingness of the Court to respond to requests whose primary goal is to "prevent (...) disputes from becoming a threat to international peace and security", in other words to settle such inter-state disputes. In his statement, President *Yusuf* distinguished between the power of the UNSC to refer a dispute to the Court to be settled in a binding manner by means of the Court's contentious procedure under Article 36 para. 3 ICJ Statute, which requires the consent of the parties, and the UNSC's power to request advisory opinions:

> "I can understand the reluctance of the Council to recommend the referral of a dispute to the Court, by the Parties concerned, unless it is clear that both Parties are ready for such a step. (...) However, the request for an advisory opinion is a different matter. Such an advisory opinion would not be binding and would not be addressed directly to States, but rendered for the benefit of the Council to clarify a specific legal issue. The Security Council would then be free to do whatever it wishes with such an opinion."[1690]

Of course, the composition of the Court has changed since then. Shortly after President *Yusuf* made these statements, Judge *Donoghue* took over as President of the Court. President *Donoghue* exhibited a much more reserved stance towards the use of advisory opinions to settle inter-state

1688 UNGA resolution 43/51 of 5 December 1988, UN doc. A/RES/43/51, paras. 15, 19.

1689 Abdulqawi Ahmed Yusuf, President of the International Court of Justice, to the Security Council, 18 December 2020, "Upholding international law within the context of fostering close co-operation between the International Court of Justice and the Security Council", 4.

1690 Ibid., 3.

disputes, as evidenced by her dissenting opinion in the *Chagos* case.[1691] Nevertheless, she could not convince the majority on the bench to follow her approach. The recent *Legal Consequences arising from the Policies and Practices of Israel* advisory opinion, delivered under the current President *Salam*, can be seen as another example of the Court being open to the use of its advisory procedure for the settlement of inter-state disputes.

The trajectory of the Court's advisory practice seems clear. The question is only if the Court will decide to openly abandon the Eastern Carelia doctrine. Such a move could convince the authorized UN organs, in particular the UNGA and the UNSC, to refer pressing legal questions at the heart of inter-state disputes more frequently to the Court. Considering the momentum that the *Chagos* advisory opinion has created to restart the stalled negotiations between the UK and Mauritius over the return of the Chagos Archipelago, such a development could prove auspicious for the international community.

B. Summary

1. **The ICJ advisory jurisdiction extends to inter-state disputes**: An interpretation of Article 96 UNC and Article 65 ICJ Statute reveals that the ICJ's subject-matter jurisdiction extends to any legal question, regardless of its connection to an inter-state dispute. While states have tried to invoke the difference in wording between Article 14 of the Covenant of the League of Nations ("dispute or question") and Article 65 ICJ Statute ("any legal question") to argue that the drafters of the ICJ's constituent instrument deliberately decided to exclude inter-state disputes from the Court's jurisdiction, there is no indication of such an intent in the drafting history.
2. **The ICJ has no discretion in the use of its advisory jurisdiction:** Despite the fact that Article 65 para. 1 ICJ Statute employs the word

1691 "Today the Court recites once again that there would be "compelling reasons" to decline to give an advisory opinion when such a reply "would have the effect of circumventing the principle that a State is not obliged to allow its disputes to be submitted to judicial settlement without its consent" (...) However, the decision to render today's Advisory Opinion demonstrates that this incantation is hollow. It is difficult to imagine any dispute that is more quintessentially bilateral than a dispute over territorial sovereignty.", see *Legal Consequences of the Separation of the Chagos Archipelago from Mauritius in 1965*, Advisory Opinion, Dissenting Opinion Donoghue, ICJ Reports 2019, 95 (266, para. 21).

"may give", the ICJ cannot decide freely to give or deny requested advisory opinions. Instead, from the ICJ's status as an organ of the UN follows a duty to comply with the request for an advisory opinion, unless "compelling", i.e., imperative reasons prohibit the Court from giving the requested opinion.

3. **The ICJ must protect its "judicial function" from harm:** The Court has identified the protection of its judicial function as one of the most important "compelling reason" for refusing requests for advisory opinions. Under its Eastern Carelia doctrine, the ICJ has held that giving an advisory opinion on a question which forms the subject-matter of an inter-state dispute without the consent of the disputing states may be prejudicial to its judicial function.
4. **The ICJ has not one but many judicial functions:** The ICJ, just like all other international courts and tribunals, has not one, but many judicial functions, including the function to settle international disputes, the function to stabilize normative expectations, the function to concretize and develop the law, and the function to control the behavior of the law's addressees.
5. **Advisory opinions on inter-state disputes do not circumvent the principle of consensual dispute settlement**: The principle of consensual dispute settlement protects states from being subject to the exercise of jurisdiction by an international court or tribunal. However, advisory opinions do not constitute such an exercise of jurisdiction, as they do not have binding force and do not become *res judicata.*
6. **The Eastern Carelia doctrine is premised on the de-facto effects of ICJ advisory opinions:** The Eastern Carelia doctrine and the Monetary Gold doctrine share certain similarities. Both doctrines insert a consent requirement of a third or affected state into the Court's jurisdictional framework and both doctrines justify this supplementary consent requirement with the need to protect the Court's judicial function. Since judgments are not binding for third parties and since advisory opinions are not binding at all, the Court's concern can only be justified by reference to the *de facto* legal effects of these judicial pronouncements. There is, however, a crucial difference between the two doctrines: In the case of the advisory jurisdiction, the ICJ, as a UN organ, has a duty to support the requesting organ's activities by giving the requested advisory opinion.
7. **The ICJ does not openly recognize its power to use its advisory opinions to settle inter-state disputes**: While the ICJ has dramatically

reduced the scope of its Eastern Carelia doctrine, the Court continues to pay lip service to it by repeating its core tenet that a state may not be forced to have its disputes settled by judicial means without its consent. The ICJ thus denies that its advisory procedure may be used to address matters which form the subject-matter of inter-state disputes. However, in the application of this doctrine, the Court uses ill-defined terms such as "broader frame of reference" and relies on the request's object and purpose even where the submitted questions are identical to the subject-matter of the underlying inter-state dispute, thereby depriving the doctrine of any real meaning. Considering the aforementioned, the Court should be open to the idea that UN organs could request advisory opinions specifically with the intention to use the opinion to settle inter-state disputes.

8. **The Court has two options: Abandoning the Eastern Carelia doctrine or strengthening it:** The best way forward for the Court would be to abandon the Eastern Carelia doctrine altogether and openly allow authorized organs to request advisory opinions on any legal question, irrespective if the legal question concerns an inter-state dispute. Another option would be to strengthen the Eastern Carelia doctrine by giving up on the "broader frame of reference" standard and go back to the Court's initial approach in the *Peace Treaties* advisory opinion, in which the Court compared the questions submitted by the authorized organ with the subject-matter of the pending inter-state dispute.

Postscript

While the work on an academic thesis must eventually come to an end, the work of the international judiciary continues. Since the completion of this book in October 2024, the ICJ has rendered two new advisory opinions[1692] and held public hearings in a third case[1693]. The purpose of this postscript is to briefly touch upon these recent developments and place them within the framework of the study.

On 23 July 2025, the ICJ has rendered its highly anticipated advisory opinion on the *Obligations of States in respect of Climate Change.*[1694] The advisory opinion was the result of a long process that began as a grassroots initiative led by law students at the University of the South Pacific, was then spearheaded by Vanuatu, and eventually gained the support of over 130 states. The proceedings sparked an unprecedented level of interest from states and international organizations alike, with 96 states and eleven international organizations presenting oral statements. The UNGA presented the Court with two questions concerning the international legal obligations of states to ensure the protection of the climate system and other parts of the environment from anthropogenic emissions of greenhouse gases as well as the legal consequences under these obligations for states where they have caused significant harm to the climate system and other parts of the environment. In answering the two questions, the Court made many important findings. Among them, the Court recognized both treaty-based and customary obligations of states to prevent significant environmental harm from anthropogenic greenhouse gases by acting with due diligence and asserted that any breach of the obligations identified in the advisory opinion could potentially constitute an internationally wrongful act which could

1692 *Obligations of States in respect of Climate Change*, Advisory Opinion of 23 July 2025; *Obligations of Israel in relation to the Presence and Activities of the United Nations, Other International Organizations and Third States in and in relation to the Occupied Palestinian Territory*, Advisory Opinion of 22 October 2025.

1693 *Right to Strike under ILO Convention No. 87*, Request for advisory opinion submitted by the Governing Body of the International Labour Office (ILO), verbatim record, CR 2025/20.

1694 *Obligations of States in respect of Climate Change*, Advisory Opinion of 23 July 2025.

in turn engage the international responsibility of the state in question.[1695] With regard to the findings of this study, the legal questions presented to the Court did not concern or even relate to a specific bilateral dispute, but rather, as the ICJ put it, "concern an existential problem of planetary proportions".[1696] Considering the abstract nature of the questions presented to the Court, the request did not pose a challenge to the Court's judicial function in the sense of the Eastern Carelia doctrine.

In the second advisory opinion rendered by the ICJ in 2025, the Court examined Israel's practice and policies after the attack of 7 October 2023, in particular Israel's adoption of legislation on 28 October 2024 curtailing the operations of the United Nations Relief and Works Agency for Palestine Refugees in the Near East (UNRWA).[1697] Just like the 2004 *Wall* advisory opinion[1698] and the 2024 *Policies and Practices* advisory opinion[1699], the request concerned elements of the ongoing Israel-Palestine conflict. As in these previous cases, Israel and (like in 2024) Hungary argued that the Court should exercise its discretion to decline to give the requested advisory opinion.[1700] However, the Court found that there were no compelling reasons to do so.[1701] The Court started by referring to its 2024 *Policies and Practices* advisory opinion,[1702] in which the Court found the request to go beyond a purely bilateral dispute, as it directly concerned the work of the United Nations. In doing so, the Court signaled its continued adherence to the Eastern Carelia doctrine in principle and its position that the UN's

1695 Ibid. (130 et seq., para. 456).

1696 Ibid. (129, para. 456).

1697 *Obligations of Israel in relation to the Presence and Activities of the United Nations, Other International Organizations and Third States in and in relation to the Occupied Palestinian Territory*, Advisory Opinion of 22 October 2025.

1698 *Legal Consequences of the Construction of a Wall in the Occupied Palestinian Territory*, Advisory Opinion, ICJ Reports 2004, 136.

1699 *Obligations of Israel in relation to the Presence and Activities of the United Nations, Other International Organizations and Third States in and in relation to the Occupied Palestinian Territory*, Advisory Opinion of 22 October 2025.

1700 *Obligations of Israel in relation to the Presence and Activities of the United Nations, Other International Organizations and Third States in and in relation to the Occupied Palestinian Territory*, Written Statement of Hungary, paras. 12 et seq.; Written Statement of Israel, paras. 59 et seq.

1701 See *Obligations of Israel in relation to the Presence and Activities of the United Nations, Other International Organizations and Third States in and in relation to the Occupied Palestinian Territory*, Advisory Opinion of 22 October 2025 (19 et seq., paras. 23 et seq.).

1702 *Legal Consequences arising from the Policies and Practices of Israel in the Occupied Palestinian Territory, including East Jerusalem*, Advisory Opinion of 19 July 2024.

long-standing involvement in the Israel-Palestine conflict elevates the conflict beyond the bilateral level. The Court then went on to address those aspects that were specific to the case at hand.[1703] Among them, the Court rejected the notion that giving the requested advisory opinion could prejudge the Court's decision of the pending *Application of the Convention on the Prevention and Punishment of the Crime of Genocide in the Gaza Strip (South Africa v. Israel)* case.[1704] In emphasizing the Court's duty to decide the contentious case solely on the basis of the evidence and arguments presented by the parties to those proceedings,[1705] the Court denied any legal or *de facto* prejudicial effect of its advisory opinions for its judgments, even as they relate to the same underlying facts. This dictum gives yet more power to the notion that the Court should reconsider its approach to requests for advisory opinions on inter-state disputes and finally abandon its Eastern Carelia doctrine.

Finally, the Court has recently concluded the oral hearings in the *Right to Strike under ILO Convention No. 87* case.[1706] The case is the result of a disagreement within the tripartite constituency of the ILO, i.e., between the member states, international employer representatives and international worker representatives, on whether the right to strike is protected under the Freedom of Association and Protection of the Right to Organise Convention, 1948 (No. 87). The request to the Court was made pursuant to Article 37 para. 1 of the ILO Constitution, according to which "[a]ny question or dispute relating to the interpretation of this Constitution or of any subsequent Convention concluded by the Members in pursuance of the provisions of this Constitution shall be referred for decision to the International Court of Justice". Notwithstanding the importance of the request regarding both the substantive issue and the ILO's decision-making process, which is usually consensus-based, it does not raise issues regarding the Eastern Carelia doctrine. As the request concerns an abstract legal question, it is similar to the 1996 *Nuclear Weapons* advisory opinion and the 2025 *Climate Change* advisory opinion.

1703 *Obligations of Israel in relation to the Presence and Activities of the United Nations, Other International Organizations and Third States in and in relation to the Occupied Palestinian Territory*, Advisory Opinion of 22 October 2025 (19, para. 24).

1704 Ibid. (20-21, paras. 30 et seq.).

1705 Ibid. (20, para. 30).

1706 *Right to Strike under ILO Convention No. 87*, Request for advisory opinion submitted by the Governing Body of the International Labour Office (ILO).

Table of cited advisory opinions, judgments and arbitral awards

A. Decisions and advisory opinions of general international courts and arbitral tribunals

Permanent Court of International Justice

Competence of the ILO in Regard to International Regulation of the Conditions of Labour of Persons Employed in Agriculture, Advisory Opinion, PCIJ Series B, 1922, 8.

Status of Eastern Carelia, Advisory Opinion, PCIJ Series B 1923, 7.

Nationality Decrees Issued in Tunis and Morocco, Advisory Opinion, PCIJ Series B No. 4, 1923, 7.

Mavrommatis Palestine Concessions (Greece v. United Kingdom), Judgment, 1924, PCIJ Series A, no. 2, 5.

Article 3, paragraph 2, of the Treaty of Lausanne (Frontier between Turkey and Iraq), Advisory Opinion, PCIJ Series B 1925, 6.

Polish Postal Services in Danzig, Advisory Opinion, PCIJ Series A, 1925, 6.

S.S. "Lotus" (France v. Turkey), Judgment, PCIJ Series A, 1927, 4.

Interpretation of Judgments Nos. 7 and 8 (Factory at Chorzów), Judgment, PCIJ Series A, 1927, 5.

Case Concerning the Payment of Various Serbian Loans Issued in France, Judgment, PCIJ Series A, 1929, 19.

International Court of Justice

Conditions of Admission of a State to Membership in the United Nations (Article 4 of the Charter), Advisory Opinion, ICJ Reports 1948, 57.

Corfu Channel (United Kingdom v. Albania), Merits, ICJ Reports 1949, 4.

Reparation for Injuries Suffered in the Service of the United Nations, Advisory Opinion, ICJ Reports 1949, 174.

Corfu Channel (United Kingdom v. Albania), Judgment on Compensation, ICJ Reports 1949, 244.

Competence of the General Assembly for the Admission of a State to the United Nations, Advisory Opinion, ICJ Reports 1950, 4.

Interpretation of Peace Treaties with Bulgaria, Hungary and Romania (First Phase), Advisory Opinion, ICJ Reports 1950, 65.

International Status of South-West Africa, Advisory Opinion, ICJ Reports 1950, 128.

Reservations to the Convention on the Prevention and Punishment of the Crime of Genocide, Advisory Opinion, ICJ Reports 1951, 15.

Nottebohm (Liechtenstein v. Guatemala), Preliminary Objections, Judgment, ICJ Reports 1953, 111.

Case of the monetary gold removed from Rome in 1943 (Italy v. France, United Kingdom and United States) (Preliminary Question), Judgment, ICJ Reports 1954, 19.

Effect of Awards of Compensation Made by the United Nations Administrative Tribunal, Advisory Opinion, ICJ Reports 1954, 47.

Judgments of the Administrative Tribunal of the ILO upon Complaints Made against UNESCO, Advisory Opinion, ICJ Reports 1956, 77.

Interhandel (Switzerland v. United States of America), Judgment, ICJ Reports 1959, 6.

Right of Passage over Indian Territory (Portugal v. India) (Merits), Judgment, ICJ Reports 1960, 6.

Constitution of the Maritime Safety Committee of the Inter-Governmental Maritime Consultative, Advisory Opinion, ICJ Reports 1960, 150.

Arbitral Award made by the King of Spain on 23 December 1906 (Honduras v. Nicaragua), Judgment, ICJ Reports 1960, 192.

Case concerning the Temple of Preah Vihear (Cambodia v. Thailand), Judgment, ICJ Reports 1962, 6.

Certain Expenses of the United Nations (Article 17, paragraph 2, of the Charter), Advisory Opinion, ICJ Reports 1962, 151.

Northern Cameroons (Cameroon v. United Kingdom) (Preliminary Objections), Judgment, ICJ Reports 1963, 15.

Barcelona Traction, Light and Power Company, Limited (Belgium v. Spain) (Preliminary Objections), Judgment, ICJ Reports 1964, 6.

South-West Africa Cases (Ethiopia v. South Africa; Liberia v. South Africa), Judgment, ICJ Reports 1966, 6.

Barcelona Traction, Light and Power Company, Limited (Belgium v. Spain), Judgment, ICJ Reports 1970, 3.

Legal Consequences for States of the Continued Presence of South Africa in Namibia (South West Africa) notwithstanding Security Council Resolution 276 (1970), Advisory Opinion, ICJ Reports 1971, 16.

Application for Review of Judgment No. 158 of the United Nations Administrative Tribunal, Advisory Opinion, ICJ Reports 1973, 166.

Nuclear Tests (Australia v. France), Judgment, ICJ Reports 1974, 253.

Western Sahara, Advisory Opinion, ICJ Reports 1975, 12.

United States Diplomatic and Consular Staff in Tehran (United States of America v. Iran), Judgment, ICJ Reports 1980, 3.

Interpretation of the Agreement of 25 March 1951 between the WHO and Egypt, Advisory Opinion, ICJ Reports 1980, 73.

Application for Review of Judgment No. 273 of the United Nations Administrative Tribunal, Advisory Opinion, ICJ Reports 1982, 325.

Military and Paramilitary Activities in and against Nicaragua (Nicaragua v. United States of America), Jurisdiction and Admissibility, Judgment, ICJ Reports 1984, 392.

Military and Paramilitary Activities in and against Nicaragua (Nicaragua v. United States of America) (Merits), Judgment, ICJ Reports 1986, 14.

Application for Review of Judgment No. 333 of the United Nations Administrative Tribunal, Advisory Opinion, ICJ Reports 1987, 18.

Applicability of Article VI, Section 22, of the Convention on the Privileges and Immunities, Advisory Opinion, ICJ Reports 1989, 177.

Arbitral Award of 31 July 1989 (Guinea-Bissau v. Senegal), Judgment, ICJ Reports 1991, 53.

Certain Phosphate Lands in Nauru (Nauru v. Australia), Preliminary Objections, Judgment, ICJ Reports 1992, 240.

Territorial Dispute (Libyan Arab Jamahiriya v. Chad), Judgment, ICJ Reports 1994, 6.

East Timor (Portugal v. Australia), Judgment, ICJ Reports 1995, 90.

Legality of the Use by a State of Nuclear Weapons in Armed Conflict, Advisory Opinion, ICJ Reports 1996, 66.

Legality of the Threat or Use of Nuclear Weapons, Advisory Opinion, ICJ Reports 1996, 226.

Gabčíkovo-Nagymaros Project (Hungary v. Slovakia), Judgment, ICJ Reports 1997, 7.

Questions of Interpretation and Application of the 1971 Montreal Convention arising from the Aerial Incident at Lockerbie (Libyan Arab Jamahiriya v. United States of America), Preliminary Objections, Judgment, ICJ Reports 1998, 115.

Land and Maritime Boundary between Cameroon and Nigeria (Cameroon v. Nigeria), Preliminary Objections, Judgment, ICJ Reports 1998, 275.

Vienna Convention on Consular Relations (Paraguay v. United States of America), Order, ICJ Reports 1998, 426 (discontinued on 2 November 1999).

Difference Relating to Immunity from Legal Process of a Special Rapporteur of the HRC, Advisory Opinion, ICJ Reports 1999, 62.

Kasikili/Sedudu Island (Botswana v. Namibia), Judgment, ICJ Reports 1999, 1045.

Arrest Warrant of 11 April 2000 (Democratic Republic of the Congo v. Belgium), Judgment, ICJ Reports 2002, 3.

LaGrand (Germany v. United States of America), Judgment, ICJ Reports 2001, 466.

Avena and Other Mexican Nationals (Mexico v. United States of America), Judgment, ICJ Reports 2004, 12.

Legal Consequences of the Construction of a Wall in the Occupied Palestinian Territory, Advisory Opinion, ICJ Reports 2004, 136.

Legality of Use of Force (Serbia and Montenegro v. Belgium), Preliminary Objections, Judgment, ICJ Reports 2004, 279.

Armed Activities on the Territory of the Congo (New Application: 2002) (Democratic Republic of the Congo v. Rwanda), Jurisdiction and Admissibility, Judgment, ICJ Reports 2006, 6.

Application of the Convention on the Prevention and Punishment of the Crime of Genocide (Bosnia and Herzegovina v. Serbia and Montenegro), Judgment, ICJ Reports 2007, 43.

Territorial and Maritime Dispute between Nicaragua and Honduras in the Caribbean Sea (Nicaragua v. Honduras), Judgment, ICJ Reports 2007, 659.

Sovereignty over Pedra Branca/Pulau Batu Puteh, Middle Rocks and South Ledge (Malaysia v. Singapore), Judgment, ICJ Reports 2008, 12.

Certain Questions of Mutual Assistance in Criminal Matters (Djibouti v. France), Judgment, ICJ Reports 2008, 177.

Maritime Delimitation in the Black Sea (Romania v. Ukraine), Judgment, ICJ Reports 2009, 61.

Dispute regarding Navigational and Related Rights (Costa Rica v. Nicaragua), Judgment, ICJ Reports 2009, 213.

Pulp Mills on the River Uruguay (Argentina v. Uruguay), Judgment, ICJ Reports 2010, 14.

Accordance with international law of the unilateral declaration of independence in respect of Kosovo, Advisory Opinion, ICJ Reports 2010, 403.

Judgment No. 2867 of the Administrative Tribunal of the ILO, Advisory Opinion, ICJ Reports 2012, 10.

Jurisdictional Immunities of the State (Germany v. Italy: Greece intervening), Judgment, ICJ Reports 2012, 99.

Whaling in the Antarctic (Australia v. Japan: New Zealand intervening), Judgment, ICJ Reports 2014, 226.

Alleged Violations of Sovereign Rights and Maritime Spaces in the Caribbean Sea (Nicaragua v. Colombia), Preliminary Objections, Judgment, ICJ Reports 2016, 3.

Jadhav (India v. Pakistan), Provisional Measures, Order, ICJ Reports 2017, 231.

Legal Consequences of the Separation of the Chagos Archipelago from Mauritius in 1965, Advisory Opinion, ICJ Reports 2019, 95.

Legal Consequences arising from the Policies and Practices of Israel in the Occupied Palestinian Territory, including East Jerusalem, Advisory Opinion, Publication in ICJ Reports 2024 pending.

Obligations of States in respect of Climate Change, Advisory Opinion of 23 July 2025.

Obligations of Israel in relation to the Presence and Activities of the United Nations, Other International Organizations and Third States in and in relation to the Occupied Palestinian Territory, Advisory Opinion of 22 October 2025.

International Tribunal for the Law of the Sea

Responsibilities and obligations of States with respect to activities in the Area, Advisory Opinion, ITLOS Reports 2011, 10.

Request for Advisory Opinion submitted by the Sub-Regional Fisheries Commission, Advisory Opinion, ITLOS Reports 2015, 4.

Dispute concerning delimitation of the maritime boundary between Mauritius and Maldives in the Indian Ocean (Mauritius v. Maldives), Preliminary Objections, Judgment, ITLOS Reports 2021, 17.

Awards of arbitral tribunals

Alabama claims of the United States of America against Great Britain, Award rendered on 14 September 1872 by the tribunal of arbitration established by Article I of the Treaty of Washington of 8 May 1871, United Nations Reports of International Arbitral Awards, Volume XXIX, 125.

Island of Palmas (Netherlands v. United States of America), Award, UNRIAA, 1928, Vol. II, 829.

Trail Smelter Arbitration (United States of America v. Canada), Award, UNRIAA, Vol. III (1941), 1905.

Chagos Marine Protected Area Arbitration (Mauritius v. United Kingdom), Award, UNRIAA, Vol. XXXI (2015), 359.

Dispute Concerning Coastal State Rights in the Black Sea, Sea of Azov, and Kerch Strait (Ukraine v. the Russian Federation), Award on Preliminary Objections, PCA Case No. 2017–06.

B. Decisions and advisory opinions of regional human rights courts

African Court on Human and Peoples' Rights

Request for Advisory Opinion by the Pan African Lawyers' Union and Southern African Litigation Center, No. 002/2012, Order.

Request for Advisory Opinion by the Socio-Economic Rights and Accountability Project (SERAP), No. 001/2013, Advisory Opinion.

Request for Advisory Opinion by the Coalition for the International Criminal Court, the Legal Defence & Assistance Project (LEDAP), the Civil Resource Development & Documentation Center (CIRDDOC) and the Women Advocates Documentation Center (WARDC), No. 001/2014, Order.

Request for Advisory Opinion by Rencontre Africain pour la Defense des Droits de l'Homme, No. 002/2014, Advisory Opinion.

Request for Advisory Opinion by the Pan African Lawyers Union (PALU) on the compatibility of vagrancy laws with the African Charter on Human and Peoples' Rights and other human rights instruments applicable in Africa, No. 001/2018, Advisory Opinion.

Request by the Pan African Lawyers Union (PALU) on the right to participate in the government of one's country in the context of an election held during a public health emergency or a pandemic, such as the COVID-19 Crisis, NO. 001/2020, Advisory Opinion.

European Court of Human Rights

Loizidou v Turkey, Judgment of 23 March 1995, Series A, no. 310.

Decision on the competence of the Court to give an advisory opinion, 2 June 2004, A47–2004–001.

Advisory opinion on certain legal questions concerning the lists of candidates submitted with a view to the election of judges to the European Court of Human Rights, 12 February 2008, A47–2008.

Advisory opinion on certain legal questions concerning the lists of candidates submitted with a view to the election of judges to the European Court of Human Rights (No. 2), 22 January 2010, A47–2010–001.

Inter-American Court of Human Rights

"Other Treaties" Subject to the Consultative Jurisdiction of the Court, Advisory Opinion OC-1/82, IACtHR Series A No. 1.

Restrictions to the Death Penalty, Advisory Opinion OC-3/83, IACtHR Series A No. 3.

Compatibility of Draft Legislation with Article 8(2)(h) of the American Convention on Human Rights, Advisory Opinion OC-12/91, IACtHR Series A No. 12.

Certain Attributes of the Inter-American Commission on Human Rights (Arts. 41, 42, 44, 46, 47, 50 and 51 of the American Convention on Human Rights), Advisory Opinion OC-13/93, IACtHR Series A No. 13.

International Responsibility for the Promulgation and Enforcement of Laws in Violation of the Convention (Arts. 1 and 2 of the American Convention on Human Rights), Advisory Opinion OC-14/94, IACtHR Series A No. 14.

Reports of the Inter-American Commission on Human Rights, Advisory Opinion OC-15/97, IACtHR Series A No. 15.

The Right to Information on Consular Assistance in the Framework of the Guarantees of the Due Process of Law, Advisory Opinion OC-16/99, IACtHR Series A No. 16.

Juridical Condition and Rights of the Undocumented Migrants, Advisory Opinion OC-18/03, IACtHR Series A No. 18.

Rights and guarantees of children in the context of migration and/or in need of international protection, Advisory Opinion OC-21/14, IACtHR Series A No. 21.

Entitlement of legal entities to hold rights under the Inter-American Human Rights System (Interpretation and scope of Article 1(2), in relation to Articles 1(2), 8, 11(2), 13, 16, 21, 24, 25, 29, 30, 44, 46 and 62(3) of the American Convention on Human Rights, as well as of Article 8(1)(A) and (B) of the Protocol of San Salvador), Advisory Opinion OC-22/16, IACtHR Series A No. 22.

The Environment and Human Rights (State obligations in relation to the environment in the context of the protection and guarantee of the rights to life and to personal integrity – interpretation and scope of Articles 4(1) and 5(1) of the American Convention on Human Rights), Advisory Opinion OC-23/17, IACtHR Series A No. 23.

Gender identity, and equality and non-discrimination with regard to same-sex couples. State obligations in relation to change of name, gender identity, and rights deriving from a relationship between same-sex couples (interpretation and scope of Articles 1(1), 3, 7, 11(2), 13, 17, 18 and 24, in relation to Article 1, of the American Convention on Human Rights), Advisory Opinion OC-24/17, IACtHR Series A No. 24.

The institution of asylum, and its recognition as a human right under the Inter-American System of Protection (interpretation and scope of Articles 5, 22(7) and 22(8) in relation to Article 1(1) of the American Convention on Human Rights), Advisory Opinion OC-25/18, IACtHR Series A No. 25.

Differentiated approaches with respect to certain groups of persons in detention (Interpretation and scope of Articles 1(1), 4(1), 5, 11(2), 12, 13, 17(1), 19, 24 and 26 of the American Convention on Human Rights and other human rights instruments), Advisory Opinion OC-29/22, IACtHR Series A No. 29.

C. Decisions of national and supranational courts

Court of Justice of the European Union

Case C-386/08, judgment of 25 February 2010, ECLI:EU:C:2010:91 – *Brita.*

Case C-363/18, judgment of 12 November 2019, ECLI:EU:C:2019:954 – *Organisation juive européenne.*

Federal Constitutional Court of Germany

FCC, judgment of the first senate of 30 July 1952 – 1 BvF 1/52 – BVerfGE 1, 396 – *Deutschlandvertrag.*

FCC, order of the plenary session of 8 December 1952 – 1 PBvV 1/52 – BVerfGE 2, 79 – *Plenargutachten Heuß.*

FCC, judgment of the second senate of 7 March 1953 – 2 BvE 4/52 – BverfGE 2, 143 – *EVG-Vertrag.*

FCC, order of the first senate of 29 April 1954 – 1 BvR 328/52 – BVerfGE 3, 377 – *Schwerbeschädigtenschutz.*

FCC, order of the plenary session of 16 June 1954 – 1 PBvV 2/52 – BVerfGE 3, 407 – *Baugutachten.*

FCC, order of the first senate of 21 October 1954 – 1 BvL 9/51, 1 BvL 2/53 – BverfGE 4, 74 – *Ärztliches Berufsgericht.*

FCC, order of the first senate of 9 November 1955 – 1 BvL 13/52, 1 BvL 21/53 – BverfGE 4, 331 – *Soforthilfegesetz.*

FCC, order of the second senate of 28 November 1957 – 2 BvL 11/56 – BVerfGE 7, 183 – *Zeugenvernehmung Verwaltungsverfahren.*

FCC, judgment of the second senate of 7 and 8 March 1967 – 2 BvR 375, 53/60 and 18/65 – BVerfGE 22, 49 – *Verwaltungsstrafverfahren.*

FCC, order of the first senate of 14 March 1967 – 1 BvR 334/61 – BverfGE 21, 209 – *Auslegung einfachen Rechts.*

FCC, order of the first senate of 20 December 1978 – 1 BvR 385/77 – BVerfGE 53, 30 – *Mülheim-Kärlich.*

FCC, judgment of the second senate of 5 December 2000 – 2 BvF 1/00 – BVerfGE 103, 111 – *Wahlprüfung Hessen.*

Supreme Court of Israel

Beit Sourik Village Council v. The Government of Israel et. al., HCJ 2056/04, Supreme Court of Israel, 20 June 2004.

Mara'abe et al. v Prime Minister of Israel et al. (Alfei Menashe), HCJ 7957/04, Supreme Court of Israel, 15 September 2005.

Supreme Court of the United States of America

McCulloch v. Maryland, 17 U.S. 316 (1819), U.S. Supreme Court decision.

Bibliography

G. Abi-Saab: Les exceptions préliminaires dans la procédure de la Cour internationale. étude des notions fondamentales de procédure et des moyens de leur mise en oeuvre, Paris 1966.

G. Abi-Saab: On Discretion. Reflections on the nature of the consultative function of the International Court of Justice, in: L. Boisson de Chazournes/P. Sands (eds.), International law, the World Court of justice and nuclear weapons, Cambridge, New York 1999, 36–50.

R. Ago: "Binding" Advisory Opinions of the International Court of Justice, 85, AJIL 3 (1991), 439.

D. Akande: The Competence of International Organizations and the Advisory Jurisdiction of the International Court of Justice, 9, EJIL 3 (1998), 437.

D. Akande: Selection of the International Court of Justice as a Forum for Contentious and Advisory Proceedings (Including Jurisdiction), 7, Journal of International Dispute Settlement 2 (2016), 320.

M. M. Aljaghoub: The Advisory Function of the International Court of Justice 1946 – 2005, Berlin Heidelberg 2006.

M. M. Aljaghoub: The Absence of State Consent to Advisory Opinions of the International Court of Justice, 24, ALQ 2 (2010), 191.

S. Allen: Self-determination, the Chagos Advisory Opinion and the Chagossians, 69, International and Comparative Law Quarterly 1 (2020), 203.

S. Allen: Reflections on the Treatment of General Assembly Resolutions in the Chagos Advisory Opinion, in: T. Burri/J. Trinidad (eds.), The International Court of Justice and decolonisation. New directions from the Chagos Advisory Opinion, Cambridge 2021, 41–50.

K. J. Alter, L. R. Helfer & M. R. Madsen: How Context Shapes the Authority of International Courts, in: K. J. Alter/L. R. Helfer/M. R. Madsen (eds.), International court authority, Oxford, United Kingdom 2018, 24–56.

K. J. Alter, L. R. Helfer, M. R. Madsen (eds.): International court authority, Oxford, United Kingdom 2018.

K. J. Alter, L. R. Helfer & M. R. Madsen: International Court Authority in a Complex World, in: K. J. Alter/L. R. Helfer/M. R. Madsen (eds.), International court authority, Oxford, United Kingdom 2018, 3–23.

J. E. Alvarez: Judging the Security Council, 90, American Journal of International Law 1 (1996), 1.

J. E. Alvarez: What are International Judges for? The Main Functions of International Adjudication, in: C. Romano/K. J. Alter/Y. Shany (eds.), The Oxford Handbook of International Adjudication, Oxford 2013, 158–176.

C. F. Amerasinghe: Jurisdiction of International Tribunals, The Hague, London 2003.

C. F. Amerasinghe: Principles of the institutional law of international organizations, Cambridge studies in international and comparative law, 36, Cambridge 2005.

C. F. Amerasinghe: Reflections on the Judicial Function in International Law, in: T. M. Ndiaye/R. Wolfrum/C. Kojima (eds.), Law of the sea, environmental law, and settlement of disputes. Liber amicorum Judge Thomas A. Mensah, Boston 2007, 119–130.

R. J. Araujo: Implementation of the ICJ Advisory Opinion – Legal Consequences of the Construction of a Wall in the Occupied Palestinian Territory, 22, BUILJ 2 (2004), 349.

A. von *Arnauld*: Völkerrecht, 5. ed., Heidelberg 2023.

A. Aust: Advisory Opinions, 1, JIDS 1 (2010), 123.

A. Aust: Modern treaty law and practice, 3. ed., Cambridge 2013.

A. Balasko: Causes de nullité de la sentence arbitrale en droit international public, Paris 1938.

M. A. Becker: Request for an Advisory Opinion Submitted by the Sub-regional Fisheries Commission (SRFC), 109, American Journal of International Law 4 (2015), 851.

D. Beetham: The legitimation of power, Issues in political theory, Houndmills, Basingstoke, Hampshire 1991.

E. Benz: The Advisory Function of the Inter-American Court of Human Rights, Beiträge zum ausländischen öffentlichen Recht und Völkerrecht, 329, Baden-Baden 2024.

M. Benzing: Evidentiary Issues, in: A. Zimmermann/C. J. Tams/K. Oellers-Frahm/C. Tomuschat/D. W. K. Anderson (eds.), The Statute of the International Court of Justice. A commentary, 3. ed., Oxford 2019.

H. C. Black, B. A. Garner (eds.): Black's law dictionary, 8. ed., St. Paul, Minn. 2007.

N. Blokker: Constituent Instruments, in: J. K. Cogan/I. Hurd/I. Johnstone (eds.), The Oxford Handbook of International Organizations, Oxford 2016.

N. M. Blokker: International Organizations or Institutions, Implied Powers (last updated 2021), in: A. Peters/R. Wolfrum (eds.), The Max Planck Encyclopedia of Public International Law 2008.

E.-W. Böckenförde: Verfassungsfragen der Richterwahl. Dargestellt anhand der Gesetzentwürfe zur Einführung der Richterwahl in Nordrhein-Westfalen, Schriften zum öffentlichen Recht, Bd. 250, Berlin 1974.

A. v. Bogdandy/I. Venzke: In Whose Name?, 23, European Journal of International Law 1 (2012), 7.

A. v. Bogdandy/I. Venzke: On the Functions of International Courts, 26, LJIL 1 (2013), 49.

A. v. Bogdandy & I. Venzke: In wessen Namen? Internationale Gerichte in Zeiten globalen Regierens, 2. ed., Berlin 2014.

L. Boisson de Chazournes, P. Sands (eds.): International law, the World Court of justice and nuclear weapons, Cambridge, New York 1999.

F. L. Bordin: Reckoning with British colonialism, 78, CLJ 2 (2019), 253.

F. L. Bordin: State Responsibility in Advisory Proceedings. Thoughts on Judicial Propriety and Multilateralism in the Chagos Opinion, in: T. Burri/J. Trinidad (eds.), The International Court of Justice and decolonisation. New directions from the Chagos Advisory Opinion, Cambridge 2021, 95–116.

A. E. Boyle & C. Chinkin: The making of international law, Foundations of public international law, Oxford, New York 2007.

C. Bradley/J. Kelley: The Concept of International Delegation, 71, Law and Contemporary Problems 1 (2008), 1.

C. Brown: Inherent Powers in International Adjudication, in: C. Romano/K. J. Alter/Y. Shany (eds.), The Oxford Handbook of International Adjudication, Oxford 2013,828–847.

C. Brown: Article 59 ICJ Statute, in: A. Zimmermann/C. J. Tams/K. Oellers-Frahm/C. Tomuschat/D. W. K. Anderson (eds.), The Statute of the International Court of Justice. A commentary, 3. ed., Oxford 2019, 1561–1590.

J. Brunnée: Consent (last updated 2010), in: A. Peters/R. Wolfrum (eds.), The Max Planck Encyclopedia of Public International Law 2008.

J. Brunnée & S. J. Toope: Legitimacy and legality in international law. An interactional account, Cambridge studies in international and comparative law, Cambridge, New York 2010.

F. Burmeister: Gutachten des Bundesverfassungsgerichts zu völkerrechtlichen Verträgen, Hamburger Studien zum europäischen und internationalen Recht, 15, Berlin 1998.

T. Burri/J. Trinidad: Dispute Concerning Delimitation of the Maritime Boundary between Mauritius and Maldives in the Indian Ocean, Preliminary Objections (ITLOS), 60, International Legal Materials 6 (2021), 969.

C. Burset: Advisory Opinions and the Problem of Legal Authority, 74, Vanderbilt Law Review 3 (2021), 621.

G. A. Caldeira/J. L. Gibson: The Legitimacy of the Court of Justice in the European Union: Models of Institutional Support, 89, The American Political Science Review 2 (1995), 356.

B. Çalı: Authority, in: J. d' Aspremont/S. Singh (eds.), Concepts for international law. Contributions to disciplinary thought, Cheltenham, UK 2019, 39–53.

B. Çalı/A. Koch/N. Bruch: The Legitimacy of Human Rights Courts: A Grounded Interpretivist Analysis of the European Court of Human Rights, 35, Human Rights Quarterly 4 (2013), 955.

M. Cappelletti: The law-making power of the judge and its limits: a comparative analysis, 8, MULR 1 (1981), 15.

A. Cassese: The Legitimacy of International Criminal Tribunals and the Current Prospects of International Criminal Justice, 25, Leiden Journal of International Law 2 (2012), 491.

L. Chenwi: The Advisory Proceedings of the African Court on Human and Peoples' Rights, 38, Nordic Journal of Human Rights 1 (2020), 61.

C. Chinkin: The East Timor Case (Portugal v. Australia), 45, ICLQ 3 (1996), 712.

C. M. Chinkin: Third parties in international law, Oxford monographs in international law, Oxford 1993.

R. Christensen: Was heißt Gesetzesbindung? Eine rechtslinguistische Untersuchung, Schriften zur Rechtstheorie, v.140, Berlin 1989.

Christian J Tams: The ICJ as a 'Law-Formative Agency': Summary and Synthesis, in: C. J. Tams/J. Sloan (eds.), The development of international law by the International Court of Justice, Oxford 2014.

Committee of Ministers: Explanatory Report to Protocol No. 2 to the Convention for the Protection of Human Rights and Fundamental Freedoms, conferring upon the European Court of Human Rights competence to give advisory opinions 6 May 1963.

J.-P. Cot & *S. Wittich*: Art. 68, in: A. Zimmermann/C. J. Tams/K. Oellers-Frahm/C. Tomuschat/D. W. K. Anderson (eds.), The Statute of the International Court of Justice. A commentary, 3. ed., Oxford 2019.

J. Crawford: Opinion: Third Party Obligations with respect to Israeli Settlements in the Occupied Palestinian Territories 2012.

J. Crawford: Brownlie's Principles of Public International Law, 9. ed. 2019.

Z. Crespi Reghizzi: The Chagos Advisory Opinion and the Principle of Consent to Adjudication, in: T. Burri/J. Trinidad (eds.), The International Court of Justice and decolonisation. New directions from the Chagos Advisory Opinion, Cambridge 2021, 51–70.

D. P. Currie: The Constitution in the Supreme Court. The First Hundred Years 1789–1888, Chicago and London 1985.

L. F. Damrosch/B. H. Oxman: Agora: ICJ Advisory Opinion on Construction of a Wall in the Occupied Palestinian Territory, 99, AJIL 1 (2005), 1.

P. d'Argent: Article 65, in: A. Zimmermann/C. J. Tams/K. Oellers-Frahm/C. Tomuschat/D. W. K. Anderson (eds.), The Statute of the International Court of Justice. A commentary, 3. ed., Oxford 2019.

M. Dawidowicz: The Obligation of Non-Recognition of an Unlawful Situation, in: J. Crawford/A. Pellet/S. Olleson/K. Parlett (eds.), The law of international responsibility, Oxford 2010, 677–686.

M. Dicosola/C. Fasone/I. Spigno: The Prospective Role of Constitutional Courts in the Advisory Opinion Mechanism Before the European Court of Human Rights, 16, German Law Journal 6 (2015), 1387.

Dinstein: The International Law of Belligerent Occupation 2009.

O. Dörr: Art. 31, in: O. Dörr/K. Schmalenbach (eds.), Vienna convention on the law of treaties. A commentary, Heidelberg, Dordrecht, London, New York 2012.

O. Dörr: Art. 31, in: O. Dörr/K. Schmalenbach (eds.), Vienna Convention on the Law of Treaties. A Commentary, 2. ed., Berlin, Heidelberg 2018.

J. Dugard: Advisory Opinions and the Secretary-General with Special Reference to the 2004 Advisory Opinion on the Wall, in: L. Boisson de Chazournes/M. G. Kohen/Boisson-de-Chazournes-Kohen (eds.), International law and the quest for its implementation. Liber amicorum Vera Gowlland-Debbas = Le droit international et la quête de sa mise en oeuvre, Leiden 2010, 403–416.

P.-M. Dupuy: Recourse to the International Court of Justice for the Purpose of Settling a Dispute, in: L. Boisson de Chazournes/M. G. Kohen/J. Viñuales (eds.), Diplomatic and judicial means of dispute settlement, Leiden 2013, 61–69.

S. T. Ebobrah: International Human Rights Courts, in: C. Romano/K. J. Alter/Y. Shany (eds.), The Oxford Handbook of International Adjudication, Oxford 2013, 225–249.

F. S. Eichberger: The Legal Effect of ICJ Advisory Opinions Redefined?, 22, Melbourne Journal of International Law 2 (2021), 1.

J. Esser: Richterrecht, Gerichtsgebrauch und Gewohnheitsrecht, in: J. Esser/H. Thieme (eds.), Festschrift für Fritz von Hippel zum 70. Geburtstag, Tübingen 1967, 95–130.

J. H. Fahner: Two Takes on Chagos. Reconciling the Advisory Opinion with the Res Judicata Effect of the UNCLOS Arbitral Award, in: T. Burri/J. Trinidad (eds.), The International Court of Justice and decolonisation. New directions from the Chagos Advisory Opinion, Cambridge 2021, 71–94.

R. Falk: The Kosovo Advisory Opinion, 105, American Journal of International Law 1 (2011), 50.

B. Fassbender: Art. 2(1), in: B. Simma/D.-E. Khan/G. Nolte/A. Paulus (eds.), The Charter of the United Nations. A commentary, 4. ed., Oxford 2024.

W. Fikentscher: Methoden des Rechts. In vergleichender Darstellung, 4, Tübingen 1977.

J. Finke: Die Parallelität internationaler Streitbeilegungsmechanismen. Untersuchung der aus der Stärkung der internationalen Gerichtsbarkeit resultierenden Konflikte, Veröffentlichungen des Walther-Schücking-Instituts für Internationales Recht an der Universität Kiel - Band 147, Berlin 2004.

G. G. Fitzmaurice: The Law and Procedure of the International Court of Justice, 29, British Yearbook of International Law (BYIL) 1 (1952), 1.

T. M. Franck: Legitimacy in the International System, 82, American Journal of International Law 4 (1988), 705.

T. M. Franck: The power of legitimacy among nations, New York 1990.

T. M. Franck: Fact-Finding in the I.C.J., in: R. B. Lillich (ed.), Fact-finding before international tribunals. Eleventh Sokol colloquium, Ardsley-on-Hudson (N.Y.) 1992, 21–32.

J. A. Frowein & K. Oellers-Frahm: Art. 65, in: A. Zimmermann/C. Tomuschat/K. Oellers-Frahm/C. J. Tams/M. Kashgar/D. Diehl (eds.), The Statute of the International Court of Justice. A commentary, 2. ed., Oxford 2012, 1605–1637.

L. L. Fuller: The morality of law, Storrs lectures on jurisprudence, 1963, New Haven, London 1969.

M. García García-Revillo: The contentious and advisory jurisdiction of the International Tribunal for the law of the sea, Leiden [etc.] 2015.

R. K. Gardiner: Treaty interpretation, 2. ed., The Oxford International Law Library, Oxford 2015.

C. D. Gaver: Dispute Concerning Delimitation of the Maritime Boundary Between Mauritius and Maldives in the Indian Ocean (Mauritius/Maldives), 115, American Journal of International Law 3 (2021), 519.

W. Geiger: Zur Reform des Bundesverfassungsgesetzes, in: T. Maunz (ed.), Vom Bonner Grundgesetz zur gesamtdeutschen Verfassung. Festschrift zum 75. Geburtstag von Hans Nawiasky, München 1956, 211–236.

W. Geiger: Abweichende Meinungen zu Entscheidungen des Bundesverfassungsgerichts, Tübingen 1989.

F. Giese: Die Verbindlichkeit gutachtlicher Beschlüsse des Bundesverfassungsgerichts, 78, Archiv des öffentlichen Rechts 3/4 (1952/1953), 389.

M. Giles Samson & *D. Guilfoyle*: The Permanent Court of International Justice and the "Invention" of International Advisory Jurisdiction, in: C. J. Tams/M. Fitzmaurice (eds.), Legacies of the Permanent Court of International Justice, Leiden 2013, 41–68.

V. Gowlland-Debbas: The Relationship between the International Court of Justice and the Security Council in the Light of the Lockerbie Case, 88, American Journal of International Law 4 (1994), 643.

C. Greenwood: Judicial Integrity and the Advisory Jurisdiction of the International Court of Justice, in: J. Grote Stoutenburg/G. Gaja (eds.), Enhancing the rule of law through the International Court of Justice. ... presented at a Conference Entitled "The International Court of Justice in the Service of Peace and Justice" which took place on 23 September 2013 at the Peace Palace at the Hague, Leiden, Boston 2014, 63–73.

D. W. Greig: The Advisory Jurisdiction of the International Court and the Settlement of Disputes between States, 15, International and Comparative Law Quarterly 2–3 (1966), 325.

A. M. Gross: The Construction of a Wall Between the Hague and Jerusalem, 19, Leiden Journal of International Law 2 (2006), 393.

J. R. Gundersen: Advisory Opinions, in: K. L. Hall (ed.), The Oxford Companion to the Supreme Court of the United States, 2. ed. 2005,p. 21.

E. Hambro: The Authority of the Advisory Opinions of the International Court of Justice, 3, International and Comparative Law Quarterly 1 (1954), 2.

Heinrich Triepel: Völkerrecht und Landesrecht 1899.

W. Heintschel von Heinegg: § 55. Vom ius ad bellum zum ius contra bellum, in: V. Epping/W. Heintschel von Heinegg (eds.), Völkerrecht, 7. ed., München 2018.

J. Heliskoski: Eastern Carelia (Request for Advisory Opinion) (last updated 2007), in: A. Peters/R. Wolfrum (eds.), The Max Planck Encyclopedia of Public International Law 2008.

G. I. Hernández: The International Court of Justice and the judicial function, Oxford United Kingdom 2014.

C. Heyns & *M. Killander*: South West Africa/Namibia (Advisory Opinions and Judgments) (last updated 2007), in: A. Peters/R. Wolfrum (eds.), The Max Planck Encyclopedia of Public International Law 2008.

M. Hilf: Gutachten des BVerfG zu völkerrechtlichen Verträgen?, 30, Zeitschrift für Rechtspolitik 7 (1997), 270.

M. O. Hudson: Advisory Opinions of National and International Courts, 37, Harvard Law Review 8 (1924), 970.

M. O. Hudson: The American Reservations and the Permanent Court of International Justice, 22, AJIL 4 (1928), 776.

M. O. Hudson: The Permanent Court of international justice. A treatise, New York 1934.

M. O. Hudson: International Tribunals. Past and Future, Washington 1944.

M. O. Hudson: The Effect of Advisory Opinions of the World Court, 42, AJIL 3 (1948), 630.

A. Huneeus: Compliance with Judgments and Decisions, in: C. Romano/K. J. Alter/Y. Shany (eds.), The Oxford Handbook of International Adjudication, Oxford 2013, 437–462.

D. Jacobs/Y. Radi: Waiting for Godot, 24, Leiden Journal of International Law 2 (2011), 331–354.

J. Jahn: Normative Guidance from Strasbourg Through Advisory Opinions, 74, Zeitschrift für ausländisches öffentliches Recht und Völkerrecht / Heidelberg Journal of International Law (2014), 821.

C. C. Jalloh: First Report on Subsidiary Means for the Determination of Rules of International Law, A/CN.4/760 16 May 2023.

R. Y. Jennings: Advisory Opinions of the International Court of Justice, in: B. Boutros-Ghali (ed.), Amicorum Discipulorumque Liber. Paix, dėveloppement, démocratie, Bruxelles 1998,531.

N. H. B. Jørgensen: The Obligation of Non-Assistance of the Responsible State, in: J. Crawford/A. Pellet/S. Olleson/K. Parlett (eds.), The law of international responsibility, Oxford 2010, 687–694.

J. L. Kateka: Advisory Proceedings before the Seabed Disputes Chamber and before the ITLOS as a Full Court, 17, Max Planck Yearbook of United Nations Law 1 (2013), 159.

V. Kattan: The Palestine question in international law, London 2008.

V. Kattan: The Chagos Advisory Opinion and the Law of Self-Determination, 10, Asian Journal of International Law (2020), 12.

A. Keene: The Forgotten Potential of the Advisory Jurisdictions of International Courts and Tribunals as Check on the Actions of International Organisations, 14, NZJPIL 1 (2016), 67.

K. J. Keith: The extent of the advisory jurisdiction of the International Court of Justice, Leyden 1971.

K. J. Keith: The Advisory Jurisdiction of the International Court of Justice, 16, AYBIL 39 (1996), 39–58.

H. Keller & *A. Stone Sweet*: A Europe of rights. The impact of the ECHR on national legal systems, Oxford 2008.

H. Kelsen: The Principle of Sovereign Equality of States as a Basis for International Organization, 53, Yale Law Journal 2 (1944), 207.

H. Kelsen: The law of the United Nations. A critical analysis of its fundamental problems, 2. ed., London 1951.

J. Klabbers: An introduction to international organizations law, 3. ed., Cambridge 2015.

E. Klein & *S. Schmahl*: Art. 10, in: B. Simma/D.-E. Khan/G. Nolte/A. Paulus (eds.), The Charter of the United Nations. A commentary, 3. ed., Oxford 2012.

R. Kolb: De la Pretendue Discretion de la Cour Internationale de Justice, 12, AJICL (2000), 799.

R. Kolb: The International Court of Justice, Oxford 2013.

R. Kolb: The Elgar companion to the International Court of Justice, Elgar Companions to International Courts and Tribunals series, Cheltenham, UK, Northampton, MA, USA 2014.

R. Kolb: Le Droit International Comme Corps de «Droit Privé» et de «Droit Public» (Volume 419), Collected Courses of the Hague Academy of International Law 2021.

H. W. Kruse: Das Richterrecht als Rechtsquelle des innerstaatlichen Rechts, Recht und Staat in Geschichte und Gegenwart, 396, Tübingen 1971.

A. Kulick: Between Advice and Miracle, 27, International Community Law Review 1–2 (2025), 33.

M. Lando: The Advisory Jurisdiction of the International Tribunal for the Law of the Sea, 29, LJIL 2 (2016), 441.

M. Lando: Advisory Opinions of the International Court of Justice in Respect of Disputes, 61, CJTL 1 (2023), 67.

M. Lando: Binding Advisory Opinions, in: R. Buchan/D. Franchini/N. Tsagourias (eds.), The Changing Character of International Dispute Settlement: Challenges and Prospects 2023, 106–134.

N. Lanzoni: The Authority of ICJ Advisory Opinions as Precedents: The Mauritius/Maldives Case, 2, The Italian Review of International and Comparative Law 2 (2022), 296.

K. Larenz: Methodenlehre der Rechtswissenschaft, 6. ed., Enzyklopädie der Rechts- und Staatswissenschaft. Abteilung Rechtswissenschaft, Berlin [etc.] 1991.

H. Lauterpacht: Private law sources and analogies of international law, London 1927.

H. Lauterpacht: Decisions of Municipal Courts as a Source of International Law, 10, British Yearbook of International Law (1929), 65.

H. Lauterpacht: The international protection of human rights, Collected courses = Recueil des cours, 070 (1947), Leiden, the Netherlands 1947.

H. Lauterpacht: The development of international law by the International Court, 2. ed., London 1958.

G. Le Floch: Le premier avis de la formation plenière du tribunal international du droit de la mer, Annuaire français de droit international (2015), 669.

O. W. Lembcke: Hüter der Verfassung. Eine institutionentheoretische Studie zur Autorität des Bundesverfassungsgerichts, Neue Staatswissenschaften, 7, Tübingen 2007.

M. Lippold: Art. 7, in: B. Simma/D.-E. Khan/G. Nolte/A. Paulus (eds.), The Charter of the United Nations. A commentary, 4. ed., Oxford 2024.

M. R. Madsen: Sociological Approaches to International Courts, in: C. Romano/K. J. Alter/Y. Shany (eds.), The Oxford Handbook of International Adjudication, Oxford 2013, 388–412.

G. Marston: The London Committee and the Statute of the International Court of Justice, in: V. Lowe (ed.), Fifty years of the International Court of Justice. Essays in honour of Sir Robert Jennings, Cambridge 1996, 40–60.

R. McCorquodale/J. Robinson/N. Peart: Territorial integrity and consent in the Chagos Advisory Opinion, 69, International and Comparative Law Quarterly 1 (2020), 221.

Mehrdad Payandeh: Klare Worte und konstruktive Ambiguität, 79, JuristenZeitung 18 (2024), 789.

M. Milanović: From Compromise to Principle, 8, HRLR 3 (2008), 411.

Z. Mollengarden/N. Zamir: The Monetary Gold Principle: Back to Basics, 115, American Journal of International Law 1 (2021), 41.

C. Möllers: Gewaltengliederung. Legitimation und Dogmatik im nationalen und internationalen Rechtsvergleich, Jus publicum, Bd. 141, Tübingen 2005.

J. B. Moore: The question of advisory opinions. Memorandum by Mr. Moore, PCIJ Series D. No. 2 1922.

H. Mosler: Art. 96, in: B. Simma/H. Mosler/R. Bernhardt (eds.), Charta der Vereinten Nationen. Kommentar, München 1991.

S. D. Murphy: Self-Defense and the Israeli Wall Advisory Opinion: An Ipse Dixit from the ICJ?, 99, AJIL 1 (2005), 62.

S. D. Murphy: International Judicial Bodies for Resolving Disputes Between States, in: C. Romano/K. J. Alter/Y. Shany (eds.), The Oxford Handbook of International Adjudication, Oxford 2013, 182–204.

R. Murray: The African Charter on Human and Peoples' Rights: A Commentary 2019.

T. M. Ndiaye: The Advisory Function of the International Tribunal for the Law of the Sea, 9, Chinese Journal of International Law 3 (2010), 565.

D. Négulesco: L'évolution de la procédure des avis consultatifs de la Cour permanente de Justice internationale, 57, Recueil des cours d'Académie de Droit International de La Haye (1936), 5.

A. Nollkaemper: International Adjudication of Global Public Goods, 23, European Journal of International Law 3 (2012), 769.

A. Nollkaemper: National courts and the international rule of law, Oxford, United Kingdom 2012.

G. Nolte: Treaties and subsequent practice, Oxford Public International Law, Oxford 2013.

G. Nolte: Third report on subsequent agreements and subsequent practice in relation to the interpretation of treaties, UN Docs A/CN.4/683 7. April 2015.

G. Nolte: Art. 2(7), in: B. Simma/D.-E. Khan/G. Nolte/A. Paulus (eds.), The Charter of the United Nations. A commentary, 4. ed., Oxford 2024.

A. Nußberger: The European Court of Human Rights, Elements of international law, Oxford 2020.

M. D. Oberg: The Legal Effects of United Nations Resolutions in the Kosovo Advisory Opinion, 105, American Journal of International Law 1 (2011), 81.

M. E. O'Connell & L. Vanderzee: The History of International Adjudication, in: C. Romano/K. J. Alter/Y. Shany (eds.), The Oxford Handbook of International Adjudication, Oxford 2013.

K. Oellers-Frahm: Multiplication of International Courts and Tribunals and Conflicting Jurisdiction, 5, MPYUNL (2001), 67.

K. Oellers-Frahm: Lawmaking through Advisory Opinions?, 12, GLJ 5 (2011), 1033.

K. Oellers-Frahm: Art. 94, in: B. Simma/D.-E. Khan/G. Nolte/A. Paulus (eds.), The Charter of the United Nations. A commentary, 3. ed., Oxford 2012, 1957–1971.

K. Oellers-Frahm: Art. 96, in: B. Simma/D.-E. Khan/G. Nolte/A. Paulus (eds.), The Charter of the United Nations. A commentary, 3. ed., Oxford 2012, 1975–1990.

K. Oellers-Frahm & *E. Lagrange*: Art. 96, in: B. Simma/D.-E. Khan/G. Nolte/A. Paulus (eds.), The Charter of the United Nations. A commentary, 4. ed., Oxford 2024.

L. Oppenheim & *H. Lauterpacht*: International Law, 7. ed., London 1948.

A. Orakhelashvili: The Concept of International Judicial Jurisdiction, 3, The Law and Practice of International Courts and Tribunals (2003), 501.

A. Orakhelashvili: Legal Consequences of the Construction of a Wall in the Occupied Palestinian Territory: Opinion and Reaction, 11, Journal of Conflict and Security Law 1 (2006), 119.

A. Orakhelashvili: The Competence of the International Court of Justice and the Doctrine of the Indispensable Party: from Monetary Gold to East Timor and Beyond, 2, Journal of International Dispute Settlement 2 (2011), 373.

M. Paparinskis: Inherent Powers of ICSID Tribunals. Broad and Rightly So, in: I. A. Laird/T. Weiler (eds.), Investment treaty arbitration and international law, Huntington, N.Y. 2012.

A. Paprocka/M. Ziolkowski: Advisory Opinions under Protocol No. 16 to the European Convention on Human Rights, 11, European Constitutional Law Review 2 (2015), 274.

J. M. Pasqualucci: The practice and procedure of the Inter-American Court of Human Rights, 2. ed., New York 2013.

A. Paulus: Art. 66, in: A. Zimmermann/C. J. Tams/K. Oellers-Frahm/C. Tomuschat/D. W. K. Anderson (eds.), The Statute of the International Court of Justice. A commentary, 3. ed., Oxford 2019.

M. Payandeh: Internationales Gemeinschaftsrecht. Zur Herausbildung gemeinschaftsrechtlicher Strukturen im Völkerrecht der Globalisierung, Beiträge zum ausländischen öffentlichen Recht und Völkerrecht, 219, Berlin, Heidelberg 2010.

M. Payandeh: Judikative Rechtserzeugung. Theorie, Dogmatik und Methodik der Wirkungen von Präjudizien, Jus publicum, Band 265, Tübingen 2017.

M. Payandeh: Art. 92, in: W. Kahl/C. Waldhoff/C. Walter (eds.), Bonner Kommentar zum Grundgesetz June 2020, 1–234.

A. Pellet: Art. 38, in: A. Zimmermann/C. J. Tams/K. Oellers-Frahm/C. Tomuschat/D. W. K. Anderson (eds.), The Statute of the International Court of Justice. A commentary, 3. ed., Oxford 2019.

A. Peters: Die Anwendbarkeit der EMRK in Zeiten komplexer Hoheitsgewalt und das Prinzip der Grundrechtstoleranz, 48, Archiv des Völkerrechts 1 (2010), 1.

A. Peters: Has the Advisory Opinion's Finding that Kosovo's Declaration of Independence was not Contrary to International Law Set an Unfortunate Precedent?, in: M. Milanović/M. Wood (eds.), The Law and Politics of the Kosovo Advisory Opinion, Oxford 2015, 291–313.

B. Peters/J. K. Schaffer: The Turn to Authority beyond States, 4, Transnational Legal Theory 3 (2013), 315.

A. Pillepich: Art. 94, in: J.-P. Cot/A. Pellet (eds.), La Charte des Nations Unies. Commentaire article par article, 3. ed., Paris 2005, 1987–1998.

M. Pomerance: The Admission of Judges Ad Hoc In Advisory Proceedings: Some Reflections in the Light of the Namibia Case, 67, The American journal of international law 3 (1973), 446.

M. Pomerance: The advisory function of the International Court in the League and U.N. eras, Baltimore u.a. 1973.

M. Pomerance: The United States and the Advisory Function of the Permanent Court of International Justice, in: Y. Dinstein (ed.), International law at a time of perplexity. Essays in honour of Shabtai Rosenne, Dordrecht 1989, 567–592.

M. Pomerance: The Advisory Role of the International Court of Justice and its 'Judicial' Character. Past and Future Prisms, in: S. Muller/D. Raic/J. M. Thuránszky (eds.), The International Court of Justice. Its future role after fifty years, The Hague 1997, 271–323.

M. Pomerance: The ICJ's Advisory Jurisdiction and the Crumbling Wall Between the Political and the Judicial, 99, AJIL 1 (2005), 26.

D. Pratap: The advisory jurisdiction of the International Court, Oxford 1972.

G. Puma: Preliminary Questions in the ICJ Advisory Opinion on the Legal Consequences of the Separation of the Chagos Archipelago from Mauritius in 1965, 79, Zeitschrift für ausländisches öffentliches Recht und Völkerrecht (ZaöRV) (2019), 841.

J. Raz: The authority of law. Essays on law and morality, Oxford 1979.

A. von Rebay/C. Oberle: Booming Advisory Jurisdiction of the International Tribunal for the Law of the Sea, 83, Zeitschrift für ausländisches öffentliches Recht und Völkerrecht / Heidelberg Journal of International Law 2 (2023), 283.

K. F. Röhl: Allgemeine Rechtslehre. Ein Lehrbuch, Köln 1995.

C. P. R. Romano, K. J. Alter & Y. Shany: Mapping International Adjudicative Bodies, the Issues, and Players, in: C. Romano/K. J. Alter/Y. Shany (eds.), The Oxford Handbook of International Adjudication, Oxford 2013.

Y. Ronen: Forum Prorogatum (last updated 2020), in: A. Peters/R. Wolfrum (eds.), The Max Planck Encyclopedia of Public International Law 2008.

S. Rosenne: Visit to the Site by the International Court, in: E. Yakpo/T. Boumedra (eds.), Liber amicorum Judge Mohammed Bedjaoui, The Hague 1999, 461–473.

S. Rosenne: The law and practice of the International Court, 1920–2005, 4. ed., Leiden, Boston 2006.

T. Ruys/A. Soete: 'Creeping' Advisory Jurisdiction of International Courts and Tribunals?, 29, Leiden Journal of International Law 1 (2016), 155.

C. Ryngaert: Jurisdiction in international law, 2. ed., Oxford monographs in international law, Oxford 2015.

J. Salmon: Who are the addressees of the Opinions?, in: L. Boisson de Chazournes/P. Sands (eds.), International law, the World Court of justice and nuclear weapons, Cambridge, New York 1999.

H. G. Schermers & *N. Blokker*: International institutional law. Unity within diversity, 6. ed., Leiden 2018.

S. Schmahl: Die Internationalen und die Supranationalen Organisationen, in: W. Vitzthum/A. Proelß (eds.), Law of Nations, 8. ed., Berlin/Boston 2019, 319–462.

H. Schulze-Fielitz: Art. 92, in: H. Dreier (ed.), Grundgesetz Kommentar 2018, 473–507.

S. M. Schwebel: Was the Capacity to Request an Advisory Opinion Wider in the Permanent Court of International Justice than it is in the International Court of Justice?, in: S. M. Schwebel (ed.), Justice in International Law: Selected Writings of Judge Stephen M. Schwebel 1994, 27–71.

I. Scobbie: International Court of Justice: Recent Cases, 42, International and Comparative Law Quarterly 3 (1993), 705.

I. Scobbie: Unchart(er)ed Waters?, 16, EJIL 5 (2005), 941.

I. Scobbie: Words my Mother Never Taught Me—"In Defense of the International Court", 99, AJIL 1 (2005), 76.

M. Shahabuddeen: Precedent in the World Court, Hersch Lauterpacht memorial lectures, 13, Cambridge 1996.

Y. Shany: The Competing Jurisdictions of International Courts and Tribunals, International courts and tribunals series, Oxford 2003.

Y. Shany: Assessing the Effectiveness of International Courts, 106, American Journal of International Law 2 (2012), 225.

Y. Shany: Jurisdiction and Admissibility, in: C. Romano/K. J. Alter/Y. Shany (eds.), The Oxford Handbook of International Adjudication, Oxford 2013, 779–801.

S. Shapiro: Authority, in: J. L. Coleman/S. Shapiro (eds.), The Oxford Handbook of Jurisprudence and Philosophy of Law, Oxford, New York 2004, 382–439.

M. N. Shaw: International law, 7. ed., Cambridge 2014.

M. N. Shaw: Rosenne's Law and Practice of the International Court: 1920–2015, 5. ed. 2016.

M. N. Shaw: International law, 8. ed., Cambridge, United Kingdom, New York, NY, Port Melbourne, VIC, Delhi, Singapore 2017.

F. B. Sloan: Advisory Jurisdiction of the International Court of Justice, 38, CLR 5 (1950), 830.

D. Snoxell: Prospect of the Chagos Advisory Opinion and the Subsequent UN General Assembly Resolution Helping to Resolve the Future of the Chagos Archipelago and Its Former Inhabitants. A Political Perspective, in: T. Burri/J. Trinidad (eds.), The International Court of Justice and decolonisation. New directions from the Chagos Advisory Opinion, Cambridge 2021, 262–279.

L. B. Sohn: Advisory Opinions by the International Tribunal for the Law of the Sea or Its Seabed Disputes Chamber, in: Moore (ed.), Oceans Policy 1999, 61–72.

J.-M. Sorel & *V. Eveno Boré*: Art. 31, in: O. Corten/P. Klein (eds.), The Vienna Conventions on the law of treaties. A commentary, Oxford 2011.

O. Spiermann: Who Attempts too Much Does Nothing Well, 73, British Yearbook of International Law 1 (2003), 187.

O. Spiermann: International legal argument in the permanent court of international justice. The rise of the international judiciary, Cambridge studies in international and comparative law, 34, Cambridge 2005.

R. J. St. MacDonald: Changing Relations between the International Court of Justice and the Security Council of the United Nations, 31, Canadian Yearbook of International Law/Annuaire canadien de droit international (1994), 3.

C. Staker: Jurisdiction, in: M. D. Evans (ed.), International law, 5. ed., Oxford, New York 2018.

K. Stern: Das Staatsrecht der Bundesrepublik Deutschland. Staatsorgane, Staatsfunktionen, Finanz- und Haushaltsverfassung, Notstandsverfassung, Band 2, München 1980.

J. Summers: Chagos, Custom and the Interpretation of UN General Assembly Resolutions, in: T. Burri/J. Trinidad (eds.), The International Court of Justice and decolonisation. New directions from the Chagos Advisory Opinion, Cambridge 2021, 9–40.

C. J. Tams: Peace Through International Adjudication. The Permanent Court of International Justice and the Post-War Order, in: M. Erpelding/B. Hess/H. Ruiz Fabri (eds.), Peace Through Law 2019, 215–238.

C. J. Tams & *J. Devaney*: Art. 50, in: A. Zimmermann/C. J. Tams/K. Oellers-Frahm/C. Tomuschat/D. W. K. Anderson (eds.), The Statute of the International Court of Justice. A commentary, 3. ed., Oxford 2019.

T. Thienel: The 'Living Instrument' Approach in the ECHR and Elsewhere. Some Remarks on the Evolutive Interpretation of International Treaties, in: J. Delbrück/U. E. Heinz/K. Odendahl/N. Matz-Lück/A. von Arnauld (eds.), Aus Kiel in die Welt: Kiel's Contribution to International Law. Festschrift zum 100-jährigen Bestehen des Walther-Schücking-Instituts für Internationales Recht. Essays in Honour of 100th Anniversary of the Walther Schücking Institute for International Law, Berlin 2014, 165–200.

T. Thienel: Drittstaaten und die Jurisdiktion des Internationalen Gerichtshofs. Die Monetary Gold-Doktrin, 192 2016.

H. W. Thirlway: The Law and Procedure of the International Court of Justice 1960–1989, 60, British Yearbook of International Law (BYIL) 1 (1989), 1.

H. W. A. Thirlway: The International Court of Justice, [Oxford] 2016.

H. W. A. Thirlway: The international court of justice, in: M. D. Evans (ed.), International law, 5. ed., Oxford, New York 2018.

H. W. A. Thirlway: Article 30, in: A. Zimmermann/C. J. Tams/K. Oellers-Frahm/C. Tomuschat/D. W. K. Anderson (eds.), The Statute of the International Court of Justice. A commentary, 3. ed., Oxford 2019.

R. Thoma: Rechtsgutachten betreffend die Stellung des Bundesverfassungsgerichts, 6 (new series), Jahrbuch des öffentlichen Rechts (1957), 161.

C. Tomuschat: International Courts and Tribunals (last updated 2019), in: A. Peters/R. Wolfrum (eds.), The Max Planck Encyclopedia of Public International Law 2008.

C. Tomuschat: Art. 36 ICJ Statute, in: A. Zimmermann/C. J. Tams/K. Oellers-Frahm/C. Tomuschat/D. W. K. Anderson (eds.), The Statute of the International Court of Justice. A commentary, 3. ed., Oxford 2019.

T. Treves: Advisory Opinions under the Law of the Sea Convention, in: J. N. Moore/M. H. Nordquist (eds.), Current Marine Environmental Issues and the International Tribunal for the Law of the Sea, Boston 2001, 81–94.

United Nations: Report of the Informal Inter-Allied Committee on the Future of the Permanent Court of International Justice, 39 Am. j. int. law S1: Supplement Official Documents 1945.

A. P. van der Mei: The Advisory Jurisdiction of the African Court on Human and Peoples' Rights, 5, African Human Rights Law Journal 1 (2005), 27.

A. P. van der Mei: The New African Court on Human and Peoples' Rights, 18, LJIL 1 (2005), 113.

W. Vandenhole: The 'J' Word, in: S. Allen/D. Costelloe/M. Fitzmaurice/P. Gragl/E. Guntrip (eds.), The Oxford handbook of jurisdiction in international law, Oxford 2019, 413–430.

I. Venzke: How interpretation makes international law. On semantic change and normative twists, Oxford 2012.

I. Venzke: Between Power and Persuasion: On International Institutions' Authority in Making Law, 4, Transnational Legal Theory 3 (2013), 354.

I. Venzke: Understanding the Authority of International Courts and Tribunals: On Delegation and Discursive Construction, 14, Theoretical Inquiries in Law 2 (2013), 381.

I. Venzke: Semantic authority, legal change and the dynamics of international law, in: P. Capps/H. P. Olsen (eds.), Legal authority beyond the state, Cambridge 2018, 102–126.

I. Venzke: Semantic Authority, in: J. d' Aspremont/S. Singh (eds.), Concepts for international law. Contributions to disciplinary thought, Cheltenham, UK 2019, 815–826.

M. E. Villiger: Art. 31, in: M. E. Villiger (ed.), Commentary on the 1969 Vienna Convention on the Law of Treaties, Leiden, Boston 2009.

M. E. Villiger (ed.): Commentary on the 1969 Vienna Convention on the Law of Treaties, Leiden, Boston 2009.

M. Virally: La notion de fonction dans la théorie de l'organisation internationale, in: M. Virally (ed.), Le droit international en devenir. Essais écrits au fil des ans, Genève 1990.

C. de *Visscher*: Les avis consultatifs de la Cour permanente de justice internationale, Recueil des cours de l'Académie de La Haye / Hague Academy Collected Courses, 1–76.

A. Voßkuhle: Rechtsschutz gegen den Richter. Zur Integration der Dritten Gewalt in das verfassungsrechtliche Kontrollsystem vor dem Hintergrund des Art. 19 Abs. 4 GG, Münchener Universitätsschriften, Bd. 94, München 1993.

G. R. Watson: The "Wall" Decisions in Legal and Political Context, 99, AJIL 1 (2005), 6.

A. Watts & R. Jorritsma: Israeli Wall Advisory Opinion (last updated 2019), in: A. Peters/R. Wolfrum (eds.), The Max Planck Encyclopedia of Public International Law 2008.

C. G. Weeramantry: Constitutional and Institutional Developments, 10, LJIL 2 (1997), 309.

K. Wellens: The UN Security Council and New Threats to the Peace: Back to the Future, 8, Journal of Conflict and Security Law 1 (2003), 15.

H. Weller: Die Bedeutung der Präjudizien im Verständnis der deutschen Rechtswissenschaft. Ein rechtshistorischer Beitrag zur Entstehung und Funktion der Präjudizientheorie, Berlin 1979.

R. Wilde: Kosovo (Advisory Opinion) (last updated 2011), in: A. Peters/R. Wolfrum (eds.), The Max Planck Encyclopedia of Public International Law 2008.

R. C. Williams: The United Nations Register of Damage (UNRoD) Rules and Regulations Governing the Registration of Claims, 49, ILM 2 (2010), 620.

M. Wind: The Nordics, the EU and the Reluctance Towards Supranational Judicial Review, 48, JCMS: Journal of Common Market Studies 4 (2010), 1039.

S. Wittich: The Judicial Functions of the International Court of Justice, in: I. Buffard/J. Crawford/A. Pellet/S. Wittich (eds.), International law between universalism and fragmentation. Festschrift in honour of Gerhard Hafner, Leiden 2008, 981–1000.

R. Wolfrum: Ad Hoc Chambers, in: J. M. van Dyke/S. P. Broder/S. Yi/C. Paek (eds.), Governing ocean resources. New challenges and emerging regimes : a tribute to Judge Choon-Ho Park, Leiden, The Netherlands 2013, 275–283.

R. Wolfrum: Advisory Opinions. Are they a Suitable Alternative for the Settlement of International Disputes, in: R. Wolfrum/I. Gatzschmann (eds.), International Dispute Settlement: Room for Innovations?, Berlin 2013, 35–67.

L. Yackle: Advisory Opinions, in: D. S. Tanenhaus (ed.), Encyclopedia of the Supreme Court of the United States 2008,pp. 34et seq.

S. Yee: Art. 40, in: A. Zimmermann/C. J. Tams/K. Oellers-Frahm/C. Tomuschat/D. W. K. Anderson (eds.), The Statute of the International Court of Justice. A commentary, 3. ed., Oxford 2019.

K.-J. You: Advisory Opinions of the International Tribunal for the Law of the Sea: Article 138 of the Rules of the Tribunal, Revisited, 39, Ocean Development & International Law 4 (2008), 360.

E. A. Young: The Supreme Court and the constitutional structure, University casebook series, New York, NY 2012.

A. Zimmermann: Uniting-for-Peace und Gutachtenanfragen der Generalversammlung. Anmerkungen aus Anlaß des Gutachtens des Internationalen Gerichtshofes zur Zulässigkeit des Sicherheitszaunes zwischen Israel und den palästinensischen Gebieten, in: K. Dicke/S. Hobe/K.-U. Meyn/A. Peters/E. Riedel/H.-J. Schütz/C. Tietje (eds.), Weltinnenrecht. Liber amicorum Jost Delbrück, Berlin 2005, 909–925.

All internet sources were last accessed on 31 October 2024.